Pierre Bourdieu

Culture and Education Series
Series Editors: Henry A. Giroux, Pennsylvania State University
Joe L. Kincheloe, Pennsylvania State University

Race-ing Representation: Voice, History, and Sexuality
    edited by Kostas Myrsiades and Linda Myrsiades
Between the Masks: Resisting the Politics of Essentialism
    by Diane DuBose Brunner
The Mouse That Roared: Disney and the End of Innocence
    by Henry Giroux
Schooling as a Ritual Performance: Toward a Political Economy of Educational Symbols and Gestures
    by Peter McLaren
Literacy as a Moral Imperative: Facing the Challenges of a Pluralistic Society
    by Rebecca Powell
None of the Above: Behind the Myth of Scholastic Aptitude, Updated Edition
    by David Owen with Marilyn Doerr
The Ethics of Writing: Derrida, Deconstruction, and Pedagogy
    by Peter Trifonas
Che Guevara, Paulo Freire, and the Pedagogy of Revolution
    By Peter McLaren

Forthcoming:

Cutting Class: Social Class and Education
    edited by Joe L. Kincheloe and Shirley R. Steinberg
Between Hope and Despair: Pedagogy and the Remembrance of Historical Trauma
    edited by Roger I. Simon, Sharon Rosenberg, and Claudia Eppert

Pierre Bourdieu

Fieldwork in Culture

edited by
Nicholas Brown
and
Imre Szeman

ROWMAN & LITTLEFIELD PUBLISHERS, INC.
Lanham • Boulder • New York • Oxford

ROWMAN & LITTLEFIELD PUBLISHERS, INC.

Published in the United States of America
by Rowman & Littlefield Publishers, Inc.
4720 Boston Way, Lanham, Maryland 20706
http://www.rowmanlittlefield.com

12 Hid's Copse Road
Cumnor Hill, Oxford OX2 9JJ, England

British Library Cataloguing in Publication Information Available

Library of Congress Cataloging-in-Publication Data

Pierre Bourdieu : fieldwork in culture / edited by Nicholas Brown and Imre Szeman.
    p. cm. — (Culture and education series)
    Includes bibliographical references and index.
    ISBN 0-8476-9388-0 (cloth : alk. paper) — ISBN 0-8476-9389-9 (pbk. : alk. paper)
    1. Bourdieu, Pierre. 2. Culture—Philosophy. I. Brown, Nicholas,
1971–   II. Szeman, Imre, 1968–   III. Series.
  HM479.B68 P54   1999
  306'.01—dc21   99–044609

Printed in the United States of America

♾ ™ The paper used in this publication meets the minimum requirements of American
National Standard for Information Sciences—Permanence of Paper for Printed Library
Materials, ANSI/NISO Z39.48–1992.

To our parents:
Lis and Steve,
Imre and Magdolna

The analysis of mental structures is an instrument of liberation: thanks to the instruments of sociology, we can realize one of the eternal ambitions of philosophy—discovering cognitive structures and at the same time uncovering some of the best-concealed limits of thought.

—Pierre Bourdieu, "Fieldwork in Philosophy"

They say that organisms that have not been exposed to microbes have weak immune systems.

—Pierre Bourdieu, *Free Exchange*

Contents

Acknowledgments and Credits

It's a truism that happens to be true: a volume like this one is the product of many more individuals than are listed on the spine. We would like to thank, first, all of the contributors for their patience as this book crawled toward publication (our fault entirely), and for the outstanding essays they contributed to this volume. We might have left them waiting even longer had it not been for Henry Giroux's enthusiasm for this project: a heartfelt thanks, Henry. At Rowman & Littlefield, we could not have asked for a better editor than Rebecca Hoogs, who kept us on course every step of the way. Finally, Jan Plug provided some important last minute help for which he has yet to be properly rewarded.

There are a number of people who participated in the original conference at Duke University that need to be thanked for the work that they did above and beyond the call of duty; of these, Priscilla Lane, Natania Meeker, and Anne Curtis deserve particular thanks.

Neither the conference nor this book could have gone forward without the generous support of Valentin Mudimbe, who spent hours discussing with us the complexities of Bourdieu's sociology, who lent his considerable cultural capital to the initial project, and who kept us philosophically honest.

Most of all, thanks to Pierre Bourdieu, whose work is of course the inspiration for everything in this volume and who generously dealt with all of our requests, reasonable or not.

CREDITS

Pierre Bourdieu. "Passport to Duke." *International Journal of Contemporary Sociology* 33, no. 2 (1996): 145–50. Reprinted by permission of the *International Journal of Contemporary Sociology*.

Bo G. Ekelund, "Space, Time and John Gardner," was previously published as "Författaren och fältets tid," in *Kulturens fält*, edited by Donald Broady. Göteborg: Daidalos, 1998. Reprinted by permission of Donald Broady.

ix

John Guillory. "Bourdieu's Refusal." *Modern Language Quarterly* 58, no. 4 (1997): 367–98. Reprinted by permission of Duke University Press.

Rob Holton. "Bourdieu and Common Sense." *SubStance* 84 (1997): 38–52. Reprinted by permission of the University of Wisconsin Press.

Caterina Pizanias, "Habitus Revisited: Notes and Queries from the Field." Portions of this essay were previously published as "*Habitus*: From the Inside Out and the Outside In." In *The Body and Psychology*, edited by H. J. Stam. London: Sage, 1997.

Carol Stabile. "Resistance, Recuperation, and Reflexivity: The Limits of a Paradigm." *Critical Studies in Mass Communication* 12, no. 4 (1995): 403–22. Reprinted by permission of the National Communication Association.

Abbreviations

References to the most commonly cited of Pierre Bourdieu's texts will be abbreviated as follows:

AR   *Acts of Resistance: Against the New Myths of Our Time.* Translated by Richard Nice. Cambridge: Polity Press, 1998.

D   *Distinction: A Social Critique of the Judgement of Taste.* Translated by Richard Nice. Cambridge, Mass.: Harvard UP, 1984.

DM   *La domination masculine.* Paris: Seuil, Collection Liber, 1998.

FCP   *The Field of Cultural Production.* Edited by Randal Johnson. New York: Columbia UP, 1993.

HA   *Homo Academicus.* Translated by Peter Collier. Stanford, Calif.: Stanford UP, 1988.

IOW   *In Other Words: Essays toward a Reflexive Sociology.* Translated by Matthew Adamson. Cambridge: Polity Press, 1994.

LSP   *Language and Symbolic Power.* Translated by Gino Raymond and Matthew Adamson. Edited by John B. Thompson. Cambridge: Harvard UP, 1991.

LP   *The Logic of Practice.* Translated by Richard Nice. Stanford: Stanford UP, 1990.

OTP   *Outline of a Theory of Practice.* Translated by Richard Nice. Cambridge: Cambridge UP, 1977.

POMH   *The Political Ontology of Martin Heidegger.* Translated by Peter Collier. Stanford, Calif.: Stanford UP, 1991.

RA   *The Rules of Art: Genesis and Structure of the Literary Field.* Translated by Susan Emanuel. Stanford, Calif.: Stanford UP, 1996.

SN   *The State Nobility: Elite Schools in the Field of Power.* Translated by Lauretta Clough. Stanford, Calif.: Stanford UP, 1996.

OT   *On Television.* Translated by Priscilla Parkhurst Ferguson. New York: New Press, 1998.

FE   *(With Hans Haake). Free Exchange.* Stanford, Calif.: Stanford UP, 1995.

I   *(With Jean-Claude Passeron). The Inheritors: French Students and Their Relation to Culture.* Translated by Richard Nice. Chicago: U of Chicago P, 1979.

R   *(With Jean-Claude Passeron). Reproduction in Education, Society, and Culture.*
         Translated by Richard Nice. London: Sage, 1977.
IRS   *(With L. J. D. Wacquant). An Invitation to Reflexive Sociology.* Chicago: U of
         Chicago P, 1992.

Other in-text references will be by title or by author and author-and-date, as determined by context.

Introduction: Fieldwork in Culture

Nicholas Brown and Imre Szeman

"Fieldwork in philosophy": this is one way that Pierre Bourdieu has described his research of almost four decades, and this phrase commanded our attention from the moment we came across it.[1] As a description of a specific form of intellectual practice, its promises are twofold. To the sterility of a philosophical practice whose abstract puzzles tend to be disconnected from the pragmatics of lived experience, the possibility of "fieldwork" suggests a fundamental reconstitution of philosophy along a different and potentially more fruitful axis. At the same time, the possibility of a fieldwork that is directly engaged with philosophical questions challenges the empiricism typical of anthropological and sociological explorations of social and cultural phenomena; in a fieldwork that is philosophical, there is never any danger that social life might be made over into a reified object to be measured and investigated in a manner too quickly called "scientific." "Fieldwork in philosophy" thus captures what has been the aim of Bourdieu's reinvigoration of the discipline of sociology in France all along: to produce a theory of social life drawn neither from the mental laboratories of philosophy, nor from the strict empiricism of much of what passes for sociological research, but from a highly theoretical mode of analysis that nevertheless pays careful attention to the complex dynamics of social life itself.

The chapters that follow are examples of what might be described as "fieldwork in culture"—the transposition of the promise of a "fieldwork in philosophy" to the examination of cultural objects and formations. The first versions of these essays were presented at a conference that we organized in 1995 at Duke University, entitled "Pierre Bourdieu: Fieldwork in Art, Literature, and Culture." The theme of this conference developed out of a sense of frustration at what we saw as the fairly limited uses that had been made of Bourdieu's ideas. Even a few years ago—perhaps due to the ways in which French thought has generally been assimilated in the North American intellectual field—most discussions of Bourdieu seemed to be stuck in a mode of what might be called the "philosophy of fieldwork," that is, a mode characterized by careful attention to and analysis of Bourdieu's theoretical concepts (*habitus*, field, etc.) in order to consider their implications for social theory.[2] As useful as we found this kind of work for understanding the possibilities and limits of Bourdieu's sociology, we thought that there were other things that could be done with Bourdieu's insights and methods. Specifically, given our own disciplinary backgrounds, we felt that there was a great deal that could be learned by engaging Bourdieu's work with the dominant discourses of literary, artistic, and cultural criticism in the North American academy. In his contribution to this volume, John Guillory has written of "what might be called a refusal of Bourdieu's sociology as simply incompatible with the project of much social and cultural theory in the United States" (19). Even in this climate of suspicion and hostility, our aim was to bring together those scholars who *were* making use of Bourdieu's work in the analysis of art, literature, and culture, in order to see what we could learn from each other about the uses to which we could put Bourdieu's work, as well as to understand better the relationship of Bourdieu's sociology to theoretical discourses that had already achieved more secure positions in the North American academy. The chapters in this volume represent the rich and varied possibilities of a fieldwork in culture that is inspired and challenged by the work of Bourdieu.

This is an opportune time to consider the possibilities that Bourdieu's sociology offers for cultural criticism. For while Bourdieu's work has never been about anything other than culture in the broadest sense, the past several years have seen the publication and translation of a number of books that promise to expand the discussion of the importance and significance of Bourdieu's work within the humanities. While a number of these texts have appeared since the chapters in this volume were first conceived, the work in this volume nevertheless collectively probes some of the tensions (which have only become more pronounced as Bourdieu has been increasingly explicit about the political commitments engendered by his work) that were already apparent in his earlier writings, and that provided the impetus for many of the essays here. It is to a brief consideration of these tensions that we would like to turn now, for they are of signal importance for the issues that animate this volume: the relationship of Bourdieu's work to other forms of cultural criticism and the promise and difficulties of using Bourdieu for an examination of cultural phenomena.

TWO SOLITUDES? SOCIOLOGY AND AESTHETICS

John Guillory links the "refusal" of Bourdieu's work in North America to what is perceived to be its pessimistic and reductive explanation of human behavior.

He suggests that the "intellectual ethos of *voluntarism*" (20) that underlies most forms of cultural and social theory in North America is fundamentally at odds with an account of society that emphasizes the continuity of social structures and their resistance to change, and that stresses the fundamentally self-interested character of subjectivity. Guillory's insight accounts in part for the difficulty of bringing Bourdieu's sociology into North American discourses on cultural phenomena; however, with respect to the study of cultural objects such as art, literature, and film, there is perhaps an even more long-standing point of refusal that is not directed specifically towards Bourdieu, but to the sociological study of art and culture in general.

The aims of the sociological study of art and literature are clear. As Janet Wolff, for example, suggests at the beginning of *The Social Production of Art*, to study art from the perspective of sociology is to argue

> against the romantic and mystical notion of art as the creation of "genius," transcending existence, society and time, and [to argue] that it is rather the complex construction of a number of real, historical factors . . . art and literature have to be seen as historical, situated and produced, and not as descending as divine inspiration to people of innate genius.[3]

The sociology of art and literature challenges those processes and modes of analysis in which the significance or meaning of a cultural object is ascertained through an immanent reading—a form of communion with the "divinely inspired" work. From the perspective of sociology, New Criticism and deconstruction are thus equally insufficient as critical practices insofar as they fail to examine the social and historical conditions of possibility of literary form itself. As Wolff suggests, it is only when art and literature are seen as the products of very specific social and historical formations that their true significance can be understood beyond the romantic fantasies concerning the unique power of art and culture that remain a part of most contemporary critical practices to this day. Even though more attention has been paid to the historical, social, and political dimensions of cultural objects over the past several decades, the "pure aesthetic" that underwrites an understanding of literary and artistic artifacts as ineffable objects demanding infinite interpretation has nevertheless continued to operate behind the scenes in both implicit and explicit ways.[4]

It is one thing, however, to say that a sociological approach to art and literature might complement other possible "readings" or approaches to a cultural text, and quite another to suggest that a sociological approach constitutes nothing less than a total explanation of the logic of cultural forms themselves. In *The Rules of Art*, at least, Bourdieu appears at times to make the latter claim. For Bourdieu, the aim of sociology is not simply to lend to various forms of "aesthetic" criticism a historical and social dimension that they often lack. Rather, a sociological approach to the study of art and literature seems to reveal the aesthetic to be nothing more than an effect of the cultural field. The aesthetic is seen by Bourdieu as perhaps the fundamental concept that allows the *illusio* of various cultural fields to function; it is a concept that gains philosophical legitimacy only through a misrecognition of the rules of the game of taste. Strictly speaking, for Bourdieu, it might be said the aesthetic *does not exist*, except as a concept that continues to be used to perpetuate the form of symbolic violence that he discusses in *Distinction*. This may seem contrary to his claim in the preface to *The Rules of Art* that "scientific analysis of the social conditions of the production and reception of a work of art, far from reducing it or destroying it, in fact intensifies the literary experience" (*RA*, xix). What needs to be stressed, however, is that what Bourdieu names here as "literary experience" is hardly the aesthetic as this has been traditionally understood. The "intensification" of literary and artistic experience Bourdieu speaks of comes about not through the sociological supplementation of other forms of criticism, but through a redefinition of the pleasure once associated with the aesthetic. In *The Rules of Art*, the aesthetic is no longer the site or the name of the particular pleasure associated with the experience of art and culture. Rather, the pleasure of the literary experience is now contained *within* the kind of sociological activity that aims to "uncover what makes the work of art *necessary*, that is to say, its informing formula, its generative principle, its *raison d'être*" (*RA*, xix). What becomes pleasurable about art is thus not aesthetic experience but the sociological demystification of this experience. Or as Allan Dunn has put it in his perceptive analysis of *The Rules of Art*, "rather than admiring or disapproving of a particular cultural performance, the sociologist is content to contemplate the social forces that made it necessary."[5]

Bourdieu's work thus represents a radicalization of a more general tendency in the sociology of art and literature. If the "meaning" of cultural objects is to be apprehended only by treating "the work as an intentional sign haunted and regulated by something else, of which it is also a symptom" (*RA*, xx), the resistance that Bourdieu's work has encountered has as much to do with its explicit threat to established forms and modes of cultural criticism as to its dissonance with the implicit and explicit politics of North American criticism. To use the insights of Bourdieu's sociology in a way that respects the overall theoretical claims of his work—that is, to use it in a manner consistent with its broad conceptual aims—while simultaneously attending to those aspects of cultural objects that can only be termed "aesthetic," would seem to be difficult indeed. In one sense, a refusal of Bourdieu's conclusions about the limits of what he sees as just so many variations of *belle-lettristisme* can be seen as an attempt to defend the logic that legitimates the *status quo* in the fields of literary and cultural criticism in North America. At the same time, however, it may be that this refusal also signals a reluctance to reduce cultural experience to its sociological determinants—a reduction that Bourdieu claims to have avoided, but of which the energy with which he has worked to dismantle the category of the aesthetic might nonetheless be considered emblematic.

It seems to us, then, that we still need to consider whether there is room for the aesthetic as such in Bourdieu's sociology. Any attempt simply to revalorize the aesthetic would open up numerous theoretical and conceptual pitfalls into which it is all too easy to stray. If we had wanted to cast ourselves outside the pale of current discourses on the study of culture, then indulging in a nostalgia for the aesthetic—a concept potentially both reactionary and mystificatory—is surely the way to go about it. But in raising this question with respect to Bourdieu's work, we have no intention of replacing Bourdieusian analysis with the forms of cultural criticism that it has quite rightly opposed. The imperative of having to think about the place of the aesthetic in Bourdieu's work comes not just from the "outside," from the need to think about the points of engagement between Bourdieu's social and cultural theory and other forms of literary and cultural theory, but from "inside" Bourdieu's work, which seems increasingly to posit a politics and ethics on an implicit aesthetics that is apparently at odds with claims he makes at other places in his work. In other words, as much as we might like to resist having to address the aesthetic at all, Bourdieu's work—and especially his most recent work—seems to generate the need for such a concept as a condition of the "socioanalysis" that he performs.

It is possible to argue that the "freedom" that Bourdieu has associated with the project of his sociology contains something of the aesthetic about it, or, at the very least, that there is no fundamental incompatibility between the "genuine freedom from one's determinations" (*RA*, xvii) offered by sociology and the possibility of aesthetics.[6] Nevertheless, rather than approaching it in an abstract, philosophical manner, we would like here to approach the question of the place of the aesthetic in Bourdieu's work in a manner that connects it—and the chapters in this book—to his most recent work. In *Free Exchange, On Television, Acts of Resistance*, and other works, Bourdieu has repeatedly drawn attention to the threat posed by contemporary "neoliberalism" or "neoconservatism."[7] In the wake of the apparent "victory" of democratic capitalism signaled by the dissolution of the Soviet bloc, the unique danger of the present moment of capitalism is that it threatens to forestall or eliminate discussions about social, political, and economic alternatives. The ideology of liberal consumerism that corresponds to "late capitalism" has sought to accomplish this either by pretending to assume its place as the "natural" order of things outside of history, or, on the contrary, by hijacking the philosophy of history, becoming the last moment of a new Hegelianism.[8] Not content merely to revel in the afterglow of the "new world order," the past decade has in fact witnessed an all-out neoconservative assault on every sphere of life not yet defined by the rationality of the market. As the century nears its end, Bourdieu has been increasingly preoccupied with the social and cultural consequences of this assault and with the attempt to map out its implications for the current division of fields that was produced at the height of modernity.

The symptomatic indications of this neoconservative offensive are visible everywhere: in the new prominence given to the stock market and to financial dealings in the media; in the reduction of what used to be collective political concerns into a personalized ethics of individual responsibility; in the discourse of privatization that has infected cultural and educational organizations; in the language of fiscal responsibility that now dominates governmental policy-making at all levels; and so on. The current phase of neoconservatism is both more subtle and more dangerous than the outright attacks on the left that took place during the Reagan and Thatcher 1980s. The conservative logic that had manifested itself in outrage over the art of Serrano or Mapplethorpe, or in impassioned defenses of the canon and of the values of Western civilization, now finds itself internalized as policy: as, for example, in the decisions by major museums to host popular shows of canonical nineteenth- and twentieth-century artists, in the elimination or merger of "nonproductive" university departments (almost always in the humanities), and in the market factors that have found their way into both academic publishing and the establishment of academic reputation. This logic is, in other words, now less recognizable as ideology than as institutional rationality. These various forms of "invisible censorship," as Bourdieu names them in *On Television*, have come insidiously to define the entire space of social possibility, with some options being ruled out immediately as "impractical" or "impossible." It is for this reason that the recent elections of purportedly left-of-center governments in Britain, Germany, and France have had little real political significance.[9] For these governments, too, must toe the line of the GATT agreement and concede the inevitability of capitalism and, ultimately, the inability of the state to intercede in the Manichean logic of the global economy.

Bourdieu's recent work constitutes both an assessment of the dangers of the present moment for various cultural fields and a call to intellectuals to respond to the threat that the market poses to contemporary cultural and intellectual production. In both cases, it is the issue of the *autonomy* of fields that has come to the fore. In "For a Corporatism of the Universal," the postscript to *The Rules of Art*, Bourdieu argues that the logic of the market produces a "threat to the most precious collective achievements of intellectuals, starting with the critical dispositions which were simultaneously the product and the guarantee of their autonomy" (*RA*, 339). Bourdieu reminds us that it is only through the "specific authority founded on their belonging to the relatively autonomous world of art, science and literature, and on all the values associated with that autonomy— disinterestedness, expertise, etc." (*RA*, 340) that intellectuals can intervene in politics *as* intellectuals. In the case of the cultural and intellectual fields, he claims that "*the threats to autonomy* result from the increasingly greater interpenetration between the world of art and the world of money" (*RA*, 344). For Bourdieu, then, the critical capacity of various cultural fields lies in inverse proportion to their penetration by the market. In *On Television*, Bourdieu shows that the impact of money on journalism has been to produce a view of the world that "fosters fatalism and disengagement, [and] which obviously favors the status quo" (*OT*, 8); in turn, he shows how the corruption of the autonomy of the journalistic field has spread into other fields of intellectual and cultural production. In a similar fashion, in his discussions with the artist Hans Haacke in *Free Exchange*, Bourdieu examines the impact of corporate sponsorship on art production. He suggests that the abandonment of the artistic field by the state has left it increasingly beholden to the whims and desires of its corporate masters, so that work like Haacke's, which criticizes and challenges the contemporary capitalist worldview, is lamentably in danger of disappearing altogether.

In light of these threats, Bourdieu calls for an "*internationale of intellectuals* committed to defending the autonomy of the universes of cultural production or, to parody a language now out of fashion, *the ownership by cultural producers of their instruments of production and circulation*" (*RA*, 344).[10] This call for a defense of the autonomy of fields should not be mistaken for a narrow defense of the privileges of the ivory tower. What is at issue here is the dissolution of the particular system of evaluation and consecration internal to each field. As the logic of the market enters these fields and renders each heteronomous, the system of symbolic rewards and recognition proper to each field begins to dissolve, with grave consequences for cultural and intellectual production. "Heteronomy arrives in a field," Bourdieu claims, "through the producers who are the least capable of succeeding according to the norms that it imposes" (*RA*, 347). This is perhaps most clearly shown in *On Television* through Bourdieu's analysis of the "fast thinkers" and "fast readers" who gain considerable symbolic capital outside of established fields through their involvement with the media. For Bourdieu, the intellectual "experts" that the media consult routinely for sound-bites are intellectuals in name only:

> They are Zolas who would publish manifestos like "J'accuse" without having written *L'Assomoir* or *Germinal*, or Sartres who would sign petitions or lead protest marches without having written *Being and Nothingness* or *Critique of Dialectial Reason*. They want television to give them a notoriety that previously only a whole, often obscure life of research and work could give. (*FE*, 52)

At issue here is not the fact that those with real knowledge on subjects of social importance are given little room to speak in fields crowded by media "experts" who may in truth have very little understanding of their purported field of expertise. Rather, what is implicitly threatened in the dissolution of the autonomy of intellectual and cultural fields, it seems, is the *quality* and *significance* of the artifacts and concepts produced within it. "Slow thinking" produces something "fast thinking" cannot, and it is the autonomy of the field that permits slow thinking to occur and enables it to be properly consecrated when its end-product is finally achieved.

There is, then, we would suggest, a new element introduced into Bourdieu's work in his attempt to resist the tyranny of the market. In the analysis of the literary field offered in *The Rules of Art*, the basic structure is familiar: the orientation of a writer towards the market (the attainment of economic capital) as opposed to the purity of the aesthetic (the attainment of symbolic capital) is seen by Bourdieu as representing the two poles of a range of possible strategies and positions that a writer might occupy within the field. Indeed, the "cynical subordination to demand" and the "absolute independence from the market and its exigencies" (*RA*, 142) finally amount to the same thing, since the symbolic capital that can be attained by taking up the position of the aesthete is also, finally, convertible into money. As Bourdieu points out, while the sales of Alain Robbe-Grillet's *La Jalousie* and Samuel Beckett's *Waiting for Godot* may initially be minuscule compared to the season's literary bestseller, their consecration as literary "classics" ensures that, over time, their sales outpace the blockbusters whose revenue is limited to the period when they first appear (*RA*, 141–53). These two poles of the field—art and money—thus together describe the structure and logic of the field, "with producers' strategies distributing themselves between the two extremes that are never, in fact, attained" (*RA*, 142).

But what originated as a structural consideration has in Bourdieu's most recent work been inflected both normatively and *aesthetically*. It is clearly no longer the case (and it may be that it never was in Bourdieu's work) that the poles of money and art are both acceptable strategies within, for example, the literary field. Bourdieu explains the need for intellectuals to defend the autonomy of the fields of cultural production as the need to prevent the "destruction of the economic and social foundations of humanity's rarest cultural achievements,"[11] and to preserve "the greatest achievements of humanity" (*FE*, 72). In his attempt to articulate a politics that might constitute an appropriate response to the dominance of the market, there is thus the emergence of a normative, even romantic understanding of the relationship between art and money. Bourdieu assumes that the greatest works of art and culture are produced at the furthest distance from the market, where they can be created purely under the influence of the imperatives generated within the particular field itself. While this claim is itself worthy of discussion, what we would like to draw attention to here is that it appears that at this point autonomy and aesthetics overlap. After all, it seems important to defend what he elsewhere calls "the forms of civilization associated with the civil state"[12] not because these are simply the by-products of strategic battles fought within specific cultural fields—which on their own are hardly significant outside those fields—but because they seem to contain some kind of intrinsic value: a value, it is worth mentioning, above and beyond the uses to which they may be put in reproducing social classes. This is, no doubt, why Bourdieu generally seems to have so little difficulty with the canonical constitution of the "great works" of human civilization, which are to be defended by intellectuals against the barbarism of the market.

The need to identify great works with those produced at the greatest remove from the market arises in Bourdieu's work as a result of an unresolved tension:

there are aesthetic claims being made, but no theory of the aesthetic to give them intelligibility. At times Bourdieu will go out of his way to distance himself from the aesthetic, even while he is aware that the claims that he makes on behalf of certain cultural forms nevertheless seem to have an aesthetic character. For example, since it is clear that the work of Flaubert has an exemplary importance for him, he suggests at one point that literary "value" might be thought of as "the investment in a work which is measured by the cost in effort, in sacrifices of all kinds and, definitively, in time . . . which goes hand in hand with the consequent independence from the forces and constraints exercised outside the field" (*RA*, 85). He similarly sidesteps the aesthetic when he identifies the mark of literary or artistic "success" with the degree to which a work manages to produce the same insights into the social world as sociology itself. This is clear in his understanding of Flaubert's *Sentimental Education* as a text that not only marks the emergence of the autonomy of the literary field but simultaneously produces an analysis of this field that parallels Bourdieu's own; it is also this bracketing of the aesthetic in favor of the sociological that he finds most appealing about the work of Haacke in *Free Exchange*, which he sees as marked above all by "a critical analysis of the art world and of the very conditions of artistic possibility" (*FE*, 1). Finally, it is apparent in Bourdieu's discussion of autonomy that what is ultimately valuable about each field having its own power of evaluation and consecration is that this ensures that the best work produced within each field succeeds. If there are "failures" in each field, it is because, above and beyond the struggle of self-interested individuals that constitute fields, they are also characterized as meritocracies that guarantee that "the highest human creations" (*OT*, 65) make their way to the top. Is there thus really no room to examine or consider what it is about a particular cultural work that makes this passage through the field possible, that gives us reason to assign greater value (contingently and historically) to one cultural object as opposed to another? Neither the accrued labor time of its production, nor its sociological dimension, nor its consecration in a field whose producers are the sole consumers seems to address this question adequately.

Nor, of course, do the traditional theories and treatments of the aesthetic. Now is unfortunately not the time to go into a detailed treatment of the question of the aesthetic as such; any discussion of the current parameters of the problem as we see them would have to take us back at least as far as Lukács's essay on reification,[13] if not indeed back to Kant himself. This brief exploration of some of the issues raised in Bourdieu's recent work is offered less as a critique of his sociology of culture than as a provocation to consider some of the problems involved in using Bourdieu's theories in conjunction with mainstream North American cultural theory. It may be that what we have identified as an unresolved tension in Bourdieu's work between sociology and the aesthetic is less significant than it might at first seem. And certainly, this tension does not rule out or render problematic the need for intellectuals to defend the assault of the market on culture.

Yet it is just this tension "inside" Bourdieu's work that necessarily seems to characterize an engagement with Bourdieu's work from the "outside" as well; to characterize, that is, the process in which the insights of his sociology are wedded to a normative and aesthetic framework that, for the most part, originates outside of it.[14]

For better or for worse, this is the manner in which Bourdieu will continue to be taken up by others; full-scale investigations of other national, literary, cultural, and artistic fields following the model of *The Rules of Art* are less likely than a borrowing of its theoretical components as a way of providing one aspect of an exploration of a literary or cultural object, period, or genre. In any case, this tension between sociology and aesthetics should be seen as productive rather than problematic. Without wishing to assume the whole burden of the deeply ideological concept of the aesthetic, it is important to remember that, as Michael Sprinker has written, "literature is both a socio-historical phenomenon, and an aesthetic phenomenon. There are differences worth insisting on between, say, *Middlemarch* and the factory blue-books on which Marx drew heavily in writing *Capital*."[15] In another context, Sprinker writes that "the tension between the aesthetic as a model of transcendental cognitive power and the aesthetic as a historical and ideological social practice remains a constitutive and productive feature of Marxist theory down to the present moment."[16] Just as in Marxist theory, the aesthetic may still have a role to play in Bourdieu's sociology—not by infusing fieldwork in culture with an unscientific, mystical element, but by drawing its attention to an aspect of the social that it has perhaps not yet properly considered.

FIELDWORK

This "reading" of Bourdieu represents merely one strand of the complex web of engagements with his thought that are produced by the chapters in this book. Indeed, it is a strand whose assumptions, far from being shared by all of the contributors to this volume, are continually probed, contested, and challenged. In order to facilitate an exploration of this web, we have divided the book into two sections. The first, more theoretical section begins with chapters by John Guillory and Carol A. Stabile, two authors who recommend—from quite different viewpoints—Bourdieu's sociology, which is often criticized for an apparent determinism, as a welcome corrective to a certain voluntarist strand in American cultural studies. Guillory, one of the keynote speakers at the 1995 conference, begins his contribution, "Bourdieu's Refusal," by finding in the refusal of Bourdieu's methodology by American cultural studies the clue to a genuine oddity in Bourdieu's thought: the lack of a theory of capital in a framework apparently dominated by metaphors of capital. For Guillory, this lack does not represent a form of "failure" on Bourdieu's part, but is inherent to the structure of Bourdieu's sociology, which reduces the relatively new zone of the capitalist market to a mere point of reference, negated in play—art, the sacred, and so on—but nonetheless the truth of all play. Guillory turns to Bourdieu's *Rules of Art* to assess the complex relationship between the reflexivity of the artist and the reflexivity of the sociologist, between the refusal of the market and the refusal of the logic of economics—and finds Bourdieu "in the end to have been on the side of the artists."

While Carol A. Stabile is also concerned to critique a certain voluntarist strand in American cultural studies, she launches her endorsement of Bourdieu's sociology not from the point of view of a literary critical field that betrays some anxiety about the "reductiveness" of Bourdieu's demystification of the aesthetic, but from a suspicion of "textualism," a tendency within cultural studies that must be seen to have its origin in literary studies. In her article "Resistance, Recuperation, and Reflexivity: The Limits of a Paradigm," Stabile finds that the field of media studies has been dominated in recent decades by a lopsided application of Gramsci's theory of hegemony, a hermeneutic practice that interprets all cultural behavior as either resistance or recuperation, subversion of or containment within a hegemonic structure that is conceived in idealistic terms, neglecting state violence and economic necessity as repressive forces. The dialectical pole of resistance is, of course, the favored moment, and Stabile stages her confrontation with this interpretive machine in an extended discussion of the situation comedy *Roseanne* and the historical moment in which it arose—both in terms of the history of the field of TV sitcoms and the history of what this particular sitcom purports to represent, the situation of working-class mothers. Stabile understands the voluntarist tendency in U.S. cultural studies as constitutive of an intellectual game homologous with a more directly economic game that must disguise necessity as choice, and she recommends Bourdieu's reflexive sociology as the antidote to an unreflective interpretive practice that ultimately serves the very social reality whose subversion it claims to celebrate.

In "Anglicizing Bourdieu," Daniel Simeoni takes on a question that has persisted at the periphery of Bourdieu's thought (see, for example, Bourdieu's own "Passport to Duke" in this volume): the issue of the possibility of its translation across national and linguistic borders, particularly into a North American Anglophone context. In the absence of a full-scale application of Bourdieu's methodologies in the English-speaking world on the order of *Distinction* or *Homo Academicus*, Simeoni turns to the translation of *Le sens pratique* for clues to the deformations Bourdieu's thought undergoes in its transfer to a different academic, linguistic, and cultural field. Simeoni argues that the attenuation of the affective element in Bourdieu's language reflects a more thoroughgoing deformation of Bourdieu's thought that is decisive for dominant Anglophone understandings of Bourdieu, and he suggests that contemporary translation practices might take a lesson from older and seemingly discredited modes of transcultural interpretation.

The question of Bourdieu's North American reception is continued in Robert Holton's "Bourdieu and Common Sense," which contests a stereotypical—or commonsense—notion of Bourdieu's thought as straightforwardly deterministic. Holton proceeds through an exegesis of *doxa*, *habitus*, and related terms to derive an understanding of the causal complexity implicit in a Bourdieusian conception of common sense. Insightfully, Holton takes Bourdieu's remarks on Heidegger as a commentary on certain (commonsense?) notions of the postmodern, finally finding that the phrase in Bourdieu reproduces an ambivalence that almost seems to inhere in the words themselves: Holton identifies Bourdieu's defense of science with Kant's *sensus communis logicus*—even as science in Bourdieu's sense starts from a decisive break with common sense.

The final chapter in this section is Jon Beasley-Murray's "Value and Capital in Bourdieu and Marx," which closes the circle by returning to an issue first brought up by Guillory: the relationship in Bourdieu's thought between cultural and economic capital. Beasley-Murray seeks to realize a possibility implicit in but not followed up by Bourdieu in his theory of cultural capital: the possibility of understanding all cultural activity (not merely consecrated forms) in terms of the creation of cultural value. Beasley-Murray begins by pointing out the fact that Bourdieu's is a theory of capital without a theory of exploitation, that is, without a notion of surplus. He describes Bourdieu's theory of cultural capital as a reintroduction of use value (practice) into the supposedly "useless" aesthetic realm, leading into a discussion of use value in Marx and its relation to labor time and surplus value. What is ultimately at stake in resituating these terms in the heart of cultural capital is a concept of cultural capital that would not only entail a study of the unequal values assigned to cultural practices, but would make possible an understanding of (and attack on) the process of cultural valorization itself.

A second, more concretely oriented section focuses on the application of Bourdieusian concepts and methodologies to various cultural fields; beyond the insights gained through each of these chapters individually, taken as a whole they convey something of the richness of Bourdieu's thought for North American research on cultural phenomena. Marie-Pierre Le Hir's "Cultural Studies Bourdieu's Way: Women, Leadership, and Feminist Theory" takes as its point of analysis a peculiar phenomenon in the U.S. academy: the "feminization of the discipline of French." Interestingly, her theoretical touchstone is less *Homo Academicus* than *La domination masculine*, which she uses to understand the "somatized," internalized, and embodied forms of domination that are at play in contemporary institutional practices. Starting from two social facts, one objective (the distribution of salaries and genders across disciplines) and one subjective (her own skepticism about the educational buzzword of "leadership"), Le Hir finds in Bourdieu's *symbolic violence* a concept that enables her to synthesize these facts in a manner congruent to Bourdieu's famous synthesis of subjective and objective knowledge in the *habitus*. In so doing, she also orients us towards a feminist theory of practice that would overcome the traditional opposition between a "feminism of equality" and a "feminism of difference." In the end, Le Hir concludes that a feminist theory along the lines suggested would neither reveal the impossibility of change nor call forth an unwarranted optimism, but would realistically address the "immensity of the task at hand."

In the art-historical study "Habitus Revisited: Notes and Queries from the Field," Caterina Pizanias begins with the suspicion that Bourdieu's sociology is more "feminist friendly" than some more readily appropriated French theory. Her discussion focuses on two very different gallery exhibits, each attempting to represent or to create "queer" communities: one, an aesthetic and representational success, was a failure in such objective terms as the length of the exhibit, public reviews, and so on; the other, a representational failure that unwittingly signifies the current limits of cybertechnology more than, as intended, the possibilities of cybercommunity, was an objective success. Pizanias argues that the vagaries of cultural consecration only make sense in terms of *habitus* and field; in this case, in terms of the changing fields of the U.S. and Canadian high-art worlds and the trajectories of various dispositions within those fields.

Paul Lopes's contribution intervenes in a debate about the origins of "modern jazz" in the 1950s, a debate whose *doxa* is that a radical stylistic rupture reflects an abrupt economic and educational shift among jazz musicians—a conclusion that is not borne out by empirical research. Lopes argues that the "modern jazz paradigm" was instead the result of changes in the field of musical production over a prolonged period, from the twenties to the rise of modern jazz in the fifties. Although Lopes's approach is essentially Bourdieusian, he also seeks to correct a tendency, noted by many of Bourdieu's critics, to assimilate all popular art to the category that another mode of cultural criticism called the "culture industry." Lopes proceeds by reconstructing the U.S. field of musical production in the early twentieth century, a field whose internal tensions ultimately produced a new term, lacking in Bourdieu's cultural analyses: "Restricted Popular Art," which exists in opposition to the more familiar categories of both "Restricted High Art" and "Industrial Art." Once this historical emergence is explained, Lopes turns to strategies employed within this subfield, in some ways answering Beasley-Murray's call for an investigation of the "alternative valorization for the concrete time of . . . disenfranchised subjects."

Marty Hipsky's work on the field of nineteenth-century novelistic production is the first of three chapters applying Bourdieusian methodology or concepts to literary subjects. In "Romancing Bourdieu: A Case Study in Gender Politics in the Literary Field," Hipsky details the literary career of Mary Arnold (Mrs. Humphry Ward) against the late Victorian British literary field. A theoretical introductory section seeks to position an approach to literature that emphasizes social and institutional processes not as a corrective but as a complement to reigning text-based and potentially idealist literary-critical methodologies. Hipsky goes on to outline the literary-historical moment of Ward's literary production, focusing in particular on the strategies available to female novelists in the period just after George Eliot's death. The narration of Ward's trajectory—from the self-styled "next George Eliot" to "modernists' lightning rod of abuse"—against this background not only reveals the limited strategies available to women writers in the context of the late Victorian cultural establishment, but also sheds light on the demise of the triple-decker novel, the decline of the lending libraries as a cultural force, the origins of the mass-market romance novel, and the widening gap between "restricted" and "industrial" literary production. Finally, Hipsky traces the end of Ward's career to the beginning of the modernist movement, finding in the position-takings of prominent female modernist writers the "determinate negation" of the position of Mrs. Humphry Ward.

Carolyn Betensky's contribution concerns George Sand's *Le Compagnon du Tour de France*, but her discussion also bears on our understanding of Bourdieu's concept of symbolic capital. She begins with Dominick LaCapra's use of the term—a use which has little strictly to do with Bourdieu's, but which nonetheless points up an absence in Bourdieu's formulation. For, in LaCapra's usage, symbolic capital marks a form of prestige that is *purely* symbolic: that is, it is only ideologically considered to be capital and is in fact the inverse of any real prestige. The "guilt economy" in which oppression is capital is not, like the cultural economy, the inversion of the market and convertible to it, but rather a purely imaginary market. In "The Prestige of the Oppressed: Symbolic Capital in a Guilt Economy," Betensky returns to the textualist methods avoided by many Bourdieusian studies, reading Sand's novel through the figure of the carpenter Pierre, a defamiliarizing presence in the upper-class milieu of the novel who unmasks the mystifications of the "guilt economy."

Bo Ekelund's "Space, Time, and John Gardner" aims to rethink the genre of the author-study along Bourdieusian lines. Ekelund begins by laying out some essential aspects of and movements within Gardner's literary career and biographical life; but rather than take Gardner's career (or his texts) as the central fact, Ekelund attempts to reconstruct the fields—relatively autonomous, but homologous and synchronized in various ways—in which Gardner made strategic choices. Indeed, Ekelund turns a defamiliarizing gaze on the notion of the "career" itself and the deformations that inevitably arise from making such a construct the engine of meaning; far from having an organic unity all its own, the career itself is produced by (even as it helps produce) the fields within which it exists. Ekelund is primarily concerned with the relationships between the U.S. literary field, in which Gardner must negotiate an awkward generational position, and the larger fields—for example, the educational and political—from which it claims its autonomy but which it must nonetheless express. Ekelund seeks to discover the "sociological truth of literary phenomena": *On Moral Fiction*, Gardner's *summa* produced at the height of his literary career, is found to be the product of an incompatibility between Gardner's own *habitus* and the objective structures of the mid-1970s U.S. literary field.

Our final entry, Pierre Bourdieu's own "Passport to Duke"—written for the original 1995 conference at Duke University—is a fitting coda, recapitulating a theme that dominated the earliest chapters in this book: the reception of Bourdieu's thought in the North American academic field. Bourdieu is primarily concerned here with the potential deformations of his work that might come about as it circulates across the Atlantic—in particular, with the way his work might be understood in the specific place and time that the conference was being held. In order to differentiate himself decisively from other French thought with which he may have been unthinkingly assimilated, Bourdieu sketches out certain elements of the post-World War II French intellectual field to demonstrate the distance that separates him from, say, a Lyotard or a Baudrillard, a Foucault or a Derrida, making the significance of his position-takings clear to a North American audience. Finally, he implicitly provides a very useful canon of his own works, a selection through which a very different Bourdieu would emerge than the figure who is known, in the United States, primarily for his 1979 *La Distinction.*

NOTES

1. Pierre Bourdieu, "Fieldwork in Philosophy," in *IOW.*
2. See, for instance, Craig Calhoun, Edward LiPuma, and Moishe Postone, eds., *Bourdieu: Critical Perspectives* (Chicago: University of Chicago Press, 1993).
3. Janet Wolff, *The Social Production of Art* (London: Macmillan, 1981): 1.
4. For example, with respect to Marxist literary criticism, a form of criticism that one might expect to have done the most to expel the specter of the aesthetic, Franco Moretti has pointed out that "even the great historical controversies, when all is said, turn almost exclusively on the reinterpretation of an extremely small number of works and authors . . . the fact is that criticism has not entirely freed itself of its old task: that of being a sort of cultivated companion to reading." *Signs Taken for Wonders: Essays in the Sociology of Literary Forms*, trans. Susan Fischer, David Forgacs, and David Miller (New York: Verso, 1983): 13.
5. Allan Dunn, "Who Needs a Sociology of the Aesthetic? Freedom and Value in Pierre Bourdieu's *Rules of Art*," *boundary 2* 25, no. 1 (1998): 99.
6. This is Dunn's main project in the essay previously cited.
7. These terms only appear as contradictions in the context of American politics; they, of course, name the same general tendency towards the market as the singular imperative of human existence, the first (neoliberalism) in the realm of economics, the second (neoconservatism) in politics. In addition to the books listed above, see "The Essence of Neoliberalism," *Le Monde Diplomatique* (December 1998), and "A Reasoned Utopia and Economic Fatalism," *New Left Review* 227 (January–February 1998): 123–30.
8. Francis Fukuyama, *The End of History and the Last Man* (New York: Free Press, 1992).
9. Bourdieu writes in *Free Exchange*: "For years I have asked myself what can be done to oppose modern forms of symbolic domination. Intellectuals—but also unions and political parties—are truly unarmed; they are three or four symbolic wars behind" (19–20).
10. See also "A Reasoned Utopia and Economic Fatalism."

11. "A Reasoned Utopia and Economic Fatalism," 127.

12. "A Reasoned Utopia and Economic Fatalism," 126.

13. "Reification and the Consciousness of the Proletariat," in *History and Class Consciousness*, trans. Rodney Livingstone (Cambridge, Mass.: MIT Press, 1971): primarily section 12, "The Antinomies of Bourgeois Thought," 110–49.

14. Dunn writes that "most American literary critics who profess allegiance to Bourdieu's work supplement his sociology with their own normative framework. . . . These critics tend to share Adorno's pessimism about the kinds of satisfactions that contemporary culture makes available, but they affirm both the possibility and necessity of radical social transformation, and this affirmation provides the concrete details of the political program that Bourdieu seems to lack" (110).

15. Michael Sprinker, "We Lost It at the Movies," *Modern Language Notes* 112, no. 3 (1997): 387.

16. Michael Sprinker, *Imaginary Relations: Aesthetics and Ideology in the Theory of Historical Materialism* (New York: Verso, 1987): 14.

PART I

2

Bourdieu's Refusal

John Guillory

And this is that famous human freedom which everyone brags of having, and
which consists only in this: that men are conscious of their appetite and igno-
rant of the causes by which they are determined.
—Spinoza

PLUS ÇA CHANGE . . .

Of the several reasons one might offer for the belated reception of Pierre Bourdieu's work in the U.S. academy—the uncertainties of translation, the difference
of the French intellectual scene, the discrepancy between the publication order
of his books in France and in the United States, the notorious difficulty of his
prose—none explains the suspicion, even hostility, with which his work has often
been greeted. Surveying the most typical misapprehensions of Bourdieu's theoretical positions, Loïc Wacquant reminds us, much in the spirit of Bourdieu, that
the reception of any foreign oeuvre is mediated by "structures of the national
intellectual field."[1] The interesting question raised by this point is why the same
field that permitted so favorable a reception of Derrida or Foucault, especially
in the humanities, should have occasioned so different a response to Bourdieu.
Wacquant observes in concluding his study that the severity of Bourdieu's "reflexive sociology," which spares neither itself nor any other intellectual project
exposure to the cold illumination of its analysis, provokes intense uneasiness
among his readers. This uneasiness must be very great indeed, if the same readers
who assimilated poststructuralist thought without being too disturbed by what
some consider to be its "nihilism" find Bourdieu altogether too bleak. Yet even
this account may not go far enough in registering what might be called a refusal
of Bourdieu's sociology as simply incompatible with the project of much social
and cultural theory in the United States.[2]

I would like to take this refusal seriously as the occasion of advancing both an
analysis and a defense of what is perceived as most problematic in Bourdieu's

19

work. This is a question not so much of how Bourdieu has been misunderstood as of how the refusal of his sociology constitutes precisely that understanding of Bourdieu called forth in the U.S. intellectual field. Let me acknowledge at the outset, then, exactly what Bourdieu's American readers refuse: his apparent reduction of social action to self-interest, in the form of the accumulation of "capital," and, further, his implicit foreclosure of any action that transcends individual interest or has progressive social change as its end. It will not do simply to argue that this understanding of Bourdieu is a misunderstanding, that concepts such as *habitus* or *le sens pratique* were intended from the beginning to supersede the notion of a "self" consciously calculating its interests. Even Bourdieu's most sympathetic readers, while granting his anticipation of the typical misreadings of his work, record a sense that his account of human motivation is profoundly reductive and pessimistic. Speaking for many, Edward LiPuma wonders how, given the terms of Bourdieu's analysis, any individual can "produce forms of thought that expose and threaten the reproduction of the class structure" (Calhoun et al., 24). It is only too easy to come away from Bourdieu with the impression that he offers a completely determinist social ontology, expressed in a fail-safe mechanism of "reproduction."[3]

Whether Bourdieu's sociology can be accurately characterized in such terms is not my primary concern here, although I hope to dislodge some assumptions underlying this response. My immediate objective is to consider the possibility that his refusal can be taken as an index of certain properties of the "national intellectual field." What seems to have troubled Bourdieu's U.S. readers most is the implication that social change cannot be the conscious and intended effect of individual or collective action. I argue that the very vehemence with which his perceived determinism is rejected can be said to express by contrast an intellectual ethos of *voluntarism*. If there is any doubt about the prevalence of this ethos in recent years, let me offer the emergence of cultural studies as a sufficient exhibit. Lawrence Grossberg's statement concerning the ends of this project would elicit broad consensus in the humanities and in some of the social sciences: "Cultural studies is a rigorous intellectual—even academic—practice which seeks to produce better knowledge of the political context of the world, knowledge which opens up new and hopefully progressive possibilities of struggle and transformation."[4] In lieu of a fuller account, I shall rely on a perception that few would now contest: it has become increasingly important to justify academic practice by asserting it as the vehicle of political transformation. We need not decide whether it is such a vehicle, or even whether it should be, to recognize how important it has become to foreground the motive of political change in academic practice.

Now it is worth remarking, before proceeding any further, that Bourdieu's sociology in no way denies the ubiquity of struggle or the fact of social change. Bourdieu offers at least an implicit descriptive theory of social change, to wit, the failure of reproduction. But he would say that such change is an effect of struggles that do not usually have as their conscious end the progressive transformation of society implied in the cultural studies project. Most change, in Bourdieu's terms, is the effect of struggles within fields that never cease to be determined by the principles of the field, even when what constitutes power or value in the field is being contested. Bourdieu's theory also allows for change as the result of struggles between fields as they interrupt or interfere with each other, but again, these struggles are not necessarily undertaken with progressive, transformative ends in view. Sometimes, of course, they are. However, one must wonder at the reductiveness of a social theory that speaks of change only as an effect of socially transformative agendas.[5] Such a concept of social action constructs it as the altruistic complement to the calculating self-interest imputed to Bourdieu's social agents. Both conceptions evacuate the large area of social action for which the motives of action are not so clearly or consciously conceived. In any case, the relegation of social change to the sphere of individual motives, good or bad, should arouse our theoretical suspicions, for it encourages a descent from the rigor of analysis to the rhetoric of praise or blame and thus links voluntarist discourse to an even less credible moralism.

Still, we are scarcely prepared yet to defend Bourdieu's consideration of the issue. All we can do at the moment is to specify what the refusal of Bourdieu in the U.S. academic field tells us about this field: its conception of change is modeled on a very old idea of social transformation that it has nevertheless repudiated in its nineteenth-century, revolutionary form. The revolutionary project has now been parceled out to the New Social Movements in their opposition to particular forms of domination: racism, sexism, homophobia, and so on. What is the relation, then, of an academic discourse that analyzes the social realm to the New Social Movements themselves, which must proceed on the assumption that things can be changed? This question has no simple answer, if an analytic account of social phenomena is expected to demonstrate what determines states of affairs.[6] Literary and cultural critics would like to believe that vanguard theoretical discourses can lead to transformative struggles, by which the various forms of domination can be brought to an end. Envisioning such a transformation has a necessary place in thought, but it does not describe how change will take place in the future or has taken place in the past. Raising social change to consciousness, or rationalizing it as a theoretically informed practice, is a project whose realization should not be confused with the mode of change in social reality.

Shall we say, then, that what Bourdieu's American readers find lacking in his sociology is this project? Whether or not it is truly absent from his work, it would certainly appear that Bourdieu's sociology is given over to a descriptive analysis of social actions that in the end (whatever the intentions of the actors) always reconstitute structures of domination. This reconstitution occurs even within and through the process of social change, which appears to have an attenuated significance by comparison with the recurrence of these fundamental structures of domination. Thus Bourdieu's readers come away with the (mistaken) impression that for him there is never any change at all, only "reproduction." But a better way to put it is, after all, in French: *Plus ça change, plus c'est la même chose.*

The French maxim raises a question somewhat deeper than Bourdieu's supposed inclination to a cynical view of human things. The recurrence of structures of domination despite manifest change is an undeniable fact of history. This question is discussed in sympathetic but not uncritical terms by the sociologist Craig Calhoun, who rightly sees it as related to the tension in Bourdieu's work between "what sorts of categories should be taken as historically specific and which as transhistorical" (Calhoun et al., 82). The tension corresponds roughly to the difference between an anthropology making universal claims about human societies and a sociology addressed to the historical question of "modernity" as the epoch characterized by continuous social change.[7] Calhoun proposes that the very rapidity of social change, which seems to have accelerated with the transition to a "postmodernism," may have prevented theorists from considering to what extent certain fundamental social relations might be reproduced despite the pace of change and behind the screen of its spectacular show. In its favor, Bourdieu's sociology draws attention to the reproduction of structures of domination. I would agree with Calhoun that by underelaborating the relation between social change and reproduction, Bourdieu arouses the suspicion that he "is saying something more trans-historical and anthropologically invariant about human actors than he lets on" (Calhoun et al., 71). While the strong emphasis on "social integration and stable reproduction" (Calhoun et al., 82) is a tendency in Bourdieu's sociology, it is not a necessary assumption.

I propose to argue that the tension Calhoun identifies between the transhistorical and the historical in Bourdieu is related to his undertheorizing some aspects of modernity as an epoch of continual change—specifically, the economic per se—while extensively elaborating other aspects, primarily the cultural. It will require some time (and the reader's patience) for me to evince the relation between this distribution of theoretical labor and the signal tension Calhoun observes. The question cannot be resolved simply by asserting that Bourdieu has neglected some relevant areas of social life. He may have done so, yet he has never claimed to produce a total theory of the social but only to construct theory as an analytic aid. Which domains of the social Bourdieu chooses to explore, and to what extent, is no doubt determined in ways (for example, the biographical) to which we can have only limited access. But the question of the distribution of his theoretical labor is raised in an especially vexing way by one of the three chief concepts in his sociology, capital (the others being, of course, *habitus* and field). Given the problem I have just remarked, it is all the more striking that the concept most resonant with historical implication is also insistently transhistorical in Bourdieu's usage. The forms of "symbolic capital" are present for him wherever there are social relations, but Bourdieu offers no independent or correlative analysis of capitalism as an economic or social system. As Calhoun shrewdly remarks, Bourdieu's account of capital lacks "an idea of capitalism" (Calhoun et al., 68).

Nor would it be possible to dismiss this problem by observing that the idea of capitalism has been elaborated elsewhere, as in Marxism. That idea is arguably missing in Marx, too; his concept was, after all, *capital*. Capitalism, as the union of social and economic systems, is even today as controverted a theoretical construct as it is an ongoing reality.

If Bourdieu is not really interested in the theory of capitalism (which seems dubious), he is certainly interested in modernity. Calhoun points out that Bourdieu's account of the multiplication and autonomization of fields is decisively oriented toward the analysis of modern society. It powerfully evokes the themes of classical sociology (Durkheim's anomie or Weber's rationalization) as well as more recent developments in social theory, such as Habermas's "uncoupling of system and lifeworld" or Luhmann's "differentiation of society." It is not just that Bourdieu's sociology lacks a historical account of capitalism that would complement his account of modernity or counterbalance his transhistorical concept of capital. The very choice of this concept to define the stakes of the "field" compels us to consider the absence of an account of capitalism deliberate. I will argue that Bourdieu refuses the problematic of capitalism—which is to say that this refusal is, in his own terms, both determined and strategic, a move in the game of sociology.

The risk in this strategy is more immediately evident than the possible gain. It seems perverse to construct the most universal account of social action by means of a concept that signals a definite historical epoch and, worse, constantly invites Bourdieu's readers to identify his construction with the rational calculation of behavior in the capitalist market. His lexical choice risks echoing the universalization of market behavior, which Western economists have been only too enthusiastic to affirm (indeed, since the collapse of the Soviet Union, to elevate to an anthropological universal). The terminological confusion troubles even his most sympathetic readers. Calhoun, for example, wonders if, after all, Bourdieu is unwittingly guilty of economism: "The motive force of social life [in Bourdieu] is the pursuit of distinction, profit, power, wealth, and so on. Bourdieu's account of capital is an account of the resources that people use in such pursuit. In this sense, despite his disclaimers, Bourdieu does indeed share a good deal with Gary Becker and other rational choice theorists" (Calhoun et al., 71).

Calhoun goes on to concede the justice of Bourdieu's rejection of the charge of economism but qualifies this concession by noting that rational choice theory is probably more sophisticated than the version of it that Bourdieu is rejecting; at least, it is no longer dependent on constructing every social action as though a fully free and conscious mind confronted the world with unlimited knowledge about possible choices. But I am less concerned with reaffirming the difference between Bourdieu and rational choice theorists such as Becker, or even Elster, than with understanding the stakes in the strategic appropriation of the concept of capital.[8] We can acquire a preliminary sense of them by noting a certain paradox both in rational choice theory and in Bourdieu's sociology. For rational choice theorists, as indeed for "free-market" economists generally, the market is the site of a certain idealized freedom; there, individual agents are free to pursue their interests, to "maximize utilities." The freedom from constraint (that is, from government interference) is also experienced in the market as a freedom of the will. The ideology of the free market has thus never dispensed with an essential voluntarism, which undergrids the methodological individualism of economics (one might invoke here both F. A. Hayek and Milton Friedman as representative of mainstream free-market economics). From the viewpoint of economics as a science, however, the freedom of the will is merely notional. In the aggregate behavior of the market's free agents, economic science discerns regularities that, insofar as they are determinable, can be said to be determined. For economics, the market is like nature, the object of increasingly mathematical description and prediction. At the same time, the quasi-religious faith of this science is that all is for the best when the market is left in its natural (that is, "free") state. The more ideologically committed free-market economists give no indication at all of recognizing the contradiction in asserting a freedom that their science disallows, but this may be the kind of philosophical question in which economists have long since lost interest.

As a social science, sociology too aspires, as Durkheim said, to treat social facts as "things"; like economics, it is forced to confront the ancient antinomy of freedom and necessity (usually updated in social theory as that of agency and structure) in its account of social action. Bourdieu hopes to overcome this antinomy—the alternatives of "social physics" and "social phenomenology"—and perhaps he does. But the durability of these ancient powers is such that his sociology continues to give the impression of reducing social life to implacable necessity. Because we are dealing with an immemorial binarism of thought, we can see why Bourdieu's account of social action in terms of symbolic capital can be confused with the individualist and voluntarist market ideology he so obviously disdains. The antinomy has the uncanny capacity to flip any social phenomenon from one pole to the other. This paradox of Bourdieu's reception suggests that his "determinist" sociology is being read as the mirror image of Western economics, for which the universalization of the market is nothing less than the maximal extension of human freedom.

I hope by this point to have established a certain understanding of the response to Bourdieu in the United States: the perception of his determinism, or economism, has as its cultural or ideological referent a voluntarism whose context is ultimately the free market. But this context need not be openly acknowledged as a condition of reception, and indeed it cannot be without calling into question that tendential voluntarism that the refusal of Bourdieu shares with economics. For this reason the misunderstanding of Bourdieu expressed in the charge of economism is always also an understanding, in that it suggests that the refusal of Bourdieu in the U.S. academy is in a deep way related to his own refusal of the problematic of capitalism, of the market in material as opposed to symbolic goods. We return, then, to the question raised above: If Bourdieu's appropriation of the concept of capital is to be read as something other than an index of his tendency toward economism, we have to consider the possibility that his disinclination to specify further the relation between capital and capitalism has a strategic value for him. The stakes of his appropriation of economic concepts are in any case very high.

CONTEST OF THE FACULTIES

In his *Outline of a Theory of Practice* Bourdieu makes the claim that "the theory of strictly economic practice is simply a particular case of a general theory of the economics of practice."[9] In strategic terms, this claim might be seen as an argument for the greater "generality" of sociology itself in relation to the discourse of economics. Sociology would then have to wrest the language of the economic away from its inherence in the "particular case": "Economic theory has allowed to be foisted upon it a definition of the economy of practices that is the historical invention of capitalism" ("Forms of Capital," 242). It has not been sufficiently appreciated that from Bourdieu's point of view economic discourse is a defective, anticipatory version of sociology. Thus Bourdieu can definitively say that "my theory owes nothing, despite appearances, to the transfer of the economic approach. And I hope one day to be able to demonstrate fully that, far from being the founding model, economic theory (and rational action theory which is its sociological derivative) is best seen as a particular instance, historically dated and situated, of the theory of fields" (*IRS*, 120). We may have difficulty imagining such a revolution in social science now that economics seems to have so successfully subordinated the other social sciences, establishing itself at once as a "science" on the natural-scientific model and as the most powerful academic presence in the domain of policy making. Yet if Bourdieu's hypothesis is correct, it will go a long way toward recasting the relation between economics and sociology as something more than a "contest of the faculties," despite being first of all such a contest. This question, in my view, goes much deeper than the common objection that symbolic or cultural capital is merely a metaphor, or an extrapolation from economic behavior, a charge that fails to grasp the social reality of the symbolic form or the extent to which Bourdieu regards sociology as a challenge to the very entitlement of economics to the language of exchange.

With this question in mind, we can take a closer look at the implications of the distinction between the general and the particular economies of practice. In his early anthropological work Bourdieu describes "archaic" (or premodern) societies as structured predominantly by a general economy of practice, regardless of whether there also exists a market for the exchange of material goods. What is most crucial to grasp about this general economy is that it operates in such a way as to "prevent the economy from being grasped *as* an economy" (*OTP*, 171). To conceive the principle of social action in the general economy (what Bourdieu calls *le sens pratique*) by analogy to the rationality of the capitalist market is to miss precisely the sense in which the "practical logic" of archaic societies utterly refuses the rational calculation of the market without ceasing to be a kind of economic practice. Only in this refusal can symbolic capital be constituted as such. The concept of capital must be understood in this usage as expressing a refusal of the calculus of accumulation and even as an implicit negation of "material" capital as a description of exchanged objects. The general economy is a negation of the particular; this is a rather different relation between the two terms than that of genus to species.

One might ask whether the form of material capital needs to become the object of thought in order to be negated. Bourdieu's answer, of course, is that the notion of practice entails no necessary reflective consciousness. *Habitus*, as a "structuring and structured structure," does not require its ends to be posited in thought to operate as a kind of "rationality." Rather, it is an embodied rationality (this is different too from an unconscious rationality, which would presumably look just like rational calculation, only "unconscious"). An important matter hinges on this question, since only the historical circumstance of rationality's development as a fully conscious process of thought (the instrumental rationality of the market) yielded a language—the economic—by means of which the rationality of the general economy could be recognized, after the fact, as a form of economic rationality. For the same reason, it was only when the form of material capital became a ubiquitous social fact that one could see that the general economy was constituted by the very negation of the form of material capital. This irony brings capital back into relation to the historical order of capitalism by making capitalism the condition for both the understanding and the misunderstanding of "economic practice" in precapitalist or noncapitalist societies. The negation of market rationality in premodern practice curiously precedes market rationality itself (or the universalized condition of commodity exchange). One might say, then, that the "idea of capitalism" is not developed in Bourdieu but that it is always implied in the description of the general economy of practice in archaic societies as a "reversed" or denied economic practice.

We will return presently to the motif of reversal. It is necessary first, however, to clarify a difficulty that arises at this juncture: everything recounted thus far leads us to believe that just as archaic societies are defined by the prevalence of the general economy or symbolic capital, so the dominance of the particular form of economic capital—material capital—has to constitute modernity itself. The very categories of the general and the particular, or the symbolic and the material, appear to be closely associated, if not identified, with the epochal concepts of the archaic and the modern. In fact, this identification is a misreading of Bourdieu, although his terminology elicits it for reasons as yet unstated. Let us pose the question that emerges here as clearly as possible: Why does symbolic capital seem constitutively primitive, when Bourdieu everywhere calls attention to the existence of such capital in the modern world, preeminently in the sphere of artistic production but pervading every practice associated with the concept of "distinction." Is one to construe those spheres of the social (or fields) in which symbolic capital is accumulated at one or more removes from the market in material goods as residual, as carrying over into modernity the same capital form, indeed the very economic form, that defines archaic societies? This would seem to be confirmed by every instance of what Bourdieu calls "consecration" in modern artistic production. The refusal of a strictly economic valuation of cultural products might be said to invoke a primitive relation to the products of labor: "The denial of the economy and economic interest which, in pre-capitalist societies, was exerted first in the very area of 'economic' transactions, from which it had to be expelled in order for 'the economy' to be constituted as such, thus finds its favored refuge in the domain of art and 'culture.'"[10] This theme is echoed in much the same terms in *The Rules of Art:* "The trade in 'pure' art belongs to the class of practices where the logic of pre-capitalist economy survives."[11] Yet the meaning of "survival" can hardly be less straightforward. Assuming that we avoid the temptation to project the practices of our own society on those of our precedessors, would we not make the converse error by construing as residually primitive every sphere of society not simply expressive of the overt rationality of the market? To be sure, we have rejoined here classical sociology's problem of the relation between traditional and modern society, which requires a rather different interpretive schema than the transition from feudalism to capitalism. Theories of capitalism are concerned with the emergence of the "restricted economy," as well as with the extension of market rationality into other domains of social exchange. But even the most ambitious rational choice theorists have not reduced every domain of the social to the quantifiable practice of maximizing utilities. If all social action were nothing but market behavior, then economics could give us a full and adequate account of the social. There would be no need for sociology at all.

The appearance of symbolic capital within modernity thus leads one to ask what kinds of archaic social relations subsist within capitalism and what the mode of subsistence is.[12] Theories of modernity and modernization have often entailed as a corollary the necessity of recognizing as apparently archaic many social forms, not only the "refuge" of art but much else besides, from the conspicuous archaism of religion to the highly ritualized practices of corporate culture. I say that these forms are "apparently" archaic because it cannot be that they exist as pure repetitions of premodern practice, without relation to the central fact of the capitalist market. It was just the ambition of classical sociology to demonstrate the refunctioning of premodern categories of "status," for instance, around the economic division of class that constituted the space of its deviation from a Marxist political economy (the preeminent example would be Weber, but one may cite Simmel and Veblen as well). Nonetheless, the question of the archaic remains a deep puzzle in social theory; it gives rise to the ambiguity of

28 John Guillory

Bourdieu's categories of general and particular economic practice, at once a distinction between genus and species and the terms of a mutual negation. Only in a society that declares its difference from all others, that apprehends itself ecstatically or tragically as under the sway of the particular social form of the capitalist market, can the antinomy of the general and particular economy emerge.

This question is either illuminated or further complicated in Bourdieu's essay "The Forms of Capital," where he defines three categories of capital: economic, cultural, and social (the latter referring to the network of familial and other institutional relations constituting social advantage of some sort). This taxonomy is at a slight tangent to the larger antithesis of symbolic and material capital, since symbolic and cultural capital are not precisely equivalent concepts. In *Outline of a Theory of Practice* symbolic capital is given the specific content of "prestige" or "honor," while cultural capital seems best exemplified elsewhere in Bourdieu's work on the educational institution (*Reproduction, Homo Academicus*), where it refers as much to knowledge, skills, or competence as to the honor or prestige that the possession of this capital can command. Cultural capital is certainly a species of symbolic capital generally, but it is a form of symbolic capital certifiable by objective mechanisms ("Forms of Capital," 247), most importantly by the credentializing function of the school. In *The Wizard of Oz,* for example, we know that the Scarecrow has more than proven his intelligence and that he has acquired considerable symbolic capital based on that personal embodied quality. He only lacks, as the Wizard says, a diploma. It is the curious property of the diploma to certify his intelligence to those who may not be familiar with the Scarecrow's accomplishments.

As good a sociologist as the Wizard, Bourdieu gives such mechanisms a crucial role in the narrative of modernization, since their emergence partly usurps the space of practical logic in its purely embodied form, reproducing the unequal distribution of capital over successive generations through institutions that work according to a principle somewhat like inheritance.[13] Hence the status concept of nobility can continue to model the possession of cultural capital (or distinction) even when that capital is acquired by inheriting not "blood" but access to educational institutions or cultivated social venues. The *differentia specifica* of cultural capital would seem to be its convertibility into material capital, and vice versa. This convertibility raises the limit on the accumulation of capital, which is no longer confined to the embodied form (as it presumably was in archaic societies). In retrospect, we can recognize at least an implicit articulation of capitalism to modernity in the invention of new forms of accumulation that overcome the limits of embodied prestige or symbolic capital and that include, above all, money itself, for which there is perhaps no limit of accumulation and which can be converted in certain circumstances into forms of cultural and even symbolic capital. In foregrounding accumulation as the end of social action, Bourdieu's conception of capitalism seems closer to that of Immanuel Wallerstein, for whom capitalism is the regime of endless accumulation, than to that of Marx.[14]

Only with the condition of convertibility can symbolic capital take the more recognizably modern form of cultural capital. It is worth insisting on this point, for the sake of reiterating the difference of symbolic capital in premodern society. There the denial of the very economic process of conversion constitutes symbolic capital as such. This denial can be so total as to govern even the exchange of material goods, which anthropology has long taught us to view in terms of gift exchange, or "potlatch." One sees why Bourdieu is so eager to rebut the charge of economism, which assumes that the point of all social action is simply to convert symbolic into material capital. His vehement rejection of rational choice theory reveals his intense theoretical investment in exploring the conditions of nonconvertibility, constraints on convertibility, or resistance to convertibility. Hence he expresses considerable disdain for Becker's well-known "human capital" theory, which always "reduc[es] the universe of exchanges to mercantile exchange" ("Forms of Capital," 242). It is as though Bourdieu were responding not so much to the social depredations attributed to capitalism's reduction of social relations to market exchanges as to the way economic theory takes that reduction as an accurate picture of social life generally. Yet the fact that Bourdieu's contempt for rational choice theory is expressed in response to the consistent tendency of his readers to confuse his argument with that very theory compels us to recognize his social theory as the mirror image of rational choice theory.

Once again we are impressed by how close the misunderstanding of Bourdieu's work is to its understanding. Nowhere is this point more evident than in the curious similitude between rational choice theory's development of a "game-theoretic" model of social action and Bourdieu's consistent preference for the analogy of the game. The philosophical example of Wittgenstein lies behind Bourdieu's use of this term, but that example may well be invoked in the background of rational choice theory, too (as in Elster's work). The analogy of the game increases the tension between sociology and economics for Bourdieu, since capital is consistently described in *Marxist* political economy as embodied or accumulated labor, set to work in a definite social relation in which productive labor is employed to further the accumulation of capital. These terms are still authoritative for Bourdieu—in "The Forms of Capital" he defines capital as accumulated labor—but they are not his usual terms. Labor may be the inner truth of social practice, but practice appears more often in Bourdieu as play, a move in a game, the "game of culture." In analogous fashion, rational choice theory renders the neoclassical economic problematic of maximizing utilities into quasi-cultural terms, in the form of game theory. What are we to make of this similitude? It is just here, if anywhere, that we shall have to distinguish rational choice theory (and economic discourse) from its mirror image in Bourdieu. What we will discover, looking into the two mirrors, is that the image of the *market* in the one finds its most effective reversal as *art* in the other. By implication, we shall not be able to take Bourdieu's ruthless reduction of the domain of art at face value; indeed, his sociology is compelled continually to return to the question of the aesthetic precisely in order to settle accounts, as it were, with the discourse of economics.[15]

Let us begin, however, by briefly recalling Bourdieu's description of archaic practice, which demonstrates that what appears to us as mere play (gift exchange, ritual practices) does a certain kind of work. When the general economy is conceived as the game of accumulating symbolic capital, practice is represented as both work and play. But understanding any particular practice is like looking at the surface of a solid figure—one side will present itself by occluding the other— and for Bourdieu the facing side is more often than not play, conceived under the general category of "competition" or a move in a game. To imagine a practice that is nothing but play (on both sides) or nothing but labor (on both sides), one has to enter fully into the universe of the capitalist market. There indeed we find a domain of practice that appears to be labor and nothing but labor—or better, "abstract labor," exchanged for a value that does not admit of accumulation for the laborers themselves. Play here approaches the zero degree. These players have no capital to play with; they have no embodied symbolic capital, and only their labor time has a market value. Analogously, it is only in this capitalist society that there is something like pure play or "abstract play," if we can allow that term to invoke the major topos of aesthetic discourse as it descends from Kant and Schiller to Bourdieu himself: "The world of bourgeois man, with his double-entry accounting, cannot be invented without producing the pure, perfect universe of the artist and the intellectual and the gratuitous activities of art-for-art's sake and pure theory" ("Forms of Capital," 242). The antinomies of work and play are thus linked to the discourses of the economic and the aesthetic, and this link has important consequences for Bourdieu's development of a sociology that aggressively appropriates key concepts of economic discourse.

One can see that a tendency in Bourdieu's sociology favors elaborating practice as a form of play whose inner truth is labor against an economism that would either reduce all practice to the explicit labor of accumulation or conceal the fact of labor altogether by representing all social action as play, as in game theory. Bourdieu's hybrid conception recognizes the complexity of social practice, its identity as both labor and play, but it may well be that capitalist society has sorted out labor and play to such a degree that they exist at special social sites in a very pure state: pure labor in Taylorized wage labor, pure unproductive play in the passive mass-mediated consumptions of "leisure." Bourdieu's greater interest in complex forms of play than in mass-media consumption directs him inevitably and repeatedly in his career to the domain of art and high culture. He is more interested in an activity such as museum going, for example, than in watching television, because aesthetic play in the former context is more interestingly complex, a labor (or game) of accumulating symbolic capital that refuses the crude calculations of market rationality. One might contrast the scene of museum going with that of the video game, which, as in the game-theoretic models of rational choice theory, gives us the simplest possible model of social action, explicitly directed toward the accumulation of profit in the mimetic form of a score. The end of museum going cannot be reduced to such a quantifiable measure of its profitability, and hence its very resistance to conversion into such terms must be seen as incorporated into the experience itself, as the sign of its innate complexity. It shares this quality of complexity with certain archaic practices, and thus a kind of rhyme between archaic practice and these complex social spaces in modernity is produced. This is why the archaic peasant's unproductive ritual can seem like "art-for-art's sake" and art like religious experience: "The world of art, a sacred island, ostentatiously opposed to the profane, everyday world of production, a sanctuary for gratuitous, disinterested activity in a universe given over to money and self-interest, offers, like theology in a past epoch, an imaginary anthropology obtained by denial of all the negations brought about by the economy" (*OTP,* 197).

What I am calling the rhyme between archaic and certain complex modern practices depends for its force, then, on the striking contrast of such practices with the overt calculation of market rationality. These practices hold the market at a distance but of course do not cancel its reality or effects. All cultural capital may be ultimately convertible, by however complexly mediated a process, into economic capital. If, as I have tried to show, Bourdieu is especially drawn to the most complex social practices, then the same tendency conversely requires that the capitalist market play the role of simplicity itself, that it operate, in other words, according to the reduced and reductive principle of what Marx called "naked self-interest." The market will then be like a *point of reference* at the center of a complexly divided social space. Bourdieu's investment in specific social fields is directly proportional to their distance from this point, with art and the institutions of culture lying at the farthest remove and the school and the family closer in. We can now see that the spatial distance of culture from the market corresponds to the temporal distance of archaic practice and that this correspondence accounts for the rhyme between them. The distance to the center, the social space that must be traversed for cultural or symbolic capital to be converted into economic, is the space in which a long and complex game is played and in which the tactic of delaying convertibility may yield the best profits in the end. Bourdieu's sociological work brings to light the identity of this game as an economy, exposing the "denial of the economy" as the move on which the game is founded. But it also enters into the spirit of this denial, into culture's repudiation of "a universe given over to money and self-interest." This universe is contracted to a point in Bourdieu's sociology, and in this way he maintains nothing less than an aesthetic distance from the market itself.

SALON DES REFUSÉS

I have now drawn attention, by what may seem an altogether too oblique itinerary, to an otherwise puzzling absence in Bourdieu's social theory: despite the fact that it relies so heavily on the concepts of capital and the market, his work is distinguished by the relative lack of commentary on economics, as an elaborated discourse, or on the economy, narrowly defined. There is a market in Bourdieu, but there is no history of capitalism; no theory of the commodity or of surplus value; no conceptualization of money or financial instruments; no banks; no corporations; no price theory; no stocks or bonds; no monopolies; no business cycles; no inflations, depressions, or recessions; no taxes or deficits; no international trade or currency exchange; no Fordist or post-Fordist modes of production. All of this, Bourdieu would be entitled to respond, is the matter of economics, not sociology. We are nevertheless forced to acknowledge that the contraction of the economic domain in Bourdieu to the dimensionless singularity of the market is the effect precisely of the commanding position of the market at the center of his social universe. Everything is either falling toward this center or struggling to escape its attraction. The impression of economic determinism conveyed so powerfully by Bourdieu's work is at least in part an effect of the market as *absent cause*. The market structures social space into "classes," which appear in turn like nature, in the sense that they are always given in his account of social action.

Even as the market is contracted to a point, what is antithetical to the market is expanded into a world, the "economic world reversed." Bourdieu's is the first major sociology since Simmel's to focus so intensively and lingeringly on the domain of the aesthetic, and like Simmel's it is deeply, though less directly, obsessed with the market. In its interest in the aesthetic, it stands in partial contrast to the work of Durkheim and Weber, who developed the discursive field of sociology primarily through the study of religion. But the rhyme between art and religion should hint at the stakes of Bourdieu's discursive strategy, which maps the social world to define once again, like the founders, the discursive territory of sociology. In the remaining pages of this essay I would like to draw out some implications of Bourdieu's interest in art, with particular reference to his most recent volume, *The Rules of Art*. This analysis will be facilitated by first situating the domain of art within the map of Bourdieu's social space, which can be resolved into four different markets:

1. The *general economy* of archaic or premodern or "nonmarket" societies, in which a practical logic prevails and in which the economy in the narrow sense is "socially repressed." The form of capital here is preeminently honor. Its accumulation is limited by its dependence on embodiment, and the conditions of its convertibility into economic capital are severely constrained.
2. The *capitalist market* proper, in which the preeminent form of capital is material goods or money, whose accumulation is virtually unlimited. Social interest in accumulation is expressed overtly, as it becomes the object of rationality in its "instrumental" or calculating form.

What Bourdieu calls the "market of symbolic goods" gives us two other markets with somewhat different principles:

3. A *mimetic market,* where cultural capital is accumulated. In this market there is no attempt to conceal the mutual convertibility of cultural and material capital; on the contrary, agents are deliberately and even enthusiastically interested in reconstructing cultural spheres as practices of rational accumulation and assured convertibility. This market corresponds to the advancing frontier of commodification, which seeks to regularize and manipulate the convertibility of cultural goods and embodied qualities, even the most accidental, such as physical beauty.[16] In the same way, wealth is convertible directly into prestige or honor, as in "lifestyles of the rich and famous." Within the mimetic market we also find Bourdieu's objective mechanisms, such as the school, which make possible ever greater accumulations of cultural capital and thus a higher rate of convertibility. In certifying qualifications or competences, the school "guarantee[s] the monetary value of a given academic capital" (*"Forms of Capital,"* 248). The mimetic market, with which Becker's human capital theory is concerned, is what gives rational choice theory its license to construct all social action as market behavior, as maximizing utilities.[17]

4. To the mimetic market Bourdieu implicitly opposes an *antimimetic market,* defining the realm of art but also that of science. In these fields (the "intellectual field," in the broadest sense for Bourdieu), where the "economic world [is] reversed," symbolic capital refuses to be assessed in economic terms. This refusal establishes a distance that must be traveled in order for conversion of symbolic into material capital to take place. Within the antimimetic market, the symbolic capital of honor or prestige can then reappear in a rather different mode than in the institutional venues dispensing cultural capital by means of objective mechanisms. This mode is linked to what Bourdieu calls "autonomy." I will suggest that Bourdieu is intensely interested in the antimimetic market's project of maintaining a distance from the capitalist market proper.

The significance of autonomy in this social mapping emerges in the following account of *The Rules of Art,* a summalike text that confirms the signal importance of the aesthetic for Bourdieu's sociology. But let us appreciate, before proceeding, the unusual perspective this focus gives us on contemporary society. If the aesthetic domain establishes a "rhyme" with archaic practice, this practice, as Bourdieu constructs it, looks very marginal at the present time. The unacknowledged legislators of the "world apart" may once have exerted their authority throughout Western high culture, but after the orgy of the eighties art scene, it may no longer be necessary to acknowledge their rules or possible to deny that the frontiers of commodification have greatly diminished art's "sacred island." Bourdieu's interest—this word should be emphasized in all its senses now—has always been in a certain construction of the aesthetic that finds its origin in the romantic period, is definitively theorized in Kant, and achieves autonomy in aestheticism, which then lays the groundwork for the avant-garde and for high modernism.

In short, a strongly invested construction of the aesthetic underlies the selection in *The Rules of Art* of its representative moment, the later nineteenth century; its representative author, Flaubert; and its representative text, *Sentimental Education.* The exemplarity of Flaubert's novel for delimiting the "genesis and structure of the literary field" is altogether too fitting, which is to say that it lends itself easily to Bourdieuian analysis. *Sentimental Education* offers us what looks like a sociological allegory *avant la lettre,* in which the protagonist, Frédéric Moreau, is set to play the game of culture with a carefully assessed stock of cultural and material capital. At the same time, the novel itself is to be understood as the stake in Flaubert's own struggle in the literary field, his reworking of the "minor genre" of the realist novel into the aesthetic object whose autonomy (art for art's sake) Bourdieu identifies with the genesis of the literary field (*RA,* 148). This excessive exemplarity is the index of a theoretical investment, since Bourdieu makes a certain dialectical advance through this text: he recovers from the same sociology of art that seemed to reduce the "love of art" to the accumulation of capital something that might be called, on the other side of this analysis, "love of art."

This is why, from the opening pages of the book, Bourdieu raises the possibility of the sociologist's identification with Flaubert: "One might think perhaps that it is the sociologist, in projecting questions of a particular sort, who turns Flaubert into a sociologist, and one capable, moreover, of offering a sociology of Flaubert" (3). Such an identification must be declined immediately, because it would render the sociologist superfluous; hence what is at stake in *The Rules of Art* is really the difference between Bourdieu and Flaubert, or between sociology and art: "It is a vision that one could call sociological if it were not set apart from a scientific analysis by its form, simultaneously offering and masking it" (31). One can hardly underestimate the extent to which Bourdieu is magnetized by this particular author and text and consequently challenged to assert a difference. Nor can one underestimate how important the moment of Flaubert's novel is to Bourdieu's understanding of the aesthetic generally. The derogated commercial genre that Flaubert elevates to a work of art thus exemplifies the principal claim of aesthetic discourse, to be "of the world and beyond it" (100). In its refusal to deliver only the pleasures of realist narrative, in its eagerness to offend the sensibilities of bourgeois consumers by representing the reality of the everyday in the most crafted and autoreferential language, Flaubert's avant-garde production goes so far as to refuse the demand for a vendible novel, which is to say that it engenders the literary field as such, art as such: "Art produces the effect of making the market disappear" (81). What is most important for Bourdieu in Flaubert's stance, however, is not just disdain for the market (which it shares with other high art forms, especially poetry) but the fact that the artwork that enacts this refusal is itself supremely accurate in its representation of the relation between culture and the market. This relation is indeed foregrounded in *Sentimental Education* and constitutes a kind of double reflexivity of subject and form. How is Bourdieu to demonstrate, then, that there is something that Flaubert does not know that sociology knows? At the least there will have to be something that Flaubert does not *say* and that sociology will have to say for him. But does this unsaid provide a sufficient reason for the discourse of sociology?[18]

These questions turn on the relation between the moment of reflexivity that gives birth to aestheticism (art for art's sake) and the moment of reflexivity in sociology, when that discourse acknowledges the social determination of the scientific field itself. Bourdieu's sociology seems dedicated to the ruthless exposure of art's claim to distance from the market. This claim is a generative *illusio,* the game of "loser takes all" (*RA,* 21) that institutes the literary field as an antimarket, the "market of symbolic goods." The self-understanding of art as autonomous is thus itself determined by the effects of a social space structured by the market and by the distribution of capital in the division of classes. I shall not be concerned here with the particulars of Bourdieu's analysis of this determination or with what he calls the "historical genesis of a pure aesthetic," or with his interpretation of Flaubert's novel, which is not at stake in this argument. I propose to bring out the circumstance that if Flaubert's novel so precisely anticipates the terms of Bourdieu's sociology, then the assertion of sociology's difference will entail not only the "reduction" of art's *illusio* but a further identification of the sociologist with the artist.

But let us clarify first the specificity of the aesthetic discourse that is to be analyzed: despite Flaubert's sociological fidelity to representing the social structures that impel or impede individuals like "particles in a force-field" (9), he implicitly claims to have transcended the force field himself and to have established at the level of the formal artwork the very freedom that his represented social world denies to the characters he creates: "Writing abolishes the determinations, constraints and limits which are constitutive of social existence: to exist socially means to occupy a determined position in the social structure" (27). The question for Bourdieu, I believe, is whether this freedom, which sociology reduces to a determination in its analysis of the aestheticist movement in its sociohistorical context—Bourdieu will say that Flaubert's position-taking in the literary field is possible by virtue of a certain position he occupies in social space—is not a prefiguration of the more real freedom of science, which includes its reflexive moment in the analysis of its determination. Is such freedom any more real than that of the artist, the maker of a world apart?

We begin to see why the question of Bourdieu's relation to Flaubert is necessarily repeated (or prefigured) in *Sentimental Education* as the question of Flaubert's identification with Frédéric. Yet it is important for Bourdieu that Flaubert is not Frédéric: "One recognizes, here again, Flaubert's fundamental relation to

Frédéric as the possibility, simultaneously surpassed and conserved, of Gustave" (27). Flaubert creates Frédéric as the figure of indeterminacy, suspended between all the possibilities—economic (business), cultural (art), or political (office)—but determined to none. Like Flaubert, he attempts to occupy "that indeterminate position, that *neutral place* where one can soar above groups and their conflicts" (26); but Flaubert intends to frustrate that intention and to exhibit his creature in the end as the figure of determined indeterminacy, as the figure who realizes the most likely possibility of his "neutral place," which is to squander his capital not in the artist's love of art but in the love of Madame Arnoux. Occupying roughly the same social position as Frédéric—at "the geometric intersection of all perspectives" (100)—Flaubert can establish his freedom only by distinguishing himself from his creation, just as Proust does later with his fictional Marcel: "It is this liberating rupture, creative of the creator, that Flaubert symbolized in dramatizing, in the shape of Frédéric, the powerlessness of a being manipulated by the forces of the field" (105).

Again, it is not my concern to assess the validity of Bourdieu's reading of Flaubert, and I have no doubt that literary critics will find Bourdieu's reading of Flaubert . . . reductive. But my point is to call attention to the structure of prefiguration that forces into the open the problem that motivates Bourdieu's reading of Flaubert and simultaneously troubles the reading of Bourdieu. For the freedom of Flaubert as novelist is like that of "Spinoza's God," who "remains immanent and coextensive with his creation" (112). Precisely because Flaubert is, in the real world, in much the same position as Frédéric, Frédéric remains always a "possibility . . . of Gustave": his fictional narrative does not become a fantasy of absolute freedom from social determination, and his "crazed love" for Madame Arnoux remains the analogue for the life of the artist, another version of determined indeterminacy. The difference between Gustave and Frédéric is not the difference between freedom and determination, then, but the difference between what Gustave knows about Frédéric and what Frédéric knows about himself.

If we are indeed to move beyond the facile voluntarism of a less sophisticated aesthetics (in which artists are gods) or a less sophisticated politics (in which social agents are undetermined), we shall have to ask what freedom is won by such knowledge. To arrive at some sense of the answer to this question, let us first grant that the freedom of the artist is not merely a false freedom and is located, for Bourdieu, in the apparent formalism of art for art's sake. It is what he otherwise calls autonomy, which has nothing to do with the freedom of the will but is a *historical condition of the literary field* and therefore itself determined. Autonomy is an aspect of the development of fields, although this development does not necessarily define a progressive evolution. Rather, we must think of autonomy as an effect of increasing social complexity and of differentiation within fields.[19] Discussing the figure of Manet (analogous in this context to Flaubert), Bourdieu locates the emergence of autonomy among those artists who "had to struggle to conquer their autonomy from the Académie. . . . the process leading to the constitution of a field is a process of the *institutionalization of anomie,* after which no one can claim to be absolute master and possessor of the *nomos*" (132). The freedom instituted by autonomy (or the "anomie" of the social total-ity) declares itself "the objective and subjective distance of enterprises of cultural production with respect to the market" (141), which again is not a godlike free-dom but the determined indeterminacy of those who recognize that art is subject to this demand. It is the freedom of the *salon des refusés,* who reject those who reject them and who establish an antithetical market in symbolic goods. The point is not, then, simply to expose this freedom as unreal, when in fact the space cleared by the refusal of market demand is precisely the space in which social determinations can be explored without wholly acceding to market demand and in which many new possibilities for the development of art are created.[20] These possibilities endure even when, as with every avant-garde, the *refusés* are eventu-ally embraced by the market itself. The point is that this freedom or autonomy is that of the knowledge differential between the commercial artist and the avant-garde, a differential that is extremely marginal and fragile and reaches its limit when autonomy is misrecognized as the absolute freedom of the artist or as the transcendence of the aesthetic domain.

It should be evident what kind of freedom is implied by Bourdieu's social the-ory: "It is within history that the principle of freedom from history resides" (248). The space in which Gustave and Frédéric are both "possibilities" is a de-termined space. In retrospect, it was perhaps too easy for Bourdieu to withhold from the artist the full recognition that autonomy itself is determined, even though aesthetic discourse obviously misrecognizes its real autonomy as freedom from determination *tout court.* Autonomy misrecognized reinstates the error of voluntarism in the aesthetic realm, as in every other. Bourdieu's struggle with this question produces in his argument something like a dialectical turn, provoked by a reconsideration in *The Rules of Art* of the old accusation that social agents in his theory always seem to act with conscious calculation (the converse, as we have seen, of the accusation of economic determinism). This question is particu-larly vexed in the context of a highly differentiated, relatively autonomous social space such as the literary field, where the choices of artists who have refused the market will always look compromised if they are seen as calculated to acquire an alternative symbolic capital. Bourdieu is concerned "above all to exorcise the alternatives of innocence or cynicism which carry the risk of introducing into the analysis—and especially *into the reading* made of it—antagonist visions of the daily struggle at the heart of the intellectual field, that of exalted celebrants, usu-ally applied to the great of the past, and that of a Thersites who arms himself with all the resources of a second-rate 'sociology' in order to discredit rivals by reducing their intentions to their presumed interests" (272).

Bourdieu goes on to invoke Spinoza's solution to the dilemma: "to substitute the often rather melancholic joys of the necessitating vision for the perverse plea-sures (always ambivalent and often alternating) of celebration and denigration."

Indeed, Spinoza seems very much behind Bourdieu's insistence that "reminding ourselves of the historical determinations of reasoning may constitute the principle of true freedom" (311). The question is whether this anamnesis is nothing other than "science," which is to say that it is not art. On this point Bourdieu arrives at a curiously revisionist insight, admitting that until he understood a certain text by Mallarmé, he did believe that being "aware of the logic of the game as such" could only "turn the literary or artistic enterprise into a cynical mystification or conscious trickery" (272). But perhaps the revisionist moment is self staged, as it seems to posit a Bourdieu who forgets or does not understand the Spinozist import of his own theory. Mallarmé plays with the possibility of dismantling the whole enterprise of making art by calling it a "fiction" and ends by simply stating that "it is a game," which is to say that the making of art is itself art. Mallarmé argues, in Bourdieu's explication, "both the objective truth of literature as a fiction founded on collective belief, and the right we have to salvage, in face of and against all kinds of objectification, literary pleasure" (275).[21] The objectification of art by sociological analysis cannot diminish the pleasure of literary art, except perhaps for unimaginative and moralistic readers.[22] So we have come full circle, to affirm the "love of art" whose inner truth as a symbolic economy was asserted in one of Bourdieu's earliest works, *The Love of Art.* The question about conscious calculation is resolved by recognizing all social action as like art, in that it is founded on *illusio,* or belief in the game. Love of art is not so very different from love of life, or at least the willingness to live it.

Playing the literary game to win in no way cancels the work of making art as an expression of "the love of art." The same must be said for the sociologist's "reductive" analysis of the literary field, or of any other social action, insofar as it is complex and not simple. The experience of reading a fiction (or the experience of any work of art) is itself the model for social action, in that it combines belief and disbelief, *illusio* and *disillusio.* Bourdieu is saying neither that calculation is all that there is nor that calculation is really unconscious, but that social action is complex in the same way that making or consuming art is complex.[23] This dialectical move displaces the economic model of social action as conscious calculation altogether or, rather, confines it to the domain of the strictly and narrowly economic, the market of material goods. But can we not say (or confirm) that in so doing Bourdieu constructs his sociology precisely to produce this distance from the narrowly economic?

The strategy of distancing is at issue if science (the science of sociology) produces this distance even more effectively than art. The advantage to be gained from the more effective strategy is greater autonomy, or greater freedom, as Bourdieu explains straightforwardly in his interview with Wacquant: "When you apply reflexive sociology to yourself, you open up the possibility of identifying true sites of freedom, and thus of building small-scale, modest, practical morals in keeping with the scope of human freedom which, in my opinion, is not that large" (*IRS,* 199). Science initiates a dialectical turn on art: as art gains its autonomy by refusing the market—the *salon des refusés*—so science gains its autonomy by insisting on the *illusio* of this refusal and bringing to light the market of symbolic goods. Only in a remotely Hegelian way is this dialectic detrimental to art. Bourdieu allows that "the literary work can sometimes say more, even about the social realm, than many writings with scientific pretensions," but "it says it only in a mode such that it does not truly say it" (*RA*, 32). But is it not the case that this science, whose name is sociology, also repeats art's gesture of refusal by taking art as the object of its analysis, and not the economy? Is there no sociology of the market of material goods? One might reply in the spirit, if not the voice, of Bourdieu: What interest can there be in "naked self-interest" if it is as simple and shallow as art is complex and profound? The richness of the sociology of art is purchased, after all, at the expense of impoverishing economics, which shrinks to the dimensionless point of the market. In exchange for its cultural poverty, however (and perhaps it is satisfied with this deal), the market acquires the force of determination and the name of the real. It is the "unsaid" in the *illusio* of art. Of course, in discovering this unsaid—"Science tries to speak of things as they are," Bourdieu writes at the end of his book, "without euphemisms"—the science of sociology also betrays its own *illusio:* science "asks to be taken seriously, even when it analyzes the foundations of this quite singular form of the *illusio* which is the scientific *illusio*" (336). In the game Bourdieu plays, I would say that the name of art is staked in a contest of sociology with economics, and if Bourdieu is destined to lose this game, he will at least be seen in the end to have been on the side of the artists.

NOTES

This chapter first appeared in *Modern Language Quarterly* 58:4, December 1997. It is reprinted by permission of Duke University Press.

1. Wacquant, "Bourdieu in America: Notes on the Transatlantic Importation of Social Theory," in *Bourdieu: Critical Perspectives,* ed. Craig Calhoun, Edward LiPuma, and Moishe Postone (Chicago: University of Chicago Press, 1993), 246.

2. Wacquant discusses typical critiques of Bourdieu's work at length. It is not my intention to respond to these criticisms, many of which have been addressed by Bourdieu himself. The refusal I speak of here is indicated as much by the relative lack of Bourdieu's influence in the United States as by published critiques of his work. It is too soon to tell whether the recent spate of translations will alter the situation.

3. LiPuma's view is shared by a number of commentators in the Calhoun volume. On the side of the social sciences, Jeffrey Alexander complains that Bourdieu "casts subjectivity in a determinate, antivoluntaristic form" and that the concept of *habitus* is only "a Trojan horse for determinism" (*Fin de Siècle Social Theory: Relativism, Reduction, and the Problem of Reason* [London: Verso, 1995], 131, 136). On the side of the humanities, Bruce Robbins writes of Bourdieu's "deep, static pessimism" (*Secular Vocations: Intellectuals, Professionalism, Culture* [London: Verso, 1993], 209). For a critique of Bourdieu

as a "conservative and normative" thinker see Bill Readings, *The University in Ruins* (Cambridge, Mass.: Harvard University Press, 1996), 106. I confine my remarks here to the North American academy, but I might have written nearly as accurately of the "Anglo-American" sense. Some aspects of the ethos described above characterize both national milieus. For example, in a generally appreciative account Derek Robbins speaks of "an element of fatalism or, perhaps of reluctant cosmic conservatism" in Bourdieu (*The Work of Pierre Bourdieu* [Boulder, Colo.: Westview, 1991], 175). As one might expect, given the different development of British cultural studies, there has been considerably more interest in Bourdieu in the United Kingdom (and in Australia) than in the United States. See in this context John Frow's quite good account of Bourdieu in his *Cultural Studies and Cultural Value* (Oxford: Clarendon, 1995), 27–47. Frow nonetheless registers the sense that Bourdieu's theory "allows for no possibility of critique and social transformation" (43). This reading is too prevalent, despite Bourdieu's careful attempts to address it, to be dismissed as a misreading. In sociological discourse the charge of determinism usually goes by the name "functionalism," as exemplified in Durkheim or Parsons. I avoid rehearsing these debates in narrowly disciplinary terms, for the sake of an audience presumed to consist largely of those in the humanities.

   4. Grossberg, "Toward a Genealogy of the State of Cultural Studies," in *Disciplinarity and Dissent in Cultural Studies,* ed. Cary Nelson and Kilip Parameshwar Gaonkar (New York: Routledge, 1996), 133.

   5. Indeed, a good deal of change has occurred in consequence of struggles undertaken to restore some previous state of affairs. But the conception of "social change" has been assimilated so entirely to a discourse of political voluntarism that even this fact has become difficult to see. Some of Bourdieu's work is concerned directly or indirectly with the significance of the sixties, May 1968 in particular (*Homo Academicus,* for example). It is not difficult to recognize his strong political investment in not taking the reactionary turn of so many French intellectuals in response to that decade's failed revolutionism. His later work attempts to see through the political voluntarism of the period to the structures reproducing the fundamental poles of dominant and subordinate groups. Whether or not Bourdieu's account of social reproduction is adequate, it certainly sets out from the fact of change.

   6. My use of "determination" with reference to the social realm is to be distinguished from the concept of "causality" in the natural-scientific sense. Determinations constrain or enable particular social actions, which is to say that in the realm of the social there is a weak causality. I believe that this usage is congruent with Bourdieu's.

   7. See, for example, the opening chapter of Jürgen Habermas, *The Philosophical Discourse of Modernity: Twelve Lectures,* trans. Frederick Lawrence (Cambridge, Mass.: MIT Press, 1987), 7–11.

   8. For a general bibliography of rational choice theory see Peter Abell, "Sociological Theory and Rational Choice Theory," in *The Blackwell Companion to Social Theory,* ed. Bryan S. Turner (Oxford: Blackwell, 1996), 252–73. Rational choice theory assumes that a scientific theory of social action must be based on the simplest possible model, according to which human beings always act to "maximize utilities." Since Bourdieu responds most directly to Gary Becker, I derive my comments on rational choice theory from his work, specifically *Human Capital: A Theoretical and Empirical Analysis, with Special Reference to Education,* 3d ed. (Chicago: University of Chicago Press, 1993); and *The*

Economic Approach to Human Behavior (Chicago: University of Chicago Press, 1976). In *Human Capital* Becker writes that his approach "follows modern economics and assumes that these investments usually are rational responses to a calculus of expected costs and benefits" (17). In *The Economic Approach* he argues that "market instruments perform most, if not all, of the functions assigned to 'structure' in sociological theories" and that "the economic approach provides a valuable unified framework for understanding *all* human behavior" (5, 14). Becker's remarks will give readers some idea of the stakes in Bourdieu's sociology and the present essay. In a "contest of the faculties," economics has for the most part displaced sociology. For Bourdieu's response to Becker see "The Forms of Capital," in *Handbook of Theory and Research for the Sociology of Education,* ed. John G. Richardson (New York: Greenwood, 1986), 241–58; Bourdieu and Wacquant, *An Invitation to Reflexive Sociology* (Chicago: University of Chicago Press, 1992), 123; and Bourdieu, *In Other Words: Essays towards a Reflexive Sociology,* trans. Matthew Adamson (Stanford, Calif.: Stanford University Press, 1990), 46–48.

9. Bourdieu, *Outline of a Theory of Practice,* trans. Richard Nice, Cambridge Studies in Social Anthropology, 16 (Cambridge: Cambridge University Press, 1977), 177.

10. Bourdieu, *The Logic of Practice,* trans. Richard Nice (Stanford, Calif.: Stanford University Press, 1990), 133.

11. Bourdieu, *The Rules of Art: Genesis and Structure of the Literary Field,* trans. Susan Emanuel (Stanford, Calif.: Stanford University Press, 1996), 148.

12. This would be a question of the "residual" in a larger sense than that intended by Raymond Williams, an epochal sense closer to Mauss or Bataille.

13. On the distinction between embodied and objectified capital see Bourdieu, "Les trois etats du capital culturel," *Actes de la recherche en sciences sociales,* no. 30 (1979): 3–6.

14. If symbolic or cultural capital can be given specific contents of prestige, distinction, and competence, Bourdieu further reduces them in "The Forms of Capital" to the single substance of "embodied" labor, which brings his theorizing into proximity with Marxism: "Capital is accumulated labor (in its materialized form or its 'incorporated,' embodied form) which, when appropriated on a private, i.e., exclusive, basis by agents or groups of agents, enables them to appropriate social energy in the form of reified or living labor" (241). This careful and perhaps surprising definition reproduces certain features of a Marxist account of capital without grounding the concept in the cycle of production, or "productive capital." Accumulation may imply "surplus value" but not necessarily the particular form of capitalism, the extraction of surplus value from wage labor. In fact, it may be better to invoke the paradigm of "mercantile" capital, in which surplus value is extracted from the process of circulation, to account for how embodied labor, in Bourdieu's sense, might enter into a cycle of accumulation (and therefore become capital).

15. Fredric Jameson speaks of Bourdieu's "blanket condemnation of the aesthetic as a mere class signal and as conspicuous consumption" (*Postmodernism: Or, The Cultural Logic of Late Capitalism* [Durham, N.C.: Duke University Press, 1991], 132).

16. One might insert the observation that capitalism depends from the start on advancing the terrain of commodification, beginning with labor, which becomes a commodity proper in the market for wage labor.

17. See Alvin W. Gouldner's work on cultural capital, principally *The Future of Intellectuals and the Rise of the New Class: A Frame of Reference, Theses, Conjectures, Argu-*

ments, and an Historical Perspective on the Role of Intellectuals and Intelligentsia in the International Class Contest of the Modern Era (New York: Seabury, 1979). Scott Lash, in his contribution to *Critical Perspectives,* "Cultural Economy and Social Change," makes some interesting remarks that extend Bourdieu's work on cultural capital to the theory of the new class (Calhoun et al., 206–7). Lash points out the considerable basis in Bourdieu, particularly in *Distinction,* on which the terms of such a theory might be worked out.

18. "In short, I believe that literature . . . is on many points more advanced than social science" (*IRS,* 208).

19. "In highly differentiated societies, the social cosmos is made up of a number of such relatively autonomous social microcosms, i.e. spaces of objective relations that are the site of a logic and a necessity that are *specific and irreducible* to those that regulate other fields" (*IRS,* 97). The concept of autonomization entails a certain complication, which tends to be elaborated for Bourdieu with reference to fields other than that of the economy per se and which gives autonomy in such fields distance from economic determination. "Obviously, in advanced capitalist societies, it would be difficult to maintain that the economic field does not exercise especially powerful determinations" (*Invitation,* 109). Nevertheless, as Bourdieu's theory demands, the economic field is itself the site of autonomy, namely, a relative freedom from determination by the political field, and this freedom is quite real, too. Should we not say that it is expressed in nothing other than the form of rational calculation, that it is the autonomy of the market? This freedom is not absolute, of course—it is not a freedom of the will—but it is the signature of the epochal nature of capitalism that market freedom is identified with freedom *tout court* and, conversely, that the dominance of the economy over other domains of the social should signify unfreedom, or determination *tout court.* The importance of this point is brought out at the end of the essay.

20. "For bold strokes of innovation or revolutionary research to have some chance of even being conceived, it is necessary for them to exist in a potential state at the heart of the system of already realized possibles, like *structural lacunae* which appear to wait for and call for fulfillment, like potential directions of development, possible avenues of research" (*RA,* 235).

21. I have argued elsewhere that the concept of pleasure is undertheorized in Bourdieu; its appearance here seems to me to belong to the revisionist moment in *The Rules of Art.* In Bourdieu's usage, pleasure is quite distinguishable from interest, which defines the project of accumulation. Capital can be accumulated and reinvested, but pleasures cannot. Rather, the interest of accumulation depends more often than not on the deferral of pleasures, sometimes even their permanent deferral, as when the accumulation of money capital becomes an end in itself. Thus the issue of pleasure raises an ultimately historical question, related to the argument made by Albert O. Hirschman in *The Passions and the Interests: Political Arguments for Capitalism before Its Triumph* (Princeton, N.J.: Princeton University Press, 1977). If pleasure occurs when accumulation ceases and consumption begins, then human beings required the institution of very specific social conditions (namely, capitalism) to cultivate the habit of accumulation and to make consumption itself into an instrument of accumulation. Hence interest is not really generalizable in anthropological terms, and the question of what limits the accumulation of symbolic capital needs a much more historical treatment than is found in Bourdieu.

22. It should be evident now why Jeffrey Alexander's complaint that Bourdieu's theory

does not allow for "altruistic behavior" or that his analysis of academics in *Homo Academicus* disallows "the possibility of sincerely held academic views" is so mistaken (151, 161 [n. 3 above]). Bourdieu's point is not that motives cannot be sincere but that one finds particular (no doubt sincerely held) views (position-takings) to be prevalent among those who share particular social locations. What is one to make of this fact? Well . . . sociology. Human beings are complex enough, Bourdieu is saying, both to believe in the game they are playing and to entertain a sense of its artificiality and fungibility.

23. It would take a more careful reconstruction of Bourdieu's itinerary than I can undertake in this essay to demonstrate this point, but it is my impression that the incorporation of Spinoza is late. In addition to the several moments in *The Rules of Art* when Bourdieu openly or tacitly invokes Spinoza (see 248, 272, 392), his appended conclusion to *Critical Perspectives* more or less translates his concepts of *habitus,* field, and capital into Spinoza's *conatus,* "a tendency" for social agents "to perpetuate themselves in their being, to reproduce themselves in that which constitutes their existence and their identity. . . . This I hold against a finalist, utilitarian vision of action which is sometimes attributed to me. It is not true to say that everything that people do or say is aimed at maximizing their social profit; but one may say that they do it to perpetuate or to augment their social being" (Calhoun et al., 274).

3

Resistance, Recuperation, and Reflexivity: The Limits of a Paradigm

Carol A. Stabile

Then-Senator Robert Dole's comments about the negative effects of Hollywood cinema, like Dan Quayle's attack on the fictional Murphy Brown several years ago, once again directed attention to the effects of media representations on that mythic entity, the American family. The public debate about such media representations has assumed a now familiar shape, with the Forrest Gumps of the Christian Coalition pontificating about the media's "nightmare of depravity," and the Nells of liberalism mouthing platitudes about "parental responsibility" (Purdum 1995, A1).

Across the overlapping areas of feminist theory, media studies, and cultural studies, shifts in media representations of gender have been theorized through a similarly dualistic framework of resistance and recuperation, a conceptualization based loosely on Antonio Gramsci's use of the term "hegemony." Meaghan Morris (1990) has described the problems that ensue from erring on either side of a similar dualism—"the banal" versus "the fatal." This polarized framework of resistant banality or recuperative fatality, however, limits the range and scope of critical analysis, with the limitations most evident in the resistance model's understanding of the relationship between economic and cultural changes. In what follows, I focus specifically on the problems that proceed from this textualist model by examining its internal limitations and the questions and lines of critical analysis it forecloses. Against this model, I argue that Pierre Bourdieu's sociological theory offers a necessary corrective to the lack of self-reflexivity and critical insight that has resulted from the dominance of this paradigm within media studies.

Contemporary conceptualizations of resistance emerge from appropriations of

44

Gramsci within cultural studies.[1] For Gramsci, hegemony described the process whereby ideology guarantees the consent of subjects to the dominant mode of production and therefore the continued functioning of the existing political and economic system. Capitalist hegemony, like capitalism itself, is a dynamic and processual entity, characterized by the ruling class's ability to persuade—rather than coerce—its subjects to consent to the existing social order. More specifically, Gramsci's writings attempted to understand the rise of fascism in Italy and its ability to win the hearts and minds of middle- and lower-middle-class men who felt crushed "between the rock of big business on the one side and the hard place of rising mass labour movements on the other" (Hobsbawm 1994, 119).[2] Writing from prison, Gramsci never underestimated the state's repressive functions and argued for a dialectical understanding of the relationship between persuasion and force in maintaining economic and political stability.

In the U.S., during the eighties, discussions of the media focused on one side of this binarism, highlighting persuasion and pleasure and generally excluding aggressive trends toward coercion and deprivation. The series of structuring binarisms that had framed previous analyses of ideology—Gramsci's delicate balance between persuasion and force, Althusser's ideological and repressive state apparatuses—in the U.S. context produced a largely single-minded attention to the persuasive aspects of society and commodity production.[3] Ideology, it was assumed, worked a lot like advertising: it persuaded subjects to buy the particular ideology on sale. The net result was a focus on the "multi-accentuality" of oppression (Fiske 1991, 464), or the ability of the oppressed to resignify (discursively) their own subordination.[4] The net deficit included a lack of attention to who was (or could be) persuaded by the ideologies on sale. In short, the focus on consent as a type of agency bypassed the fact that consent is, *in and of itself,* a marker of economic privilege, as is the privileging of consent to the exclusion of coercion within critical theory. The more distant subjects are from economic necessity, the more consent becomes a possibility. Consent is guaranteed for those who can afford to consent, or for those class factions for whom some marginal gain in privilege or a minor addition to existing privilege appears possible. In the case of those more remote from economic and cultural capital, coercion continues to be the operative term.

A proliferating number of articles in academic journals illustrate appropriations of hegemony that foreground resistance (and subversion) against recuperation (and co-optation or complicity).[5] In these, texts from popular culture allegedly illustrate the struggle for resistance and progression against the recuperative (and conservative) elements of hegemony. In feminist theory, the majority of analyses of media texts have used the term "hegemony" to highlight discursive contestations over gender relations, as well as female spectators' "counterhegemonic" reading practices.

John Fiske has been the most consistent and resilient practitioner of this resistant strain of media criticism. In his much-criticized essay on "Madonna," Fiske

(1989, 107) claims that despite the patriarchal context (indeed, because of it), Madonna's videos enable girls "to see that the meanings of feminine sexuality *can be* in their control, *can* be made in their interests, and that their subjectivities are not necessarily totally determined by the dominant patriarchy." He concludes that "Madonna's popularity is a complexity of power and resistances, of meanings and countermeanings, of pleasures and the struggle for control" (113). In "Radical Shopping in Los Angeles: Race, Media and the Sphere of Consumption," Fiske (1994, 485) takes the argument for resistance one step further, claiming that " 'Looting' gives the oppressed access to both commodities and public speech."

Feminists have criticized Fiske for his voluntarism and its displacement of the relations of force that reproduce sexist ideologies.[6] The emphasis on resistance, however, has influenced feminist media studies in similar ways. Christine Gledhill (1988, 68), endorsing a model of "pleasurable negotiations," argues that Gramsci's theory of hegemony provides a more appropriate model than that of " 'dominant ideology'—with its suggestion either of conspiratorial imposition or of unconscious interpellation." In search of an elusive feminist agent, Gledhill describes hegemony as "the ever shifting, ever negotiating play of ideological, social and political forces through which power is maintained and contested" (68). She claims to be concerned with "ideological effects" (73), but since ideologies and relations of force are considered to be fundamentally unstable, such effects are indeterminate. "Critical readings made under the rubric of negotiation offer not so much resistant readings, made against the grain, as animations of possibilities arising from the negotiations into which the text enters" (87).

In a similar attempt to negotiate between the poles of resistance and recuperation, Valerie Hartouni (1991, 50) writes that media narratives about motherhood seek "to recover and stabilize what is perceived as having become temporarily decentered, and in this they are clearly and blatantly reactionary." At the same time, she maintains that these reactionary representations contain "contradictions that cannot be resolved or suppressed, a fracture in the dominant discourse that suggests a dramatic weakening of its strength, a disruption in privileged narratives that renders them highly vulnerable to contestation." The intellectual and political benefits that proceed from such vulnerabilities are unclear, although as Gledhill (1988, 74) observes, this animation of possible meanings does ensure continued publication and employment for academics.

In "Hegemony in a Mass-Mediated Society," Celeste Michelle Condit (1994, 226) takes this largely idealist position one step further, arguing that hegemony arises "on the basis of a plurivocal set of interests, not a single dominant interest." In her version of hegemony, Gramsci's model offers a "springboard for a model of evolutionary social change produced by the interaction of multiple contesting groups." Although Condit nods in the direction of existing constraints on media access and the power of corporate interests in controlling media debates, she claims that traditional versions of hegemony do "not account sufficiently for women as active constructors of their own interests" (219).

The limits of a model based on resistance/recuperation, regression/progression, crisis/containment, elide the connection between the economic and its relations of force and the ideological and its persuasive aspects (as in Condit's depiction of women as "active constructors"). For the recuperative pole, hegemony figures as the stable, traditional status quo against which the chaotic forces of instability and unrest must struggle. The resulting concept of a "backlash" not only presumes that progress has been made, but that the stability and immutability of the existing social order depend on resolving contradictions in favor of the past and tradition. This reduces the productive and dynamic characteristics of capitalist economies to a plodding process of continual restoration. Against an equally transparent background, resistant readings promote a logic of political progression. Shifts in ideology appear as fissures or cracks in hegemony: potential faultlines through which the dominant order can be contested, undermined, or in the case of liberal pluralism, expanded.[7] A reading of resistance thus pursues a direct logic of cause and effect: resistance is the necessary *reaction* to hegemonic attempts at containment, power is maintained and then contested, and contradictions appear that cannot be suppressed.

Since the thrust of the analysis is to prove or disprove a logic of ideological progression/regression (which is then interpreted as political progression), a reading of resistance either erases the relationship between the text and wider context or reduces it to a fairly transparent causal relationship. Within the textualist paradigm, resistance is narrowly synchronic in its scope and does not promote a historicized understanding of the relationship between economic and ideological shifts. In short, when representational shifts are theorized as reflecting revolutions or changes in ideology, the subsequent analysis does not account for external shifts, correspondences, and dissonances in other fields, nor for the historicity and materiality of the fields themselves.

READING ROSEANNE, WRITING RESISTANCE

I wanted to create a three-dimensional female person to be on television because I was so damned sick of all the bullshit portrayals of women and mothers in sitcoms. They were either too passive or always absent in the lives of the family. The truth is, the mother is the center of the family. (Roseanne Arnold, in Janos 1993, 133.)

[Women] are doing everything—raising kids, working full-time, keeping a house, supporting their other friends, dealing with family problems. And they did it with this stoic but fatalistic frame of mind. "Well, hell, it can't get any worse." So what are you going to do but laugh? (Matt Williams, in Finke 1989, 10)

> *Roseanne* has held up a mirror to the people and culture of the last decade
> of the twentieth-century, and the reflection is often bittersweetly accurate.
> (Mayerle, 1991, p. 85)

The family situation comedy has been historically "one of television's preferred modes for addressing the nation's families" (Spigel 1992, 154). As such,
it is also one of the primary sites for excavating the recent history of gender ideologies. The sitcom *Roseanne* offers a concrete illustration both of the limitations
of the resistance model and the benefits of exploring what Bourdieu describes as
homologies between fields. Mainstream media critics agree that *Roseanne*
marked a turning-point in sitcom history as well as generic conventions, particularly in its representation of family life and gender roles. *New York Times* writer
John O'Connor observed that "this sitcom refuses to act like most of the
others. . . . This is not *Leave it to Beaver,* obviously. It's also not *All in the Family*" (1991, 27). *Time* magazine remarked that *Roseanne*'s "grungy ambiance and
gleeful puncturing of TV ideals of happy domesticity have made it the most daring new sitcom of the fall" (Zoglin 1988, 88).

Mainstream accounts of the show repeatedly showcase its resistant, oppositional, and progressive content, as well as the equally resistant intentions of Arnold herself as auteur. Kathleen Rowe's (1995) analysis of *Roseanne* reproduces
the logic of these mainstream accounts through the framework of resistance. In
Rowe's analysis, resistance has more to do with Arnold's intentions and persona
(or Arnold as agent) than it does with audiences' reception of these representations. Since Arnold does not conform to cultural ideals of femininity or generic
conventions of sitcom mothers, the logic of resistance positions her as transgress-
ive: "Out of Arnold's ease with her body comes her power not only to resist
objectification but also to name her own experience, to create herself" (Rowe
1995, 65). Because of this, Arnold produces a fiction "based on an explicitly
feminist and working-class point of view" (82). Judine Mayerle (1991, 71) casts
Roseanne in an equally distinctive light. Not only does the sitcom reflect "the
growing influence of women in the production of primetime television programming," it also "achieves a gritty texture of character and setting that viewers recognize as similar to the fabric of their own lives (for example, its lead characters
sit at a messy table in their cluttered kitchen and argue about who left toast
crumbs in the butter)."

My point here, and following Bourdieu, is not that such readings are wrong,
in any strict sense of the word. Rather, the point has to do with the relationship
between mainstream and academic accounts, both of which produce "unruliness"
as resistance. If the purpose of critical analysis is to provide an explication of the
program, the resistance model falls short of this goal, since in the end, academic
critics tell us little more about what *Roseanne* does—or how it functions in a
larger political and economic context—than do spokespersons for the mainstream media.

Considering *Roseanne*'s representation of gender in a way that does not succumb to an ideologistic, progressivist logic of textual resistance received from the media industry itself would involve two related moves. First, the analysis would have to provide both diachronic and synchronic readings of media texts, while at the same time accounting for the objective, material conditions of the production of texts within a larger historial context. Second, the analysis would have to be self-reflexive, insofar as the theorist would have to be able to theorize the ways in which her own theoretical categories are themselves structured and limited by her field, its historical context, as well as its relation to other fields.

Bourdieu's work offers some valuable methodological and theoretical insights for such a project. Randal Johnson describes Bourdieu's theoretical project as a "radical contextualization" that

> takes into consideration not only works themselves, seen relationally within the space of available possibilities, and within the historical development of such possibilities, but also producers of works in terms of their strategies and trajectories, based on their individual and class habitus, as well as their objective position within the field. (*FCP*, 9)

As Bo Ekelund (1995, 18) puts it, a field is "a sociologically semi-autonomous object of study within which the values governing and constituting the field are constantly in the process of being created by and through the struggle over these same values among all the agents operating within the field." Following Bourdieu, fields are primarily sites of struggle over specific kinds of power. The field of media production, for example, is driven by an economic logic. Struggles over power within the field (what kinds of programs are produced, what programming gets the best time slot, and so forth) are based on struggles for economic capital.

The logic that structures power struggles within the field of academic production is semi-autonomous from that of the field of media production, involving struggles over forms of capital specific to the academic field. Intellectuals "are a dominated fraction of the dominant class" (*IOW*, 145). They are dominant insofar as cultural capital is concerned, but are dominated "in their relations with those who hold political and economic power" (145).[8] Struggles over power in the field of academic production are struggles over cultural capital. A logic of anti-economism informs these struggles (unlike media producers, academics are not "in it for the money"), while the attendant illusion of distance from matters economic obscures the fact that cultural capital is only capital insofar as it can be converted into economic capital at some point. For instance, although academic publishing does not result in immediate financial rewards, it can translate into prominence in one's field (a form of cultural capital), which can then be "cashed in" for promotions, paid lectures, and so forth (forms of economic capital).

An understanding of ideological shifts as shifts across fields (the field of media

production, the field of media studies, and the field of economic relations that
encompasses both of these) uncovers the homologies, or the relationality, that
exist among and between fields. Each field has properties and a logic specific to
itself (although fields as a whole ultimately serve to reproduce class relations);
yet the processes of reproduction are necessarily progressive and productive.
Changes within the field produce seemingly "new" positions that effectively
reproduce the logic of the field, but fields do not operate on the principle of stability associated with tradition. Because they are infinitely dynamic, and are structured around "the power relations among the agents or institutions engaged in
the struggle" (*FCP*, 73), strategies of subversion (or partial revolutions) are a necessary part of the logic of fields. Nevertheless, if agents "are not to incur exclusion from the game itself, these strategies have to remain within certain limits"
(74).

Obvious strategies of subversion can be perceived in the mass media themselves, where a given television program, magazine, or other commodity can be
successful only insofar as it distinguishes itself from other such commodities,
while at the same time remaining within the limits of the game. If a sitcom, for
example, did not fulfill the fundamental logic of distinguishing itself from other
such programming, while at the same time remaining comprehensible within the
terms of the genre itself, it would be subject to exclusion from the game and the
field (generally through cancellation).

A similar process of distinction operates within the field of the academy, where
a textual analysis must either legitimize the text itself as distinct from other texts
(as subversive or resistant) or its analytic approach as distinct from other such
available approaches (as in Condit's distinction between traditional versions of
hegemony and her own unique rendering of it). Distinction is, in fact, the name
of the academic as well as mass media game, and those struggling for success or
popularity in both fields are "able to unseat the 'establishment' only because the
implicit law of the field is distinction in all senses of the word" (*FCP*, 135).[9]

At this point, we need to turn to the field of media production in order to better
understand *Roseanne*'s particular brand of "distinction." I have mentioned that
the primary logic structuring the field of media production is profit.[10] While this
statement may appear remarkably banal, this economic logic structures the field
in a number of more or less complicated ways, ways that necessitate an understanding of the immediate context of the program and its historical precedents
(understandings that the largely abstract resistance model does not provide). First
of all, *Roseanne* premiered in 1989 and was among the first network programs to
reflect the effects of deregulation of the cable industry on network programming.
Rowe remarks that "Arnold's move to network TV can be attributed in part to
the symbiotic relationship between standup comedy and cable television" (1995,
70), but this symbiosis took place against a complicated economic background.
The fate of the networks has become more precarious since Congress passed the

Cable Act in 1984, effectively deregulating the industry, and since the fourth network, Fox Broadcasting Company, began broadcasting in 1987.[11] Where in 1979, more than 90 percent of all prime-time viewers were watching CBS, NBC, or ABC, by 1992, that percentage had plummeted to 40 percent (Snyder 1991).

The traffic between standup comedy and cable on one hand and network sitcoms on the other (*Roseanne, Seinfeld, Ellen, Home Improvement,* and *All-American Girl*) reflects the larger changes in the industry. First of all, standup comedy is extremely cheap to produce, as are sitcoms based on standup acts. Second, cable, as a privately owned medium, has not had to conform to the regulations on network programming, such as content or language. In order to remain competitive with both cable programming and the no-censorship, tabloid style of Rupert Murdoch's Fox network, network programming has had to push the limits of existing conventions and regulations.

Arnold and her managers took advantage of this conjuncture. Her HBO special, "The Roseanne Barr Show," was broadcast in 1987, shortly after Fox launched a line-up that included the ironic and controversial *Married . . . With Children. The Roseanne Barr Show* significantly did not follow the conventions of standup comedy routine; it was designed as a television sitcom rather than a standup act. Marcy Carsey and Tom Werner (producers of *The Cosby Show*) signed Roseanne Arnold within the year and ABC aired the first episode in 1988. *Roseanne*'s production and success consequently owed much to these changes in the material circumstances of network programming and the successful marketing of the "domestic goddess" as star.

At this point, advocates of the resistance model would argue that *Roseanne*'s popularity and the progressive content of the show exceed the purview of such an admittedly reductive and materialist analysis, especially insofar as an economic analysis supposedly does not account for a text's popular appeal. However, the resistance model legitimizes its references to "the popular" and to resistant audiences/readers through a highly speculative mode of argumentation. That is, the anti-empiricism that underpins the resistance model and its narrow focus on interpretive methods actually constructs a mass, active audience that bears little relation to reality.

How do we know, for example, that a particular program is popular? How do we know who a given program's audience actually is? Since the resistance model does not involve empirical work, but "cultural interpretation," we must assume that critics receive the categories of "popular" and "audience" from the media themselves, where popularity and audience demographics are determined by the A. C. Nielsen Company's rating system.[12] However, widespread disagreement abounds in the media industry regarding the reliability of the Nielsens. Nicholas Schiavone, vice president of media and marketing research at NBC has said, "The [Nielsen] system is not accurate. We have demonstrated that Nielsen has no apparent commitment to responsible methodological research" (in Snyder 1991, 8).

Even the company's hasty introduction of the "peoplemeter" (a small box on the television set that allows participants to log in data by pushing buttons, as opposed to keeping a viewing diary) in 1986 did not resolve the following problems. First of all, the Nielsens sample only four thousand households out of a total of twenty million (with the selection of Nielsen "families" further limiting the sample); second, neither diaries nor peoplemeters are used consistently by participants; third, the peoplemeter does not account for new technologies such as VCRs, split screens, miniature televisions; and finally, the Nielsens simply cannot obtain meaningful data from the growing practice of channel-surfing or grazing. In reality, the Nielsens may well be little more than the universal equivalent for advertising costs, as agreed upon by the networks and advertisers.[13] Even if the Nielsens do indicate whether a given program is delivering its target audience, their concepts of audience and popularity are much more narrow than the versions deployed by media critics. According to Feuer (1984, 3), "The crucial change that began to occur around 1970 was a de-emphasis on numbers and a greater emphasis on 'demographics,' that is, directing television shows toward specific audience groups." With the intensification of this trend in the targeting of niche markets, television programming has been moving toward forms of narrowcasting in response to advertising demands.[14] The central question posed within the industry is not the audience as a quantity, but the audience as a quality: is a given program delivering consumers with the requisite economic profile and consumption habits? Popularity is evaluated within the parameters of market segmentation and not, as proponents of the resistant reader would have it, on the basis of "mass" or widespread appeal.

Strategies for attracting the desired demographics also vary historically and in relation to changes in the lives of target audiences. *Roseanne*'s success on network programming, for example, involved demands for reaching the growing ranks of middle-class working women (generally considered by advertisers to be one of the most valuable audiences). The resistance model forgets the dynamic and productive (if comparatively brief) history of sitcoms as a genre and their relation to the advertising industry.[15] Because of the genre's purpose—to deliver audiences to advertisers and to instill attitudes appropriate to shifting circumstances of production and consumption—sitcoms have had to incorporate changes in material gender relations to fulfill this objective. The formative years of the genre coincided with the dismissal or demotion of many of the twenty million female workers who had been employed during World War II to postwar suburban housing. Episodes of programs such as *The Donna Reed Show* (1958–1966), *The Adventures of Ozzie and Harriet* (1952–1966), *Father Knows Best* (1954–1963), *Leave it to Beaver* (1957–1963), *Life with Father* (1953–55), and *The Marriage* (1954) addressed a middle-class audience (particularly women) that was adjusting to massive postwar changes.

As the fifties progressed, the sitcom family became increasingly more homogenous as it increasingly addressed a more homogenous audience. In place of ethnic sitcoms such as *Mama* (1949–1956) and *The Goldbergs* (1949), set within the context of urban tenements and extended families, there was a shift to an ever more nucleate suburban family, in which mother was a housewife and father a white-collar worker. In fact, according to George Lipsitz (1990, 92), "After 1958, network television eliminated urban ethnic working-class programs from the schedule." As more and more middle-class women entered the work force in the late sixties and early seventies, the sitcom had to adjust to further changes in order to maintain its demographics. It would be unrealistic, not to mention economically unsound, for producers to cling to a nuclear ideal that had less and less resemblance to the lives of the very consumers it wished to reach.

Of the fifties sitcom, Mary Beth Haralovich (1992, 112) has observed, "an ideal white and middle-class home life was a primary means of reconstituting and resocializing the American family after World War II." If the fifties family sitcom reflected the move of its target audiences from urban and rural areas to the suburbs, and middle-class women's adjustment to postwar downgrading, unemployment, and a narrowly domestic existence, *Roseanne* can be seen to serve a similar function within, however, a very different economic landscape. Evaluating *Roseanne* in terms of whether the program's content is progressive or regressive obscures the changes in the field of media production. For example, to contrast the character Roseanne to previous sitcom moms produces an elaborate reading of Roseanne's distinction from a "traditional," and apparently stable and monolithic, sitcom mom (be she June Cleaver, Carol Brady, or Claire Huxtable). Here, the historical aspects of genre and advertising are reduced to a linear logic of ideological and political progression, at the end of which stands Roseanne. In addition, when we consider *Roseanne* strictly in terms of its resistance to, or distinction from, previous family sitcoms, we also erase the fact that this sitcom reflects changes in its target audience: middle-class women, ages eighteen to thirty-nine.[16] The resistance model sidesteps these points by adopting the progressive and productive logic of the field of media production itself.

If we understand *Roseanne*'s representation of gender as a response to shifts in audience demographics, as well as shifts in the wider economic situation of this audience, our analysis of the program correspondingly shifts. Female and feminized labor participation among the middle classes has become economically necessary, both in terms of U.S. service sector jobs and international manufacturing (where its devalued status has served to drive the real wages of all employees down). Some feminists argue, as does Naomi Wolff (1994), that this is a progressive change resulting from feminist demands for equality. This argument, however, is blind to the class and race specificity of its own claims, as is the argument for *Roseanne* as a resistant text.

The specificity of *Roseanne*'s audience is mirrored in the program's racially homogenized version of the working class. During the show's first season, when Roseanne worked at the Wellman factory, the show did occasionally feature an African American couple, Vonda and Phil, and a Latino couple, Juanita and Emilio. African Americans occasionally appear on episodes (D.J. once appeared with an African American friend who disappeared after another episode), but the show no longer features African Americans, much less Latinos, in recurring roles. Indeed, the only "differences" represented on the program are increasingly those of erotic orientation and gender, both of which can be successfully severed from economics and class position. The program has highlighted employment and financial problems, but the overall trajectory of the show is one of upward mobility. Roseanne has progressed from being a factory worker to an entrepreneur of loose-meat sandwiches, while the program on the whole has moved away from economic issues to interpersonal, familial conflict and biological reproduction.

By looking at female labor force participation, we can see the kinds of universalization at work in the sitcom, as well as feminist analyses of the sitcom as resistant. At the turn of the century, 40.7 percent of African American women participated in the labor force, according to U.S. Census sources. This figure remained fairly stable, with the lowest figures occurring during World War II. By 1980, African American women's labor force participation rose to 53.5 percent. In contrast, European American women's labor force participation was a mere 16 percent in 1900, rising gradually with the most dramatic increase between 1970 and 1980, when it reached 49.4 percent. Where African American women's labor force participation increased only 12.6 percent during an eighty-year period, that of European American women increased 33.4 percent. Although women's participation in the labor force increased across the board during this period, the increase was most dramatic for a particular group of women. Thus, the argument that women have only recently been able to enter the work force (and that, moreover, they have done so on the basis of choice) makes the experience of one group of white women stand in for the experiences of all women. From an advertising perspective, this makes perfect sense. After all, these—and not poor or working-class women of color—are the very women who are the target audience for *Roseanne*. But to make broad claims about progress for women as a category, claims based on demographics and ratings, is extremely problematic.[17]

The construction of *Roseanne* as a working-class, feminist sitcom, both by academics and mainstream writers, marks another, related site of convergence between critical and popular understandings of the text. What does it mean, in a culture so resistant to narratives of class relations, when a text is celebrated as an "honest portrayal of blue-collar family life" (Zoglin 1988, 88), particularly at a moment in time when the number of blue-collar jobs has dramatically decreased and when large numbers of poor and working-class women are African American and Latina? In a society where references to class position are so consistently repressed—or where what constitutes "working-class" identity is so heatedly debated among intellectuals—it is remarkable indeed that media critics and academics alike repeatedly characterize Roseanne as a "working-class housewife" (O'Connor 1991, 27) or "a hit blue-collar situation comedy" (Mayerle 1991, 71).

Indeed, the show's central conflict is characterized as class: "Every Tuesday night at nine, Americans by the millions tune in to watch the Conner family cope with the problems of class in all its connotations" (Sessums 1994, 60). Yet unlike working-class representations such as that of *All in the Family,* in which "the working class became, for many middle-class liberals, a psychic dumping ground for such stylish sentiments as racism, male chauvinism, and crude materialism: a rearguard population that loved white bread and hated black people" (Ehrenreich 1989, 120), *Roseanne* takes on issues that apparently represent a more progressive political agenda: family violence, aging, infertility, birth control, menstruation, masturbation, and unemployment. Her character has smoked pot, kissed another woman, and fantasized about Fabio. In addition, *Roseanne* was the first primetime sitcom to feature both a gay man and a lesbian in recurring roles (neither character appeared with any regularity in the 1994–1995 season).

When class is interpreted on *Roseanne,* it is understood primarily through codes of taste, rather than economic issues, particularly in more recent episodes. For instance, the Conners are self-avowed couch potatoes whose taste in programming ranges from reruns of *Bonanza* to soap operas and sports. They consume large amounts of junk food, including chocolate pudding "with real candy bars in it"; they usually order take-out fast food for dinner, a menu occasionally supplemented with Roseanne's admittedly awful meat loaf. In short, the Conners conform to certain class stereotypes: they are large, loud, lascivious, and simply do not look or speak like other television characters. *Newsweek* described the program as focusing on

> . . . working-class folks, warts and all. Roseanne and Dan are hefty. They don't just yell at each other; they bellow. Their kitchen is a mess—archeologists would have a field day digging through the layers of junk on that dinette. ("A Real Stand-up Mom," 62)

Time said of Arnold, "With her rolypoly figure and truck-driver's tongue, she is hardly your standard-issue TV mom" (Zoglin 1988, 88), as if size signified class position.

Rowe (1995, 82) claims that "the strong working-class coding . . . further distances middle-class audiences from [Roseanne's] critique." My point is not to deny some "authentic" representation of contemporary working-class culture that *Roseanne* falls short of; my concern is the claim that *Roseanne* represents the working class. First, that *Roseanne* represents economic instability or that Roseanne Conner is a working mother does not mean that the sitcom expresses the reality of working-class existence. Few middle-class women can afford to remain home with young children at this point in time (a point made abundantly clear by women's descent into poverty either through child-bearing or divorce). This fact can only be rendered novel for those groups of women whose formative experiences include a family that could actually survive on a single income (and given the history of female employment in white and African American working-class homes, *Roseanne*'s situation would not appear all that novel). Rather than reflecting some "authentic" working-class culture, *Roseanne* reflects the economic predicament of the middle classes at a specific historical moment (a middle class currently confronting chronic unemployment and debt). It represents, in other words, the precarious position of this middle class—a precariousness expressed on the show in 1991, when Roseanne observed, "Well, middle-class was fun."

THE RESISTANCE INDUSTRY

Gramsci would remind us that if capitalism is to maintain the consent of the middle class, it must package its (economic) necessities in terms of the middle class's political and ideological gains. The notion of "against the grain readings" in the resistance model coincides with this aspect of capitalist hegemony, by implying that traditional ideologies of gender, race, sexuality, and class are always already contested and ultimately lead to progress in these areas (as it has, but only for certain middle- and upper-middle class women). The concept of recuperation, which engenders such resistance, elides the dynamism of the field of economics by ascribing conservativism to ideology. Ideology is seen to function effectively insofar as it upholds tradition. The framework of resistance effectively overlooks the ways in which ideology secures the economic not necessarily in terms of overcoming ideological contradictions in favor of tradition, but in resolving or repressing ideological contradictions through a logic of progression. Tradition has an economic stake only as long as it supports and maintains economic interests. Although feminists have documented how traditions have proved entirely disposable from the perspective of capitalist imperialism, we have yet to understand similar processes at work, such as the wholesale destruction of African American, Native American, and working-class traditions in U.S. culture.[18]

Consequently, a reading of resistance reproduces the progressivist logic of capitalist democracies, wherein women now have the choice to parent and hold jobs, while the concept of recuperation—by highlighting the conservative and preservative elements of hegemony—disregards the fact that there can be no return to the traditional nuclear family *because it is no longer economically feasible.* The fundamental contradiction within the governing logic of progression is that poor and working-class women (many of them women of color) have generally worked outside the home, although few would render their alienated and often desperate labor in terms of "choice." Because media texts depict women's attempts to work and parent, it is presumed that women's position in society—as a whole—has visibly improved. An episode from the 1994–95 season, which featured highlights from the sitcom's history, vividly illustrates these points. In the tag sequence, Arnold (appearing as Roseanne Arnold and not Roseanne Conner) returns to the set of her kitchen to find it occupied by mothers from previous sitcoms. Comparing her character and her own economic situation as sitcom star to that of her predecessors, Arnold triumphantly concludes, "Anyway, on my show, I'm the boss and father knows squat" (March 1, 1995). An analysis of this sequence as resistant does not understand that the model uses an inappropriate form of metonymy: one that universalizes from a narrow range of experiences.

Contemporary struggles over the family and gender in the media actually illustrate the process whereby capitalist economies package their necessities in terms of women's gains. By universalizing a dramatic shift for a very specific group of women, *Roseanne* addresses a specifically middle-class audience (an audience that necessarily includes media theorists). It tells us that it is acceptable to complain, that the burdens are often immense, but that in the end, if we work hard and keep trying, the system will reward us—a point illustrated by the program's trajectory of upward mobility. As *Newsweek* put it, "Back-sass [for Roseanne] is a survival mechanism; without it, the pressures of making ends meet would be too much" ("A Real Stand-up Mom," 62). The show also offers the comforting reassurance that feminism has seeped into the media industry's consciousness and that social relations can be improved through struggles within this field.

Because of their textualist focus, models of resistance only refer to objective conditions of production insofar as these can be used to support the existence of resistance. Material constraints on both media production and knowledge production are displaced by reference to active audiences and individual viewers and readers—a view commensurate with with the media's myth of the active consumer, but one that tells us little about the role of the audience as commodity in contemporary society.

The resistance/recuperation framework cannot reveal that what is being packaged as choice is in fact an economic necessity in a system that now offers middle-class women the dubious advantage traditionally available to poor and working-class women: that of working two full-time jobs, one with low wages and the other with none. To reduce the problem to a question of recuperative or resistant qualities is to miss the point entirely (and to miss our own participation in the construction of a fictive agency), because such contestations over gender are not about restoring June Cleaver or advancing feminist ideologies. Instead, they are about producing the productive woman. Within the field of media production, *Roseanne* reassures middle-class women that their everyday experiences are neither alienating nor unique, but normal, natural, and entirely surmountable. Within the imbricated fields of media and academic production, *Roseanne*'s "resistance" deflects attention from the wider economic field in which so many of the world's women confront dire material conditions. In place of the distinctive superwoman of the eighties, who vowed that she could have it all, we now have the survivalist woman, who has no choice but to make a virtue of necessity. Discussions of textual resistance make a similar virtue of necessity by recognizing neither the existence of this particular homology, nor the political and economic interests it finally serves.

The poles of resistance and recuperation account for neither the productive aspects of the field of media production, nor the productive mandates of the field of academic production. Given the logic of both fields, necessitating that moves must be novel or otherwise distinct from previous moves, recuperative readings of media texts occur much less frequently than resistant readings. The resistance model, in contrast, is particularly productive in Bourdieu's sense, since it enables the critic to remain within the limits of the critical game, while at the same time rendering and legitimizing ever more complicated, novel, and distinctive variations on resistance.

The relationality among fields is extremely relevant for media studies, for as consumers of the media and as academics studying the media, we inhabit both fields. This double occupancy makes it particularly difficult to recognize that fields are only *semi*-autonomous from one another, and that homologies—or "resemblance in difference"—exist between the larger economic and political field, the field of media production, and the field of the academy. These homologies "affirm the existence of structurally equivalent—which does not mean identical—characteristics in different groupings" (*IOW,* 140–41), of which the resistance model is one example. As critics, we are implicated in a logic of distinction that structurally resembles that of the field of media production. Our interest in resistance, which offers the opportunity to display our own creative skills and thus distinguish our own work, results from our positions in our fields and is at once ideological (a tacit acceptance of the rules of the game) and economic (if we do not "contribute" to our fields, that is, play by the rules, we are less likely to get jobs and/or tenure, thereby risking exclusion from the game itself).

The mediations between the field of media production and the academic field (expressed partly through the anti-economism of intellectual practices) engender an illusion of autonomy from the larger economic and political context. For instance, resistance, or what Jane Feuer (1995, xiv) has described as a shift in emphasis "away from analyses of how texts position the viewer and toward what the viewer does with the text," gained prominence during the 1980s, at a time when the U.S. was moving toward a more overtly repressive and authoritarian political regime and when political resistance of all sorts was apparently on the wane. Few would disagree that the eighties were a period of intensifying attacks on women and people of color, or that cuts in social spending ensured that more and more people were living in conditions of abject poverty. Yet the eighties, as viewed in the media, were also years of increasingly opulent and spectacular programming, from *Lifestyles of the Rich and Famous* to prime-time soaps such as *Dynasty, Dallas,* and *Falcon Crest.* To read feminist work on the media and popular culture in the eighties was to enter a world similarly rich, albeit in resistance and progressive contradictions. Here, the resemblance in difference inheres in the inversion of social reality in the mass media, an inversion which is then reproduced in the field of the academy.

Bourdieu (*HA*, 1) warns us that when we analyze the social world of which we are a part, we must confront "the special difficulties involved first in *breaking* with inside experience and then in reconstituting the knowledge which has been obtained by means of this break." Textual analyses lodged within the framework of resistance/recuperation close off this first self-reflexive rupture with inside experience, because the critic enjoys the illusion of a position outside the range and reach of the media, from which she can diagnose resistance. The resultant analyses cannot address the possibility of the critic's own pre-constituted interest in resistance, an interest that may very well proceed not from scholarly inquiry, but from the practical dictates of both the field of media production and that of academic production.

In order to understand the homologies between and among fields, then, media analysts must understand the logic of the field occupied by their object of study, as well as the logic structuring their own field. Such an analysis does not entail incriminations of, or excuses for, individual agents within those fields, but an awareness that

> the thinker is less the subject than the object of his most fundamental rhetorical strategies, those which are activated when, led by the practical dispositions of his habitues, he becomes inhabited, like a medium, so to speak, with the requirements of the social spaces (which are simultaneously mental spaces) which enter into relation through him. (*POMH*, 105)

Since the resistance model has more than a passing resemblance to the very rhetoric used by the media industry to promote and market its commodities, understanding the homologies between our field, the field of media production, and the larger economic field would give us strategies for recognizing and analyzing what are, in effect, dangerous points of convergence.[19]

The implications of this form of analysis, however, pose a serious threat to our belief and investments in a number of illusions about academic work and the function of the field of the academy in contemporary U.S. society. Bourdieu's reflexive sociology forces us to theorize agency—be it our own, or that attributed to consumers of the mass media—within the constraints exercised by structuring structures. The grim vision that proceeds from this theorizing might be, in fact, too dismal for many academics to contemplate; but as Bourdieu (*LP*, 133) reminds us, "The most successful ideological effects are the ones that have no need of words, but only of *laissez-faire* and complicitous silence."

NOTES

This chapter first appeared in *Critical Studies in Mass Communication* 12, no. 4 (1995). It is reprinted by permission of the National Communication Association.

1. See Harris (1992) for a historical account of Gramsci's influence on media studies.

2. I am not arguing against Gramsci's theory of hegemony *in toto.* Rather, I am contending that these applications of Gramsci have serious limitations when monolithically applied to contemporary media studies in the United States. First of all, Gramsci's analysis continues to provide one of the most powerful ways of understanding how consent to fascism was generated among specific groups of people. There is much that this theory could illuminate about the contemporary resurgence of fascism and the ascendance of militia movements and fundamentalism in the U.S., as well as the attraction of these for white lower and middle-class factions. It remains unclear, though, how helpful this model can be when applied to contemporary media and/or those groups of people for whom coercion is the order of the day. In addition, Gramsci composed these texts under the watchful eyes of prison censors, which has resulted in conflicting interpretations of his work. For further discussion of such issues (as well as the benefits of Gramscian insights), see Harris (1992), Quintin Hoare and Geoffrey Nowell Smith's preface to *The Prison Notebooks* (1989, pp. ix–xv), Anderson (1977), as well as Marcia Landy's important analysis of Gramsci's work (1994).

3. Christopher Simpson (1994) provides insights into the development of a similar paradigmatic focus on persuasion within communications research and its connections to the military-industrial complex.

4. As in Schulte-Sasse (1987).

5. In both *Cultural Studies* and *Cultural Critique,* for example, a very tiny proportion of articles deal with repression in the U.S. *Cultural Studies* published 148 articles between 1989 and 1994, two of which dealt with surveillance and/or force. From 1985 to 1994, *Cultural Critique* published a total of 225 articles, only 20 of which can be even remotely construed as dealing with relations of force (most of those even peripherally dealing with force, moreover, appeared in two special issues on war). Even *Media, Culture, and Society* and *Social Text,* both of which tend to have a more political and economic slant, underwent a shift during the eighties toward culturalism and the politics of consumption. Anthologies from the eighties also demonstrate the pervasiveness of this framework. See, for example, Gamman and Marshment (1989); Gledhill (1987), particularly essays by Maria LaPlace and Linda Williams; Pribram (1988), and Schwichtenberg (1993).

6. Meaghan Morris's "Banality in Cultural Studies" is among one of the most influential critiques of Fiske's work.

7. Such fault-lines have yet to produce a quake. Despite assertions about fractures, fault-lines, and fissues, resistant readings exist in a perpetual state of immanence.

8. "Cultural" or "symbolic" capital is distinguished from economic capital in Bourdieu's work in the following terms: "Symbolic capital is credit, but in the broadest sense, a kind of advance, a credence, that only the group's belief can grant those who give it the best symbolic and material guarantees" (*LP,* 120).

9. See Fellman (1995) for a discussion of related issues.

10. *The Wall Street Journal* and *The Economist* are very clear on this point. It would seem that only "liberal" media (such as *the New York Times*) and academic journals consider that there are more complicated motives at stake.

11. Fifth and sixth networks, owned respectively by Warner Brothers and Paramount (UPN), launched their first programs in autumn 1994. In August 1995, the Walt Disney Company acquired ABC, while Westinghouse acquired CBS, events that signal further changes in the function, structure, and fate of the networks.

12. Eileen Meehan (1993) provides an invaluable evaluation of historical and economic changes in the relationships among the Nielsen rating system, gender, and genre.

13. Only the A. C. Nielsen company and advertisers benefit from this system right now. The drop in network ratings and related drop in advertising dollars during the late eighties has soured the networks on this system. During the first quarter of 1990, for example, after Nielsen reported an unprecedented drop in television viewing, the three major networks had to refund between $150 and $200 million to advertisers in "make-goods" (in effect, refunding advertisers for audience guarantees that the Nielsens claimed had not been delivered).

14. Arbitron, Nielsen's major competitor in terms of local ratings in 1995, tested the "ScanAmerica" system in Denver, in order to provide ever more precise demographics. "ScanAmerica" maintains peoplemeters, but has added an in-home scanner that reads the bar codes on grocery products. Participants in the study have to scan every grocery item that enters their homes in order to tell advertisers where television viewers are buying their products.

15. Haralovich (1992), Lipsitz (1990), and Spigel (1992) provide excellent analyses of sitcom history, while Wright (1981) gives a historical account of the suburbs.

16. According to Weiss (1994, 71), "Typical households of *Roseanne* fans have an annual income of $50,000. They support gay and abortion rights, but see themselves as more conservative than liberal."

17. Feuer (1995, xxiii) is particularly self-reflexive on this point: "If I do not discuss the reception of TV programs by groups totally disenfranchised in the eighties—poor blacks, the homeless, the elderly—it is not because I consider them insignificant, but rather because I am interested in groups the industry tried to address."

18. See Nash and Fernández-Kelly (1983), Fuentes and Ehrenreich (1984), and Ong (1991) for descriptions of capitalism's relationship to tradition.

19. In order to understand a text, then, it is necessary to perform what Wacquant describes as a "twofold hermeneutic" in which "we decode the author's mental space" while at the same time we "attain some knowledge of the scholarly space in which his or her writings become inserted" (Bourdieu and Wacquant, 1992, p. 233). It is a matter, in short, of situating an understanding of both texts and contexts within the objective positions and subjective dispositions that structure academic work.

BIBLIOGRAPHY

Anderson, P. (1977). The antinomies of Antonio Gramsci. *New Left Review, 100,* 5–78.

Arnold, R. (1994). *My lives.* New York: Ballantine Books.

Barr, R. (1989, July 31). What am I anyway, a zoo? *The New York Times,* p. A15.

Berenstein, R. (1990). Mommie dearest: *Aliens, Rosemary's Baby* and mothering. *Journal of Popular Culture, 24*(2):55–73.

Bourdieu, P. (1984). *Distinction: A social critique of the judgment of taste.* Cambridge, MA: Harvard University Press.

———. (1988). *Homo academicus.* Stanford, CA: Stanford University Press.

———. (1990a). *In other words: Essays towards a reflexive sociology.* Stanford, CA: Stanford University Press.

————. (1990b). *The logic of practice.* Stanford, CA: Stanford University Press.

————. (1991). *The political ontology of Martin Heidegger.* Stanford, CA: Stanford University Press.

————. (1993). *The field of cultural production.* New York: Columbia University Press.

Bourdieu, P. & Wacquant, L. J. D. (1992). *An invitation to reflexive sociology.* Chicago: University of Chicago Press.

Brown, M. E. (1994). *Soap opera and women's talk: The pleasure of resistance.* Thousand Oaks, CA: Sage Publications.

Condit, C. M. (1994). Hegemony in a mass-mediated society: Concordance about reproductive technologies. *Critical Studies in Mass Communication, 11*(3):205–230.

Cowie, E. (1980). The popular film as a progressive text—a discussion of *Coma. M/F, 3/ 4,* 59–81.

Douglas, S. J. (1993). Will you love me tomorrow? Changing discourses about female sexuality in the mass media, 1960–1968. In W. S. Solomon and R. W. McChesney (Eds.), *Ruthless criticism: New perspectives in U.S. communication history* (pp. 349–373). Minneapolis: University of Minnesota Press.

Ehrenreich, B. (1989). *Fear of falling: The inner life of the middle-class.* New York: Harper Perennial.

————. (1992, March 2). Double-talk about "class." *Time,* p. 70.

Ekelund, B. C. (1995). *The pathless forest: John Gardner's literary project.* Uppsala, Sweden: Acta Universitatis Upsaliensis.

Ellsworth, E. (1986). Illicit pleasures: Feminist spectators and *Personal Best. Wide Angle, 8*(2):45–56.

Fellman, G. (1995). On the fetishism of publications and the secrets thereof. *Academe, 81,* 26–35.

Feuer, J. (1984). MTM enterprises: An overview. In J. Feuer, P. Kerr, and T. Vahimagi (Eds.), *MTM: "Quality" television* (pp. 1–31). London: BFI Books.

————. (1995). *Seeing through the eighties.* Durham, NC: Duke University Press.

Finke, N. (1989, January 26). The blue-collar backgrounds behind a blue-collar hit. *Los Angeles Times,* sect. 10, p. 10.

Fiske, J. (1989). *Reading the popular.* London: Unwin Hyman.

————. (1991). For cultural interpretation: A study of the culture of homelessness. *Critical Studies in Mass Communication, 8*(4):455–474.

————. (1994). Radical shopping in Los Angeles: Race, media and the sphere of consumption. *Media, Culture, and Society, 16*(3):469–486.

Fuentes, A. and Ehrenreich, B. (1983). *Women in the global factory.* Boston, MA: South End Press.

Gamman, L. and Marshment, M. (Eds.). (1989). *The female gaze: Women as viewers of popular culture.* Seattle, WA: The Real Comet Press.

Gledhill, C. (1988). Pleasurable negotiations. In E. D. Pribram (Ed.), *Female spectators: Looking at film and television* (pp. 64–89). London: Verso.

Gledhill, C. (Ed.). (1987). *Home is where the heart is: Studies in melodrama and the woman's film.* London: British Film Institute.

Gramsci, A. (1989). *Selections from the prison notebooks* (Q. Hoare and G. N. Smith, Eds.). New York: International Publishers.

Haralovich, M. B. (1992). Sit-coms and suburbs: Positioning the 1950s homemaker. In L.

Spigel and D. Mann (Eds.), *Private screenings: Television and the female consumer* (pp. 111–141). Minneapolis: University of Minnesota Press.

Harris, D. (1992). *From class struggle to the politics of pleasure: The effects of Gramscianism on cultural studies.* London: Routledge.

Hartouni, V. (1991). Containing women: Reproductive discourse in the 1980s. In C. Penley and A. Ross (Eds.), *Technoculture* (pp. 27–56). Minneapolis: University of Minnesota Press.

Hobsbawm, E. (1994). *The age of extremes: A history of the world, 1914–1991.* New York: Pantheon.

Janos, L. (1993, February). Roseanne Arnold: The queen of awesome. *Cosmopolitan,* pp. 132–135.

Johnson, R. (Ed.). (1993). Editor's Introduction: Pierre Bourdieu on art, literature, and culture. In P. Bourdieu, *The field of cultural production* (pp. 1–25). New York: Columbia University Press.

Kaplan, E. A. (1992). *Motherhood and representation: The mother in popular culture and melodrama.* New York: Routledge.

Landy, M. (1994). *Film, politics and Gramsci.* Minneapolis: University of Minnesota Press.

Leibman, N. C. (1988). Leave mother out: The fifties family in American film and television. *Wide Angle, 10*(4):24–41.

Lesage, J. (1982). The hegemonic female fantasy in *An Unmarried Woman* and *Craig's Wife. Film Reader,* 5, 83–94.

Lipsitz, G. (1990). *Time passages: Collective memory and American popular culture.* Minneapolis: University of Minnesota Press.

Mayerle, J. (1991). *Roseanne*—how did you get inside my house? A case study of a hit blue-collar situation comedy. *Journal of Popular Culture, 24*(4):71–88.

McDaniel, J. (1991, January 1). Roseanne sings a new tune. *Ladies Home Journal,* pp. 173–174.

Meehan, E. R. (1993). Heads of household and ladies of the house: Gender, genre, and broadcast ratings, 1929–1990. In W. S. Solomon and R. W. McChesney (Eds.), *Ruthless criticism: New perspectives in U.S. communication history* (pp. 204–221). Minneapolis: University of Minnesota Press.

Morris, M. (1990). Banality in cultural studies. In P. Mellencamp (Ed.), *The logics of television* (pp. 14–43). Bloomington: Indiana University Press.

Nash, J. and Fernández-Kelley, M. P. (Eds.) (1983). *Women, men and the international division of labor.* Albany: State University of New York Press.

Naurechas, J. (1987). Mother and the teeming hordes. *Jump Cut, 32,* 1.

O'Connor, J. J. (1991, August 18). By any name, Roseanne is Roseanne is Roseanne. *The New York Times,* pp. A26–27.

Ong, A. (1991). The gender and labor politics of postmodernity. *Annual Review of Anthropology, 20:*279–309.

Ortner, S. B. (1989–90, Winter). Gender hegemonies. *Cultural Critique, 14,* 35–80.

Patton, C. (1989). Hegemony and orgasm—or the instability of heterosexual pornography. *Screen, 30*(1–2):100–112.

Playboy interview: Roseanne and Tom Arnold. (1993). *Playboy, 40,* 59–74.

Pribram, E. D. (Ed.) (1988). *Female spectators: Looking at film and television.* New York: Verso.

Przybylowicz, D. (1989–90, winter). Toward a feminist cultural critique: Hegemony and modes of social division. *Cultural Critique, 14,* 259–301.

Purdum, T. S. (1995, July 11). Clinton takes on violence on TV. *New York Times,* p. A1.

A real stand-up mom. (1988, October 31). *Newsweek,* p. 62

Rowe, K. K. (1995). *The unruly woman: Gender and the genres of laughter.* Austin: University of Texas Press.

Schulte-Sasse, J. (1988, fall). Can the disempowered read mass-produced narratives in their own voice? *Cultural Critique, 10,* 171–199.

Schwichtenberg, C. (Ed.) (1993). *The Madonna connection.* Boulder, CO: Westview Press.

Sessums, K. (1994, February). Really Roseanne. *Vanity Fair,* pp. 59–116.

Simpson, C. (1994). *The science of coercion.* New York: Oxford University Press.

Slingo, C. (1981). 9 to 5: Blondie gets the boss. *Jump Cut, 24/25,* 1, 7–8.

Snyder, A. (1991, April 21). Trouble in Nielsenland. *Home: The Newday magazine,* p. 8.

Sobchack, V. (1986, Fall). Child/alien/father: Patriarchal crisis and generic exchange. *Camera Obscura, 15,* 7–36.

Spigel, L. (1992). *Make room for TV: Television and the family ideal in postwar America.* Chicago: University of Chicago Press.

———. (1993). Seducing the innocent: Childhood and television in postwar America. In W. S. Solomon and R. W. McChesney (Eds.), *Ruthless criticism: New perspectives in U.S. communication history* (pp. 259-290). Minneapolis: University of Minnesota Press.

Spigel, L. & Mann, D., (Eds.) (1992). *Private screenings: Television and the female consumer.* Minneapolis: University of Minnesota Press.

Weisblat, T. (1994, spring). What Ozzie did for a living. *The Velvet Light Trap, 33,* 14–23.

Weiss, M. J. (1994). *Latitudes and attitudes: An atlas of American tastes, trends, politics, and passions.* New York: Little Brown.

Wolff, N. (1994). *Fire with fire: The new female power and how to use it.* New York: Ballantine.

Wright, G. (1981). *Building the dream: A social history of housing in America.* Cambridge, MA: MIT Press.

Zoglin, R. (1988, December 5). Sharp tongue in the trenches. *Time,* p. 88.

4

Anglicizing Bourdieu

Daniel Simeoni

LANDMARKS

This chapter focuses on a particular case of cultural displacement, that is, the transpositioning of *styles of thinking* out of their home environments into foreign host settings. In the broadest sense, I will be addressing the difficulty of how to describe and how to identify what regulates such concepts, models, (poly-)systems, structures, patterns, and other principles of explanation and action as flourish in the social sciences and cultural studies, beyond the national/state borders within which they were initially designed to make sense. Underlying this concern is a working hypothesis: The languages of knowledge were born into national/state communities; therefore the latter's differentiated histories can go a long way towards explaining the scholarly (and more generally, epistemic) dispositions of their native and affiliate members.

Against this background a number of interesting questions can be raised. How likely is it that the much-praised principles of action and perception defining scientific activity in general, including the social and "human" sciences, will override the dispositions inscribed in every one of us, from our earliest youth, by means of the particular institutions within which we were brought up, trained, and educated? How truly universal is a practice of science derived from, and giving rise to, different styles of thinking? Is it true, for example, as intimated recently by E. Le Roy Ladurie, that when a French historian and a Japanese historian meet at a colloquium, they speak the same "language," that is, communication between them is unhampered and therefore they truly understand each other? In a sense, the interrogation overlaps with and expands on a query formulated a few years ago by Pierre Bourdieu regarding sociological practices:

"Is it possible to circumvent the barrier of the nationalisms that hinder the free circulation of ideas and set back the unification of a sociological problematic, that is, the formation of a worldwide space of social-scientific discussion and critique?" (Wacquant 1991, 374).[1] In other words: Can social scientists "who come from different countries and different intellectual traditions . . . *s'entendre*, as we say in French, that is, both *hear* one another and *agree* with each other, at least enough to enter into constructive dialogue?" (373). Asking such questions is another way of saying that a lot of work may be needed before such mutual understanding takes place and, indeed, the most that Bourdieu was willing to commit himself to then was "a working *dissensus* founded upon the critical acknowledgement of compatibilities and incompatibilities" (384).

The perspective adopted here has been designed to be tested on a multitude of objects. Its validation will depend on how successful it is in accounting for special cases of cultural transfer: authors, works, particular ideas dominant or in vogue at any point in time. I will just begin delineating the contours of one such case study: Bourdieu's own works across borders, that is, specifically, the circulation of his ideas in English-speaking environments.

Arguably, Bourdieu's theses on the distribution of cultural capital and the development of knowledge within the boundaries of state-regulated societies could help illuminate that kind of transcultural transfer, including that which bears on his own work. At the same time, because his model is also sociohistorically constructed, it cannot evade the transpositioning difficulty that plagues other explanatory or reading systems. The thesis I would like to defend here is that Bourdieu's approach retains an unresolved tension that is an integral part of the theory of knowledge that he proposes. This tension, understandable as a result of the particular history of the French state and the peculiar relation that Bourdieu entertains to it, points to a specific difficulty in the task of transpositioning it whole, out of its original frame or national/state sphere of influences, into other fields of forces. The same observation goes, of course, for all theories of social knowledge and understandings of practice, including the more objectivist. While this is not meant to suggest that conceptual transpositioning in the social sciences and the humanities is doomed to failure, it alerts us to the fact that the difficulties, due to the ways in which cultural transfer operates, are, each time, specific. Characteristically in Bourdieu's case, it is that primary tension—to be apprehended within the context of the theory—which ought to be kept in focus if we want to understand what really happens as the model migrates.

The research program just sketched out exceeds the scope of a single essay. To produce a thorough treatment of transcultural transfer applied to the works of social science, even limited to a single author, is a task of such magnitude that only a book-size development could begin to accomplish it. Even then, it is not quite certain that the result would be fully satisfying (see C. Charle's cautionary preface to that effect, 11–13). As it stands, this chapter complements and echoes Wacquant's original treatment of the same issue. Starting from Bourdieu's general claim that "the meaning of a work (artistic, literary, philosophical, etc.) changes automatically with each change in the field within which it is situated for the spectator or reader" (1983, 313), we might postulate a logic of "foreign trade" in the circulation of ideas based on "the necessary interferences and disjunctures between the objective position (and therefore meaning) of the imported work in its native intellectual space and the position (and correlative vision and interpretive strategies) of its consumers in the receiving academic space" (Wacquant 1993, 236). We may also accept the view that "the structures of national intellectual fields act as crucial mediations in the foreign trade of theories." For all those reasons, internal and external, it has been "difficult for Anglo-American scholars to get a full grasp of the overall structure and meaning of Bourdieu's sociology" (Wacquant 1993, 246).

On the other hand, Wacquant's claim that Anglo-American sociologists have "overlooked" Bourdieu's empirical research sounds strange. The argument may even be inconsistent with the idea that Bourdieu's work—like anybody else's—is perceived and assessed in its host settings through colored lenses manufactured locally. Indeed, if "the meaning and function of a foreign work is determined as much by the field of destination as by the field of origin" (Nice 1990 [1980], 1), that is, if "the receiving country acts in a manner of a prism that selects and refracts external stimuli according to its own configuration" (Wacquant 1993, 247), and finally, if that field of destination is also the home base of empiricism (and increasingly so, at this particular juncture when "a new hegemonic alliance is being struck between all manners of empiricist methodology"—see Wacquant 1991, 381), then one would expect that dimension of Bourdieu's research at least to have been recognized and duly assessed by peers. It is not difficult in fact to find references to Bourdieu's empirical work, most notably *Distinction*, in journals or Ph.D. theses. Further, even if such references were missing in evaluative articles, this would not necessarily be a sign of indifference. On the contrary, it might signal that that work is not controversial, or that it would require painstaking analyses to confirm or undo it, or more likely that protocols permitting comparative work across borders are not easily designed. An example is the deafening silence surrounding *Homo Academicus*, perhaps related to the particular structures of the education system in the United States: How do we go about collecting the basic information when "the policies of educational institutions themselves [allow them to] keep secret the kinds of data which would shed light on who gets admitted to them and who does not—and why," and we might add crucially, who runs them (Wolfe 1998)?

How do we evaluate the higher-order neo-Whorfian (or Humboldtian) claim, then, that "the schemata of academic perception and appreciation inculcated through graduate training and durable immersion in the specific universe . . . shape the assimilation of foreign intellectual products" (Wacquant 1993, 241), thereby frustrating communication and generating misunderstandings? Ideally, implementing such an evaluation would require a comparison of the work accomplished in, for example, *La distinction* with its homologues in other national/state settings.

Indeed, a number of attempts have been made in the last decade, starting with Gartman (1991) and Erickson (1991), to replicate in a more focused manner the kind of study conducted in France based on data collected from 1963 to 1975. But replication for comparative purposes is a difficult exercise when it touches on cultural cognition. What criteria of differentiation regulate "similar" usual practices in different countries? It is far from clear, for example, what status "culture" has across societies. Is it justifiable to construct an image of the overall social space, based on the same universal opposition of cultural and economic capitals everywhere? Whether such a contrast can be made operational *across borders*, indeed whether French, German, North American, let alone "postcolonial" or multicultural societies can manage it in mutually intelligible ways, remains to be seen. There is no reason why comparative work should be ruled out (see, for example, Casanova 1997 for an extreme case of such extension), but prior reflection on how to work out the relevant homologies is a clear *sine qua non*.

Since no work commensurable with *Distinction* (1979), *Homo Academicus* (1984), or *La noblesse d'État* (1989) has yet seen the light of day outside France, I have opted for a purely language-based approach to transfer. For all its inherent limitations, the study of existing translations of canonical works in the social sciences and the humanities with a view to assessing their "translatability," that is, the degree of their effective transpositioning into new host environments, is an acceptable comparative method—perhaps the next best alternative to full-fledged empirical comparison of constructed data and their extension across cultural fields. To quote from Hinkle (89): "Translation from one language to another, and more specifically from one intellectual and linguistic context to another, entails not merely a substitution of words but a transformation of ideas, styles of thinking, modes of expression, indeed a whole context of mental imagery and assumptions many of which may be unnoticed by the writer, the translator, and the reader." Furthermore, nothing in language-based inquiry is antithetical to the sociologist's investigation of social facts: "In connection with the social world, *words are the makers of things*, for they produce the consensus on the existence and meaning of things" (Bourdieu 1994, 138; my emphasis). "Words" here does not refer to the formal structuring of language as studied by mainstream linguistics, but to the regulations of *parole* (speech, oral and written): "the power principle mobilized [in certain ways of using words] is to be looked for beyond the words themselves, within the mechanism that produces both the words and those who speak and hear them" (Bourdieu 1989, 63).

Empirical-hermeneutic research of the kind sketched out in this chapter can be viewed as a long-range mode of inquiry; an easily accessible, admittedly provisional, way of addressing issues of principle regarding the material conditions of possibility of a *transfert des œuvres et des textes*: what hard facts of language—

lexical, stylistic, matricial, and argumentative—related to the *habitus* of those involved are induced by representations of social-science informational capital beyond the home base? What does the very act of translating imply for the integrity and consistency of the works, as well as for the overall rhetoric of scientificity attached to them (see also Venuti)?

In this perspective, any work produced in a specified environment at any point in time can be deemed representative, simply by virtue of its "being there," not an ad hoc construct but a social fact. The proven "shifts" or "non-obligatory deviations" (Toury, 50) brought about by translation may be taken as indices of the *difficulty* in the transfer of culture-bound forms—those very same forms Hinkle envisions in the above quotation as "whole context[s] of mental imagery and assumptions." It is important to keep in mind that no judgment of value can be attached to such shifts. A shiftless translation, if such a thing existed, would come down to transliteral, transideational replication. To translate is by definition to "transposition," that is, to transform the original. Neither can the sheer stigmatization of "loss" in translation be a sound approach, as noted by Cronin. Losses can just as well be viewed as gains from within the relevant framework—that of the receiving field and terms of destination.

BOURDIEU'S FIELD THEORY:
TOOLS FOR A TRANSBORDER HERMENEUTICS?

Experientially, we have a pretty good idea of how things work in everyday practice. The informants interviewed by Bourdieu's team (1993) did not require a special metalanguage to actualize and objectify the relations that the sociologist otherwise must strive to bring to light with a heavy conceptual apparatus. There seems to be a hermeneutics of *ordinary expert reading and understanding*, running across and narrowing down the subject/object divide. The opening of Bettelheim's "Reflections," for example, illustrates this correspondence. Reader and writer, interpreter and informant, Bettelheim and Freud, share the same frame of reference: "As a child *born into* a middle-class, assimilated Jewish family in Vienna, *I was raised and educated* in an environment that was in many respects identical with the one *that had formed* Freud's background. *The culture that was transmitted to me in my home, then in secondary school, and finally at the University of Vienna*, had changed very little since Freud's student days, fifty years earlier. So *it was natural* that from the time I began to think on my own I read Freud. . . . Understanding Freud's writings was considerably facilitated . . . by my study of psychoanalysis in the same unique Viennese cultural climate in which Freud *worked and thought*" (my emphases).

In a sense, Bourdieu's model simply illuminates what goes on in the practice of everyday life. Theoretically, it partakes of a long continental European tradition (not only sociological or anthropological but also linguistic and philosophical) of devising a metafunction to the power of two—a paramimetic device—that comes as close as possible to the primary metafunction that agents already implement as a matter of routine in their daily lives. The kind of *Vermittlung* (Cassirer, 6–7) through which Bourdieu's theory mediates social events, his interpretive prism, was designed to project an organization of things reproducing the peculiar logic of events that we-as-social-beings instill into the social world (which may explain why many view his work as tautological). His social grammar is built so as to "leak" as little as possible. This is due in large part to the functionality of the *habitus*, a concept pivotal in articulating objective and subjective referents, which seals the theory–practice continuum and prevents theory from living an independent life.

Similarly, the ordinary act of translating can be viewed as a secondary function of a "translating *habitus*" construed both as the vessel and the vehicle of whatever norms are active in the target field (Simeoni 1998). This working hypothesis is functional and, as a complement to the more traditional polysystemic reading used in translation studies, it helps gently nudge the analysis away from the dynamic interplay of systems, back to the real-life behavior of the agents concerned (beginning with the translator). In Toury's terms (11–12): In the particular semiotic subtype related to the coexistence of semiotic systems de facto represented by the coexistence of different natural languages, every operation of transfer (such as translation) entails specific relationships between the respective positions of each and every entity in the system within which they are inscribed. This is quite abstract, but the process thus identified by Toury following Even-Zohar (1978) from the vantage point of the objectivist structuralist, is easily rephrased in a way more attuned to personal experience, drawing from Bourdieu's model of engaged practice.

What is carried out in translation is, first, the coming together of two contexts of mental imagery and assumptions mediated by two *habitus*, the writer's and the translator's, then the transfer of the former by the latter's *truchement* into a new field of forces and positions. On the source side, the writer's *habitus* may have been motivated by a whole aggregate of meaning-making references derived from a generalized *pensée d'État* (or any corresponding hierarchical order). Facing it is the target environment—a historical, sociologically explainable product, in a polysystemic reading the "primary" or dominant system in the source-target relationship, that is the one that prevails on both counts of practice and theoretical reading (see Toury 1995, chapter 1)—often presumed by critics and players alike to be in a relation of perfect co-reference vis-à-vis the source side. This is a quixotic presupposition that most attempts at translation make and, interestingly, it is also the basis for Wacquant's denunciation, the "moral of the story" about his stigmatization of Anglo-American (mis-)understandings of Bourdieu. It is almost like overhearing the wrathful spirit of Nabokov (512) demanding faithful translations of poetry, with only the "gleam" of one textual line on top of the page, and the rest hosting a copious apparatus of footnotes. Wacquant is less of a purist than Nabokov, but the presupposition, that the two worlds—that of the original work and that of the host field—*ought to* be homologous and the gap between them annihilated, is the same: ". . . intellectual products such as social theories should, whenever possible, be exported with as much of their native 'context' as possible (if in miniature in the form of a select intellectual self-accounting, preface to foreign readers, and so on), and imported with full awareness of the distortions induced by the mediating interests of, affinities with, and biases built into the objective relations between producer, intermediary, and consumer" (1993, 247).

This never happens. Operating as it were at an unconscious level in the *habitus* of the translator, target norms will have the upper hand: Phenomenologically, the translator's *habitus* overrides the writer's by default. That is why it is so frighteningly consistent. Even objective inconsistencies ("objective" by some external plan of rationality) become, in this reading, subject-mediated *consistencies*. Thus when Parsons translates Weber's *Gründe* ("grounds" or "reasons") and *Ursachen* ("antecedents") as the "cause" or "causal explanation" in the singular, it does not have to be out of some conscious wish to "Parsonize" the original, it is North-American sociology's state-induced style of thinking feeding its modal agents' interests, while transpositioning the coherence of Weber's ideas (*"trans-cohering"* them) relentlessly page after page. And it will take Gisela Hinkle, an outsider positioned at a distance from the (modal) *habitus* in the field of destination and partaking of the source field on account of her dual identity as a German American, to uncover the workings of that *habitus*. Even then, this will hardly suffice for the transpositioned *personae* of Weber, Freud or, for another canonical figure extensively naturalized, Foucault (see, for example, Chambon, forthcoming), to rid themselves of their newly habituated consistency and suddenly go native. Why should they?

Although he does not seem to have expressed himself directly on this theme, Bourdieu has been skirting the issue of translation when dealing with the conundrum of being understood in "unfamiliar countries":

> It is evident that the structures of thought that I am going to put to work in my discourse, the oppositions that I use, are historically constituted. The categories of thought through which you are going to listen to what I say to you are also situated and datable. . . . I think that we are all provincials, enclosed in particular intellectual traditions, and that we are all threatened by a form of intellectual ethnocentrism. . . . If I wanted to advance a modern version of the theory of national character . . . it would begin, for me, with a theory of the educational systems in as much as they are formative of the structures of understanding, and constructive of our taxonomies (translation in Boyne, 38–39).

Translation, when applied to explanatory models, concepts, and more generally, alternative ways of doing science, presents specific problems, not least for

Bourdieu's theory itself. The contents of such notions as "field," "capital," "modal *habitus*," homologies of "positions," "dispositions," and "stances" (*prises de position*), their dependence upon "l'État," that is, a whole network of thinking styles embodying a force dynamics marked by the peculiar workings of French society, those constructs may resist transfer. Bourdieu's ideas have evolved over the years, and there seems to be one critical difference between the Bourdieu of 1977 who wrote "Sur le pouvoir symbolique" and today's analyst of the "bureaucratic field" (Boyne), a difference that may require, as well as complicate, the treatment and inclusion of transborder data within the theory. Fields in the later work are not simply a methodological device, a projection of the theoretician's organizing imagination intent on bringing order to the surrounding *hyle*. They are deemed to be *state-inferable constructions* (1991) co-elaborated by increasingly administrative structures of power interiorized by people and thus regulating social life. The type of transfer called for by Bourdieu, clearly of a relational nature as he recommends adjusting one's glasses to the principles of differentiation relevant to other societies, poses similar problems for the practical application of the model across borders as for purposes of textual translation.

TRANSLATION AND THE SYSTEMS-THEORETICAL BIAS OF COMMON PRACTICE

Weber's works were translated after World War II, at a time when his reputation had long been established. The first translations of Freud's works into English were not controlled by the Strachey team, but were the product of A. J. Brill's penmanship. Even then, Brill could not have ignored the importance of the pioneering work he was translating in 1913 (*Die Traumdeutung* was published in 1900). Brill was an established psychoanalyst, and Freud was that rare theorist who seemed at the time to create his interpretive system out of nowhere. In contrast, Bourdieu's translations saw the light of day before he acquired the fame that is his today (Sheffy), and his work was teeming with scholastic references to the social sciences and the philosophical field. Translators may have had little or no idea of the extent to which their transpositioning attempts would reverberate eventually across disciplinary boundaries. Bourdieu's works have had one chief translator into English, Richard Nice, with whom the author is said to have worked closely (Barret-Ducrocq, 197 et seq.), but counting others who have toiled on his prose produces an unusual crowd: Matthew Adamson, M. C. Axtmann, J. Bleicher, R. Boyne, Lauretta C. Clough, Peter Collier, Claud DuVerlie, Susan Emanuel, Priscilla Ferguson, E. Foster, Sian France, R. Hurley, R. Johnson, Gisèle Sapiro and Brian McHale, W. Leeds-Hurwitz, C. Majidi, Channa Newman, Charles Newman, Juliette Parnell, Gino Raymond, K. Robinson, A. C. M. Ross, R. Swyer, R. Teese, C. Turner, Loïc Wacquant, J. Wakelyn, J. C. Whitehouse, Y. Winkin, Colin Wringe, and many others of whom I am not aware at the time of this writing (the list is from Clough, 44). For translation studies, this profusion is a boon. Anglicizing Bourdieu has resulted in uneven, heterogeneous styles. If the analogy I have been drawing between textual translation and conceptual transpositioning holds, the translated material may even suggest pathways for a refined definition of the notions of "field" or "system," based on what takes place *between* as much as within them.

Sociologists have never had a good press in terms of how they treat "style." An exchange of letters between W. G. Runciman and Edward Shils in the mid-sixties dealt with just this issue. To Runciman's "Why do sociologists write such bad prose?" (45), Shils responded with his own typology of the "major vices of sociological language. One is its use of neologisms which startle by their own novelty, and offend by their inelegance. Another is vagueness; a third is stylistic and grammatical awkwardness. A fourth is pretentiousness: things could often be said less portentously" (88). While Runciman summarily dismissed the option that there might be national characteristics to "bad prose" in the first page of his essay, he did so only after referring to the habitual complaints that American and German social scientists are perhaps most "to blame." Be this as it may, we would expect the protagonists to have become somewhat blasé, so it is interesting that Bourdieu's rhetoric, sometimes in the original French but more frequently in its Anglicized mould, keeps being denounced as notoriously "difficult." This is noted by Wacquant (1993, 237, 249) who recalls Jenkins's stigmatization of *Homo Academicus* in 1989, as a book "written in a language so obscurantist, so dense and so ugly that the effort of reading the damned thing will probably . . . heavily outweigh any final benefit." Michael Luntley of the University of Warwick, in a review of the translation of *Le sens pratique* (448), offers another example of the kind of reaction elicited by Bourdieu's writing: "LP [*The Logic of Practice*] is not an easy read. The language of the book contains some of the worst excesses of academy-speak which continually prompt the desire, in this reader at last, to put the book down and turn to something more profitable. That is an unfair reaction, but it is difficult to avoid. In reading this book, one frequently has to engage a theoretical, not practical mode of reading in which one has consciously to decode not only the hinted metaphorical meanings, but also the syntax and punctuation."

This is intriguing. Bourdieu has always claimed to be mindful of facilitating communication. The following is a typical passage, but other equally reflexive examples of such thoughtfulness are easy to come by (see, for example, the foreword to *Choses dites*): "It is already an important contribution to all communication, especially to pedagogic communication, to say, 'Bear in mind that what you say involves categories and structures of thought, and that you should work to improve your comprehension of such categories, in whose name you are going to understand, or at least think that you do' " (Boyne, 38–39).

The English preface to *Distinction: A Social Critique of the Judgement of*

Taste, written in 1984 and translated by Richard Nice, must be seen as a landmark in this regard. It reveals both a compulsive desire to be understood, and a disenchanted awareness that comprehension—to borrow from Culioli's felicitous formulation—may be but a particular case of misunderstanding. In the preface, the notion of "modal *habitus*" later refined in *La noblesse d'État* (for example, 256) is already transparent. The concept was developed in order to better assert the effort of the analyst in recording, making sense of, and qualitatively assessing the individual differences (of which lexico-stylistic variation is an integral part) denoted by the agents' distinctive positions. In the preface, Nice's Bourdieu, a transposed sociologist writing in English about French society in the sixties for an American readership (the book was published by Harvard University Press), reviews some of the features of his own *habitus* as a writer—this "most absolute system of censure" internalized and acknowledged as a matter of course, by himself as well as by those whose behavior *Distinction* was designed to elucidate. Already an interference in the *textual* process of translating, those features raise a formidable obstacle to *conceptual* transpositioning away from their original base.

As could be expected, this section of the preface introduces the notions of a hierarchy of tastes and preferences culturally modulated, as well as a correspondence between the variation induced and the socially differentiated positions of those concerned, all against the background of coherent social spaces constructed in the act of research as (specialized) fields. Vis-à-vis the question of transfer between (nation-bound) systems of references, Nice himself had already voiced his opinion in his own translator's foreword to *Outline of a Theory of Practice* (1977). In the last two paragraphs, he emphasized the inevitability of *referential distortions* brought about by *conceptual* transfer. Source *references*, he said, shall be perceived and interpreted differently in the field of reception. The author of *Esquisse d'une théorie de la pratique* having set for himself the task of "thinking the unthinkable," that is, of questioning the unquestioned in French society, how could the conditions for homologous, equally subversive reading be conceived of in another cultural ensemble whose agents organized their lives and had their lives organized according to different criteria of differentiation and judgment? Under growing pressure to explain his ideas abroad, Bourdieu has tended lately to advocate reading modes inspired by structuro-relational principles, in order to preclude the temptation of false "essentialist" readings (Sapiro and McHale 1991; Bourdieu 1994). This does not make the finality of transposition any easier. If the meaning of an item or node in the system depends on its position in the overall structure, to reexpress that meaning in another context requires a solid sense of how the systems differ in the first place.

The criteria for self/other differentiation in the unconscious game of distinction, that is, those criteria constitutive of the main axes of differentiation in French society in the sixties and seventies, are said to vary considerably from one society to another: "The system of distinctive features that express or reveal economic and social differences (themselves variable in scale and structure) varies considerably from one period, and one society, to another." Thus the little "game" of guessing the actual homologies has all the characteristics and "dangers of a facile search." Having said that, Bourdieu embarks on exactly this kind of search. Further, in the preface, he takes up the idea first brought forth by Nice. Specifically, he stratifies the difficulty likely to be experienced by his American and other English-speaking readers in three layers: the *form*, the *style*, and the *conception* of the book.

The "form" must be relocated in the context of its sociogenesis: "[the form of the book] depends on the laws of the market on which it is offered." Considerations relative to style follow closely: "My long, complex sentences may offend." The theme is that of a sociostylistics in which the syntax and substance of arguments are iconic. The length of sentences is said to be motivated: "They were constructed *with a view to* reconstituting the complexity of the social world in a language capable of holding together the most diverse things while setting them in rigorous perspective" (my emphasis). One may wonder at this postcripted intentionality, and prefer Halliday's insight (1971; 1988; 1994) that there is a formal correspondence between the *way* things are said and *what* is being said, at least for those creative writers who produce original work, in literature or in the social sciences. One need not consciously mould one's style after another's ideas for such coherence to co-occur: "the how of the saying" is ipso facto "the what of the saying" (Geertz). Lévi Strauss's native could not fail to be the "cerebral savage," his detached style—*le regard éloigné*—following suit, any more than Bourdieu's narratives of social relations could avoid being reflexive and, as a result, maximally inclusive—some say proustian. Similarly, as much as he tried to distance himself in his formative years from the two poles or modal styles of thinking and writing exemplified in France by Sartre and Lévi-Strauss (see, for example, 1980, 51–86), Bourdieu was also careful to import some of their insights. Bourdieu's "take" on things is actually often most inclusive when it is exclusionary. Hence the Prévert-like appearance of his acknowledged influences, sometimes decried by observers as baffling and baroque (see, for example, Wacquant 1993, 237), when in fact he retains scrupulously only what is consistent with his systemic construal, denouncing the traits he disagrees with. This is something we all do as a matter of course, only with a lesser capacity for synthesizing genres. Keeping the project coherent while discouraging misinterpretations has entailed a very personal, sophisticated, highly charged style of writing.

Lastly, and perhaps most importantly, the reader of *Distinction*'s preface is warned: "I realize how much the specificity of the French intellectual field may have contributed to the conception of the book." The last paragraph opens on a note of disillusionment: "At all events . . ." The impression is one of self-conscious melancholy; overcome by the realization of the gulf between referential systems, the author will play the game, but the style of the preface shows more than a little reticence. Similarly, Wacquant (1993) has referred to what he sees as "a disenchanting questioning of the symbolic power of intellectuals." Bourdieu closes then on what constitutes in 1984 the core of his teaching, that which must be preserved at all cost for his work not to have been in vain: "the *project* of a critique of culture."

What are we left with then, in the end? The sociologist of society internalized by its agents, of *Fremdzwänge* turned *Selbstzwänge*, remains alone, facing his object. It is quite an astonishing paragraph: to be delivered proselytically across the Atlantic and beyond, yet suffused with an unmistakably continental European mood. The critical project turns out to be expressed in the most abstract mode. Its grounding is in philosophical studies: Kant's critique of Reason. At that point, the American reader, and perhaps even more so his British and former British Empire counterparts may be under the impression that the conception of the book, after all, is hardly French; the intellectual field wherein it was devised is European, with a strong continental flavor. The last sentence evokes "the only rational basis for a truly universal culture."

Going back to Nice's 1977 foreword, let us ask ourselves now about the kind of referential shifts involved in the transpositioning of a continental European mould into a constellation of perceptions cohering into a renewed map of postcolonial "Englishness." Can the Reason of Kant and the Enlightenment as the "only rational basis" of culture retain the practical force it had in its original system of references, once it undergoes transfer to its new host context? Are we sure that the universalization of a critical project taking for its unique reference European "reason"—*raison, Vernunft*—will translate as a matter of course into an American, British, Irish, Canadian, or Australian context, not to mention other ethnically distinct yet perfectly anglicized projects of emancipation? Does transfer have that kind of leeway? If so, then how? Think of Noam Chomsky's habitual dismissal of French styles of thinking as "weird" (see, for example, Barsky, 196), a gut reaction by a Bertrand Russell follower that can hardly be explained away on idiosyncratic grounds. There is more at stake here than the technical issue of transferring idioms. What if the "reason" valued in Cambridge was not quite the "raison" invoked in Paris? Nor "ethics" "l'éthique," any more than "law" is "la loi" or "culture" "Kultur"? Of course, Bourdieu builds up his case. The American reader (or other) will see through the Enlightenment references without difficulty. But the fact remains that such categories are more than semantic; they are categories of persuasion working their way through society until they become fully internalized and incorporated by less than perfectly bilingual/bicultural agents. As shown in the Parsonian naturalization of Weber, they evade even the consciousness of the alert.

This is the double bind of transpositioning processes: once the project of a "realpolitik of reason" is understood to belong to continental Europe, how can it be "translated" to speak to monolingual sociologists trained in a different environment, other than as a curiosity? Is not the undertaking a parochial attempt or, worse, will it not be taken by some as a neocolonial return of the repressed by one of Europe's leading thinkers? On the other hand, if it turns out to be effectively transpositioned as the "rational project" into which the translator willed it, the universal search may be thwarted in return. For if the goal is to universalize the project, how will the modal *habitus* of the monolingual non-European reader react to the hand extended to him from Europe? This is no idle question, for the "project" is explicitly relativized by Nice's Bourdieu: Each reader, it is suggested, should "reproduce on his or her behalf the critical break." On the surface, this seems to require that the epistemological break be appropriated at will by each and every one concerned. The goal is the same, but the means and dynamics are many: as diverse as there are readers? Bourdieu cannot ignore the tyranny of field-logic. He writes through the modal reader. The epistemological break has got to be "americanized" in the first place. *Distinction*'s North-American readers should see their reading styles redistributed as a function of the positions *they* occupy within the local field(s), that is, according to the relations *they* entertain to the dominant, modal reading in those fields.

What the English preface to *Distinction* proposes to its variously distributed foreign readers is a universal critical project: to replicate for their own benefit the kind of critique developed in the book for the particular case of France, this time on the basis of whatever higher principles of social differentiation are at work in the U.S., Canada, Britain, etc. If the project is highlighted in the book by reference to the Enlightenment, it is because the author was born, raised, and educated in a system of socialization steeped in the reference. Bourdieu's commitment to the emancipatory project of a social critique is inseparable from this referential base viewed in a European perspective. This is transparent in his reflexive argumentation: *I come from a certain location in social space and I have been trained in a certain tradition; I am acutely aware of this, both in my fieldwork and with my peers, and I wish others would objectify their own training and* habitus *through similar awareness, thus performing a true and honest socioanalysis.* It is a deeply felt, engaged project of emancipation, in which the affect plays a primordial role.

Since the mid-eighties, however, writing more and more for Anglo-American audiences, Bourdieu seems to have opted for another reading principle. The structural principle has taken on center stage again, emphasizing a prior aspect of the theoretical work, the predilection for orderly construction, in which the European reference, nominally at least, is downplayed. The dynamics of fields has been foregrounded, more than the changing contents assigned to the nodes. The inflection may have been motivated by the persistence of misunderstandings, both in France and elsewhere. But it is also possible that translations accentuated this shift. It is this aspect of Bourdieu, at any rate, that has been retained and commented upon most by his Anglo-American critics, often to distance themselves from it. The anglicized Bourdieu has been seen primarily as a systems theoretician whose production, in English-speaking forums, has been compared to that of Giddens or Schmidt, occasionally to Even-Zohar's semiostructural work, leading commentators at times "to attribute to [him] exactly the type of mechanistic, objectivist structuralism that he discarded and self-consciously set out to overcome in the mid-sixties" (Wacquant 1993, 239). Perhaps more in accordance with the theory, this dissonance may have followed from a deeper misapprehension revealing a clash of ingrained habits and preferences: a disseverance of (source and target) modal *habitus* causing distinct repositionings. The preference for systems-theoretical readings in English-speaking forums may be a cultural artifact.

Perhaps the role and import of what I have called the practice of cultural transpositioning will be clearer if we go back to the passage in *Le sens pratique* quoted earlier as stigmatized by Michael Luntley. It is important to stress from the outset that the translator's *personal* mediation, his signature, is not at issue. Nice's performance—like that of any seasoned translator—must be understood as an outcome shared with a multitude of other agents: the author, the university press that signed the contract, editors, proofreaders, the myriad intervening hands in the collective process of publishing—making public—the typed submission (on all those points, compare, for example, Chartier on authorship and the circulation of books in the modern period and, specifically on the subject of translation, Robinson), and whatever perception of the readership all concerned may have entertained before the decision was made to go the galleys. We know for example from Nice himself (1996, 143) that the title in English—*The Logic of Practice*—was not his choice. His original proposals, *Sense in Practice*, or *Making Sense of Practice*, "were rejected by the publisher on the grounds of obscurity."

The English version of how the concept of *habitus* is accounted for is given in the appendix to this chapter, together with the original French. The slimming factor, or quantitative loss of words, common from French into English, is well within average (115 < 131 = 12% reduction). Yet the original flows more smoothly, its contents are clearer, the presence of the author more "felt." The style in *The Logic of Practice* does not correspond to what one likes to imagine in France as the so-called "Anglo-Saxon" style of writing, in which sentences never end, abstract nouns of Latin stock abound, and the complexity of logical articulations renders the syntax somewhat opaque. Together, these make for an arduous task for the reader. I am not saying that Bourdieu's style in *Le sens pratique* is representative of French sociological writing, or even that it serves as the modal reference for aspiring sociologists. His sentences are longer than average. But his style works. Communication is unhampered. It seems justified to ask, then, what happened to this definition of the *habitus* in the course of its being transpositioned into the host environment, which detracted from the relative fluidity of the original and turned it into the kind of "academic-speak" denounced by Runciman? Short of segmenting the text, many inflections were accomplished in the process of transfer.

Lexically first: a number of ellipses were performed on the original: (1) from "le travail . . . nécessaire pour que . . . les structures objectives *parviennent à* se reproduire" to the leaner "work . . . needed in order for objective structures . . . *to* be reproduced" a subtle shift has taken place, which attenuates the effort implied in the structural reproduction of societal manners; emphatic reformulations such as "maintenir [les institutions] *en activité, en vie, en vigueur"* or "l'état *de lettre morte, de langue morte"* are reduced to: "keep them *in activity"* and "the state *of dead letters."* Not only does the relative emphasis in the original lose strength, (3) the rhythmic *energy* and the *dynamics* inherent in the process of social habituation are gone. The same transformation is borne out by three more ellipses, less "lexical" than "rhythmic" perhaps, since the functions of the phrases in question led them historically to delexicalization. Thus "que sont," "par là," and "s'y trouve" disappear from the English version, because of their void status (for a comparable assessment of discourse particles, see, for example, Even-Zohar 1990). Delexicalization ought not to be equated with stylistic redundancy. Often, original texts derive their dominant flavor from such terms.

Bourdieu's expressiveness is not typical of social scientists. M. A. K. Halliday was able to contrast successfully the synoptic constituency of "written style" with the "choreographic" nature of spoken language. By this standard, Bourdieu's written style is quite unusual, in that the dynamic expression of his ideas rather evokes what Halliday sees as the defining quality of *speech,* that is, "the ability to 'choreograph' very long and intricate patterns of semantic movement while maintaining a continuous flow of discourse that is coherent without being constructional" (1985, 224). The difference with truly spoken style of course is in the degree of construction. Bourdieu does construct his sentences in a very elaborate manner. But overall, his style is uncannily informed with orality. He is best read aloud.

The foregoing analysis is supported by many other features. Not only the lexis and rhythm, the syntax also is inflected. Three types of syntactic shifts stand out: (1) whereas in French "les structures . . . *se* reprodui[sent]" and "l'*habitus . . . se* constitue," the English text proposes "structures . . . *be* reproduc*ed,"* and "the *habitus . . . is* constitut*ed";* (2) "arrach*er* (les institutions)" and "faire revivre [leur] sens" are recast somewhat euphemistically as: "pull*ing* them" and "reviv*ing* [their] sense"; (3) in "the *habitus . . .* through *which* agents partake of the history," *which* refers less obviously to an animate antecedent than *qui,* in "l'*habitus,* par *qui* les agents participent de l'histoire." A back-translation would be just as likely to yield the more detached "par *lequel"* or even "par *quoi"* as the more involved "par *qui"* of the original. These syntactic shifts—passivation of an otherwise self-agentive process, substitution of nonfinite dependency for infinitive autonomy, mitigation of the relative-pronoun personalization of the *habitus*—are consistent with the lexical and rhythmic inflections previously noted.

Barely noticeable individually, these translational shifts together snowball into a formidable effect that is easily identifiable: *most affective components are gone.* Specifically, the rage with which Bourdieu enunciates the continuous reactivation of individual, personal dispositions within institutions ("en activité," "en vie," "en vigueur," "arracher," "faire revivre"), as a social magic of legitimation, loses much of its force. This rage is not only the mantle in which the "substance" of ideas would be clothed. It is part and parcel of his teaching. It disappears from the passage analyzed, as in most cases when translation operates from French into English.

Could the translation have been otherwise? Of course, but the conditional makes the question irrelevant. The point is never what translations might have been or might be like, but what they are or were. A translation is what is taken to be so at a given point in time, in a given society, under the prevailing circumstances. Translations are social facts (Toury) and it is a vain exercise to wish they had been otherwise. They should be regarded as they were by those who first mediated and vetted their coming into being. Nice's competency is not in question: he has translated most of the major books written by Bourdieu, and he is now in the process of translating his latest, *Méditations pascaliennes.* Besides, as we already noted above, to say that a translation has been defective in letting go some of the characteristics of the original text implies that it was also creative, within the limits prescribed by prevailing norms. Critics of translations focus on what they prefer to view as the failings of the individual translator, when in fact they are distancing themselves from the positive values of a particular cultural field. Far from the individual translator's gesture being the issue, it is the *norms* that led him or her as well as all involved in the translation event that bear responsibility for the final form. Otherwise the translation would not even have seen the light of day.

The style of the social scientist has come to be rehabilitated recently as an integral part of the social-science capital s/he helps transmit (Geertz, 68; Le Goff, 53). For the translator, focusing on the style of the social scientist *qua* author requires, first, paying special attention to the presence or absence of modality markers understood as part of an "extended" or "discourse modality" (Maynard; Chambon and Simeoni): mood, aspect, auxiliating devices, grammatical metaphor, the order in which arguments are introduced in the clause, the way traditional parts of speech supporting the inner voice of the writer are foregrounded or, on the contrary, disappear from view—all those meaningful symbols and symptoms expressive of the author's distinctive stance against the uniformity of the shared dialectal resources available to him. Rachel May (especially chapter 3) has documented the effects of ignoring those "little words" while translating nineteenth-century Russian novels, yet this bias did no deter generations of English readers from enjoying the works of Tolstoy, Dostoievskij, Turgeniev, or Gogol, although their prose was as equalized in the English version as it was different in the original.

Because of the specific national histories of social-science scientificity (Heilbron), the task of providing "acceptable" translations of marginal styles (Toury, 75), that is, styles peripheral in terms of their not being raised yet to modal status, has become near impossible. The practice has favored transpositioning patterns that work well as long as the author's style does not swerve too far from normative types in the target environment. Whenever the authors have been innovators, not only in substance but in styles of thinking—as was the case with Freud or Weber and more recently, Bourdieu—the task of the translator, working on the frontline as a potential bridgemaker for several conflicting *habitus,* has been a nightmare.

Rereading the preface to *Distinction* after this linguistic detour is illuminating. One by one, the author resists the temptations and "dangers" of finding correspondences between his work in the original French and its putative replications in other national settings. The criteria for differentiation cannot be assumed to be the same; the form, the style, the conception of the book are none of them essential to the project. System and properties must adjust to the conditions prevailing in the host culture. Bourdieu's moral imperative is as follows: Cast doubt on the phenomena that surround you, including those most familiar, for you have been led to take them for granted by the magic of the modal *habitus* conveyed by your country's institutions. The core of the project then is a *stance,* an attitude, a *posture* both involved (in the sense of being *physically* engaged, invested, and interested in the field) and detached (being able to visualize and comprehend the relative positions of participants). Of this ambivalent stance of "involvement" and "detachment" (as opposed to the scholastic point of view), it seems that the latter has received the most attention, resulting in the concept of position being interpreted topologically, as a berth, a slot in social space, although Bourdieu repeatedly distanced himself from the idea that one side of this schizoid stance could be separated from the other (Bourdieu 1980; Boyne). Translation by itself cannot account for this bias (and for an inclusive explanation of external reasons for Bourdieu's difficult reception in North America, see John Guillory's chapter in this book) but if we recognize that the setting of translational parameters is all but arbitrary and the principles guiding its coming into being are shared by all as a function of their socioculturalized *habitus,* it is easy to understand how all influences conspire to make the objective form of the translated product a test of the latter's transpositionality.

It is his complex and altogether rather strange, self-ascribed posture, both intellectual and affective, it-focused and I-focused, objective and subjective, structural and phenomenological, detached and participatory, that grounds Bourdieu's interpretation of the notion of *habitus.* The construct is threefold: (1) incorporated as *hexis;* (2) language structure inflected with rhythm, pitch, and tone of voice; (3) theoretical principle. It has given rise to the baffling concept of "positional pain" (*suffrance de position*), a notion difficult to figure out from either of the two poles of involvement or detachment taken separately. Embodied, word-based, and theoretical, that posture is at its best in spoken form, much easier to decode at each of the constituent levels. It is also possible that spoken "I"-forms, unlike the seemingly idiosyncratic redundance of modality markers punctuating endless sentences, can circulate more freely across borders. The issue of translation as a difficulty of transpositioning situated stances may find a partial solution here.

An interesting question is whether Bourdieu—and other similarly positioned authors in the social sciences—might be better served by an interpreter, rather than by translation in the modern sense of the term. It is doubtful that the agents concerned in the field (beginning with the author himself) would tolerate such freedom in the process of transpositioning the "original" ideas and model. The history of translational practices, since Jerome first set the frame for all Western attempts at appropriating figures of authority, has caused the cultural status of translators to founder as they were made to believe at every stage of the process that their proper place was at the back. Counterexamples such as the Ciceronian practice four centuries before the Hyeronimian turn, or translating in twice or three times as many words as the original (as is common on the fringes of the Empire even today), paradoxically provide directions for a renewed practice of translation. Iconoclastic as it may appear, the rationale for such a counterpractice is not easily dismissed: it might lead to an improved circulation of knowledge across borders.

CONCLUSION

The regularities in nonobligatory deviations uncovered in translation analysis are too recurrent to be simply a matter of chance. The polysystemic reading of trans-lational equivalences is thereby confirmed. Refracting the facts of translation as I have done through Bourdieu's model of cultural transfer—bringing the model to bear on theory taken as its own object—produces similar findings. With one major difference: the focus moves back from the systems-theoretical dimension to *the agents' viewpoint*, with minimum loss or distortion in the analytical proc-ess. On the other hand, the vicissitudes of Bourdieu's works in English transla-tion, compounded with the negative reactions they trigger, signal that this focus is downplayed at a cost as the writer's engagement undergoes transfer from the French intellectual field to its anglicized host settings. As the affective compo-nent of Bourdieu's style disappears in the early translations, the iconicity of the message is lost.

Things are more complex, however, in reception. For there is little doubt that those readers similarly positioned somewhere along the same imaginary line de-scribing Bourdieu's trajectory in the original field of forces (it does not matter where on the line; the vernacular style of Bourdieu's teaching, the pervasive oral-ity of his books, have preserved traces of his earlier positioning), those readers thus dispositioned away from the mainstream, in the margins of the field of desti-nation, may paradoxically be in a better position to re-inject the missing affective component into the truncated model. Such a reading, which could be labeled "ad-equate," is hardly a matter of individual choice. The configuration leaves open all sorts of more or less "acceptable" readings, equally accountable for in theory yet too centrifugal not to blur the message of universalization. Perhaps in this recognition we can find a key to Bourdieu's peculiar disenchantment.

APPENDIX: *HABITUS: THE LOGIC OF PRACTICE, LE SENS PRATIQUE*

Produced by the work of inculcation and appropriation that is needed in order for objective structures, the product of collective history, to be reproduced in the form of the durable, adjusted dispositions that are the condition of their functioning, the *habitus*, which is constituted in the course of an individual history, imposing its particular logic on incorporation, and through which agents partake of the history objectified in institutions, is what makes it possible to inhabit institutions, to appropriate them practically, and so to keep them in activity, continuously pulling them from the state of dead letters, reviving the sense deposited in them, but at the same time imposing the revisions and transformations that reactivation entails. (*The Logic of Practice*, 57)

Produit du travail d'inculcation et d'appropriation qui est nécessaire pour que ces produits de l'histoire collective *que sont* les structures objectives *parviennent à* **se** reproduire sous la forme des dispositions durables et ajustées qui sont la condition de leur fonctionnement, l'habitus, *qui* **se** constitue au cours d'une histoire particulière, imposant sa logique particulière à l'incorporation, *et par* **qui** les agents participent de l'histoire objectivée dans les institutions, est ce qui permet d'habiter les institutions, de se les approprier pratiquement, *et par là* de les maintenir *en activité, en vie, en vigueur*, de *les arrac***her** continûment à l'état *de lettre morte, de langue morte*, de faire *revivre* le sens *qui s'y trouve* déposé, mais en leur imposant les révisions et les transformations *qui sont* la contrepartie et la condition de la réactivation. (*Le sens pratique*, 96; my emphasis)

NOTES

1. Since this essay hinges on the issue of translation, texts in the non-English original language will be listed in the bibliography by author, and English translations will be cited by translator. It follows that the citation format established at the beginning of this volume for Bourdieu's works will not be used in this chapter.

BIBLIOGRAPHY

Barret-Ducrocq, Françoise. "Les sciences humaines au carrefour des langues." In *Traduire l'Europe*, edited by Barret-Ducrocq. Paris: Payot, 1992.
Barsky, Robert F. *Noam Chomsky: A Life of Dissent*. Toronto: ECW Press, 1997.
Bettelheim, Bruno. "Reflections: Freud and the Soul." *New Yorker* (March 1982): 52–93. Published in book form as *Freud and Man's Soul*, New York: Vintage Books, 1984.

Bourdieu, Pierre. "Sur le pouvoir symbolique." *Annales* ESC 3 (1977): 405–11.

———. *La distinction*. Paris: Minuit, 1979.

———. *Le sens pratique*. Paris: Minuit, 1980.

———. "The Field of Cultural Production, or the Economic World Reversed." *Poetics* 12 (1983): 311–56

———. *Homo Academicus*. Paris: Minuit, 1984.

———. "Avant-propos," in *Choses dites*. Paris. Minuit, 1987.

———. *La noblesse d'État: Grandes écoles et esprits de corps*. Paris: Minuit, 1989.

———. *Cours*. Collège de France, 1991.

———. *Raisons pratiques: Sur la théorie de l'action*. Paris: Le Seuil, 1994.

———. "Esprits d'État: Genèse et structure du champ bureaucratique." *Actes de la recherche en sciences sociales* (1996/97): 49–62.

Bourdieu, Pierre, et al. *La misère du monde*. Paris: Le Seuil, 1993.

Boyne, Roy. Translation of Bourdieu's "Thinking About Limits," *Theory, Culture, and Society* 9 (1992): 37–49.

Brill, A. J. Translation of *Freud's Die Traumdeutung: The Interpretation of Dreams*. London: George Allen & Unwin Ltd.; New York: The Macmillan Company, 1913.

Campbell, Peter. Translation of Le Goff's "Comment écrire une biographie historique aujourd'hui?": "Writing Historical Biography Today." In *Current Sociology* 43, no. 2/3 (1995): 11–17.

Casanova, Pascale. *Le champ littéraire international*. Doctoral thesis, EHESS (Paris), 1997.

Cassirer, Ernst. *Philosophie der symbolischen Formen*. Erster Teil: Die Sprache; Darmstadt: Wissenschaftliche Buchgesellschaft, 1964 [1923].

Chambon, Adrienne S. "Foucault's Discursive Genre and the Cultural Challenges of Translation." *Proceedings of the 6th International Symposium on Social Communication* (Santiago de Cuba, January 1999), forthcoming.

Chambon, Adrienne S., and Daniel Simeoni. "Modality in the Therapeutic Dialogue." In *Studies in Discourse and Grammar: Linguistic Choice across Genres: Variation in Spoken and Written English*. Amsterdam and Philadelphia: John Benjamins Publications, 1998.

Charle, Christophe. *Les Intellectuels en Europe au XIXème siècle: Essai d'histoire comparée*. Paris: Éditions du Seuil, 1996.

Chartier, Roger. *Le livre en révolutions: Entretiens avec Jean Lebrun*. Paris: Editions Textuel, 1997.

Clough, Lauretta C. *Translating Pierre Bourdieu: Reverence and Resistance*. Ph.D. thesis. University of Maryland, 1997.

Cronin, Michael. "Shoring up the Fragments of the Translator's Discourse: Complexity, Incompleteness, and Integration." *Meta* 40, no. 3 (1995): 359–66.

Elias, Norbert. "Problems of Involvement and Detachment." *British Journal of Sociology* 7 (1956): 226–52.

———. "On the Sociogenesis of the Concepts 'Civilization' and 'Culture.'" In *The Civilizing Process*. Oxford, U.K., and Cambridge, Mass.: Blackwell, 1994 (1939).

Erickson, Bonnie H. "What Is Good Taste Good For?" *Canadian Review of Sociology and Anthropology* 28, no.2 (1991): 255–78.

Even-Zohar, Itamar. "Translation Theory Today: A Call for Transfer Theory." Paper presented at the Colloquium on Translation Theory and Intercultural Relations, held at the Porter Institute for Poetics and Semiotics in collaboration with the M. Bernstein Chair of Translation Theory, Tel Aviv University (27 March–1 April). *Poetics Today* 2, no. 4 (1978): 1–7.

———. "Void Pragmatic Connectives." *Poetics Today* 11, no. 1 (1990): 219–46.

Gartman, David. "Culture as Class Symbolization of Mass Reification? A Critique of Bourdieu's *Distinction.*" *American Journal of Sociology* 97, no. 2 (1991): 421–47.

Geertz, Clifford. *Works and Lives: The Anthropologist as Author.* Stanford, Calif.: Stanford University Press, 1984.

Gogol, Sheila. Translation of Johan Heilbron's *Het Ontstaanvan de sociologie: The Rise of Social Theory.* Minneapolis: University of Minnesota Press, 1995.

Guillory, John. "Bourdieu's Refusal." In this volume 19–43.

Halliday, M. A. K. "Linguistic Function and Literary Style: An Inquiry into the Language of William Golding's *The Inheritors.*" In *Literary Style: A Symposium.* London and New York: Oxford University Press, 1971. Reprinted in slightly abridged form as "The Syntax Enunciates the Theme." In *Rules and Meanings*, edited by M. Douglas. New York: Penguin, 1973.

———. *Introduction to Functional Grammar.* London: Edward Arnold, 1985.

———. "Poetry as Scientific Discourse: The Nuclear Sections of Tennyson's In Memoriam." In *Functions of Style*, edited by D. Birch and M. O'Toole. London and New York: Pinter Publishers, 1988.

———. "The Construction of Knowledge and Value in the Grammar of Scientific Discourse, with Reference to Charles Darwin's *The Origin of Species.*" In *Advances in Written Text Analysis*, edited by M. Coulthard. London and New York: Routledge, 1994.

Heilbron, Johan. *Het Ontstaanvan de sociologie.* Amsterdam: Prometheus, 1990.

Hinkle, Gisela J. 1986. "The Americanization of Max Weber." *Current Perspectives in Social Theory* 7 (1986): 87–104.

Le Goff, Jacques. 1989. "Comment écrire une biographie historique aujourd'hui?" *Le Débat* 54 (1989): 48–53.

Luntley, Michael. "Practice Makes Knowledge?" *Inquiry* 35 (1992): 447–61.

Manheim, Ralph. Translation of Cassirer's *Die Philosophie der Symbolischen Formen: The Philosophy of Symbolic Forms.* Vol.1: *Language.* New Haven and London: Yale University Press, 1953.

May, Rachel. *The Translator in the Text: On Reading Russian Literature in English.* Evanston, Ill.: Northwestern University Press, 1994.

Maynard, Senko K. *Discourse Modality: Subjectivity, Emotion, and Voice in the Japanese Language.* Amsterdam/Philadelphia: John Benjamins Publishing Company, 1993.

Nabokov, Vladimir. "Problems of Translation: *Onegin* in English." *Partisan Review* 22, no. 4 (1955): 498–512. Reprinted in *Theories of Translation: An Anthology of Essays from Dryden to Derrida*, edited by Rainer Schulte and John Biguenet. Chicago: University of Chicago Press.

Nice, Richard. "Translator's foreword" to *Outline of a Theory of Practice*, by P. Bourdieu. Cambridge: Cambridge University Press, 1977.

———. Translation of Bourdieu's "Preface" to *Distinction: A Social Critique of the Judgement of Taste.* Cambridge: Harvard University Press, 1984.

———. Translation of Bourdieu's *Le sens pratique: The Logic of Practice.* Stanford: Stanford University Press, 1990 [1980].

———. "Myths, Loose Fits and Near Misses: Some Highlighting Problems in Translating French Social Science." *Palimpsestes* 2, no. 5 (1996).

Robinson, Doug. "The Invisible Hands that Control Translation." In de *Quaderns. Revista Traducció* 1. Universitat Autònoma de Barcelona, 1998.

Runciman, W. G. "Sociologese." *Encounter* 25, no. 6 (1965): 45–47.

Sapiro, Gisèle, and Brian McHale. Translation of Bourdieu's "First Lecture: Social Space and Symbolic Space: Introduction to a Japanese Reading of Distinction" and "Second Lecture: The New Capital: Introduction to a Japanese Reading of State Nobility." *Poetics Today* 12, no. 4 (1991): 627–38, 643–53.

Sheffy, Rakefet. "Rites of Coronation." Review of *An Introduction to the Work of Pierre Bourdieu*, edited by R. Harker, C. Mahar, and C. Wilkes. *Poetics Today* 12, no. 4 (1991): 801–11.

Shils, Edward. "The Ways of Sociology." *Encounter* 28, no. 6 (1967): 85–91.

Simeoni, Daniel. "Translating and Studying Translation: The View from the Agent." *Meta* 40, no. 3 (1995): 445–60.

———. "The Pivotal Status of the Translator's *Habitus*." *Target* 10, no. 1 (1998): 1–39.

Strachey, J., et al. Translation of Freud's *Complete Works*. Standard Edition. London: Hogarth Press, 1953–66.

Toury, Gideon. *Descriptive Translation Studies and Beyond*. Philadelphia: John Benjamins Publishing, 1995.

Venuti, Lawrence. *The Scandals of Translation*. London and New York: Routledge, 1998.

Wacquant, Loïc. Translation of Bourdieu's "Epilogue: On the Possibility of a Field of World Sociology." In *Social Theory for a Changing Society*, edited by Pierre Bourdieu and James S. Coleman. New York: Russell Sage Foundation, 1991.

———. "Bourdieu in America: Notes on the Transatlantic Importation of Social Theory." In *Bourdieu: Critical Perspectives*, edited by Craig Calhoun, Edward LiPuma, and Moishe Postone. Cambridge: Polity Press, 1993.

Wolfe, Alan. "Affirmative Action: The Fact Gap." Review of *The Shape of the River*, by William G. Bowen and Derek Bok, and *The Black-White Test Score Gap*, edited by Christopher Jencks and Meredith Phillips. *New York Times Book Review* (October 25, 1998).

5

Bourdieu and Common Sense

Robert Holton

I

The term "common sense" has a long and complex history. Its roots go back to the Greek terms *koinos nous* (common mind—the mental equipment we all, presumably, bear), *koine aisthesis* (common perceptual sense, on which I will elaborate below), and *koine ennoia* (common notions, beliefs, or ideas). The Latin term *sensus communis* uneasily combines all these senses, a fact that accounts perhaps for some of the continuing vagueness of its definitions (Bugter, 83–84). In one form or another, the phrase has never gone out of use, but as a result of its complex history, it does seem to carry contradictory meanings. Sometimes common sense is that plain feet-on-the-ground sense of reality available to any clear-thinking person, which can emerge when all the fancy talk of the so-called experts is swept away. Alternatively, common sense is quite the opposite: that collection of provincial, conventional wisdom, superstition, and false consciousness that can be recognized as such and overcome through rigorous thought, rationality, and science. Does common sense refer to those universal properties of mind, rationality, and sense that all humans have in common? Or does it signify the fact that we are all members of particular and specific social and historical communities of sense and knowledge?

It is instructive to note that while Samuel Johnson's famous kick at a stone has long been understood as a defense of common sense against Berkeley's philosophy, Berkeley himself understood his own philosophical work to be a defense of common sense. While skeptical commonsense thinking, with its ability to debunk and demystify, found Enlightenment defenders and champions from Descartes to Voltaire to Thomas Reid, a concurrent strain of philosophical inquiry—

sometimes including the same thinkers—understood common sense itself to be that body of received ideas that must be overcome by means of skeptical philosophical reflection. More recently, G. E. Moore has explored the articulation of common sense in ordinary language, while Chomsky's work has occasioned a related debate on the idea of common notions and innate knowledge. An excellent example of what W. B. Gallie refers to as an essentially contested concept (157–91), the notion of common sense continues to permit a wide variety of definitions and approaches, both positive and pejorative.

While Bourdieu does not use the term "common sense"—a translation from *sense commun*, or occasionally *bon sens*—as often as some others such as *habitus* or *doxa*, it does occur quite frequently in his work and is, in fact, closely related to both these terms. In his use, the phrase "common sense" includes a great deal: it includes those things commonly known or even tacitly accepted within a collectivity; it also includes the consensus of the community as articulated in a variety of public discourses; and finally, it includes the sense of community that this commonly shared sense of the world provides. In some ways, of course, this meaning is quite far removed from some of the term's sources, the Greek *koine aisthesis* or Aquinas' similar *sensus communis*—the sense of which, it was thought, provides a unified and integrated interpretation of the information receieved by the five primary senses. On the other hand, in Bourdieu's work— particularly in *Distinction*, his study of taste—it *does* appear that some aspects of one's fundamental understanding of the world of taste, smell, sight, and so on *are* structured or even produced to some degree by something like common sense, in that one's very perception of the world is profoundly socially structured. While Bourdieu's idea of a tacit and embodied common sense may perhaps, in its lack of clear articulation, have something in common with Kant's notion of *sensus communis* as a set of "obscurely represented principles" of judgment based on feeling rather than clearly articulated concepts (Kant, 75), there remains at least one significant difference in that for Bourdieu, common sense is historically and culturally grounded in specific communities. The appeal, for instance, as in Kant, to any form of Universal Community of Humanity is rather more difficult to make.

Another key Bourdieusian concept, the *habitus*, has a similar reference and overlaps somewhat with common sense in that it suggests an agent with a relatively determined and socially constructed set of embodied dispositions. "One of the fundamental effects of the orchestration of habitus," writes Bourdieu, "is the production of a commonsense world endowed with the objectivity secured by consensus on the meaning of practices and the world" (*OTP*, 80). A central distinction, however, is that the *habitus* refers principally to the structured nature of specific, individual agency, while common sense is, of course, a communal rather than an individual property. In any case, both *habitus* and common sense involve the constitution of a common "world of already realized ends—procedures to follow, paths to take" (*OTP*, 53). A general but fundamental agreement thus exists within a community on the range of desirable goals and the strategies available to achieve them, and on the range of undesirable outcomes and the strategies available to avoid them. This commonsense world consists of an implicit and explicit dimension, each of which complements the other: the implicit involves "the simplicity and transparency . . . the feeling of obviousness and necessity which this world imposes" (*LSP*, 131). The explicit includes the articulation of this consensus in the public act of naming the world, "legitimate naming as the official . . . imposition of the legitimate vision of the social world . . . which has on its side all the strength of the collective . . . of common sense" (*LSP*, 239).[1]

What Bourdieu calls "the conductorless orchestration" (*OTP*, 59) of the social world is made possible by the circularity of the relation between the agent (whose experience is structured by her/his social position within a historically-situated collectivity) and the world (whose contours are experienced and interpreted in relation to socially approved and legitimized taxonomies). In his discussion of Bourdieu and Wittgenstein, Charles Taylor uses a similar metaphor: at the level of practice, the common rhythms of dialogical action, like the conductorless orchestration of the social world, are made possible by a shared understanding so powerful that Taylor even refers to those who participate as a common agent (51–53). Since it structures my sense of possibility, my list of available choices (what Bourdieu in a discussion of Flaubert calls "the space of social possibles" [*FCP*, 162]) and removes other possibilities, my commonsense view of the world thus attains the power of a self-fulfilling prophecy. And the self-fulfillment of the prophecy itself strengthens my common sense, which will be seen in retrospect to have been right. And all of this is reinforced by my community—family, friends, media, and so on—who live in a universe quite similar, for all its variations, to mine.

II

Such a world would, however, appear to be oppressively determined, offering little possibility for innovation, progress, or hope. Is there no mechanism whereby people or groups of people can question their experience, critique their world? Bourdieu's work has frequently been criticized on precisely these grounds. Terry Eagleton, for example, questions whether, in Bourdieu's theory, there is any room for "dissent, criticism and opposition" (Bourdieu and Eagleton, 114). Axel Honneth characterizes Bourdieu's human agents as merely "unconscious bearers of interest calculation" (Honneth, Kocyba, and Schwibs, 42). Richard Jenkins remarks that, given Bourdieu's model of structure and agency, "it is difficult not to perceive them as bound together in a closed feedback loop, each confirming the other" (82). And Morag Schiach suggests that Bourdieu's "analyses serve to specify the terms of our enclosure rather than to offer us any escape" (219).

I am not sure what it would mean to escape, actually escape from all such forms of enclosure within networks of community affiliation, and Bourdieu in fact speaks elsewhere about the "pernicious utopianism" of some forms of liberation thought (Honneth, Kocyba, and Schwibs, 40). Bourdieu maintains that there are, nonetheless, several ways in which the apparently rigid determinism of this enclosure by common sense can be affected and altered. One factor that disturbs the relentless determinism and stasis, perhaps the most trivial in some ways, is the need for distinction that Bourdieu sees as basic to social identity: in order to assert our distinctiveness we constantly find, create, and extrapolate ways to distinguish ourselves from others both within and beyond our communities of identity. In this category we might include fashions, clothes and hair styles, for example, which must continue to change and evolve in order to make the desired personal statement. And it can be argued, of course, that intellectual styles and artistic fashions follow the same logic of change as a means of maintaining their value within the market for symbolic goods. This demand for innovative thought does, however, have the effect of calling into question the common sense of the dominant traditions, thereby opening the possibility of valuable new insight.

More important though, as Bourdieu asserts in the discussion of *doxa* in *Outline of a Theory of Practice*, is that objective social crises—whether political or economic, whether natural, military, or technological—may put the practices of common sense into question, thereby undermining its self-evidence and leading to a sense of the possible insufficiency or arbitrariness of *doxa*. Such a crisis can alter the social field so radically that the "feedback loop," as Jenkins puts it, is simply dysfunctional and, because "the routine adjustment of subjective and objective structures is brutally disrupted" (*IRS*, 131), the common sense of yesterday becomes inapplicable today. Alterations in the objective social conditions of the world that cannot easily be subsumed within the categories of the old common sense—famine, war, economic collapse—necessitate a reexamination of those notions and a gradual elaboration of a new *sensus communis*. If common sense is to a great degree produced in response to objective social and historical conditions, then its modifications will occur in concert with alterations in those conditions.[2]

And finally—although I do not take this list to be exhaustive—cross-cultural contact may, by simple comparison, expose the arbitrariness of social categories and procedures. Trained as an anthropologist, Bourdieu is familiar with a broad range of cultural differences and effects produced when one culture is exposed to another. "When you are in the preconstructed, reality offers itself to you," writes Bourdieu (1992, 44). But in the unfamiliar territory of cross-cultural contact, however, the social nature of the preconstruction of the world can become apparent in a way that is "hidden from indigenous perception" (1992, 44). In other words, the local nature of specific cultural systems can be revealed in the juxtaposition of different intellectual communities, different cultures, different communities of sense, different aesthetic communities, all of which bring into focus the different "theses implied in a particular [and different] way of living" (*OTP*, 168). Descartes himself, in the *Discourse on Method*, makes a similar point in discussing his travels: "The greatest profit to me was, therefore, that I became acquainted with customs generally approved and accepted by other great peoples that would appear extravagant and ridiculous among ourselves, and so I learned not to believe too firmly what I learned only from example and custom" (9).[3]

A culture tends to see its own way of life as "natural," even divinely sanctioned: for Vico, for instance, common sense *was* directed by a conductor: "the common sense of the human race," he argues, is "taught to the nations by divine providence" (63). Much later, just as Marx reversed Hegel's idealism and Nietzsche posited the creation of God by man, Durkheim inverted this notion of a divine origin of common sense, analyzing instead the social sources of religious belief. Common sense, rather than being a divine sanction for a way of life, appears as an expression of social unity (331). Durkheim considered religion as an articulation of "the collective sentiments and collective ideas which make [a culture's] unity and its personality" (475). Such expressions of tribal unity are rather easily disturbed in the cosmopolitan conditions of modernity, and cross-cultural contact can reveal the degree to which one's commonsense world, far from being divinely ordained, is arbitrary, humanly constructed, and therefore susceptible to change.

Given these qualifications, it appears that common sense, the sense of reality or of the world's limits (*OTP*, 167) as Bourdieu describes it, is not so monolithic as it sometimes appears, but has more than a single modality of existence, and might be related to Bourdieu's tripartite model of social discourse. The first category is *doxa*, which includes unexamined and unspoken presuppositions about the world, all that which we take for granted—those "theses tacitly posited on the hither side of all inquiry," as Bourdieu puts it (*OTP*, 168).[4] Contrasted to the realm of *doxa* is the realm of opinion, the speakable, and this is divided into two: orthodoxy is conservative and looks backward to the reestablishment of previous *doxa* and its tacit beliefs and naturalized conventions—in short, a nostalgia for some version of the "good old days." Heterodoxy pulls in the other direction, contesting not only the conservatism of orthodoxy but also presenting the possibility (or threat) of drawing more doxic foundations into the realm of discourse and opinion, the realm of the speakable (*OTP*, 164–69).[5] In either case though, whether the attitude is an affirmation of doxic traditional common sense or a challenge to it, as Toril Moi writes, "these two positions more or less explicitly recognize the possibility of different arrangements. To defend the 'natural' is necessarily to admit that it is no longer self-evident" (1026).

It must be noted, at least in passing, then, that the closed feedback loop image is, once again, less than adequate: the possibility exists of a heretical disruption of the enchantment of *doxa* and consequently a heretical movement into heterodox discourse. At one extreme of heterodoxy, there is simple disagreement over the interpretation of some aspects of the world; at the other, there is the vertiginous moment Bourdieu alludes to "when the meaning of the world slips away" (1985, 203). In the latter case, two possibilities present themselves: the breakdown of the *sensus communis* and the restructuring of the community. Interestingly, according to Bourdieu, this is one of the moments when the poet's function of naming the world for the community—and by extension the artist's function of representing the world—has been crucial, has contributed much more than a unit of exchange value in the circulating economy of cultural capital. Still, whichever is the result, or (more accurately perhaps) whatever combination of rethinking and restructuring results, the effect is change, both at the level of the social and at the level of the individual. And to a greater or lesser degree such adjustments are, in one form or another, always underway in all historical cultures.

A brief comparison may help to shed some light on this problem. While Bourdieu has often been accused of an excessive determinism, of a closed and oppressive view of the social and the individual, Bakhtin is rarely seen in this light. Yet their work shares some important features. For Bakhtin as for Bourdieu (particularly in *Language and Symbolic Power*), language is immediately related to common sense and social power: "We are taking language not as a system of abstract grammatical categories," writes Bakhtin, "but rather language conceived as ideologically saturated, language as world view" (1981, 271). Voloshinov/Bakhtin's statement that the sign is the site of the class struggle (Voloshinov, 23) is related to the detailed work Bourdieu has done in *Distinction*, examining the valences of various social signifiers in the systems of taste, while Bourdieu's general position concerning the struggle to impose the legitimate meaning and names of the world echoes Bakhtin's insight as well. Furthermore, although Bakhtin's model of discourse is a two- rather than three-part model, it presents some striking similarities. His monologic cultural moment can be related at times to Bourdieu's *doxa*, and at other times to orthodoxy. And his heteroglossia is related to Bourdieu's heterodoxy: the effect of heteroglossia is, Bakhtin writes, to "wash over a culture's awareness of itself and its language . . . and deprive it of its naïve absence of conflict" (1981, 368). Anticipating in part Bourdieu's notion of the cultural arbitrary, the relativizing recognition of the variety of cultures, Bakhtin notes that the passage to heteroglossia occurs when a community "becomes conscious of itself as only one among other cultures and languages" (1981, 51). Heterodoxy and heteroglossia imply, then, a crisis in the common sense of the world and in the community that has been constituted by that common sense.[6]

Bakhtin's and Bourdieu's views on the relation of art to overall culture display a remarkable similarity as well, most notably in a rejection of the limitations of formalism. In "Content, Material, and Form in Verbal Art," Bakhtin attacks the attempt to found an autonomous aesthetic or to understand a work of art without reference to its culturally-specific location: "A work is alive and valid," observes Bakhtin, "in a world which is also both alive and valid" (1990, 275) and must be understood within the context of the cognitive and ethical structures of that world. Bourdieu, in *The Field of Cultural Production*, examines the historicity not only of the work of art but also of the "pure gaze" itself (254–66). And finally, both Bakhtin (Bakhtin and Medvedev, 61) and Bourdieu (*FCP*, 33–34) discuss the failure of the Russian formalist notion of defamiliarization—not unrelated to what might in Bourdieu's terms be called dedoxification, or the move toward heterodoxy—to address the more generally political aspects of this process of articulating what was once a matter of tacit and commonsense knowledge. While Bourdieu's model does emphasize the processes of social reproduction more than Bahktin's, this ought not to obscure their shared concern with the dynamics of cultural struggle and historical change.

It is worth pointing out as well that Bourdieu's position here is not far removed from some versions of postmodernism that examine the coexistence of differently constructed social worlds, again not a position usually associated with oppressive forms of determinism. Certainly, the solipsistic claims of some postmodernists to the effect that there is, essentially, no reality beyond that projected or constituted by subjective cognition are well beyond Bourdieu's more cautious break with traditional epistemologies. And Bourdieu has not been unwilling to condemn what he sees as the nihilistic relativism of postmodern theory (see "Passport to Duke," in this volume). Some postmodern theory might be characterized in the same terms he employed in describing "conservative revolutionaries," like Heidegger, who opt to jump "into the fire to avoid being burnt, to change everything without changing anything, through one of those *heroic extremes* which, in the drive to locate oneself beyond the beyond, unite and reconcile positions verbally, in paradoxical, and magical propositions" (*POMH*, 62). On the other hand, he insists that epistemological "absolutism is clearly based on the absolutization and the naturalization of a [particular] historical culture. . . . [T]here is no absolute, universal point of view" (*FE*, 62). Bourdieu takes up a position in the middle, accepting cultural difference but basing it on more or less objective and knowable conditions, open to divergent perspectives and realities but eschewing the idea that radical relativism can be a consequence.[7]

In Bourdieu, as in Bakhtin, there is the possibility—even the historical necessity—of a constant destabilization and a constant modification of common sense. It is evident in the very idea of heterodoxy and, in an extreme form, in the idea of the meaning of the world slipping away. The world's meaning must continually be reaffirmed and/or reconstructed as common sense precisely because it is a historical world constantly open to challenge and to struggle, because the possibility continues to exist that its meaning may slip away, because it is in the interest of some that certain aspects of its meaning should slip away and be replaced with other meanings. It is not surprising that a social system should have a powerful mechanism built in to guarantee its continuance—indeed, as Marx and Althusser point out, a society that lacked such a mechanism of reproduction would not last long. But to admit this is not to abandon the possibility of change. "I think," Bourdieu says in conversation with Terry Eagleton, that "the capacity for resistance . . . was overestimated (Bourdieu and Eagleton, 114), particularly in the 1960s when, for a while at least, it appeared that changing the world might easily be accomplished. Still, a corrective to this naivete need not entail a collapse into its opposite—into a sense that, as one of Bourdieu's critics put it, "all is for the worst in the worst possible world" (*IRS*, 79). In various attempts to clarify the concept of the *habitus* is a historical product: neither complete nor sealed off from further development, it is "*an open system of dispositions* that is constantly subjected to experiences, and therefore constantly affected by them in a way that either reinforces or modifies its structures. It is durable but not eternal!" (*IRS*, 133). As long as history and personal experience continue, and as long as a multiplicity of fields exists, each providing a variety of positions, new possibilities and creative adjustments of the *sensus communis* are themselves in fact demanded by the very complex and dynamic structure of his determined system.

To view history itself as the agent of change, however, is to adopt too passive and abstract an attitude to social processes. Bourdieu's attempt to navigate between the Scylla of naive utopianism and the Charybdis of automaton determinism leads him to argue that for an objective crisis to accomplish positive change, it should be in combination with dedicated and conscious activity carried out by agents in a variety of spheres—including the scientific and the artistic. With the tools provided by social science, for example, we can explore "a rational and politically conscious use of the limits of freedom afforded by a true knowledge of social laws and especially of their *historical* conditions of validity" (*IRS*, 197). Like the *habitus*, then, social laws are neither immutable nor transhistorical. They operate within the framework of a given *sensus communis* and are dependent on that common sense for their continued existence. Still, scientific knowledge enjoys a relative stability: "it remains that [science] has its own *nomos*, its (relative) autonomy, which insulates it more or less completely from the intrusion of external constraints" ("Passport to Duke," 245).[8] What is both necessary and possible is to make visible the specific social laws that constrain us as a preliminary to the attempt to reduce their more negative aspects, and Bourdieu speaks of the capacity of science to carry forward such a program. What such an emancipatory science demands "first and foremost," writes Bourdieu, is "a break with common sense (*IRS*, 235).[9]

On the other hand, scientific reason, with its capacity to objectify for the purposes of analysis, could itself be considered another kind of common sense, one referring to the universal human property of reason—what Kant calls *sensus communis logicus,* to distinguish it from either *sensus communis aistheticus* (138) or from common sense as Bourdieu himself uses the term. It is on this point, perhaps—Bourdieu's affirmation of such a form of common sense (as a common human capacity for reason) and his insistence on the privileged epistemological status of science, that Bourdieu is furthest from what he has referred to as the "neo-nihilist current called postmodernism" (1992, 46). While Bourdieu himself does not use the term common sense in this way, it is this use of reason which, according to Kant, delivers one from prejudice and superstition—the lower form of common sense—a deliverance he names "enlightenment" (136–37). This term has come to figure prominently, if often negatively, in postmodern theory—and enlightenment (or some version thereof) seems to be Bourdieu's goal in seeking a break with common sense.[10]

If social science and rationality offer one avenue for an exploration beyond the limits of common sense, the arts provide another. Far from simply functioning always as a badge of honor in a game of social one-upmanship, literature, according to Bourdieu, "is on many points more advanced than social science, and contains a whole trove of fundamental problems . . . that sociologists should make their own" (*IRS*, 208). Given Bourdieu's concern with practical consciousness, it is not surprising that he sees the novel as a space in which the experience of the social subject and the rules of the field in which he/she functions can be examined. And *Free Exchange*, one of his most recent books, is a lengthy discussion with contemporary artist (and coauthor) Hans Haake of the critical strategies and situations available to contemporary artists and intellectuals if they are to move beyond "the tired litanies of . . . the cult of the artist and the work of art" (*FE*, 116) and toward an art that can, among other things, "give full symbolic effectiveness to [the] unveiling of social mechanisms" (109).

III

There is a final version of common sense that I would like to address briefly in conclusion, and it also concerns this problem of the need to break with common sense. In some ways, Bourdieu's use of the term common sense to refer to the sense of reality of specific communities is similar to Gadamer's (itself borrowing from Vico). It seems, however, to be almost a relationship of mirrored opposition: while Gadamer emphasizes the enabling aspects of the *sensus communis*, Bourdieu emphasizes its limits. Gadamer argues that common sense is not necessarily that ordinary sense of reality that must be escaped by means of reason, nor is it the light of common reason that can help us escape our sense of reality: it is instead

the sense that founds community . . . what gives the human will its direction is not the abstract universality of reason but the concrete universality represented by the community of a group, a people, a nation, or the whole human race. Hence developing this communal sense is of decisive importance for living. (21)

While Gadamer sees the positive way in which common sense is constitutive of the community's traditions and way of life, and values it as a balance to the excesses of scientific methodology, Bourdieu sees it most often as an obstacle to be overcome, and values scientific methodologies precisely for their ability to break down common sense. The former could be said to value the determinacy and stability that is involved in being born into a society, a tradition, a culture. Bourdieu, on the other hand, chafes at this: "I am often stunned by the degree to which things are determined," he admits. "I do not rejoice over this. Indeed . . . I find it particularly unbearable. As an individual I personally suffer when I see somebody trapped by necessity" (*IRS*, 200).[11] This difference between Bourdieu and Gadamer recapitulates Bourdieu's own distinction between orthodoxy and heterodoxy: the former a conservative tendency to preserve traditional common sense because of its contribution to the way of life, the latter a heterodox tendency to call such cultural foundations into question because they limit our ability to think the reformation of that way of life.

On the whole, Bourdieu's work posits a common sense that does not enable as much as it constrains. He points to the centrality of the broadly social struggle over the production of common sense, to the determinist tendency that a strong theory of common sense entails, and to the necessity of a break with common sense as a precondition for understanding the dynamics of the social world. His own detailed studies focus on the structures of constraint much more than on the necessary conditions for change. It is an open question at this point whether or not Bourdieu's models will be as productive in understanding and in bringing about change as they have unquestionably been in understanding systems and the mechanisms of cultural reproduction. But that is nevertheless what must be attempted: it's just common sense.

NOTES

Work on this chapter was carried out with assistance from the Social Sciences and Humanities Research Council of Canada and from Okanagan University College. My thanks as well to Natasha Tusikov for her assistance. This essay first appeared in *SubStance* 84 (1997): 38–52. It is reprinted by permission of the University of Wisconsin Press.

1. In Quebec, where I have been living, the very real possibility of the breakup of Canada and the establishment of Quebec as an independent nation provides an example of different versions of common sense, different communities of sense, and their attempts to impose the legitimate, indeed legal, definitions of the political world.

2. In his study of social discourse, Angenot similarly notes the effect of the simple passage of time on common sense. With a bit of historical distance, he writes, one sees that "the number of contentions and ideas that seem to us today to be banal or at least probable, if not obvious to all, were at the time literally unthinkable, even for the most progressive minds. . . . One should keep in mind that if it is quite easy to point to the 'limits of consciousness' for our immediate predecessors, it is not so easy for us to remove ourselves from our present hegemony" (9). His study of printed material of 1889 reveals, among other things, that as the nuances of meaning shift, humor can rapidly become unfunny, grand dramatic displays no longer provoke the desired response, realistic narrative loses its realism and betrays its artifice, and so on (11).

3. In the same passage, however, Descartes's understanding of the term common sense is shown to differ from Bourdieu's. Descartes ridicules the thinker whose ideas are

"far removed from common sense" and whose motive for such thinking is vanity "since he then needs so much more wit and skill to make them seem plausible" (9).

4. Bourdieu's emphasis on the relationship between *doxa* and common sense has its roots in the classical philosophical tradition. In his discussion of *sensus communis*, Schaeffer notes that *"common sense* is often given as the translation for Plato's term, *doxa*, the common opinion of the ordinary man. It means, in Platonic philosophy, hearsay or illusory knowledge built upon fleeting sense impressions" (2).

5. Angenot, who acknowledges the influence of Bourdieu's work on his own, argues that "the sayable" is a complex realm "made out of regulated antagonisms between conflicting images, concepts, cognitive discrepancies and incompatibilities that are relatively stabilized without ever reaching a state of equilibrium." Through all of this, "something like a hegemony can be identified, producing arbitrations between conflicting discourses, concealing topical axioms and basic principles of social verisimilitude, universal taboos, and censorships that mark the boundaries of the 'thinkable' " (4).

6. See my *Jarring Witnesses: Modern Fiction and the Representation of History* for an extended discussion of this point.

7. The version of postmodernism to which Bourdieu responds is that characterized by Teresa Ebert as ludic postmodernism, an ironic deconstruction of signifying systems that cannot or does not aspire to "provide the basis for a transformative political practice." She contrasts this to a version with which Bourdieu might sympathize more, a resistance postmodernism that begins with the understanding that signifying systems themselves are one of the sites of a larger social struggle (Ebert, 293).

8. The "truths that are produced in this relatively autonomous field [of social science] can be historical through and through, as is the field itself," he writes, "without for that being either deducible from historical conditions or reducible to the external conditions they impose, because the field opposes to external forces the shield, or the prism, of its own history, warrant of its autonomy, that is, the history of the 'languages' (in the broadest possible sense of the word) specific to each field or subfield" (*FE*, 9).

9. Bourdieu is close to Gramsci on this point. Gramsci describes common sense as "fragmentary, incoherent," "a conception of the world uncritically absorbed" (419), and opposes it to the coherent and consistent forms of thought that must call it into question: "the starting point must always be that common sense which is the spontaneous philosophy of the multitude and which has to be made ideologically coherent" (421).

10. In a passage cited earlier, Bourdieu speaks of the commonsense world providing "procedures to follow, paths to take" (*OTP*, 53). In his discussion of common sense, Clifford Geertz cites Wittgenstein's metaphor of language as a set of detours and side roads that we use. "We see the straight highway before us, but of course we cannot use it, because it is permanently closed" (127). Does Bourdieu's appeal to science and his call for a break with common sense (*IRS*, 235) suggest that some stretches of the straight highway can be used after all? And his repeated insistence on breaking with common sense, his consistently pejorative use of the term, suggests that it is certainly desirable to abandon the side roads of common sense for the high road of truth.

11. In his discussions of science, Bourdieu frequently opposes science not only to common sense but also to national tradition—even intellectual tradition and culture. The ethnocentrism of national cultures is opposed to the universalism of science, particularly as it transcends national boundaries and participates in international discussion. This seems

to be one of the reasons for Bourdieu's personal participation in a journal such as *Liber: The European Review of Books.*

BIBLIOGRAPHY

Angenot, Marc. "The Concept of Social Discourse." *English Studies in Canada* 21, no. 1 (March 1995): 1–19.

Bakhtin, M. M. *The Dialogic Imagination.* Translated by Caryl Emerson and Michael Holquist. Austin: U of Texas P, 1981.

———. *Art and Answerability: Early Philosophical Essays.* Edited by Michael Holquist and Vadim Liapunov. Translated by Vadim Liapunov and Kenneth Brostrom. Austin: U of Texas P, 1990.

Bakhtin, M. M., and P. N. Medvedev. *The Formal Method in Literary Scholarship: A Critical Introduction to Sociological Poetics.* Translated by Albert J. Wehrle. Baltimore: Johns Hopkins, 1978.

Bourdieu, Pierre. *Outline of a Theory of Practice.* Translated by Richard Nice. Cambridge: Cambridge UP, 1977.

———. "The Social Space and the Genesis of Groups." *Social Science Information* 24, no. 2 (1985): 195–220.

———. *The Logic of Practice.* Translated by Richard Nice. Stanford: Stanford UP, 1990.

———. *Language and Symbolic Power.* Translated by Gino Raymond and Mathew Adamson. Edited by John B. Thompson. Cambridge: Harvard UP, 1991.

———. *The Political Ontology of Martin Heidegger.* Translated by Peter Collier. Stanford: Stanford UP, 1991.

———. "Thinking about Limits." *Theory, Culture, and Society* 9 (1992): 37–49.

———. *The Field of Cultural Production.* Edited by Randal Johnson. New York: Columbia UP, 1993.

———. "Passport to Duke." In this volume.

Bourdieu, Pierre, and Terry Eagleton. "*Doxa* and Common Life." *New Left Review* 191 (1992): 111–21.

Bourdieu, Pierre, and Hans Haake. *Free Exchange.* Stanford: Stanford UP, 1995.

Bourdieu, Pierre, and L. J. D. Wacquant. *An Invitation to Reflexive Sociology.* Chicago: U of Chicago P, 1992.

Bugter, S. E. W. "Sensus Communis in the Works of M. Tullius Cicero." In *Common Sense: The Foundations for Social Science,* edited by Frits van Holthoon and David R. Olson. Lanham, Md.: University Press of America, 1987.

Descartes, Rene. *Discourse on Method and Meditations.* New York: Liberal Arts Press, 1960.

Durkheim, Emile. *The Elementary Forms of Religious Life.* Translated by Joseph Ward Swain. New York: Free Press, 1965.

Ebert, Teresa. "Writing in the Political: Resistance Post(modernism)." *Legal Studies Forum* 15, no. 4 (1991): 291–303.

Gadamer, Hans-Georg. *Truth and Method.* Second edition. Translated by Joel Weinsheimer and Donald G. Marshall. New York: Crossroad, 1989.

Gallie, W. B. *Philosophy and Historical Understanding.* New York: Schocken, 1964.

Geertz, Clifford. *Local Knowledge: Essays in Interpretive Anthropology.* New York: Basic Books, 1983.

Gramsci, Antonio. *Selections from the Prison Notebooks of Antonio Gramsci.* Edited and translated by Quentin Hoarre and Geoffrey Nowell Smith. New York: International Publishers, 1971.

Holton, Robert. *Jarring Witnesses: Modern Fiction and the Representation of History.* New York: Harvester Wheatsheaf, 1995.

Honneth, Axel, Hermann Kocyba, and Bernd Schwibs. "The Struggle for Symbolic Order: An Interview with Pierre Bourdieu." *Theory, Culture, and Society* 3, no. 3 (1986): 35–51.

Jenkins, Richard. *Pierre Bourdieu.* London: Routledge, 1992.

Kant, Immanuel. *Critique of Judgement.* Translated by J. H. Bernard. New York: Hafner, 1951.

Moi, Toril. "Appropriating Bourdieu: Feminist Theory and Pierre Bourdieu's Sociology of Culture." *New Literary History* 22 (1991): 1017–49.

Schaeffer, John D. *Sensus Communis: Vico, Rhetoric, and the Limits of Relativism.* Durham, N.C.: Duke University Press, 1990.

Schiach, Morag. "Cultural Studies' and the Work of Pierre Bourdieu." *French Cultural Studies* 4, no. 3 (1993): 213–23.

Taylor, Charles. "To Follow a Rule. . . ." In *"Bourdieu: Critical Perspectives*, edited by Craig Calhoun, Edward LiPuma, and Moishe Postone. Cambridge: Polity Press, 1993.

Van Holtoon, Frits, and David R. Olson. *Common Sense: The Foundations for Social Science.* Lanham, Md.: University Press of America, 1987.

Vico, Giambattista. *The New Science of Giambattista Vico.* Translated by Thomas Goddard Bergin and Max Harold Fisch. Ithaca: Cornell UP, 1968.

Voloshinov, V. N. *Marxism and the Philosophy of Language.* Translated by Ladislav Matejka and I. R. Titunik. New York: Seminar Press, 1973.

Wittgenstein, Ludwig. *Philosophical Investigations.* Translated by G. E. M. Anscombe. Oxford: Blackwell, 1972.

6

Value and Capital in Bourdieu and Marx

Jon Beasley-Murray

The concept of "cultural capital" is among Pierre Bourdieu's most distinctive contributions to critical theory. The term has found remarkable success, and has probably been taken up and disseminated more than any other item from his critical terminology; *habitus*, for instance, has scarcely demonstrated such widespread appeal. Cultural capital has even inspired a book of its own (John Guillory's *Cultural Capital*). Faced with this reception of the term, Bourdieu himself would no doubt be the first to see this as a distortion and to agree with Loïc Wacquant's criticism of the way in which his work "has typically been apprehended in 'bits and pieces' " (*IRS*, 4). Moreover, he would be likely to ascribe such an imbalanced reception of his work to limited reading (as he does in "A Reply to Some Objections," 107) or "*fast-reading*" ("The Economy of Symbolic Goods," 93) on the part of critics and followers alike. But such criticism of Bourdieu's readers would be unfair and, more to the point, would fail to account sufficiently for the seductions that the term undoubtedly exerts. Moreover, it would also miss the fact that Bourdieu himself is arguably equally seduced by what the concept promises, and that even in his own work, Bourdieu fails to make the concept fully live up to its promise.

This paper will examine the concept of cultural capital within the framework of Bourdieu's project to construct a "general theory of the economy of practices" (*LP*, 122). I am sympathetic to this project, but I argue that it requires that we examine Bourdieu's understanding of capital more closely, and that Bourdieu's neglect of the strictly economic is a serious weakness in his attempt to construct this general economy. In particular, and comparing Bourdieu's analysis of capital with that of Marx, I note that despite Bourdieu's gestures towards something like a Marxist labor theory of value, in fact his use of the concept "cultural capital" fits badly with the Marxist conception. More strikingly still, it appears that Bourdieu's "capital" is in practice closer to the economic category of "wealth," and as such fails to enable an account of the accumulation of surplus (and hence either profit or exploitation). However, I propose a means by which to conceive of a theory of cultural capital along lines suggested but not followed by Bourdieu, to incorporate a theory of exploitation, and to resolve what is a significant ambivalence that runs through Bourdieu's work as a whole. This draws on Moishe Postone's emphasis on the importance of time within Marx's work, to supplement Bourdieu's own analysis of the role of time's productivity and to understand capital in general as a particular form of the regulation of time.

THE EFFECT OF CULTURAL CAPITAL

The strange effect of the term "cultural capital" among practitioners of cultural theory is largely a matter of its apparent capacity to bridge the constitutive divide between the humanities and the social sciences: at a stroke it seems to reintegrate economics with the study of culture. At the same time, the term also seems to encapsulate the specific object of study for Left social criticism, that is, the interrelations between the economic or material and the cultural or abstract. In that it both crosses anxiously patrolled disciplinary borders and also offers a new center to a project of political investigation, the term both troubles and soothes. However, given the current (particularly U.S.) context in which a humanities-based, yet purportedly political, cultural studies has long forgotten to take seriously social-scientific disciplines, let alone political economy, "cultural capital" may provide only the soothing fantasmatic seal of political rigor without ever provoking anxiety over the disciplinary and epistemological stakes of this terminology.[1]

While this may be the danger, Bourdieu adamantly denies the suggestion that "cultural capital" is an empty metaphorical gesture towards scientificity and radicalism, just as he denies the term's purely literalist tendencies towards economism. In response to such criticisms, Bourdieu answers that cultural capital is a particular "form" of capital, convertible with but irreducible to economic capital, itself only another form of capital. He argues that this generalized usage of the concept of capital

is not a metaphoric usage . . . one can use the concept in its generality so long as one specifies, very precisely, the logics of the different forms of capital, their specific functions, etc. . . . One important argument, of a primary pragmatism in favor of this usage, is that it was not born from theoreticist speculation, and that if one challenges this concept one is no longer able to understand a certain number of important things. ("L'avenir des ideologies," 53–54)[2]

For Bourdieu it is, then, simple observation that shows that cultural capital is fully capital; understanding its logic as a logic of capital (if specific to a particular field) offers direct analytical gains. On this basis, it is possible to understand both the structure of the social field and the various position-takings within it in terms of the differing absolute volumes of capital held by particular agents, and in terms of the differing composition of particular agents' capital assets, which will be made up of varying proportions of cultural and economic capital (as in the chart in *Distinction*, 128–29). Class hierarchy (and class alliances or disputes) can therefore be understood in terms of multidimensional space, rather than in terms of simple linearity. The notion of cultural capital's convertibility with economic capital also enables struggles within a particular class to be understood now as struggles over "the conservation or transformation of the 'exchange rate' between different kinds of capitals" ("Social Space and Field of Power," 34). Pragmatically, one could imagine that political phenomena such as populism, in which agents appear to contradict their class interests, could now be understood without reference to theories of "false consciousness" that simply reintroduce an absolute (yet, ironically, reductionist) account of the distinction between the economic and the cultural.

However, it is not mere pragmatism that determines Bourdieu's unmetaphoric use of the concept "cultural capital." Pragmatically, after all, interdisciplinary metaphorical slippages can sometimes seem to work wonders; yet it is this mystifying use of economic language that Bourdieu wishes to refute. Rather, the argument for cultural capital *as* capital crucially underpins his social analysis, even if this fact remains undertheorized in Bourdieu's work. For it is upon the basis of his analysis of different but convertible forms of capital—its "three fundamental guises" ("The Forms of Capital," 243) of economic, cultural, and social capital—that he outlines his overarching project of a "general theory of the economy of practices . . . [requiring us] to abandon the economic/non-economic dichotomy [in favor of] . . . a science capable of treating all practices" (*LP*, 122). The concept of cultural capital enables this general theory's articulation; were cultural capital categorically distinct from other forms of capital (were it not fully capital), the "economic/non-economic dichotomy" would resurface and a general theory would be unthinkable.

I will argue that such a general theory is possible—and therefore that cultural capital is indeed a form of capital—but that there are serious flaws in Bourdieu's own version of this general theory. Moreover, these flaws derive, ironically, from his inconsistent use of the term "capital." In other words, Bourdieu does more or less outline a general political economy of practices and capitals, one that encompasses the specific political economy of strictly economic capital, but he is unable to account for all sectors of this economy. Rather, in Bourdieu's understanding of the general economy, the market subsumes all other sectors at the expense of an understanding of production and so, most crucially, of surplus. After all, capital is distinguished from value or wealth, for instance, insofar as it implies surplus and therefore exploitation. To reintroduce the concept of surplus, I argue for a critique of Bourdieu's general political economy, one that might then historicize the specific modes and mechanisms of production and capitalization, and thus enable us to conceive of alternative ways in which this general economy might be structured. I hope to move towards such a critique through Marx's similar critique of the political economy of capitalist economic relations, in which Marx identifies the form and means of capital's exploitation as resting in a specific form of alienation.[3]

BOURDIEU AND MARX: CAPITAL AND SURPLUS

The relation between Bourdieu and Marx is somewhat fraught. On the one hand, Bourdieu is usually taken—particularly if not exclusively in the Anglophone world—to be working within a Marxist or post-Marxist paradigm. Thus, for instance, Bridget Fowler is quite prepared to claim that in his analysis of culture "there is an equivalence between Bourdieu's approach and Marx's method in *Capital*. . . . Bourdieu's method is to use Marx's critique in another sphere of production in the bourgeois period, that of cultural goods" (43). Equally, John Guillory states that "the theory of cultural capital belongs to the general field of what in France goes by the name of 'post-Marxist' thought" (*Cultural Capital*, viii). After all, work such as Bourdieu's and Jean-Claude Passeron's *Reproduction* bears striking similarities to the Althusserian critique of schools as "ideological state apparatuses"; in a book such as *Distinction,* Bourdieu seems clearly to be advocating a Marxist reading of the political field (397); while even the simple mention of capital as a means by which to understand culture conjures up a Marxist appeal to the priority of the economic—as he himself often enough seems to confirm. Bourdieu may even have been a member of the French Communist Party cell at the *Ecole normale* (see Jeremy Lane's "Pierre Bourdieu in Context," 20, note 3). On the other hand, Jeremy Lane notes the diversity of interpretations placed on Bourdieu's politics, from the attack mounted on his work on education by former student Christian Baudelot who deserted him to join the Althusserians ("Un Etrange Retournment?" 21) to his characterization as either postmodernist or as anti-postmodern rationalist ("Pierre Bourdieu in Context," 2–7). Lane himself argues persuasively that "the tendency to locate Bourdieu's work on education and culture within a Marxist or *marxisant* tradition . . . has overlooked the central importance . . . of a classically French Republican political vision to Bourdieu's thinking in this area" ("Un Etrange Retournment?" 4).

I would argue that, again, these different receptions of Bourdieu's work are less misreadings than they are symptomatic of a fundamental ambivalence exhibited by Bourdieu himself. It is true that most recently he has seemed to lean towards the classical Republican tradition with a series of declarations in favor of "universaliz[ing] the conditions of access to the universal" (*OT,* 66; see also

Acts of Resistance and, earlier, the conclusion to *The State Nobility*). Still, it is hard to see this as any resolution of the questions he himself poses elsewhere, and the claim for example that "the highest human products . . . were all produced against market imperatives" (*OT,* 27) is the suspension of an earlier ambivalence over the relation between cultural capital and value rather than its transcendence. Once the "highest human products" are also seen as products destined for a market system, albeit a "market of symbolic goods" ("The Market of Symbolic Goods") obeying the specific logic of cultural rather than economic capital, such goods can only be definitively regarded as produced "against market imperatives" if markets in which cultural capital is dominant are regarded as qualitatively distinct from markets in which economic capital is dominant—if, in other words, "cultural capital" is once more taken as a metaphoric term.

Indeed, Bourdieu's ambivalence centers around the concept of cultural capital, which seduces by offering on the one hand a democratizing equalization of cultural value (all cultural practices are instances in which the same form of value is at stake, if in differing quantities) and on the other a measure of the degrees of difference between cultural values (all cultural practices are instances in which differing quantities of the same form of value are at stake). If the theory of cultural capital is unable to encompass equally a theory of exploitation (as an indication of the difference that such differences make) then it is unable to adjudicate between the claims of distinction and equality. Republicanism, then, steps in to offer an apparent resolution by claiming that cultural value can be made available to all in equal measure—but only by denying any real relation between cultural and economic capital.

Given that Republicanism cannot resolve the questions raised by the use of the term cultural capital, I suggest that making sense of the concept must involve a further investigation of its compatibility with a theory of economic capital that also involves a theory of exploitation. Thus we will be taking up the traces of Bourdieu's Marxism (however ambivalently he may hold to it) and forced also to look at economics (however much Bourdieu, strangely, shirks the subject). For there are various moments at which Bourdieu gestures towards a more or less straightforward Marxist account of social structure. It is significant also that he never offers any clear *non*-Marxist account of the relations between economics and culture.

Thus several times, and in quite conventional Marxist terms, Bourdieu asserts the general primacy of the economic, in the Althusserian turn of phrase that economic capital is "always at the root in the last analysis" ("The Sociologist in Question," 33). It is true that elsewhere he is more circumspect, as where he admits that "in advanced capitalist societies, it would be difficult to maintain that the economic field does not exercise especially powerful determinations" while simultaneously asking "should we then for that reason admit the postulate of its (universal) 'determination in the last instance'?" (*IRS,* 109). This, however, may still be in accord with a developed theory of cultural capital once it is realized that the economic field is but a part of the general economy of practices (and hence "economic theory . . . [but] a particular instance, historically dated and situated, of the theory of fields" [120]). If there is a parallelism between the cultural and the economic marked by the presence of specific forms of capital in both fields, rather than a dependency of the former on the latter, then what is at issue is the determination of the economic *within* the cultural, in other words the nature of cultural capital itself.[4] Thus the economic could be seen as determinant in particular situations even if this was an economic logic proper to the field of culture.[5] Again, however, this argument could only be sustained so long as cultural capital was clearly also fully capital.

At the one point at which Bourdieu theorizes the general nature of capital, he seems remarkably close to Marxist orthodoxy as he provides what is essentially the labor theory of value:

> Capital is accumulated labor (in its materialized form or its "incorporated," embodied form) which, when appropriated on a private, i.e., exclusive, basis by agents or groups of agents enables them to appropriate social energy in the form of reified or living labor. ("The Forms of Capital," 241)

But the proximity to orthodoxy is misleading. Indeed, it is startling that Bourdieu here provides what in the labor theory of value is, precisely, a definition of *value* rather than a definition of capital. For the essence of the labor theory of value is that it defines *value* as accumulated labor. But value is quite distinct from capital (even if capital depends upon value), in that capital, for Marx, is the result of a *process* in which "value . . . becomes value in *process* . . . and as such capital" (*Capital*, 256; my emphasis). Bourdieu does mention such a process of valorization or exploitation by adding a description of appropriation to his definition. But this is an *addition*: he here defines capital as contingently rather than necessarily related to appropriation. Appropriation, in other words, is exterior (and as such other) to capital: "Capital is accumulated labor . . . *which, when* appropriated . . ." [my emphasis] rather than *that is* appropriated. As such, this definition of capital, cultural or otherwise, forestalls any understanding of surplus value or valorization, which is what "converts [value] into capital" (*Capital*, 252). For Marx, this process whereby capital is *produced* is the production process itself; in contrast, what Bourdieu outlines here is rather a theory of (unequal) *distribution* of capital effected through appropriation. As John Guillory has pointed out in this volume ("Bourdieu's Refusal"), Bourdieu's definition here "reproduces certain features of a Marxist account of capital without grounding the concept in the cycle of production or 'productive capital' " (41n14).[6] By subsuming capital into a definition of value, Bourdieu passes over the passage between value and capital, and between capital and value, and hence production and valorization disappear from his framework.[7]

VALUE: USE VALUE AND TIME

If Bourdieu's own definition of capital leads to a consideration of value,[8] it should prove useful to reinvestigate the theory of value in political economy. From a consideration of value we may then be able to return to capital; for the moment, however, it is clear that "cultural capital" as used by Bourdieu unsettles value theory more than it has (yet) added to any understanding of capital. Moreover, this accords with the general reception of Bourdieu's work inasmuch as it is taken as a critique of (aesthetic) value by means of a critique of the school system's legitimation of middle-class culture (in *Reproduction*) and by means of a critique of taste (as in *Distinction*). However (again), if cultural capital is to be a concept appropriate to a *general* theory of economic practices, in which there would be no clear dichotomy between the aesthetic and the strictly economic, then the use of the term must also imply an analysis of the relation between value in political economy and value in aesthetics.

John Guillory attempts such an analysis. He argues that the concept of cultural capital forces a reconceptualization of the relations between the two components of value—use value (value realized in use) and exchange value (realized in exchange)—and therefore of the law of value within capitalist economies, understood as the dominance of exchange over use in the pursuit of profit. Both use value and exchange value are implied in any economic exchange. Marx points out that consumers exchange in order to obtain goods (food, clothing) whose value lies in the use that the consumer can make of them; the capitalist, on the other hand, exchanges in order to realize capital, expressed in the exchange value of the goods sold.[9] In capitalism, the economy is organized around and driven by exchange rather than use. Guillory points out that, in line with this law of dominance, "political economy relegates use value to a domain of subjectivity, which it cannot enter into the equation of exchange value." Guillory goes on to establish the connection between value in culture and in economics as constituted by the fact that "*both* aesthetics and economics were founded in contradistinction to the concept of use value" (*Cultural Capital*, 302). The aesthetic disposition demands a disavowal of utility—and hence what Bourdieu will criticize as the cult of disinterest. Thus both Kant in aesthetics and Adam Smith in economics bracketed utility to establish their fields of study.[10] Bourdieu, however, refuses to bracket utility in this way.

Bourdieu's innovation is to reintroduce use value *through the concept of cultural capital* into the discourses of both aesthetics and economics, unsettling and potentially "debasing" each. The introduction of "cultural capital" to analysis of the cultural field enables the argument that cultural appreciation is far from disinterested, that indeed taste conforms to a market system, if with its own logic and its own specific form of capital. But while Bourdieu is prepared to carry out the rupture of aesthetics in his critique of Kant, emphasizing the ways in which cultural products are used for particular interests, he remains strangely loath to discuss economics strictly speaking: "I shall not dwell on the notion of economic capital" (*IRS*, 119); "As regards economic capital, I leave it to others; it's not my area" ("Sociologist," 32). No doubt in part it is this reticence that preserves Bourdieu's ambivalence over his relations to Marxism on the one hand and French Republicanism on the other.[11] Yet surely it is time equally to consider Bourdieu's possible effect upon political economy. I suggest that the most profound effect of his work is its enabling us to reintegrate and reconceive use value within the circuits of both cultural *and* economic capital. Bourdieu shows that common to utility in both spheres is the particular role of *time*; equally, then, I will argue that common to the exploitation involved in both cultural and economic capital is a particular operation performed upon "concrete time."

As Loïc Wacquant notes, "Bourdieu's interest in time is a long-standing one, going back to his days as a student of philosophy in the 1950s. . . . It is in good part by restoring the temporality of practice that Bourdieu breaks with the structuralist paradigm" (*IRS*, 137, note 91). In other words, central to any general economy of practices would be this restoration of temporality: "practice unfolds in time and it has all the correlative properties . . . that synchronization destroys" (*LP*, 81). Thus Bourdieu's analysis of the gift exchange in *Outline of a Theory of Practice* argues that Lévi-Strauss collapses time in his account and is therefore unable to understand the "misrecognition of the reality of the objective 'mechanism' of the exchange, a reality which an *immediate* response brutally exposes" (5–6; my emphasis). The economy of symbolic capital analyzed here depends upon the intervention of time to be effective—time that separates discrete practices, allows room for strategy, and enables the nature of the exchange to be misrecognized. Bourdieu argues that this same logic of practice (and denial of interest) now "expelled" from the "area of 'economic' transactions . . . finds its favoured refuge in the domain of art and 'culture,' the site of pure consumption—of money, of course, but also of time" (*LP*, 133–34). In other words, cultural capital operates according to this same logic of delay, denial, and misrecognition made possible above all by the intervention of time.[12] By contrast, Bourdieu makes clear that in economic exchange, and thus in exchange value, the "temporality of practice" is eliminated.

This "concrete time" of strategy, of the interval, opposed as it is to the synchronization of exchange, marks the specificity of use and of use value.[13] In both the cultural and economic fields, concrete time defines utility, and thus has to be bracketed. In and for the field of culture, a consideration of time threatens to reveal the workings of calculation and of interest—determining the appropriate and most profitable moment to reciprocate in the gift exchange, for instance—and has therefore to be denied. Aesthetics suggests that the appreciation of culture is immediate and hence disinterested and leads to what Bourdieu terms the "ideology" or "cult of the 'gift' " that denies the time-consuming labor of "apprenticeship" required to accumulate cultural capital (*R*, 129, 130). In and for the field of economics, on the other hand, it is the moment of calculation that is instantaneous. Even though economics is an art of forecasting and perhaps long-term investment, its time is abstract and is measured out in increments (discount rates and APRs). Payment has to be punctual while, as Michel de Certeau observes, the unpredictable time and rhythms of use in consumption, the "*ways of using*" commodities, "paradoxically . . . become invisible in the universe of codification and generalized transparency" (35). Concrete time, then, can be contrasted to the "abstract time" of the contract instituted in and through exchange.

This is clear in any analysis of simple commodity exchange and use: whereas a given commodity can be exchanged (can realize its exchange value) at any time and in a legal instant, it is used (it realizes its use value) according to a temporality or a set of rhythms that may be determined by the particularity of the commodity itself, or of its user(s). Let us examine such a simple exchange. If I buy *Great Expectations* at a bookstore, I pay for it at the cash register and its exchange value is realized in an instant. As far as the bookstore is concerned, they will total all such exchanges made on a given day or during a given quarter to determine the total balance of transactions more or less irrespective of which particular book I have bought and when, except insofar as they are concerned with replacing their stock and whether their profits are increasing or decreasing. On the other hand, I may take the book home and read it, or not, at my leisure according to a temporality determined both by the structure of the novel and by the interruptions of my everyday life.

Traditionally, only the exchange at the cash register and its attendant calculations concern economics. In Marxist terms, the price paid is related to the book's value, which is a combination of: the value of its means of production; the value of the variable capital (wages) required for the reproduction of the socially necessary labor time; and the value of the surplus, which is more or less equal to profit. Everything else in the exchange concerns use value—why I should want to read Dickens rather than William Gibson, say, or whether I enjoy the book or not—and does not enter into the calculations of traditional economics. On the other hand, for Bourdieu this is only the beginning of the story: selecting and then reading the book require a certain amount of cultural (particularly linguistic) capital, and the benefits of such an investment yield an amount of cultural capital that may acquire a new form of exchangeable value at an academic dinner party or job interview, or if I pass an exam or am granted an educational diploma. This is the case even (and especially) if in buying the book I am not considering that it might bring me such temporal benefits: my attitude to it is likely to be that much more casual and thus "natural" if I deny interestedness; if I am already familiar with other Dickens novels, it is that much more likely that I will be able to adopt such an attitude.

Thus whereas for an orthodox economist the choice of *Great Expectations* over *Neuromancer* or the reading history of the customer are of no concern, for the economist of cultural capital such distinctions are the essential points of analysis. Indeed, Bourdieu appears to overturn the common economistic conception that use is the immediate and uncomplex satisfaction of need: Bourdieu restores time and strategy (thus, concrete time) to a consideration of the exchange process. He points to the fact that the initial, economic, exchange only initiates a process as a result of which use value may be transformed into a new form of value and thus may produce cultural capital, at a scene removed from the initial, economic exchange. It is important to note that the realization of cultural capital on my part is not guaranteed and depends not only on the book I have chosen but also on my use of the book and my ability to put it to use. Use value is not equivalent to cultural capital.[14] Cultural capital and economic capital, and the processes that produce them, may in some sense mirror each other, but this is far from saying that all aspects of social exchange that are ignored by political economy are then taken up by cultural economy, or vice versa. The question now then is that of the relation between these two processes: is the first, economic, realization of capital (on the part of the bookseller) really equivalent to the second, the realization of cultural capital (at the job interview or wherever)?

SOCIALLY NECESSARY LABOR TIME AND SURPLUS VALUE

Here we return to Marx. For the erasure of use value from economics has been far from absolute. Marx's essential difference from classical economics lies not only in his recognition of the role of surplus (and hence exploitation), but also and concomitantly in his acceptance of use value as an economic category in certain decisive circumstances.[15] Marx argues that "nothing is . . . more erroneous than to assert that the distinction between use value and exchange value, which falls outside the characteristic economic form in simple circulation . . . falls outside it in general" (*Grundrisse*, 646). Moreover, his stress on use value and his stress on exploitation are part of one and the same argument: Marx understands the process of capitalist production and exploitation itself in terms of a contradiction between use value and exchange value—a contradiction that is also, as we have seen, one between abstract and concrete time.

In the *Grundrisse*, Marx asks: "Does not use value as such enter into the form itself, as a determinant of the form itself . . . in the relation of capital and labour?" (267). Marx is particularly concerned with the exchange between capital and labor, and with the special property of labor power as a use value. In the labor process, capital takes advantage of the fact that the use value of labor power is distinct from its exchange value. The use value of labor power for the capitalist consists in the fact that it is able to valorize more capital than is necessary for its own subsistence:

the value of labour-power, and the value which that labour-power valorizes in the labour-process, are two entirely different magnitudes; and this difference was what the capitalist had in mind when he was purchasing the labour-power. . . . it is a source not only of value, but of more value than it has itself. (*Capital*, 300–301)

It is this discrepancy between the use value of labor and its exchange value that is the source of surplus value and hence profit: surplus value arises as the difference between the capital input to the production process (the combination of constant capital and variable capital, the latter paid as wages and hence as labor power's exchange value) and what is produced (as realized in the sale of the produced commodities, which incorporate constant capital valorized by labor power in the production process). As the commodities produced in this process are sold by capitalists to realize this surplus, the labor they incorporate is alienated from the workers, presented to them (in the market) as an object for consumption; the total value of the commodities is measured in terms of the amount of dead labor time they incorporate.

Most important for our present analysis is that this process of exploitation is enabled through positing abstract time as the measure of value. In other words, the exchange of labor power for its value as the wage is an abstraction of value measured in terms of socially necessary labor time. Hence the labor theory of value: value is not merely accumulated labor, but rather an accumulation of quantifiable labor, with socially necessary labor time as its measure. It is this abstraction that enables both the extraction of surplus and its mystification as an alienated, fetishized relation. The phrase "socially necessary labor time" signifies not only that the *quantity* of labor time is socially determined to be "necessary," but more importantly still that the very *form* of quantification as labor time is also (socially and thus systematically) determined as "necessary." Socially necessary labor time is not simply a quantification of time, but in this very quantification constitutes a change in time's quality. As Moishe Postone argues, "this category represents the transformation of concrete time into abstract time in capitalism" (301). This is the essence of alienation and hence exploitation, which results from the fact that the concrete time characterizing the use of labor power (the rhythms and particularities of the working day) is transmuted into the quantifiable abstract time deemed socially necessary for its reproduction (so many hours per week at so much per hour). Moreover, reciprocally capitalism's abstract time comes to dominate and influence the concrete time insofar as the rhythm of events (or practice) comes to be determined increasingly by the dictates of abstract time. For example, capitalist demands for efficiency may involve speeding up the labor process (and thus a densification of concrete time) or a particular mode of time regulation outside of the production process (in schools or hospitals or even holiday camps) thus generalizing social alienation and determining in part developments within the field of culture. As Postone puts it: "It is the temporal dimension of the abstract domination that characterizes the structure of alienated social relations in capitalism" (191).

Yet however much abstract time may tend to influence or determine concrete time, the two forms of time are permanently in contradiction. This is a contradiction that parallels the contradiction between labor power's use value and its exchange value and likewise (and as an integral part of the same process) is made productive for capital. For the abstract quantification of time is socially constituted as insufficient to represent the full amount of concrete time (use value) expended over the working day: a surplus is produced, less or more according to the working day and the socially determined productivity of the branch of production in which the labor process is taking place. The surplus, which is essentially surplus time, time wasted, from the point of view of the worker, is then the source of surplus value and the transformation of value into capital. While it is true that *all* his or her working time is alienated from the point of view of the worker, it is so only thanks to the specific surplus labor time in which "the worker does indeed expend labour-power, he does work, but his labour is no longer necessary labour, and he creates no value for himself" (*Capital*, 325). It is this surplus, as we have seen, that drives the whole system. The fact that this contradiction determines that all labor time is alienated (and, in influencing concrete time more generally, tends towards the alienation of everyday life) marks capitalism's distinction from other modes of production such as feudalism, in which there is a separation between necessary labor time (in which the peasant works for him- or herself) and surplus labor time (in which he or she works for the feudal landlord). It is in this sense that capital is a "social relationship" (*Capital*, 998) that it thus permeates the social world. I want to suggest that *exactly the same process* of valorization, determined by a specific contradiction between concrete time and abstract time, constitutes cultural capital. Cultural capital arises from the fact that only a certain proportion of the activities that make up the concrete time of use value are valorized by the agents of cultural accreditation.

THE STRUGGLE AGAINST VALORIZATION

Just as economic capital is a result of the constitutive under-valorization through abstraction of concrete laboring (that is, sensuous) activity, so cultural capital has to be understood not in terms of productive or unproductive activity (for consumption through use is only secondarily productive) but in terms of precisely this mechanism of under-valorization. By "under-valorization" I mean the process by which activity is not rewarded according to what it is worth. The fact that labor struggles have consistently been fought over the wage and the length of the working day demonstrates the ways in which workers have focused on precisely this index of valorization, asserting their own mechanisms of auto-valorization in contradistinction to the abstract and constitutively exploitative valorization of capital. As Marx notes, "The establishment of a normal working day is the result of centuries of struggle between the capitalist and the worker" (*Capital*, 382).

But we should also note that this struggle has not merely been to reduce the absolute amount of labor time or the proportion of surplus to necessary labor; also at stake have been precisely the "normalization" of the working day and the imposition of socially necessary labor time as measure of value. Peter Linebaugh describes the struggles against the institutionalization of the wage on the part of the eighteenth-century British working class: as the "customary appropriation," which workers had taken to be part of their legitimate remuneration, was criminalized, so "money rationalized class society" and the "monetary abstracting of human labour as wages" (440) instituted a new regime of discipline (in which the efforts of Jeremy Bentham, inventor of the panopticon, were instrumental). This, Linebaugh argues, "foreshadowed the discipline of the industrial order: punctuality and obedience to the factory clock; . . . a continuous working day; . . . a new language in refraining from profanity; . . . and . . . the punctilious recognition of *meum et tuum* even when property was socialized in production" (441). None of this was imposed without a fight, as is evidenced by the constant attempt to discipline London's "many-headed multitude" through the "thanatocracy" of Tyburn's gallows (42).

Likewise, cultural struggles over valorization for "non-canonical" works or subaltern cultural practices are also struggles over the proportion of surplus to "socially necessary" activity in the everyday lives of the masses of the population. They are struggles over the mode and extent of the conversion of the concrete time of use into the abstract time of exchange. Attempts to expand the canon or to introduce to it works or practices that are more widely read or seen or performed are thus attempts to ensure their valorization. They are a demand that the time that these practices entail should be recognized, above all by the institutions of accreditation charged with the consecration, and as such valorization, of cultural production. In other words, struggles over multiculturalism and so on that express themselves as a demand that hitherto unvalued or undervalued cultural practices should be valorized are an indirect recognition of the productivity of consumption—of the productivity of what aesthetics and political economy demean or ignore by bracketing as simple utility.

After all, consumption and production are immediately the same activity: Marx recognized that production can also (and simultaneously) be described as the process by which the worker "consumes the means of production with his labour, and converts them into products with a higher value than that of the capital advanced. This is his productive consumption" (*Capital*, 717). What Marx did not recognize, however, was that what he called the worker's "individual consumption," outside the labor process, should also be seen as productive. Marx saw this individual consumption as taking up "the time in which he belongs to himself, and performs his necessary vital functions outside the production process" (717). However, this depiction implies that the worker is absolutely without culture, a creature of necessity alone.[16] Bourdieu's theory of cultural capital (if not, admittedly, always his practice of cultural analysis) enables us rather to see consumption outside the workplace as likewise productive consumption and not simply as need-driven utility. The concept of cultural capital makes this process visible—even as political economy and aesthetics occlude and ignore the practices that occupy this concrete time in which we take the otherwise dead labor and accumulated cultural capital in books, videos, and other products of earlier cultural production and "awaken them from the dead, change them from merely possible into real and effective use-value . . . infused with vital energy" (*Capital*, 289). In short, as de Certeau argues, far from locating production only in the process that produces *economic* capital:

> In reality, a rationalized, expansionist, centralized, spectacular and clamorous production is confronted by an entirely different kind of production, called "consumption" and characterized by its ruses, its fragmentation (the result of the circumstances), its poaching, its clandestine nature, its tireless but quiet activity, in short by its quasi-invisibility, since it shows itself not in its own products (where would it place them?) but in an art of using those imposed upon it. (31)

Bourdieu's theory of cultural capital enables us to see de Certeau's description of consumption as a "different kind of production" as no metaphor, for it shows that this production takes place within an entire system of valorization, to which the struggles over cultural value also point.

Bourdieu points out that the state and, particularly, its educational system are key agents in the valorization of cultural capital. Bourdieu is thus right to insist that institutions such as the school are not the sites of cultural capital's distribution, but the sites of its valorization. Guillory, among others, confuses the issue by claiming that "the school . . . regulates and thus distributes cultural capital *unequally*" (*Cultural Capital*, ix) and that "the school's historical function [is that] of distributing, or regulating access to, the forms of cultural capital" (vii), defining capital in terms of this unequal distribution (61). Many things are distributed unequally (from freckles to snow showers) but that does not make them capital. Bourdieu might elsewhere, as we have seen, define capital in terms of distribution (though at least he describes this uneven distribution as appropriation), but for very pragmatic reasons, perhaps the same pragmatic reasons that lead him to insist that "cultural capital" is no metaphor, he does *not* see the school system's primary function in terms of distribution. Rather, Bourdieu emphasizes that the school operates upon preexistent inequalities, "legitimating the reproduction of the social hierarchies by transmuting them into academic hierarchies" (*R*, 153). Were the school system to work through simple unequal distribution, this would be all too soon and all too easily recognized as simple injustice. The state school system in particular, with which Bourdieu is always above all concerned, does not and cannot discriminate through unequal distribution, as on the whole it has to treat all students alike in order to maintain the aura of objectivity and disinterest that then allows misrecognition of the fact that, owing to pre-

existent inequalities in inherited capital, not all students are in a position to respond alike to this uniform treatment, and not all cultures that they bring to the
school are valorized alike by the same uniform process of valorization. Moreover,
the school is especially ruthless in devaluing the dispositions it itself distributes—for example by "denigrating a piece of academic work as too 'academic'
[and thereby] . . . devalu[ing] the culture it transmits" (*I*, 21)—in favor of those
that are gained outside of the formal education system. It is true that Bourdieu's
use of the term "consecration" rather than valorization is often ambiguous, as
when he suggests that the school "awards qualifications durably consecrating the
position occupied in the structure of the distribution of cultural capital" (*LP*, 125;
translation modified), but this would lead to a truly functionalist and circular account in which the school would be fully dependent upon a prior distribution of
capital, and its legitimation (consecration) would be a matter of simply passive
recognition. If the school, rather, is seen as the site of valorization—where students can never be certain of the extent to which their dispositions (expressing
their experience and *habitus*) will be valorized—then we can better understand
the way in which it also becomes a site for struggle over, precisely, its mechanisms of valorization.

The state, then, which Bourdieu terms "the central bank of symbolic credit"
(*The State Nobility*, 376), is crucial to the valorization process. The "*state magic*"
of "*validation*" (376) indicates its role in the creation of cultural capital; here the
market—or the "free market" at least—is much less important than it is in the
valorization of economic capital.[17] Paradigmatically (if not uniquely), through its
institutions, concrete cultural wealth (to use Postone's distinction between wealth
and value) is subjected to the abstract and seemingly objective social transformation into value. As a result of such operations, it will turn out that cultural activity—concrete time—spent reading *Great Expectations* may be socially determined as necessary activity, while the time spent reading *Neuromancer* may
remain relatively undervalued, or completely surplus. The state, then, tends to
anchor the market of symbolic and cultural goods, indirectly providing a capital
fund and so defining and regulating cultural flows and exchanges. It is true that
the state does not have a complete monopoly (nor are its institutions monolithic),
and that there are other, more or less competing, institutions of accreditation and
valorization: the time spent with *Neuromancer* may be valorized at one site of
accreditation more than it is elsewhere, and there is a certain amount of revers-
ibility or play possible within the system. Moreover, valorization is not identical
with sale, and the price of cultural goods or competences may still vary. In other,
less centralized markets, the gap between cultural value and price may enable
negotiation according to supply and demand: this then opens up a new form of
transformation problem, as also a relatively fluid space for speculation, quick
profits, advantageous conversions into other forms of capital, and so on.

However, the fact remains that Bourdieu consistently focuses his attention on
the ups and downs of these more or less volatile cultural markets at the expense
of analyzing the mechanisms of valorization itself, as the source of exploitation

and surplus. Though, as Marx acknowledges in volume 3 of *Capital*, the market has real effects in value formation, especially insofar as the composition of value varies across different sectors, his critique of political economy is formulated to demonstrate that attempting to equalize demand with supply alone is impossible reformism, and that such minor disequilibria are not the source of value. Rather, a critique of the general political economy of practices shows that what is at issue is the form of the law of value itself, as a process of conversion or valorization through abstraction, which Bourdieu too uncritically accepts, as when in *Distinction* he effectively negates the very idea of the dominated class's cultural wealth on the basis that it is not valorized in this way. Perhaps Bourdieu in the end (and as a consequence of his Republican impulses) simply sets too much stock by the way in which the state valorizes cultural capital, and hence fails to investigate other modes of valorization and other institutions that provide compensatory or even completely alternative valorization for the concrete time of subaltern or other otherwise disenfranchised subjects. Nor, then, does he look at what could be termed the auto-valorization of cultural practices that expresses a refusal to labor or work for cultural capital.

Yet, contrary to his apparent functionalism, much of Bourdieu's work must also be seen as structured precisely around the possibility of a crisis in this law of cultural value. Both *Distinction* and *Homo Academicus* are effectively traumatized by the experience of 1968. Both books were researched before but written after this date, and amount at least in part to a retrospective attempt to understand this generalized revolt against precisely the law of value as a determination of socially necessary time—time to wait for a degree, to wait for a job. In describing "the collective disillusionment which results from the structural mismatch between aspiration and real probabilities," Bourdieu sees, if only temporarily, an

> anti-institutional cast of mind [that] points towards a denunciation of the tacit assumptions of the social order, a practical suspension of doxic adherence to the prizes it offers and the values it professes, and a withholding of the investments which are a necessary condition of its functioning. (*D*, 144)

Working more fully through a critique of the general political economy of practices towards which Bourdieu points us, and attempting to understand better the interrelations between and mutual determinations of the various forms of capital—now understood as immanently implicated rather than in any relation of exteriority—it might now also be possible to analyze moments of rupture such as the events of 1968 in France, Italy, and elsewhere as assaults on the general law of value. In the end, after all, socialism is not about struggles over the proportion of socially necessary labor time to surplus labor time. Rearranging the canon (for instance) does not in itself threaten the law of cultural value; if anything, it legitimates the institutions of valorization and consolidates the dominance of cultural capital. Socialism, rather, is about an attack on the law of value itself. In the cultural sphere, this would imply an affirmation of all the ways in which we use and live our everyday life. Taking seriously Bourdieu's theory of cultural capital might, then, be one approach to understanding what is at stake in such a struggle.

NOTES

I would like to thank Imre Szeman and Nicholas Brown for providing me with the opportunity to present an earlier version of this article at the conference, "Pierre Bourdieu: Fieldwork in Culture," at Duke University in April 1995, and Fredric Jameson for his response to the paper on that occasion. Many people have read and commented on this paper in its various drafts. My thanks go especially to the following: Susan Brook, Sabine Engel, Kathy Green, David Harvie, Jeremy Lane, Alberto Moreiras, Tom Schumacher, and Imre Szeman. Also to the economists: Steve Keen for his very helpful suggestions on the dialectic of use value and exchange value (and for discussing theories of marginal utility); and Massimo de Angelis for originally pointing me in this line of enquiry by asking me what I meant by capital in discussing Bourdieu. Massimo, I hope you're happy now!

1. Calls for analysis of political economy by cultural studies theorists such as Meaghan Morris and Lawrence Grossberg make them exceptions that prove the general rule that cultural studies has long since discarded serious study of economics. Grossberg writes that "cultural studies must explicitly return to questions of economics, to questions that were strategically bracketed at various moments of its history" (17). My argument would be that an unexamined use of terms such as "cultural capital" may introduce the aura of economics all the better to bracket off the real questions it poses.

2. My own translation. This quotation comes from discussion of a paper by Bourdieu, later published as "On the Fundamental Ambivalence of the State," though the discussion itself remains unpublished.

3. It is important to note—and I thank David Harvie for this reminder—that economic capital is of course not essential for exploitation. There is exploitation in noncapitalist modes of production (feudalism, for example), and there are noncapitalist forms of exploitation within capitalism (women's unpaid domestic labor). It is then immediately obvious that an expanded notion of capital, which might account for such noncapitalist exploitation, could also entail a significant revision of what is meant by "capitalism" itself.

4. Of course, the Althusserian approach also appears indefinitely to postpone that "last" analysis. Bourdieu's incorporation of the economic into the cultural, via the concept of cultural capital, could be seen as making the economic equally determinant in the *first* analysis.

5. This could be said to be the case in Bourdieu's analysis of Kabylia insofar as he demonstrates the economic logic that underlies gift exchanges, even though that logic is the logic of symbolic rather than financial (or "strictly" economic) capital. Bourdieu describes the way modernization processes entail the abstraction of strictly economic logic from the realm of symbolic capital to constitute a separate, economic field. This then leaves culture as a sphere apart, in which economic calculation remains hidden. Complicating this analysis of the genesis of the economic field, however, is the fact that Bourdieu

appears to offer a quite different (in fact, diametrically opposed) analysis in "The Market of Symbolic Goods."

6. Guillory therefore suggests that "it may be better to invoke the paradigm of 'mercantile' capital . . . to account for how embodied labor, in Bourdieu's sense, might enter into a cycle of accumulation (and therefore become capital)." As I argue below, however, such an approach would ignore the importance of the state for Bourdieu's analysis, especially for Bourdieu's account of capital's valorization.

7. Another way of putting this is that Bourdieu here implies that capital always pre-exists appropriation (rather than being its product). For Marx, too, capital may, and almost always does, pre-exist a given production process—in the form of fixed capital such as machinery or materials. However, the point is that that capital does not produce value; it merely remains constant. Marx, moreover, understands primitive accumulation as the process that lies outside capitalism but also founds it to initiate the production process; Bourdieu, on the other hand, seems to have no place for primitive accumulation as he seems to imply that capital is simply always already present. Where he does discuss "the primitive accumulation of cultural capital" he does so in terms of "the total or partial monopolizing of the society's symbolic resources" (*The Logic of Sense*, 125), which again hardly explains how these resources *become* capital.

8. And Bourdieu understands value itself, we can now see, in a framework reminiscent more of Ricardo than of Marx: Bourdieu defines value in terms of labor but not labor *power*.

9. The distinction between these two perspectives upon exchange is expressed in the difference between the circulation C-M-C, for which "consumption, the satisfaction of needs, in short use-value, is . . . its final goal" and M-C-M (or, more properly, M-C-M', given that the capitalist hopes to make a profit by realizing surplus-value in exchange value) whose "driving and motivating force, its determining purpose, is . . . exchange-value" (Marx, *Capital* 250).

10. Obviously, utility is defined differently in each field, and indeed the fields are (as Guillory argues) something like mirror images of each other "separated at birth" (*Cultural Capital*, 303). Within the cultural field, utility is defined in terms of calculation, distinguished from the natural and unmediated appreciation of the work of art; in economics, utility is defined in terms of natural and unmediated consumption of the commodity, distinguished from the calculation associated with exchange value.

11. The question as to *why* Bourdieu should opt for silence on economics is interesting, if somewhat outside the scope of this paper. What seems clear, however, is that what is at stake in this decision is as much the analysis of culture as it is the analysis of the economy: in other words, the effect of a silence on economics is equally, and with perhaps more important implications for Bourdieu, a silence on aspects of culture. By ignoring the question of exploitation, and focusing rather on appropriation as extrinsic to the capital relation, Bourdieu also keeps his relative silence on popular culture. Or, as Jeremy Lane suggests,

> Couldn't it be argued that this relates to his desire, when all is said and done, to retain some notion of the inherent value of "legitimate" culture, so that changing the contingent conditions of unequal distribution and appropriation of cultural capital, rather than attacking what it is that is counted as "legitimate culture," remains Bourdieu's ultimate goal? This, of course, would relate to Bourdieu's constant hostility to

the notion that popular cultural forms, rather than legitimate culture, should be valorized. (personal communication)

At the same time, it should be noted (as I argue below) that Bourdieu's analysis of the school system recognizes that schooling cannot simply be the site and means of cultural capital's unequal *distribution*. But Bourdieu's silence on economics in part prevents him from recognizing the consequences of that insight.

12. The specificity of cultural capital vis-à-vis symbolic capital is that the former can be accumulated; literacy, for instance, therefore "ensure[s] the perpetuation of cultural resources which would otherwise disappear with the agents who bear them" (*LP*, 125).

13. Moishe Postone defines concrete time as "the various forms of time that are functions of events. . . . The modes of reckoning associated with concrete time do not depend on a continuous succession of constant temporal units but either are based on events . . . or on temporal units that vary" (201).

14. Just as exchange value is not equivalent to economic capital. But this is a misleading parallel, because the point is that both use value and exchange value enter into the production of both cultural and economic capital; in both cases, what is important, as I argue further on, is the contradiction between use value and exchange value (as expressed in the abstraction of concrete time).

15. Though it is true that this remains unrecognized by a long line of traditional Marxists (as Steve Keen argues).

16. Ironically, of course, this is also something like the attitude Bourdieu takes in *Distinction*; were he to have resolved his ambivalence over the precise nature of cultural capital, however, he would not be able to take such a position.

17. Here then I would quibble again with Guillory when he talks of "the commanding position of the market at the center of [Bourdieu's] social universe" ("Bourdieu's Refusal," 32). The point at least is that the cultural market bears very little resemblance to the free market envisaged by orthodox economics, and the state plays a much greater role. Indeed, as I suggest further on, Bourdieu should probably be criticized for adhering overmuch to the state's role in the valorization of capital, which thus blinds him to the effectivity of subaltern practices.

BIBLIOGRAPHY

Bourdieu, Pierre. *Outline of a Theory of Practice.* Translated by Richard Nice. Cambridge: Cambridge UP, 1977.

———. *Distinction: A Social Critique of the Judgement of Taste.* Translated by Richard Nice. Cambridge, Mass.: Harvard UP, 1984.

———. "The Forms of Capital." Translated by Richard Nice. In *Handbook of Theory and Research for the Sociology of Education*, edited by John G. Richardson. New York: Greenwood, 1986.

———. *The Logic of Practice.* Translated by Richard Nice. Stanford: Stanford UP, 1990.

———. "A Reply to Some Objections." In *In Other Words: Essays Towards a Reflexive Sociology*, translated by Matthew Adamson. Cambridge: Polity, 1990. 106–19.

———. "The Sociologist in Question." In *Sociology in Question*, translated by Richard Nice. London: Sage, 1993. 20–35.

———. *The State Nobility: Elite Schools in the Field of Power.* Translated by Lauretta Clough. Stanford: Stanford UP, 1996.

———. *Acts of Resistance: Against the New Myths of Our Time.* Translated by Richard Nice. Cambridge: Polity, 1998.

———. "The Economy of Symbolic Goods." Translated by Randal Johnson. In *Practical Reason: On the Theory of Action.* Cambridge: Polity, 1998.

———. "On the Fundamental Ambivalence of the State." Translated by Roger Beebe with Helen Thompson. *Polygraph* 10 (1998): 21–32.

———. "Social Space and Field of Power." Translated by Randal Johnson. In *Practical Reason: On the Theory of Action.* Cambridge: Polity, 1998.

———. *On Television.* Translated by Priscilla Parkhurst Ferguson. New York: New Press, 1998.

Bourdieu, Pierre, and Jean-Claude Passeron. *Reproduction in Education, Society, and Culture.* Translated by Richard Nice. London: Sage, 1977.

———. *The Inheritors: French Students and Their Relation to Culture.* Translated by Richard Nice. Chicago: U of Chicago P, 1979.

Bourdieu, Pierre, and Loïc Wacquant. *An Invitation to Reflexive Sociology.* Chicago: U of Chicago P, 1992.

de Certeau, Michel. *The Practice of Everyday Life.* Translated by Stephen Rendall. Berkeley: U of California P, 1984.

Fowler, Bridget. *Pierre Bourdieu and Cultural Theory: Critical Investigations.* London: Sage, 1997.

Grossberg, Lawrence. "Speculations and Articulations of Globalization." *Polygraph* 11 (spring 1999): 11–48.

Guillory, John. *Cultural Capital: The Problem of Literary Canon Formation.* Chicago: U of Chicago P, 1993.

———. "Bourdieu's Refusal." In this volume, 19–43.

Keen, Steve. "The Misinterpretation of Marx's Theory of Value." *Journal of the History of Economic Thought* 15, no. 2 (fall 1993): 282–300.

Lane, Jeremy. "Pierre Bourdieu in Context: Ethnology and Sociology in the Era of French Late Capitalism." Unpublished Ph.D. thesis. University of Stirling: June 1998. London: Pluto, forthcoming.

———. " 'Un Etrange Retournement'? Pierre Bourdieu and the French Republican Tradition." Unpublished manuscript, 1999.

Linebaugh, Peter. *The London Hanged: Crime and Civil Society in the Eighteenth Century.* Cambridge: Cambridge UP, 1992.

Marx, Karl. *Grundrisse.* Translated by Martin Nicolaus. London: Penguin, 1973.

———. *Capital.* Vol. One. Translated by Ben Fowkes. New York: Vintage, 1977.

Morris, Meaghan. "Banality in Cultural Studies." *Discourse* 10, no. 2 (spring/summer 1988): 3–29.

Postone, Moishe. *Time, Labor and Social Domination: A Reinterpretation of Marx's Critical Theory.* Cambridge: Cambridge UP, 1993.

Wallerstein, Immanuel, moderator. Colloquium on "L'avenir des ideologies, les ideologies de l'avenir." Session 5 with Pierre Bourdieu, Toni Negri, and others. 13 March 1993. Typescript transcription courtesy of Pierre Bourdieu.

PART II

7

Cultural Studies Bourdieu's Way: Women, Leadership, and Feminist Theory

Marie-Pierre Le Hir

One of the most exhilarating experiences in adopting and applying Pierre Bourdieu's way of thinking (of "practicing Cultural Studies Bourdieu's Way") is the discovery of relations where they are least expected. In the first part of this chapter, I describe two seemingly unrelated aspects of my professional life, one related to research, the other to committee work on campus, in order to retrace that experience. This narrative then serves to identify questions and properties that, I believe, feminist theory cannot afford to overlook. Finally, I revisit these questions from a Bourdieusian perspective, focusing on the usefulness of the concepts of "male domination" and "symbolic violence" for a feminist theory of practice.[1]

PART 1: TWO WAYS TO APPROACH A PROBLEM

My current research project deals with the discipline of French and the question of its relation to cultural studies. Although this topic may not seem to have much to do with feminist theory at first, it does, nonetheless, in two ways. The objective link between the two is provided by a study on the production and placement of Ph.D.s in French (1980 and 1991) I conducted several years ago (see table 7.1). The subjective link is less obvious and would probably not figure in this chapter at all, were it not for the recognition that revealing the contradictory nature of a woman's experience of the academic world (in this case, my own) is a useful way to identify a significant task for feminist theory: the challenge of developing a

123

Table 7.1   The Feminization of a Discipline: Ph.D. Production in French (1980–1991)
[Numbers in parens refer to women]

	1980–85	1986–91	1980–91	%
MIDWEST:	179 (118)	189 (131)	368 (249)	24
NORTHEAST:	303 (201)	269 (184)	572 (385)	37
SOUTH ATLANTIC:	146 (99)	116 (85)	262 (184)	17
PACIFIC COAST:	108 (73)	94 (61)	202 (134)	13
ROCKY MOUNTAIN:	22 (13)	21 (16)	43 (29)	2
SOUTH CENTRAL:	42 (30)	39 (28)	81 (58)	5
	800 (534)	728 (505)	1528 (1039)	
Total % of women Ph.D.s:	67%	69%	68%	

theoretical framework flexible enough to take the subjective dimension of experience into account and sophisticated enough to account for it.

Let me begin with a brief presentation of the results of my study on Ph.D. production: between 1980 and 1985, 67% of the 800 Ph.D.s granted in French in the United States were granted to women. Of the 64% of the new Ph.D.s who found tenure-track positions in the U.S., almost 64% were women. Similarly, between 1986 and 1991, 69% of the 728 Ph.D.s granted in French were granted to women; and of the 416 new Ph.D.s who secured a tenure-track position, 66% were women. While this study failed to take into consideration important distinctions of a qualitative nature (that is, in which type of institutions these tenure-track positions were filled) its results are striking enough to lead to conclusions about the feminization of the discipline of French.

It has often been pointed out that female students tend to favor the arts and the humanities. It is also well known that among these disciplines, French has long exerted a particular attraction.[2] Today, the feminization of the humanities has reached such proportions that it is beginning to make headlines in the national press: "Colleges in the U.S. Are Beginning to Ask: 'Where Have All the Men Gone?' " the *New York Times* reported in a December 6, 1998, front page article.[3] Commenting on this trend in this article, feminist scholar Catherine R. Stimpson acknowledges that "[t]here may be a bias against the liberal arts, a feeling *that real men don't speak French*, that in the 20th century these are women's topics." If the figures presented above seem to lend additional support to the old American stereotypes equating Frenchness and femininity,[4] they also point to a new phenomenon. In the past, students of French may have been young women, but until recently, their teachers were predominantly males. Today for the first time, women are poised to occupy even the "leadership" positions in French.

How can we make sense of these trends, and what do they mean for the future of the discipline? Should professors of French make a conscious effort to hire male colleagues? Should they start aggressively recruiting male students? Should they fight the stereotypes by pointing out that *real men do speak French* in France? Should they perhaps go so far as to argue that France is actually such a male-dominated society that women there are currently mobilizing against "the 'masculinization' of power" (Gaspard, 93)?[5] Or should they, as women and perhaps feminists, simply rejoice that in at least one academic discipline in the U.S., there are, or will soon be, a great number of women leaders? Personally, I see two kinds of obstacles to this rejoicing: first, my awareness that an academic discipline perceived as a women's discipline tends to lose its prestige; and second, and no less important, my subjective resistance to the rhetoric of "leadership." As we will see below, these issues are more closely related than it would seem.

Subjective Resistance to the Rhetoric of Leadership

Enshrined as it is in American academic discourse, the concept of "leadership" can be found in any institution of higher education's mission statement: the stated goal of colleges and universities is to produce "leaders for tomorrow." "Leadership" is also a serious area of scholarship: over seventeen hundred bibliographical entries listed under that rubric in the library catalog at my institution.[6] But my personal relation to the term "leadership" is at best ambiguous, torn as I am between a sense of duty that forces me to accept the rhetoric of leadership, and the inner feeling that "leadership" is just another buzzword, or at least a term that does not belong to my own vocabulary. When the issue comes up at committee meetings I feel like a fraud: I listen politely but I want to protest. Images of a gesticulating "führer" (the leader *par excellence*) come before my eyes and I wonder why I am apparently the only person troubled by that word. I say nothing, however, thinking that my uneasiness is probably related to my European upbringing. But is it really? I can't even think of a French equivalent for "leadership."

In the English/French dictionary, "leadership" is translated as "militaire, commandement" (command, military term). Does it mean, then, that my "leadership" problem has more to do with gender than with culture? If the term has such obvious military connotations, women's resistance to the rhetoric of leadership may be more universal than I first thought. After all, exclusion from the military and from warfare has been the single most universal constant in women's history, and still today, the military remains one of the few social fields where vocal resistance against women's presence can be heard. Could "leadership" be an alien concept not only for me, but for women in general? An immediate objection comes to mind: the military does not constitute a universal experience for men either, particularly not in the U.S. where there is no mandatory military service. Still, the possibility cannot be rejected offhand: first, because I am apparently not the only woman bothered by the rhetoric of "leadership";[7] and second, because contemporary feminist scholarship on women leadership lends support to that claim by consistently pointing to the analogy between the business world and the military.

Scholarship on women leadership comes almost exclusively from the business field. The authors of *Feminine Leadership: How to Succeed in Business without Being One of the Boys* argue that women are at a disadvantage in a business world that draws "heavily on the military model . . . in terms of organizational structure and leadership style" (24). But even a study that approaches the issue of women leadership from a totally different angle, *Breaking the Glass Ceiling: Can Women Reach the Top of America's Top Corporations?* presents corporate culture as a foreign, masculine, and hostile environment that has yet to be conquered by women. Moving from personal intuition to preliminary research, I have found out so far, first, that "leadership" is viewed as a serious issue overall—judging by the sheer quantity of writings devoted to it; second, that although resistance to the *doxa* of leadership appears to be primarily gendered as feminine, the subjective forms it takes vary greatly among women, from my largely unreflected uneasiness with a term I perceive as foreign to my own life to the collective experience of leadership as a realm of exclusion for women in the business field; third, that in that particular case, "leadership" is no longer understood in its doxic sense, but rather as an expression of a social problem: the lack of women's representation at the top of the professional ladder—in other words, one of the most important feminist issues.

Structural Resistance to Women's Leadership

There is no agreement in the studies mentioned above on how to address and solve the problem of leadership thus defined, that is as a problem of underrepresentation of women at the top. In fact, this scholarship faithfully reproduces the traditional divide between feminism of equality and feminism of difference that has existed within women's movements for almost two hundred years.[8] Marilyn Loden, the author of *Feminine Leadership,* argues that women must acknowledge their difference if they ever want to change a masculine business environment styled on the military model. Women, she insists, are naturally inclined to do things differently from men, and they should do so. Taming one's feminine tendencies and copying male leadership styles represent a bad choice, if only because any particular quality that is perceived as positive in a man automatically translates into a negative one in a woman.[9] Women might as well play their own game; that is, focus on getting their own leadership style accepted (see table 7.2).[10] Feminists of difference such as Loden do not question the notion that differences exist between men and women. On the contrary, they seek to identify, emphasize, and valorize these differences so as to better eliminate biases against women. Because women's dispositions are different, but just as valuable as men's, they argue, the

Table 7.2   Male and Female Leadership Models

Masculine Leadership Model (p. 26)	*Feminine Leadership Model* (p. 63)
Operating Style	
Competitive	Cooperative
Organization Structure	
Hierarchy	Team
Basic Objective	
Winning	Quality Output
Problem-Solving Style	
Rational	Intuitive/Rational
Key Characteristics	
High Control	Lower Control
Strategic	Empathic
Unemotional	Collaborative
Analytical	High Performance Standards

Source: Londen, Marilyn, *Feminine Leadership: How to Succeed in Business without Being One of the Boys.* New York: Times Books, 1985.

social world can only benefit from making use of two sets of values and behaviors instead of just one.

Feminists of equality are critical of this endorsement of difference and aware of the risk of essentialism it contains. They have traditionally sided with Simone de Beauvoir and countered that "one isn't born a woman, one becomes a woman." Gender being for them a social construction, they have consistently rejected the logic of complementarity and encouraged women to prove that they are men's equals by competing on their turf, in "hard" disciplines such as science, math, politics, business, or engineering. Historically therefore, their struggle has been waged against laws and regulations that barred women from entering certain fields and professions, the reasoning being that once women are free to study and profess in any field they wish, there will automatically be women leaders everywhere. The struggle for equality is therefore premised on the assumption that equal, nondiscriminatory treatment of women is a necessary and a sufficient condition to make the professional, including the academic, world as hospitable and profitable for women as for men. As Toril Moi notes, Simone de Beauvoir was already convinced in the 1940s that professional women of her generation had already "gagné la partie"—"won the game" (Beauvoir in Moi, 1032). Fifty years later, however, feminists of equality are still struggling to understand what went wrong.

Breaking the Glass Ceiling, for instance, is haunted by this question: how can we explain, that "despite the passage of time, the increasing number of women in management and professional positions and the replacement of over-fifty male executives with younger men, the 'glass ceiling' continues to exist"? How can we account for the fact that "so little has changed in terms of representation of women in the executive ranks of most companies in America" (xii)? The authors, Ann Morrison, Randall White, and Ellen van Velsor do not quite know how to answer these questions. But they are sure that women must resist the siren song of gender difference. Although "it has now become fashionable to say that differences are beneficial, that women will complement men in the management ranks and bring a healthy balance to business," they write, women should not forget that, historically, these "perceived differences have been used to keep women out of management" (48–49). Besides, they ask, referring directly to *Female Leadership*, what is the basis for these alleged differences between men and women? "[O]nly a few examples and opinions" (49), in other words, a new mythology that "real" scholarship can easily refute. Citing the results of psychological and behavioral tests they administered to executive men and women, they conclude that there are "only a few statistically significant sex differences" (50), and that "on most of the measures examined, men and women did not score differently" (51). For them, therefore, the handicap women face in the corporate sphere is not that they are women, but rather that they are perceived as women, that is judged according to gender stereotypes and expected behaviors. Women, they conclude, cannot afford to ignore the fact that "perception is reality." If they want to succeed, to be top executives, they must make the most of the "very narrow band of acceptable behavior" (55) that corporate culture has to offer them. *Breaking the Glass Ceiling*'s primary goal is therefore to help them overcome the real handicap of perceived womanhood through some concrete, practical "lessons."

PART 2: AND WAYS TO SOLVE IT

Toward a Feminist Theory of Practice

By revealing how politically urgent it is for women in the business field to find explanations and solutions to the problem of their underrepresentation, these studies have the merit of bringing to light the very concrete nature of that problem. To say that much is to recognize that feminist theory cannot afford to be purely theoretical, that it must be able to look back at the social world, not only in order to register structural differences between fields, but also to explain why it is, for instance, that in a discipline like French, women may become leaders, while in a discipline like management they may not. More sophisticated feminist scholars in the humanities may mock the prescriptive tone of these studies and the contradictory nature of the suggested solutions (women should be themselves on the one hand; women should adjust, on the other). But it seems to me that the same contradictions are embedded in contemporary feminist theory. What makes them invisible in that case is, in fact, the very theoretical nature of this feminist discourse; that is, the privilege theory grants itself to stay away from anything empirical.

It is also relevant to point out that for all its critical sophistication, feminist theory continues to reproduce the opposition noted above between feminism(s) of difference on the one hand and feminism(s) of equality on the other. To wit, Rita Felski's effort, in a recent issue of *Signs*, to rethink "the *doxa* of difference," in an attempt, as Ien Ang correctly suggests in her commentary on Felski's essay, "to reinstate the importance of 'the seemingly obsolete issue of equality' " (57). If feminist theory is to make headway, this great divide must be overcome. One way to do just that is to recognize that, as interdisciplinary and international as it might be in comparison to other fields, feminist theory is also an academic field (in Bourdieu's sense) and that, as such, it is subject to its own logic. Once it is acknowledged that the periodic revolutions leading to the replacement of "the doxa of equality" by the "doxa of difference," or vice versa, have to do, in part, with that logic, that they are the structuring devices by which a field reproduces itself and maintains its integrity, it becomes easier to neutralize these effects and thereby also to make stronger theoretical claims.

This does not mean, however, that the opposition between "equality" and "difference" becomes irrelevant. Rather, I suggest that it ought to be rethought as the particular form of a more general opposition, the antagonism between subjectivism and objectivism. In *Logic of Practice*, Bourdieu acknowledges the individual contributions of these two modes of knowledge. The significance of subjectivist approaches lies in their efforts to retrieve "the primary relationship of familiarity with the familiar environment" (*LP*, 25), in their acknowledgment of the primacy of that dimension of social life. It is this "truth" that Rosi Braidotti wants to articulate when she emphasizes "the need to practice feminist subjectivity in such a way as to allow . . . inner multiplicity, which is also a way to resist the rationalistic pull toward the closure of fixed identity" (Braidotti, 33). Feminism of difference may not always regard sexual difference as inscribed in nature; it may or may not proclaim that there is an "essence of femininity."[11] But it is always a form of subjectivism insofar as it seeks to retrieve the truth of woman's experience, or more recently, the truths of women's experiences.

Objectivism, by contrast, is premised on a rupture with that "primary relationship of familiarity with the familiar environment" (*LP*, 25), the scientific imperative on which it is founded demanding a "radical discontinuity between theoretical knowledge and practical knowledge" (*LP*, 26). By breaking with immediate experience, objectivism marks a first important step toward understanding the social world: it provides classifications and rules that undergird rationalist discourse. For instance, to negate women's difference on the basis that apparent differences are just social constructs and to try to elucidate the principles of these

constructions is a more scientific attitude than the posture that consists in celebrating that difference. Although it may also take many forms, feminism of
equality is concerned with charting out the social world for gender-based inequalities—and therefore perhaps better prepared for collective political action than
feminism(s) of difference. Feminists of equality's refusal to acknowledge differ-
ence(s) may serve as a deterrent against the proliferation of stereotypical images
of women, or as a means to hold the social world accountable for the claims it
makes. As Joan Scott points out, feminism of equality has an interest in upholding "fictions"—the "fiction . . . that individuals have no sex, even if sex is the
basis for discrimination against them in the political realm" (Scott, 86); or, in the
case of the French "*paritaires*," upholding the national fiction of equality, so as
to better use it as a political weapon. Because it is founded on a bracketing out
of immediate, lived experience, because it refuses to dwell on differences other
than the ones that can be perceived objectively, feminism of equality is indifferent to the goal of accounting for the totality of women's experiences. Conversely,
if the merit of subjectivism is to focus on a dimension of social experience absent
from objectivist constructions, its disadvantage is to be condemned to the mere
description of subjective experiences as they are apprehended. Ien Ang's theory
of "incommensurability," for instance, stands as a particularly good example of
subjectivism's strength, its ability to express the incommensurabilty of experience,[12] but also of its failure, of its inability to explain what makes these experiences possible or incommensurable. In that respect, Felski's critique that "we
are now in a postmodern condition where female difference has fragmented into
multiple differences and any appeal to general ideals or norms can only be considered politically questionable and theoretically naive" (1) appears quite justified.

Rita Felski's essay, "The Doxa of Difference," is also indicative of a desire to
have it both ways that I find quite legitimate: there is nothing wrong with wanting
to retain the gains made possible by subjectivist criticism while at the same time
feeling the need to change the way things are, and therefore with seeking to work
within a more scientific, objectivist framework. Felski herself, however, is the
one who rejects the notion of overcoming the antagonism of these two modes of
knowledge. Mindful of the deconstructive precept that holds that "dualisms cannot be overcome, but at best displaced" (17), she points out in a footnote "that
any argument that claims to overcome binary oppositions inevitably sets up a
new opposition between binary and non-binary thought" (17). This may be true
within a purely theoretical framework that reduces the world to discourse, but not
in a conceptual framework that makes a distinction between discursive constructions of "the real" and "the real" itself. Bourdieu's theory of practice has the
power to overcome the antagonism between objectivism and subjectivism because it makes that difference, or more precisely because it sees their antagonism
for what it is, a false opposition. As different as they may seem at first, these two
modes of knowledge have in fact more in common than first meets the eye: they

are both the product of scholarly labor, the product of scholarly points of view, and as such "both equally opposed to the practical mode of knowledge which is the basis of ordinary experience of the social world" (25). This insight carries with itself a methodological imperative: the necessity, mentioned earlier, to practice self-reflexivity; that is, to conceive of scholarly labor not only as an intellectual activity, but also as a point of view issued from a particular position within in a particular field itself structured in a particular way at a given moment in time and in relation to other points of view. It helps us recognize, for instance, the incommensurability of experience between "Third World" *people* and so-called "Third World" *critics*, but on the other hand also the commonality of experience between "Third World" and "First World" *critics* as participants engaged in the same field (the field of criticism, that is, *not* of world politics).

The concept of field is also methodologically relevant in another respect, namely in the invaluable help it provides in constructing objects of studies. I am thinking here in particular of the necessity to do away with some of the glaring contradictions that can be found in feminist or postcolonial discourse. How can one, for instance, claim to recognize the "limitations of essentialist notions of female experience" (Felski, "Doxa of Difference," 4) and at the same time continue to operate with such categories as "the white woman" or "the black woman"? Similarly, what is the point of developing theories of hybridity if they do not eliminate dubious concepts such as "the colonizer" and "the colonized"?[13] If "the doxa of difference" reveals its limitation in such moments, its inability to transform theoretical insights on difference into a practice of difference, thinking in terms of field and *habitus* offers a way out of this dilemma. Applying Bourdieu's mode of thinking makes it possible not only to heed Chandra Mohanty's call for "context-specific, differentiated analyses of the ways in which women are produced as a sociopolitical group within particular historical and cultural locations" (as summarized by Felski, 10), but also to give oneself the means to situate these "objects of knowledge" in time and space, so as to acknowledge their singularities.[14] Finally, and this is the point I want to develop below, Bourdieu's theory of practice is also a feminist theory of practice.

Male Domination as a Trans-Historical Constant

Having moved far away from the concrete questions raised earlier, let me recall them now. Feminist theory should be able to deal with the kind of subjective contradictions described in my narrative on leadership, or more generally, to explain "female subjects [as] a multiplicity split within itself" (Braidotti, 33). But it should also have the ability to account for "the hold of patriarchy in Western democracies" (Cornell, 48), that is, for the kind of structural discrepancies noted earlier (women's underrepresentation in fields of power), as well as feminism's inability "to sustain itself as a movement and transmit its lessons to the next generation" (Cornell, 48).

Implied in the first objective is the necessity to work within a conceptual framework that grants at least some kind of priority to sexual difference or gender: envisioning female subjects as a "multiplicity split within itself" is not necessarily to make that condition of experience an exclusive attribute of female subjectivity, but it is to recognize sexual difference or gender as a fundamental "principle of vision and division"—Bourdieu's phrase. Feminists' theories of difference of Lacanian origin—such as Cornell's or Braidotti's—do so by building on a theoretical legacy in which "sexual difference . . . historically and conceptually functions . . . as the privileged signifier of difference" (Braidotti, 37). For more equality-minded feminists like Rita Felski, this "Lacanian view of history and culture as fundamentally phallocentric" ("Doxa of Difference," 6) is unacceptable: it wrongly asserts that "the multitudes of women in history who engaged in cultural activities—the artists, the revolutionaries, the mothers, the teachers—[were] really nothing more than the passive vehicles of phallocentrism" (6).

Bourdieu's theory of male domination does not escape this kind of criticism, and he is well aware of it. "La domination masculine," in fact, opens with the acknowledgment that feminist critics' suspicion toward male writings on sexual difference is entirely justified.[15] Conscious of the risk of essentialism attached to such a notion, he nonetheless insists that male domination is and remains the most universal form of domination: we cannot afford to overlook "the impact of an institution inscribed for thousands of years in the objectivity of social structures and the subjectivity of mental structures" ("La domination," 1). It is only by recognizing male domination for what it is, "a trans-historical constant," that we can begin to examine how it has been produced throughout history; that we can address the crucial questions "of the historical labor, always started anew, that is necessary to wring out male domination from history, and of the historical mechanisms and actions responsible for its seeming de-historicization" (*DM,* 110).

In a rather bold move, Bourdieu turns away from the object of study that would seem most obviously relevant: male domination today, in contemporary societies. Instead, both *The Logic of Practice* and *La domination masculine* are based on case studies conducted among the North African people of Kabylia, a social world where, he argues, male domination continues to impose itself doxically, as it has around the Mediterranean for thousands of years:[16] "This universe of discourses and rituals entirely oriented toward the reproduction of a social and cosmic order founded on the ultra-consequential affirmation of the primacy of malehood provides the interpreter with a magnified and systematic image of the 'phallo-narcissistic' cosmology that still haunts our unconscious" ("La domination," 4).[17] The goal of these studies is not really to describe cultural practices that have withstood the test of time in a particular society (anthropology for anthropology's sake), but more importantly to discover fundamental principles that are still operative today in gendering processes and gender relations.

From a methodological point of view, the turn to Kabylia is a strategical move aimed at "objectifying the subject of scientific objectification," that is, at enabling the "interpreter"—who, as man and woman, has "the historical structures of the masculine order" embedded in him- or herself "in the form of unconscious schemata of perception and appreciation"—to better neutralize this masculine order (*DM*, 11). Bourdieu's critique of psychoanalytical criticism hinges on that point: "it tends to use certain categories of perception and thought as heuristic devices (*instruments de connaissance*) instead of taking them as objects of study (*objects de connaissance*) ("La domination," 4).[18] The essentialism that makes Lacanian criticism unacceptable to many feminist critics (including Braidotti) originates for Bourdieu in its resistance to objectification. Instead of repressing this male unconscious, therefore, Bourdieu sets out to lay it bare, examining its "magnified image" in Kabyle society. *Two Categories*

What distinguishes his theory of male domination from others is its ability to explain the genesis and the persistence of this universal phenomenon, no longer understood as an essentialist construct but rather as a thoroughly historical phenomenon, as history to be recovered. Male domination is originally the product of an arbitrary, socially constructed division of human beings into two fundamental categories. Like many anthropologists and feminist critics, Bourdieu views the incest taboo, which Lévi-Strauss regarded as the founding act of society, as the *Incest Taboo* historical basis for the division between males and females, and for women's original exclusion from the public sphere. The exchange imperative embedded in the incest taboo feeds an economy of exchanges in which men function as subjects of exchanges, women as objects. This logic of exchange forms the basis of the social construction of relations of kinship and marriage, which universally assigns to women the status of objects of exchange and defines them in relation to men's interests—that is primarily as daughters, sisters, and wives who take their husband's name. For Bourdieu, however, women do not primarily represent an economic asset, or a means to accumulate economic capital. They are, rather, symbolic instruments meant to increase men's prestige and network of social relations since in precapitalist societies symbolic and social capital are the dominant forms of capital. It is because their function is to contribute to the reproduction of men's symbolic capital that women cannot participate as subjects in the economy of symbolic exchanges. As a rule, this exclusion is more likely to be expressed openly and granted legal status in societies or segments of society where symbolic capital remains the dominant form of capital. The exclusion of all female faculty and students from Kabul University in Afghanistan a few years ago provides a revealing example of the threat educated women pose in a society still largely based on an economy of symbolic exchanges. But even in societies that ostensibly grant primary importance to the accumulation of economic capital, women may still function as symbolic instruments, as means of increasing men's symbolic capital.[19]

The historical reproduction of this gendered order is facilitated by the fact that the relation that defines some agents as subjects and others as objects is not perceived as a form of domination, that its violence is "somatized." Although there is nothing "natural" about this division—it is not founded in nature—it becomes naturalized as sexism, "the hardest form of essentialism to uproot because the labor that aims at transforming an arbitrary historical product into nature finds in this case a plausible basis in the very real effects thousands of years of socialization of the biological have produced in the bodies and the minds" ("La domination," 12).[20]

By approaching male domination in a thoroughly historical manner, Bourdieu is in a position to recognize that the specific manifestations of this trans-historical constant differ with time and place in terms of forms of expression and degree of obviousness, thereby opening up spaces for resistance, that is to say, for women's history.[21] Nonetheless, what interests him in particular are the invariants, such as gendering, the process of social construction of sexual difference, which always occurs through differentiation from the other socially constituted sex. In any given society, practices suitable to one's sex are encouraged and improper behavior discouraged, particularly in relation to the opposite sex; it is this apprenticeship in the legitimate uses of the body—excluding "from representations and practices everything that might evoke, particularly among men, properties assigned to the other category" ("La domination," 20)—that leads to the production of feminine women and of virile men. Since gendering is based on prohibitions regarding the other sex, "gendered bodies are necessarily politicized bodies, an embodied politics" (20).

The fundamental distinction between males and females in terms of socialization is that only boys are raised to acquire "the sense of honor that incites to rivalry with other men," the desire to dominate, the will to and love of power, which Bourdieu calls "libido dominandi": "[m]an holds the domination monopoly because he is trained to recognize the social games in which domination is at stake" ("La domination," 24). As a rule, the male *habitus* is built and realized only in relation to the reserved space in which the serious games of competition are played—games of honor like war, or, in differentiated societies, "all the games that offer fields of action to the libido dominandi in all its forms (economic, political, religious, artistic, scientific, etc)." One of the most interesting aspects of Bourdieu's theory of male domination is that men do not have it as easy as we could think. First, because, as we saw, they too have to be socialized—learning how to dominate is, in the end, just as difficult as learning the opposite—even if the anticipated benefits are not comparable. Second, because men are prisoners of their domination. Unlike women, they have the obligation to be taken by the seriousness of the serious social games if they want to conform to the definition of manhood. Third, because women represent a danger to their sense of honor, and not only in the sexual sense.

As a rule, women are socialized for a selfless, maternal role, and "being trained to grant others' worries priority over their own, when they participate in serious games, it is by proxy, that is in an exterior and subordinate position," through the emotional bond they have with male players (their fathers, husbands, sons, bosses). Those who managed to take their distance from that bond however, have a great strength: their lucidity, the entirely negative privilege of not being duped by the games in which male privileges are fought over, of not being taken by them, at least not directly. Like Virginia Woolf's Mrs. Ramsey in *To the Lighthouse*, the character Bourdieu chooses to illustrate this point, they can "watch the man-child's desperate efforts to play man and the despair that accompanies his failures with amused sympathy" ("La domination," 24). It is interesting to note here that unlike Rita Felski, who contends that "it is only certain women who have the luxury of perceiving the male/female divide as the foundational division simply because their own privileged class or race position remains unmarked and hence invisible" ("Doxa of Difference," 7), Bourdieu's analysis seems to grant women at large that ability.[22]

Symbolic Violence

Bourdieu accounts for the "hold of the patriarchy," the persistence of forms of male domination in contemporary Western societies, in part through symbolic violence, a milder form of violence that cannot function without the complicity of the oppressed to their own oppression, but that remains invisible to them. The fact that overt oppression is the most obvious form of domination does not mean that it is the only form of domination, or the most prevalent in modern societies. It remains nonetheless a dominant explanatory model for many feminist critics, those who portray women as victims of the patriarchy, the media, the beauty industry, and so on. Susan Faludi's popular concept of "backlash," for instance, is related to this model insofar as it seeks to explain women's failure to make headway in the 1980s in America through the "cold war against women" discreetly but relentlessly fought by conservative men at a time when the feminist movement was losing its momentum. The notion of "backlash" is based on a voluntarist understanding of social relations (since it implies a conscious effort on the part of these individuals to put women back in their place) and on an analytical model that conceives of relations of power in a Manichean way, as a relation between an active, powerful male agent and a passive, weak feminine one. The concept of symbolic violence is a most welcome alternative to that model.

Relations of domination, Bourdieu explains, work best when they are "somatized, that is inscribed as active ingredients in the bodies—in the way people stand, walk, move, gesture—as well as in the minds that perceive them" ("La domination," 29). Symbolic violence, which "is legitimate because it is mis-recognizable as violence and therefore mis-recognized," is "a body knowledge that entices the dominated to contribute to their own domination by tacitly accepting, outside of any rational decision or decree of the will, the limits assigned to them" (12). In the case of women, he argues, this type of bodily self-censure is more likely to surface "in the presence of men and in public places" and to be expressed through "modesty, timidity, or embarrassment."[23]

The political implications of this short analysis are rather staggering: "the liberation of victims of symbolic violence cannot be accomplished by decree" ("La domination,"12). The problem of underrepresentation of women in certain academic and professional fields thereby receives a clear answer: it is not the product of exclusion, but of "self-exclusion." As proof of the validity of this claim Bourdieu notes that "this embodied self-censorship is never quite as easily observed as when external constraints are lifted and formal liberties granted (right to vote, right to education, access to all professions including political ones): self-exclusion, often in the form of a 'vocation' or a 'calling' (negative as much as positive) takes over" (12). This self-exclusion can take the form of women "dropping out of the management rat race," as observed by the authors of *Breaking the Glass Ceiling*.[24] But the type of self-exclusion Bourdieu has in mind is probably best illustrated by the "negative and positive vocations" that make women "choose" certain professions over others, or concentrate in certain fields, like French, while avoiding others. Column 1 in table 7.3, which reproduces statistics from the 1996 *Chronicle of Higher Education Almanac* on the men-to-women ratio in various academic areas, provides a rough illustration of this phenomenon,[25] highlighting the striking underrepresentation of women professors in certain academic disciplines, like engineering, natural sciences, social sciences and business. Symbolic violence, in short, can be as efficient a form of violence as oppression, but it is much more difficult to detect.

For all its superficial resemblance to theories of oppression that put the blame on the victim, Bourdieu's approach differs significantly from them. For one thing, the function of the concept of symbolic violence is not to reinforce relations of domination by presenting them as inescapable or as eternal. Rather, it is to serve as an analytical tool, as a way to identify them, often where they are least expected, as a preliminary step toward their elimination. The fact that Bourdieu's theory of male domination is part of a larger theoretical ensemble serves as a safeguard against essentialism in many respects: because symbolic violence is not a concept devised to deal exclusively with the problem of male domination, but rather with all types of relations of domination (race, class, age, etc.), its protects against generalizations. Similarly, since gender is only one of the constitutive elements of a female *habitus*, there is no way to predict the effects of symbolic violence for women as a whole: "where one female agent will 'give in to timidity'" and be "betrayed by a body that recognizes an interdiction and acknowledges calls to order," another *habitus*, "product of a different history, will see injunctions and stimulating encouragements" ("La domination," 13).

What is still missing from this account of male domination, however, is some kind of explanation as to the genesis of the gendered *habitus* in modern societies. We may accept Bourdieu's description of the Kabyle world with its social rituals related to the fetishism of virility and the separation from the maternal world as

Table 7.3   Gender, Academic Disciplines and Potential Earnings

		Column 1		Column 2
Academic disciplines:	*Full-time faculty members*	*Men*	*Women*	*Average full professors' salaries at 4-year institutions*
Engineering:	24,680	93.5%	6.5%	Engineering: 75,598
Natural Sciences:	101,681	80.5%	19.1%	Sciences: 63,161
Social Sciences:	58,526	73.1%	26.9%	Social Sciences: 59,822
Business:	39,848	70.0%	30.1%	Business: 70,049
Fine Arts:	31,682	67.8%	32.2%	Fine Arts: 53,239
Communications:	10,344	56.9%	34.1%	Communications: 54,591
Humanities:	74,086	59.2%	40.8%	Humanities: 57,730
Education:	36,851	49.9%	50.1%	Education: 55,086
Health Sciences:	77,996	50.5%	49.5%	
Other:	27,466	66.2%	34.8%	
Occupationally specific programs:	15,395	84.9%	15.1%	
Agriculture and home economics etc.:	11,466	76.2%	23.8%	
Law:	7,337	65.1%	33.7%	
Total	526,222	67.5%	32.5%	

Sources: "Characteristics of Full-Time Faculty Members with Teaching Duties, Fall 1992." *Chronicle of Higher Education Almanac,* September 2, 1996 (from: U.S. Department of Education, "Faculty and Instructional Staff: Who Are They and What Do They Do?" (Study based on 817 colleges; full and part time; lecturers, no graduate students); "Average Faculty Salaries by Rank in Selected Fields at 4-Year Institutions, 1995–96" Source: College and University Personnel Association. *Chronicle of Higher Education Almanac,* September 2, 1996.

a means to institute man's domination by designating him as dominant early on in life, but it is not our world.[26] We may also accept the notion that centuries of history are embedded in our mental structures, but in that case, how are they activated in societies where rites have lost their magic, becoming parodies of former rites—think of bachelor parties or Christmas? In modern societies such as France, Bourdieu contends, the reproduction of the gendered order is assured through social institutions; it is "orchestrated" by the family, the church, the school, and the state.[27] All contribute to perpetuating the principle that arbitrarily divides the world in two and assigns only to males the social games that are worthy of being played.[28] Referring to Nancy Chodorow's work, he presents the family as the place where "the early experience of the sexual division of labor and of the legitimate representation of this division imposes itself" (*DM*, 92)—and where the most visible forms of male domination can still be observed (*DM*, 10). While no longer so overtly misogynous as in the past, the (Catholic) church continues to "act on the historical structures of the unconscious, notably through the symbolism of its sacred literature and liturgy" (*DM*, 93). As for the modern states, "they have inscribed all the fundamental principles of the androcentric vision in their family law, and particularly in the rules that define the legal status (*état civil*) of citizens" (94). Even government reproduces the "archetypal division between masculine and feminine," with its conservative, masculine right, and its liberal, feminine left (94). The educational system, which for Bourdieu plays a primary role in reinforcing the dominant principle of vision and division, also "inscribes the presuppositions of the patriarchal representation in its own hierarchical structures, all sexually connoted" (94).[29]

One of the most interesting insights to be gained from Bourdieu's work is indeed that the invisible line separating males from females is to be found everywhere, for instance in the academic field in the opposition between "hard," dominant disciplines like business, and "soft," dominated disciplines like French. Although they are no longer directly linked to sexuality proper, these "oppositions inscribed in the structure of social fields support and feed cognitive structures, practical taxonomies, often registered in systems of qualifying adjectives that allow for the production of value judgements, ethical, aesthetic and cognitive" (*DM*, 112). Seen from the dominant pole of the field, from the point of view of business or industrial leaders for instance, "the intellectual appears . . . as a being endowed with properties clearly marked as feminine, unrealism, angelism, irresponsibility (as evidenced in situations where such leaders take it upon themselves to lecture intellectuals and artists, and, as men typically do with women, 'to let them know what the real world is about' " (113). As dominated disciplines, the humanities seem to share the feminine privilege of lucidity, and therefore perhaps also the distinction of holding some kind of monopoly on critical thought. Like women, they are associated with symbolic rather than other forms of capital; like women, they tend to be involved only by proxy in the social games deemed most important.

Surveys like the one on "Pay and Benefits of Leaders at 475 Private Colleges and Universities," published in the October 23, 1998, issue of *The Chronicle of Higher Education* provide insights into the nature of the games deemed particularly worthy of being played (medicine and business) in the American academic field. The existence of these professional fields reserved almost exclusively to males delineates in a concrete fashion the arbitrary division of the world into two gendered halves. But such studies also show that the gendered hierarchies Bourdieu views as essential to the reproduction of our social unconscious divide all academic fields and disciplines: in medicine, for instance, surgery ranks higher than pediatrics.[30] Before reaching conclusions about the global feminization of a dominated discipline like French—as I did a little hastily at the beginning of this paper—then, a study of the structure of that field ought to be conducted to determine whether the most prestigious positions—those connoting intellectual achievement in the form of theoretical work, as well as the leadership positions associated with prestigious schools or departments—are occupied by males or females.

CONCLUSION

Bourdieu has repeatedly asserted that his work is bound to produce "disenchanting effects," and his examination of male domination is certainly no exception: the very analysis that has the merit of offering a clearer understanding of crucial feminist issues also has the disadvantage of making them appear more complex than they would first seem. As a result, concrete questions that appeared quite natural and pressing at first often lose their validity: in the absence of a more specific analysis of the distributions of positions in French, for instance, it becomes premature to ask the concrete, political question of whether an effort should be made to attract more males to the discipline. Much of the frustration produced by Bourdieu's work has to do with the realization that knowledge does not automatically translate into change. The perceived foreignness of the concept of leadership described at the beginning of this essay makes more sense once it is understood as constitutive of a female *habitus*, as the lucidity of "the spectator observing the storm from the security of the shore." But what to do concretely with that knowledge is unclear. As Toril Moi suggests in her comments on this aspect of Bourdieu's theory of male domination, no precise line of action, no recommended behavior, can be derived from this analysis. The problem is still there: "[w]omen who laugh at male self-importance in university seminars may find themselves constructed not as lucid critics of male ridicule, but as frivolous women incapable of understanding truly serious thought" (Moi, 1031).

Similarly, the very sophistication that makes this analytical approach so well equipped to resist essentialism seems radically inimical to immediate, concrete feminist action. It is intellectually gratifying to know that gendering tends to make women elect disciplines that do not have the "libido dominandi" as an entry prerequisite; that women are differently positioned in disciplines that are relatively close to (or far from) the pole of power in the academic field; that the relative liberty I have not to grant as much seriousness to the issue of leadership as women in the business field has as much to do with the fact that I am positioned in a discipline located far away from the pole of power as it has to do with gender; that for women in disciplines close to the field of power, this "liberty"—actually a virtue made out of necessity—is not an option, since failure to take the discourse on leadership seriously entails exclusion; or to understand, therefore, why all literature on that topic comes from the business field. But the realization that in any field, and in the social field at large, women are "still are separated from one another by economical and cultural differences that affect, among other things, their objective and subjective ways of experiencing and challenging male domination" (*DM*, 101) makes the goal of a unified feminist politics seem more elusive.

Observations of this kind are typically used to conclude that Bourdieu is "determinist," his theoretical focus on "reproduction" being perceived as antithetical to the goal of social change. But the perception that there is no room for change in Bourdieu's work is quite unjustified. In order to counter it, we may turn the tables around, and argue, as John Guillory does in this volume (see "Bourdieu's Refusal"), that, in the humanities in the U.S., "the very vehemence with which his perceived determinism is rejected can be said to express by contrast an intellectual ethos of *voluntarism*" (20)."[31] We may also consider that feminist theories and practices that appear quite subversive at first may turn out later to still be prisoner of the same voluntarist vision.[32] Or we may simply point out that Bourdieu himself conceives of his "knowledge revolution" as a contribution to feminist struggles, that he would like to see it "have an impact in practice, and in particular in the conception of strategies aimed at transforming the current state of material and symbolic power relations between sexes" (*DM*, 10).

What his work reveals, in the end, is less the impossibility of change than the immensity of the task at hand since "[o]nly a collective action aimed at organizing a symbolic struggle capable of questioning practically all the tacit presuppositions of the phallo-narcissistic vision of the world can lead to a rupture of the quasi-immediate agreement between embodied structures and objectified structures" ("La domination," 31). His conviction that social progress cannot happen overnight[33] seems justified in light of the difficulties that pave the road, and foremost among them, of the problems specific to the political field[34]—such as the uncanny ability political struggles have to produce effects where they are not intended.[35] As difficult to accept as it may be, cautious optimism may be indicated rather than revolutionary fervor in that case.

NOTES

1. Bourdieu's work on "Male Domination" was first published in article form in *Actes de la Recherche en Sciences Sociales* in 1990. It served as the basis for "Male Domination Revisited," published in the *Berkeley Journal of Sociology*, and his 1998 book, *La domination masculine (DM)*.

2. Lawrence Kritzman writes that in the postwar years "the study of French was first a mark of class status (the unfortunate syndrome of associating French with *finishing school*)" (9) [italics mine].

3. This lead story in the December 6, 1998, issue of the *New York Times* was based on a story first published in the June 6, 1997, issue of *The Chronicle of Higher Education* [italics mine].

4. See Levy, "Représentation." Bourdieu also argues that "in the field of international relations, . . . France occupies a position that can be qualified as 'feminine' in comparison with other countries, United States, England or Germany," a contention based on a study

by N. Panayotopoulos that shows that "in very different countries, Egypt, Greece or Japan, boys tend to go to these countries, girls to France, and also that students will go to the United States or England to study Economics, Technology and Law, and to France to study Literature, Philosophy and Humanities" (*DM*, 112, note 39). Unless otherwise indicated, translations are mine.

5. On this point, see the series of articles published in *differences: A Journal of Feminist Cultural Studies* on the issue to the French "parity movement," an organization mobilized around a single demand: the fifty-fifty representation of men and women in elected political assemblies.

6. Compared to these seventeen hundred entries for "leadership" in general, only fifty titles are listed under the rubric of "women leadership" in the library catalog at my institution.

7. See Morris, "Leaders, Leaders Everywhere."

8. See Scott, "Querelle des Femmes."

9. "[A] businessman is aggressive, but a businesswoman pushy; he's good on details, she's picky; he exercises authority diligently, she's power hungry . . ." (Loden, 38).

10. Loden would view my instinctive resistance to "leadership" as justified because "leadership" is overdetermined as masculine. But she would also emphasize my failure to envision "leadership" along feminine lines.

11. Although she does not like to see their work criticized as essentialist, Braidotti is vulnerable to Felski's critique that her work seeks to "recover the feminine within sexual difference, to generate an autonomous female imaginary" (Felski, "Doxa of Difference," 4).

12. Here is a striking example: "The subjective knowledge of what it means to be at the receiving end of racialized othering—whatever it means to individual people of color—is simply not accessible to white people, just as the subjective knowledge of what it means to be a woman—whatever it means to individual women—is ultimately inaccessible to men" (Ang, 60).

13. Consider, for instance, the following sentence in which Felski summarizes of one of the critiques of the concept of hybridity: "In this context, the trope of hybridity has been subject to criticism for effacing material conflicts between the colonizer and the colonized and denying the agency of the oppressed" ("Doxa of Difference," 14).

14. See Bourdieu, *La misère du monde*.

15. "Le soupçon préjudiciel que la critique féministe jette souvent sur les écrits masculins à propos de la différence entre les sexes est fondé" ("La domination," 4). See also *DM*, 123.

16. Or at least continued to do so in the 1950s when Bourdieu was conducting this research.

17. "Cet univers de discours et d'actes rituels tout entiers orientés vers la reproduction d'un ordre social et cosmique fondé sur l' affirmation ultra-conséquente du primat de la masculinité offre à l'interprète une image grossie et systématique de la cosmologie 'phallonarcissique' qui hante aussi nos inconscients" ("La domination," 4).

18. The direct reference to Lacan is omitted in the recent book version but it should be mentioned nonetheless as an example of Bourdieu's dismissiveness of Lacanian theory—and in particular of the analyst's inability to neutralize his own male unconscious. Bourdieu begins by quoting the following passage from "La signification du phallus" in La-

can's *Écrits*: "On peut dire que ce signifiant [le phallus] est choisi comme le plus *saillant* de ce qu'on peut *attraper* dans le réel de la copulation sexuelle, comme aussi le plus symbolique au sens littéral (typographique) de ce terme, puisqu'il y équivaut à la copule (logique). On peut aussi dire qu'il est par sa turgidité l'image du flux vital en tant qu'il passe dans la génération" (Lacan, 111). He then derides Lacan's reliance on "witticisms"—the "mots d'esprit" highlighted by Bourdieu in the quote—which, according to him, "only serve to give the appearance of logical necessity, or even scientificity, to social phantasms that can only be avowed in this scientifically sublimated form" ("La domination masculine," 4).

19. A passage from *Breaking the Glass Ceiling* points to the persistence of this economy of symbolic exchanges at the very heart of the business world. Having observed the central role that male sponsorship plays in women executives' ascent to the top, the authors wonder what motivates certain male executives to act that way. Their answer is that only executives who can afford to take the risk in the first place do so; for those executives whose power and prestige will not suffer if the sponsoring fails, the gains will be "more power and recognition, a grateful and up-and-coming executive, and the respect of their colleagues for spotting talent and for engineering the protégée's advancement for the good of the company" (132)—in other words, symbolic profits. In this example, there is something profoundly shocking in the suggestion that self-interest provides a better explanation than generosity for the male executive's behavior. In fact, everything stands in the way of recognizing this relation as a relation of domination.

20. As other forms of essentialism that "aim at attributing a biological nature to historically instituted social differences," Bourdieu mentions "ethnic or class racism."

21. For Bourdieu, in fact, the most important factor of change with regard to male domination is the result of the "the immense critical work of the feminist movement" (*DM*, 95).

22. While space does not allow me to develop this point, I think that an analysis of literary female characters, whether poor or rich, black or white, would confirm that claim. I am thinking in particular of female characters in Sembene Ousmane's or Maryse Condé's novels (*Xala, God's Bits of Wood, Ségou*) who are not white, educated, or rich but who share this lucidity, even if it is to various degrees.

23. "These bodily emotions, which may surface even outside the situations where they are required, are as many forms of anticipated acknowledgment of a bias, as many ways of subjecting to the dominant vision, even in spite of oneself, as many ways of feeling, sometimes as an interior dilemma and a splitting of the self, the subterranean complicity of social censorship and a body that resists the orders of consciousness and will" ("La domination masculine," 12–13, author's translation).

24. The paradox noted here is "why female managers and professionals are leaving many corporations at a higher rate than men" (Morrison et al., 6–7).

25. Rough, because to measure accurately the extent of the discrepancy that even such a cursory study reveals, one would have to abandon creative categories such as "health sciences"—which grant equal representation to nursing and medicine—and, more generally, any type of classification that fails to take into account the relation between gender and rank.

26. For Bourdieu, these rites do not establish a discontinuity between past and present, they do not mark the passage from boy to man, but rather, they reproduce the fundamental

divide of the social world in two, reinforcing the line of separation between men and women by distinguishing between those who are worthy of being subjected to them, on the one hand, and those who are not, on the other.

27. See "Le travail historique de déhistoricisation," in *DM*, 90–95.

28. It is so, Bourdieu explains, because the fundamental law of all serious games is the principle of equality in honor (isotomia): a challenge, if it is not addressed to a peer, to a man of honor, is not a challenge.

29. Bourdieu notes that the educational relation is founded on the same dichotomy: "the homology between the relation man/woman and the relation adult/child" (*DM*, 93).

30. Of the 234 "leaders" mentioned in the survey of thirty-nine research institutions I and II, less than 3 percent are women.

31. Singling out the emergence of cultural studies as particularly illustrative of that "ethos," and noting that "it has become increasingly important [in the U.S.] to justify academic practice by asserting it as the vehicle of political transformation," Guillory, echoing Bourdieu, cautions against "[l]iterary and cultural critics [who] would like to believe that vanguard theoretical discourses can lead to transformative struggles, by which the various forms of domination can be brought to an end" (21).

32. "Judith Butler herself now seems to reject the voluntarist vision of gender she seemed to propose in *Gender Trouble*, when she writes: " 'The misapprehension about gender performativity is this: that gender is a choice, or that gender is a role, or that gender is a construction that one puts on, as one puts clothes in the morning' " (quoted in Bourdieu, *DM*, 110, note 36).

33. "Only if it truly takes into account all effects of domination . . . can political action . . . probably in the long run . . . contribute to the progressive withering of male domination" (*DM*, 124–25).

34. See "Political Representation" (171–202) and "Delegation and Political Fetishism" (203–19), in *Language and Symbolic Power*.

35. Several illustrations of this problem can be found in *La domination masculine*. For instance, the struggle led by French feminists who demand equal representation of men and women in politics (parity) "has the merit of recalling that the universalist principle that founds constitutional law is not as universal as it seems" (*DM*, 124); but for Bourdieu, it may also serve to "reinforce the effects of another form of fictive universalism, insofar as it is bound to privilege women who come from the same regions of the social space as the men who are currently holding dominant positions" (124). Similarly, gays and lesbians—whose identity as a group is defined against "the dominant definition of the legitimate form of [sexual] practice as a relation of domination of the masculine principle (active, penetrating) over the feminine principle (passive, penetrated)" (130)—are thereby situated at the forefront of the symbolic struggles against the phallo-narcissistic vision of the world and in a position to contribute to the universalization of this struggle. But the fragmentation and ghettoization of the movement may well produce the opposite effect.

BIBLIOGRAPHY

Ang, Ien. "Comments of Felski's 'The Doxa of Difference': The Uses of Incommensurability." *Signs: Journal of Women in Culture and Society* 23, no. 1 (autumn 1997): 5–64.

Bourdieu, Pierre. *The Logic of Practice*. Stanford: Stanford UP, 1990.

————. "La domination masculine." *Actes de la Recherche en Sciences Sociales* 81/82, 1990: 2–31.

————. "Male Domination Revisited." *Berkeley Journal of Sociology: A Critical Review* 41 (1996–97): 189–203.

————. *La domination masculine*. Paris: Seuil, Collection Liber, 1998.

————. *The Logic of Practice*. Stanford: Stanford UP, 1980.

Braidotti, Rosi. "Comments of Felski's 'The Doxa of Difference': Working Through Sexual Difference." *Signs: Journal of Women in Culture and Society* 23, no. 1 (autumn 1997): 21–40.

Cornell, Drucilla. "Comments of Felski's 'The Doxa of Difference': Diverging Differences." *Signs: Journal of Women in Culture and Society* 23, no. 1 (autumn 1997): 41–56.

Felski, Rita. "The Doxa of Difference." *Signs: Journal of Women in Culture and Society* 23, no. 1 (autumn 1997): 1–21.

————. "Reply to Braidotti, Cornell, and Ang." *Signs: Journal of Women in Culture and Society* 23, no. 1 (autumn 1997): 64–69.

Gaspard, Françoise. "Parity: Why Not?" Translated by Jennifer Curtiss Gage. *Differences: A Journal of Femininst Cultural Studies* 9, no. 2 (1998): 93–104.

Gose, Ben. "Liberal-Arts Colleges Ask: Where Have the Men Gone?" *Chronicle of Higher Education*, June 6, 1997, A 35, 36.

Guillory, John. "Bourdieu's Refusal." In this volume.

Kritzman, Lawrence. "Identity Crises: France, Culture, and the Idea of the Nation." *SubStance* 76/77, nos. 1 and 2 (1995): 5–20.

Lacan, Jacques. "La signification du phallus." *Écrits II*. Paris: Editions du Seuil, 1966 (Collection Points): 103–15.

Levy, Francine. "La représentation (très) féminine du français-langue-étrangère." *The French Review* 66, no. 3 (February. 1993): 453–65.

Loden, Marilyn, *Feminine Leadership: How to Succeed in Business without Being One of the Boys*. New York : Times Books, 1985.

Moi, Toril. "Appropriating Bourdieu: Feminist Theory and Pierre Bourdieu's Sociology of Culture." *New Literary History* 22 (1991): 1017–49.

Morris, Polly. "Leaders, Leaders Everywhere." *The New York Times*, August 3, 1998: A21.

Morrison, Ann, Randall White, Ellen Van Velsor, and the Center for Creative Leadership. *Breaking the Glass Ceiling: Can Women Reach the Top of America's Top Corporations?* Addison-Wesley Publishing, 1992.

Scott, Joan Wallach. " 'La Querelle des Femmes' in the Late Twentieth Century." *differences: A Journal of Femininst Cultural Studies* 9, no. 2 (1998): 70–92.

8

Habitus Revisited: Notes and Queries from the Field

Caterina Pizanias

INTRODUCTION

During the 1990s, discussions of identity, race, gender, ethnicity, and sexuality have increasingly taken *center* stage in the Canadian academic, artistic, and public domains. The search for and validation of identity have emerged as distinctive features of political as well as artistic discourses: identity matters, and culture is seen as central to identity formation and sustenance. My general interest as a scholar has been to lay the grounds for a systematic exploration of how aspects of gender, race, sexuality, and ethnicity are negotiated within contemporary art worlds—social spaces that are fundamentally hierarchical, agonistic, rule bound, and Eurocentric. Specifically, my research has focused on the ways in which women artists have negotiated the obstacles of an increasingly challenging and challenged identity discourse and art practice. Regarding my present involvement with theories of the "body," I am simply responding to the preoccupation of women artists, themselves immersed in examinations of the symbolic significance of the gendered body, both as a metaphor of social relations and as a sensory and sensual being. I am particularly interested in what goes on in the "gap" between the discursive construct, "the body," and the affective experience of embodiment.

In the 1990s, examinations of the body have become productive sites for analyzing aspects of contemporary culture in general, and issues of identity and difference in particular. They have also become battlegrounds for position-claiming within both the public arena and feminist disciplinary and artistic practices: the body has been made to carry so much of the "burden of truth" (Probyn 1991, 111). Once I became immersed in the contemporary field of "body art"—art

145

that is mostly installational and highly sexualized, such as performance, video, cybernetic, and combinations thereof—I realized that the time had come to re-read, rewrite stories, shift alliances, change positions and in the process create spaces for movement within, around and across the already "given and said" about art practice and sociology. And long before I had become interested in body art, I had already committed myself to recording the work of contemporary women artists, to concentrating on synchronic tensions rather than diachronic breaks, to understanding agency as it plays itself out among agents who have no say in the establishment of the artistic field. My theoretical motivation has been to solve contextual puzzles and to be of use to the community of women artists.

Throughout all this, my feminism, which implies the need for yet-to-be-realized structural changes, has brought me time and again to Pierre Bourdieu. Although it is true that Bourdieu's artistic preoccupations have mostly centered around classical modernist concerns and that his aesthetic experiences have been understood as involving experiences of form, his treatments of the field and its affiliated concepts have proven to me their efficacy, malleability, and transportability by their usefulness in examinations of contemporary determinate situations where real agents struggle for innovation and legitimation.[1] In his essay on philosopher Martin Heidegger, Pierre Bourdieu speaks of discourse as being "the product of a compromise between an expressive interest and a censure constituted by the very structure of the field within which the discourse produces itself and within which it circulates."[2] My project is such a product. I have appropriated Bourdieu's concepts of the field and *habitus* in order both to document and to analyze contemporary artistic phenomena, but also to reopen questions generally considered resolved or nonresolvable within sociology and art and culture—questions of value, identity, power, and community.[3] This essay is a report on this ongoing journey through various fields of artistic production. It articulates my present position—that of itinerant academic—and my rhetorical strategies will reflect my appropriation of canonical texts, tempered by my acquired "disposition" of a "novice" (awaiting "consecration" to the ever-decreasing available spaces within the North American academy) and the "functioning ethos" of feminist politics.

This chapter started its life in response to a call for papers for the April 1995 conference entitled "Pierre Bourdieu: Fieldwork in Culture," held at Duke University.[4] At the time, I felt compelled to enter the fray of tallying up the blind spots and filling in the lacunae in Bourdieu's work, while steadfastly proclaiming my hunch that his conceptual formulations are more "feminist friendly" than are those of Michel Foucault. I could and can sustain that Janus-like "novitiate" space partly because "novices"—if they are to succeed in their initiation efforts—must follow the lead of those holding "consecrated" positions, and partly because of the number of years I have spent in the field putting Bourdieu's formulations ("Trois états," 1979, 3–6) "to work" without ever becoming disappointed. At the same time that the discourses of "otherness" and "body art" were gaining *center* stage, a peculiar form of academic discourse has been developing around Pierre Bourdieu: concurrent with the exponential growth of the English translations of his works were the efforts to discredit him for having failed to examine or do whatever each of his detractors was examining or doing in their own practice.[5] He may have attained this dubious status because of his "methodological polytheism" (Wacquant 1992, 30), or his "quasi-monomaniacal insistence on the necessity of the reflexive turn" (42), or his long-winded paragraphs, or his abrasive characterizations of other theorists. Whatever the reason(s) might be, finding faults with or giving underhanded compliments to his work has become a discursive field of its own within English-speaking academic fields. This chapter is presented as a "time out" from the discursive agonistics and one-upmanships, a time instead to be used to tell you some stories from the field. They are about my encounters with two artistic projects by two women artists in two different North American artistic fields.

historically it is the body of the other that is made to tell the truth of the time.

—Elspeth Probyn[6]

The most important gift feminism has given to women is permission to tell our own stories, to break the age-old taboo of silence. During the formative years of second-wave feminism, before its intellectualization by postmodernism and psychoanalysis and before theories of the body became the vogue in the art world, New York artist Carolee Schneemann was breaking taboos (when breaking taboos still made sense, in the 1960s) and telling stories about the female body in her performance work, as early as 1963, by deploying her eroticized body in/ as her work. She has described her work of that period as making "a gift of my body to other women: giving our bodies back to ourselves" (1979, 194).

Giving their bodies back has been the core of the artistic work of *Kiss & Tell,* the lesbian collective of Persimmon Blackbridge, Lizard Jones, and Susan Stewart based in Vancouver, Canada. *Kiss & Tell* started as a group in 1984 and its political roots are in the antipornography movement. *Drawing the Line* (1988) was the group's first collaborative artistic effort. A photo installation of one hundred photographs of Persimmon and Lizard taken by Susan, it covered a wide variety of lesbian erotic images—inviting the viewers to see/think/decide how far the "line" can be drawn before censorship may begin. Their second, and most controversial, work was the video *True Inversions* (1993), created and first shown at the Banff School for the Arts, as part of a live performance that included video projections. Their book, *Her Tongue on My Theory* (1994), is the best source of documentation, description, and reflection on their work. Their work is shown, performed, and/or written with intellectual clarity and wit, consciously working against the grain and the law, employing and marking the "unmarked" in the service of political commitment toward their queer community.

Most of the women in "Lovers and Warriors" are lesbians, and for lesbians the mere experience of being "seen" in a context we create and control is a unique and powerful experience. Representations of lesbians created by lesbians are extremely rare and difficult to find, even for lesbians. Until very recently, the possibility of discovering lesbian texts relied on the ability to de-code meanings, deeply imbedded to the point of assimilation, in heterosexual productions. Part of what I hope to accomplish with this work is to explore what a lesbian text might look like as it occupies a traditional form, in this case, classical photography. The second part of this equation is the occupation of public space in a bid to overturn exclusion. Toward that end I have enlisted the support and help of the women in these photographs, women whose stake in being visible is as urgent as my own.[7]

That is how Susan Stewart introduced her solo work, a photo installation entitled *Lovers and Warriors: Aural/Photographic Collaborations* (1993), shown in an alternative gallery in Vancouver in 1993. The installation was produced in collaboration with twenty-five women from within Vancouver's queer community, whose ages ranged from nineteen to fifty. Their races represented the gamut of the city's multiethnic community and they were sexually polymorphous—dykes, butches, femmes, transgendered individuals, S and M practitioners, and sex workers, as well as women scarred by disease or violence. Susan had long collaborated with these women on community issues; none of them was trained as an artist. But she believed that even though they did not see themselves as artists, they had skills to explore issues of gender, marginality, and the politics of photographic representation, especially of lesbians. All of them wanted to "claim back" queer bodies and their pleasures, desires, and fantasies from their "fashionable," mainstream appropriations. Appropriating queer bodies, habits, and stories has been rather *de rigeur* in North America, except that the images produced are of a sort that can easily be consumed by the mostly homophobic "male gaze." Stewart worked closely with her collaborators over a period of three years, first by showing them her previous work, so that they knew what sort of art she produced. Then, if they were still interested in continuing with the project, they chose how they wanted themselves to be "represented"—the setting, the personas, the costumes—as well as the stories they wanted told about their lives. Stewart photographed and taped the stories. The women had the final say as to approval of the photos shown, and some withdrew from the project altogether.

The installation consisted of seventy-five black-and-white photographs accompanied by an hour's audiotape of stories. When it was shown, the photographs—exemplary specimens of modernist style—were arranged on all the gallery walls, and headphones were available so visitors could (if they chose) listen to the narratives as they were looking. Neither the photographs (arranged in groups of varied numbers) nor the stories were homogeneous in their content, making clear to the viewers that there is no "core" lesbian identity, psyche, body, pleasures, or memories. Stewart made sure not only that marginalized women were able to tell their stories within a "consecrated" space, but also, by recording the stories non-con-

Above: *Prometheus* (1993) 16″ × 20″. Page 150: *Janet* (1993) 16″ × 20″. Both photos are black and white silver prints by Susan Stewart. Courtesy of the artist.

secutively vis-à-vis the photographs on the wall, she effectively disrupted our culture's pervasive habit of putting faith in the "truth" of the image, and posited that lesbians should be able to tell different stories about their bodies and pleasure, stories that undermine the status quo (queer or not). Susan told me that she "felt there were lots of stories, little fragments I was interested in expressing among friends, who I felt were remarkable people who are completely unrepresented culturally. Putting it together, I thought would be a fascinating mix."[8]

It was a fascinating story, but it was a story told out of its time. After that one showing, whose opening was celebrated in grand and joyous style by the collaborators and their friends, the exhibit was quietly (no reviews) and quickly closed down. Both the queer and the straight community had problems with the exhibit's treatment of sexual difference, not as a resolved narrative but as a question posed. The queer memories and stories—clear and powerful—and images—visually bold and exciting—were spoken and shown neither as deviant nor as watered-down metaphors within disciplinary boundaries: they were given as "jolts" for the jaded eyes and inattentive minds of "anything goes" postmodernity. As if claiming the position of the speaker for her unconsecrated friends was not "uppity" enough, Stewart's decision to "scramble" the narrative channels between the visual/formal (modernist) aspect of the installation and the aural telling of stories from the sexual underclass of mainstream society brought about a "punishment" that was both swift and expected: uppity artists and unruly genders were sent back into their closets. *Lovers and Warriors*, now renamed *Queer Ethnographies,* has started a successful run in Germany: In May 1997 it was shown to positive reception at the West Werk Gallery in Hamburg, and it had another run at the Frauen-*Kulturzentrum* in Munich during autumn 1997.

A hi-tech aborigine tripping-walkabout on the WWWeb
land in the long gone 90's. Accidentally I swallow my golf
ball-size camera. Caught in my throat,
dis-framed. Spit out the camera, I
split my legs.
Legs wide open at the end of the
bowling lane, the ball runs toward me. . . .
HACK THE CODE, BOWL ME OVER.

—Shu Lea Cheang, 1995[9]

Bowling Alley: Power, Access, and Desire[10] is an interactive/collaborative installation organized by the Walker Art Center in Minneapolis, Minnesota, in fall 1995 and winter 1996. It linked the museum with a local bowling alley and the World Wide Web. Shu Lea Cheang is an artist who describes herself as a "cyberhomesteader managing a digital existence via an e-mail address." She sees the Internet as being "mostly about community" and on a number of occasions has described the bowling lane as a "concept for an old communal space where locals meet face-to-face for a night out. Stretching the concept, taking my imagery of the bowling lane as my imagery of the information superhighway, I am trying to construct a new form of community in cyberspace."[11] Cheang, a native of Taiwan, has been living and working in New York since 1979. She is a founding member of the *Paper Tiger Television Collective* and has produced *Deep Dish TV,* a national satellite public-access network. Before coming to Minneapolis, she had been exhibited at the Whitney Museum of American Art, the Museum of Modern Art, the New Museum of Contemporary Art, the International Center of Photography Midtown, the Brooklyn Museum, the Studio Museum in Harlem, and the American Museum of the Moving Image, as well as in many of New York's "in" alternative galleries. She has also exhibited in other major U.S. art *center*s, such as San Francisco, Los Angeles, Chicago, and Boston, and has participated in international shows in Portugal, France, Germany, Austria, Japan, and Australia. She has received federal (NEA) and foundation (Rockefeller) grants for her work.

For the *Bowling Alley*, Cheang came in 1994 to Minneapolis to meet with a number of gay, multiracial, lesbian, transgendered artists from a variety of media; she chose ten with whom she was to work via e-mail, and built "her" cybercommunity. Out of a three-month collaboration, a 226K e-mail correspondence record was amassed. While in Minneapolis, she shot ten brief Quicktime movie vignettes from scenarios developed in collaboration with the ten artists. When some of the artists balked, Cheang exhorted them to "Write me a bedtime story"—"Drop that damn 10-pound ball and be lifted into cyberspace where we can *play*. . . . You're claiming a bowling lane/a new communal space on the net. In the cyberzone, *identity is in disguise. Power play, power abuse,* which do *you* choose?" (emphasis mine). In the accompanying catalogue, we learn from Marlina Gonzalez-Tamrong, the installation's curator, that Shu Lea took "their words and images which she transforms and incorporates into the complex, multifaceted operation of the installation."[12] The complexity was negotiated with the help of an installation cybernetic architect, and three web artists. The installation's costs came close to a quarter of a million dollars[13] and were financed by a variety of telecommunication companies.[14] Describing this installation will require extra space, and patience from the reader.[15]

For the project's run in Gallery 7 at the Walker Art Center, a fifty-foot-long lane was built from stainless steel. On this a bowling ball traveled continuously back and forth at high speed and even higher noise levels; at the end of the steel lane a video player projected random images from the Quicktime movies made of the participating artists ready to bowl, bowling pins, and bits of texts jumping all over the wall, such as *"open those holes," "Deep Penetration," "Slam," "three fingers deep," "What comes to your mind before all breaks loose?"* Gallery 7 at the Walker was connected with Lane 5 at the Bryant Lake Bowl and visitors in Gallery 7 could watch a live video-transmission of bowlers on Lane 5; the latter, if they bowled expertly—that is, if their balls did not jump lanes—could effect random changes on the video projections within Gallery 7. A Macintosh Power Book computer sat on what looked like an actual bowling-alley scorekeeping table. If a gallery visitor became bored being dependent on someone bowling successfully on Lane 5 to activate visual changes, she or he could either watch the ball go back and forth on the steel lane or "bowl online" by using the computer. Bowlers who dropped by the site via the web could choose among a menu of options to also bowl and effect visual and textual changes projected onto the walls of Gallery 7.

Let us now take a "virtual" walk through the sites. Let us start in Gallery 7 and let us pretend our visit takes place during the *Alley's* run. Nothing much will be happening other than the ball going up and down if we are visiting Gallery 7 during hours when no one is bowling on Lane 5 or participating via the Internet; conversely, at other times, people might be bowling effectively on Lane 5, and/ or "invading" from their home computers and no one may be present in Gallery 7 to witness or effect visual and textual changes. Next, let us pay a visit to the Bryant Lake Bowl. This alley, like so many others once the domain of greasy fries and draught beer, is now the hip, happening hangout of the "cool" crowd. Some might be bowling on Lane 5 and effecting changes on the Quicktime vignettes or the texts provided by the collaborating artists.

And then we can finally move on to the persons at home—like myself—who can visit the website. Before I could join this community on the superhighway I had to be connected to the web, had to have learned of the project through an art-affiliated source (cybernetic or not), and had to have at least Netscape Navigator 1.1, 4MB of RAM, a fast modem, and unlimited time, patience, and stamina to sit in front of my monitor hoping to enter the site at a time when the server was not down, or when the screen did not freeze on me.

Upon entering the site, one is given preliminary descriptive statements about the project and asked to "join the ever-formulating self-scrambling, hypertexts on POWER, ACCESS & DESIRE." There are five icons to choose from: *Overview* (of the Bowling Alley three-site installation); *Spare* (which traverses the Minneapolis Ten's texts); *Next* (which continues through a single message); *Write-In* (by which to write into the site, adding to the body of alien texts); and *Strike* (which remixes a scramble of Minneapolis Ten and alien texts).

After the *Overview*, which responds every time, the next icon that almost always opens up is the *Strike*; quite a few times I entered *Spare*, a couple of times I entered *Write-In*, but not once did I get into the *Next*. The option I wanted to exercise most was *Write-In*, thinking and hoping that I might get some text with a semblance of sequence, with fonts that were readable, and have a two-way exchange—however fluid or fragmented—so that I might get a sense of, or join, this community). After many attempts I decided that I must be doing something wrong (or not doing something necessary), so I then solicited the help of a friend with a faster computer and a better disposition to surf the net—and between the two of us, we got a better "hit" record. But even with a better record of opening boxes, my interactivity level did not change at all: I could not go back to a specific image or text if I wanted to, could not click on a particular artist, and when I was given (twice only) the opportunity to "write-in," my text was swallowed up, probably to be spit out during some other random encounter with the program. There was never two-way communication. Although as a person signing on from home I was not passive in a literal sense, I was not allowed to chat, choose, or contest—I was simply the "hired labor" activating the program. But I pressed on, entering the site, hoping to get better at deciphering and decoding the "texts" that changed every ten seconds, interrupted by images of body parts, bowling balls, and pins fluttering all over. No matter how many times I tried to get a "taste" of this community, I could not do so. The construction of this cyber-community was designed in such a way that Shu Lea Cheang, her ten Minneapolis collaborators, and the website's engineers, architects, and designers were the only persons allowed access and membership. The rest of us were programmed to be spectators of fragmented bodies and heteroglossic texts, very carefully controlled by a solid logocentric design funded by a coterie of corporations not known for their ethos of social and political progress. *Bowling Alley* ran its full course, and Shu Lea Cheang, supported by another Rockefeller Foundation grant, is working on her next cyberart project—about the violent death of Brandon Teena, a transgendered person from Nebraska.

Space does not allow me to carry out a more complete analysis of the two projects presented above, but if we are to make any sense of their differences, we need to take a short diachronic break into the historical and national beginnings of their respective artistic fields. According to authors such as Andreas Hüyssen (1990), Serge Guilbaut (1985), and Peter Bürger (1990), the modernity that began its trajectory in the 1850s in Paris was led "inexorably to New York—the American victory in culture following on the heels of victory on the battlefields of World War II" (Hüyssen 1990, 241). Before the modern landed in New York, both the United States and Canada had looked out toward Europe for patterning their art institutions and for legitimating their aesthetic choices. During the last quarter of the nineteenth century, the role that the state was to play as patron of the arts was bifurcated: in the United States the funding of public museums was quickly taken up by wealthy industrialists, while in Canada the state has remained—steadfastly following the lead of nineteenth-century Britain—virtually the sole patron of the arts, with some occasional corporate sponsorship. Three of the (still) leading institutions—all in New York—were established during the interwar years: the Museum of Modern Art in 1929, the Whitney Museum in 1930, and the Guggenheim in 1939. All three exhibited and collected living artists, thus upsetting the structural balance that had existed, up to that point, among bohemian artists, galleries that promoted them, and museums that conserved their "consecrated" art. Each museum's institutional concerns reflected the concerns of their founding families, and their role in the wider society was rather limited. The effect that the Great Depression had on American society was to be felt in the art worlds also (Harris 1993). The widening social use of and role for the arts had its beginnings in the Works Projects Administration, where the government "hired" artists to create art that reflected "Americanism" and became a matter of national pride. Similar changes took place in Canada, but to a much lesser degree. The closest thing to the "robber barons" of the United States that Canada could claim were the viceroys managing the Canadian Pacific Railway, who at about the same time were giving "free" passage across Canada to artists interested in painting "picturesque" renditions of the Rocky Mountains—renditions that were to be used in the establishment of a "national culture" in Canada (see Tippett 1990; Pizanias 1993).

This turn of events, which provided steady employment for many artists (more in the United States than in ~~Canada~~, resulted in a new series of structural changes in the artistic fields—especially in New York, where artists were seen as "social assets" and not mere "bohemians" (Zukin 1982). This increase in numbers and social status furthered still more the competition between museums and galleries for artists and patronage. In the years after World War II this competition reached such a "frenzy" that museums became "promoters" of artists and artistic styles rather than "conservers" of "consecrated" art (Zukin 1982, 430). Zukin quotes a curator from the MOMA as describing the rapid change of styles, stars, and general hype as "pure publicity" and "fashion" (430).[16] In Canada, meantime, a "pro-American" sentiment was growing in the central plains, fuelled more by an "anti-eastern" (Canada) sentiment than by an affinity with what was happening in New York (Pizanias 1993). Canada's artists still looked outward, but this time their "gaze" was split—looking to England but mostly to New York.

The 1960s were heady times for the arts in the United States (Zukin 1982; Hüyssen 1990; Dinkla 1996). A number of concurrent events were taking place, changing the overall ethos of American society and in the process leaving their mark on the arts. The anti-Vietnam War movement, along with movements led by blacks and women, brought about changes in the education system which resulted in the democratization and professionalization of the arts, which in turn brought about changes in the structure and capital of the artistic field. More departments of art were established, and they graduated more agents to fill positions in an expanding field, "making cultural consumption both accessible to many people . . . and thus lucrative to business investors" (Zukin 1982, 425). In 1960, the National Endowment for the Arts and the Humanities was established, with an arts policy described by one of its deputy chairs as "not one that has evolved in order to address the needs of the arts in particular, but rather as a cockleshell bobbing in the wake of many much larger vessels of public policy" (Cohnstaedt 1989, 52).[17] As more players and agendas entered the field, New York's major museums underwent another crisis of identity: not only did museums act as galleries, curators as critics, critics as curators, and artists as both critics and curators in the established institutions and the exponentially emerging "parallel" or "artist-run" spaces (Zukin 1982, 431), but the circulating capital remained the same, making competition more fierce. As a result, some New York artists, influenced by the "Duschamp-Cage-Warhol axis" (Hüyssen 1990, 240) tried to revive the heritage of the European avant-garde by attempting to integrate, once again, art and life. But their efforts to incorporate the popular expressions of pop, rock and roll, and sexual liberation movements were quickly absorbed by the entertainment industries. In 1957, Canada got its NEA equivalent, the Canada Council, resulting from internal squabbles about cultural identity among its "founding peoples" (the French and English) and the ever-increasing number of new immigrants from non-European countries of origin. The difference in political temperament between the two countries is exhibited in a statement on the council's arts policy, as one that "protected artists and arts organizations from decisions politically, rather than artistically based" (Cohnstaedt 1989, 52).[18] In any event, the end of the 1960s found artists on both sides of the forty-ninth parallel safely ensconced within the middle class. As Zukin tells it, the transformation of the artists "from 'beat' to 'bohemian' to middle class" was finally complete (1982, 435).

The 1970s found North American art worlds populated by many more participants, competing for increasingly diffused rewards (because of the lack of changes in the circulating capital) and overlapping spaces of the possible. During this time, the problematic of "otherness" (Hüyssen 1990, 269) asserted itself in the social and cultural arenas—notions of gender, ethnicity, race, sexuality, and a host of similar "markings" took *center* stage. They were (and still are) mostly examined within variants of ahistorical postmodernism that fit snugly within the basic apolitical character of North American public culture. Under the general rubric of "postmodernism," questions of power, subjectivity, and postcoloniality have succeeded in raising doubts and effectively destabilizing the *textual* authority of modernism. I claim that despite the fact that the number of exhibits by women, persons of color, and other minorities has steadily increased, most of them are politically "marked" as "separate but unequal" exhibits that take place during Black History months, Native Awareness weeks, and other similar events (Berger 1992)—in other words, a game of "musical chairs has been played in the last quarter of a century." Queer art has managed to avoid this sort of segregation but did not escape the ire of the political right, which has succeeded in undermining the public funding support for the arts in both Canada and the United States, even though funds going to queer minorities are minuscule. They have succeeded in their efforts for basically two reasons: one, because high art does not occupy the privileged space it used to (Hüyssen 1990, 269) and two, because its public has shrunk to its lowest levels—art and its public do not pose a political threat to the reinvigorated political right.

DISCUSSION

Crisis is a necessary condition for a questioning of doxa but it is not in itself a sufficient condition for the production of critical discourse.

—Pierre Bourdieu[19]

Both of the artists I have discussed are lesbians. They use various technologies in their installational and collaborative practice and are committed to exploring aspects of queer desire as well as bettering the social lot of queer communities.

Both attempted to answer the question, "What is queer?" The visual aesthetic sensibility of the projects I presented is basically modernist in nature. Stewart's photographs for *Lovers and Warriors* are classically shot, processed, and framed black-and-white photographs. And despite *Bowling Alley's* MTV/videogame character, a character seen by Cheang as evidence of having overcome the high versus low (art), private versus public, and other such modernist binarisms— remains resolutely modernist: I, the cyberbowler-viewer, am stuck in front of a rectangular two-dimensional computer screen, manually moving a mouse, focusing my penetrating gaze on disembodied body parts, fragmented texts, and abstract images, all of them chosen and prearranged for my passive consumption, delivered to me in a moment-by-moment linear mode, when the system was not crashing—which, more often than not, it was.

Despite the commonalities among the artists and in their projects, a host of dissimilarities can also be detected. Although Stewart's collaborators came from outside the artistic community, she gave them total creative freedom in putting forward images of themselves and in speaking their heretical life stories toward the construction of enunciative positions as multiply marked "singular" bodies and subjects. In providing "speaking" places for her collaborators, Susan Stewart crossed boundaries between life and art by turning the material of life into the material of her art. In the process not only did she claim legitimacy for her heterodoxical project, but her doing so was a real (however unconscious) power play at rearranging the field—immediately recognized as such, which is why her silencing was prompt and effective. On the other hand, Shu Lea Cheang's collaborators were carefully culled from an already-consecrated pool of artists; they were given instructions on what to imagine (power, access, desire) and how (in cyberspace).[20] Their contributions were appropriated by Cheang—fragmented bodies, stories, texts—and incorporated into a "cool" cyberdesign of a dystopian community where embodiment is a database, desire lacks unity, all newcomers' access is severely limited, and, as such, power lacks any counterforce. Her fragmented narratives are never reconciled, her body parts never hold together. By trying so hard to incorporate into her art the postmodernist tenets of fragmentation and heteroglossia, she succeeds in giving us another instance of somatophobia (very modernist) and consequently of (very postmodernist) apolitical indifference. Despite her radical rhetoric, Cheang is "typical of the 'cool' deracinated bohemian of the metropoles" left only with "nostalgia for integration and a cult of the utopian community" (Fowler 1997, 24), nostalgia that fails to give us any points of purchase for feminist involvement(s).

New York has managed, over the years, to hold on to its excess of capital, which has been circulating among its (still modernist) institutions on a rather steady basis—despite minor crises of identity and/or public funding. The field there has been able to weather rhetorical attacks on its institutions and practices because it has successfully isolated itself from the real problems, such as poverty, of the wider social field. Over the years this removal from the vicissitudes of life has engendered an apolitical *habitus*; which is why the crises experienced in contemporary artistic fields cannot produce a "critical discourse" (Bourdieu, cited in Moi 1991, 1027). For example, despite the fact that many more women have taken up positions of power—as, for instance, curators or directors of galleries and museums—the "stars" of the field are still men, exceptional cases such as Cheang's notwithstanding. The institutions that train artists and/or develop the hard- and software of cyberart are capitalist, patriarchical, and least interested in aspects of art as/in technology. The mechanisms of selection still in place reward competencies that will reproduce the status quo, with an occasional controversy tolerated—controversies have been good for business (Rissatti 1990; Lemmon 1993–94). Vancouver, on the other hand—sitting on the other side of the continental margin—has only one major institution, the Vancouver Art Gallery, an institution dependent on public support and not keen on any controversy, especially on queer identity. Having an M.A. from New York University accompanied by a series of exhibits at all major New York museums, as well as museums in San Francisco, Los Angeles, Chicago, Boston, Minneapolis, and a host of other cities across Europe and Asia engenders a different *habitus* and allows one to amass the right capital, in contrast to having an M.A. from the University of British Columbia and a series of exhibits in parallel or artist-run galleries in Canada, Australia, and Germany. Both artists exhibit the embodiment of a post-1960s North American field *habitus* based on dispositions acquired through a shared training in the dominant discourses of art history and criticism; but as we saw, there exist also enough differences in the national fields and respective local art and queer communities to allow for specific agent differences, as in Susan Stewart's case, to develop a critical–oppositional sense to the "game of art" that offered a faint glimpse (and a hope) that a political critical dialectic may yet be developed.[21] The same hope is held out for the cyberians but not before they let go of the clichés fed to them by the technocrats regarding the dissolution of all the social shackles awaiting us all—especially minorities—in cyberspace.

I would like to believe that even in the rather impressionistic description and discussion above, the reader will see how Pierre Bourdieu's theoretical constructs allow one to describe differences and to detect changes in the structural distribution of capital and their manifestations in practice (*habitus*). Neither the fields nor capital and *habitus* remain static within the changing wider social field. Of course, we would not know that from reading some of the latest entries into the discursive Bourdieuland, such as those by Judith Butler (1996, 1997) or Bridget Fowler (1997), with the first one toiling in the epistemological realm of examining *habitus* as truth[22] and the other still filling the lacunae in Bourdieu's work and trying to salvage for pop culture a position of radical critique. A welcome change has been seen in David Swartz's *Culture and Power* (1997) and the contributions to the *Modern Languages Quarterly* (1997), especially those by John Guillory and Toril Moi (as always) in the ever-increasing Bourdieusian scholarship in the United States. What is at stake here is not *habitus* as conceptual truth, but *habitus* as generator of the multiple strategies within an agent's trajectory through a field that is not static. And it is this doubleness of the *habitus* in Bourdieu's schemata that allows one to have a foot both in and out of the field, in and out of deconstruction. Understanding *habitus* as practical mastery, one can occupy the internal position of a participant in a field and the external position of a critical observer. At the present moment, when we have given up the "truth" of the grand narratives and we continue thus to describe ourselves as de-centered and fragmented, we need to develop a feminism that can discover new centers and defend certain truths on which we may ground a better common future.[23] Pierre Bourdieu's efforts to transcend gaps between practical knowledge and universal structures carry the promise of "bring(ing) the undiscussed into discussion" (Moi 1991, 1027), which reproduces on another level the doubleness of *habitus*. And as long as the artistic field acts as "sacred island systematically and ostentatiously opposed to the profane, everyday world of production, a sanctuary for gratuitous, disinterested activity in a universe given over to money and self-interest" (*OTP*, 197), we can neither resolve the contradictions between everyday life and art, nor afford to remain lost in theoreticist examinations of the field and *habitus*—if we are interested in political changes. See you in my field travels.[24]

NOTES

The writing of this chapter was made possible by the support of the Calgary Institute for the Humanities, University of Calgary, while I was a visiting research fellow in 1997. For the history of this chapter, see note 4.

1. See Bourdieu and Delsaut 1975; Bourdieu 1979a, 1979b, 1980, 1985, 1991, 1994, and 1996.

2. Pierre Bourdieu, quoted in Derek Robbins 1991, 4.

3. See Pizanias, 1996a, 1996b.

4. Subsequently, a version of it was "performed," using slides and narratives as shown and heard in the exhibit's one-and-only showing, under the title "Telling Sexual Stories: The Politics of Art, Community, and Identity" as the "Saturday Seminar on Pierre Bourdieu" in autumn 1995, in Vancouver. Reworked again, it was published in the journal *Theory and Psychology* 6, no. 4 (1996): 647–65, under the title "*Habitus*: from the Inside Out and the Outside In." It was reprinted in *The Body and Psychology*, edited by Henderikus J. Stam, London: Sage, 1998: 141–59. Subsequent to my residency at the Banff School of the Arts, the "cyber" aspects of the research were added. First, I tried my ideas at the Sixth Biennial Symposium on Arts and Technology in New London, Connecticut, in the winter of 1997 under the title "The View from Nowhere: Digitalization, Body Art, and the Symbolic Economies of Cyberspace"; later, I presented an enlarged version— "Considering the Prospect(s) of On-line Fields of (Techno)-Cultural Production"—at the conference on "Bourdieu: Language, Culture, and Education" at the University of Southampton in spring 1997.

5. To get a flavor of this problematic, see and compare Nice (1978), Wacquant (1992, 1993), and Bourdieu (1993).

6. Probyn 1991, 115.

7. Stewart, artist's statement for *Lovers and Warriors* exhibit, private correspondence.

8. Stewart, interview with the author, Vancouver, 3 October 1995.

9. Cheang, artist's statement appearing on the exhibit catalogue and the opening page of the website.

10. I was first introduced to the project during my residency at the Banff Centre for the Arts in fall 1996 by Shu Lea Cheang, who was also a resident. *Bowling Alley* can be found on the Internet at http://bowlingalley.walkerart.org.

11. Cheang, installation catalogue, no pagination.

12. Gonzalez-Tamrong, in installation catalogue.

13. Cheang, quoted in Caniglia 1995, 21.

14. "*Bowling Alley* was made possible through the patronage of AT&T/New Visions. ISDN custom and Single Line Service was provided with the assistance of Interprice Networking Services from US. West. Additional support for the exhibition has been provided by Dayton's AT&T Laboratories, gofast.yet Inc., ICONOS, Minneapolis College of Art and Design, and Minneapolis Tele-communications Network" (from the installation catalogue).

15. For detailed discussion see Pizanias, "Considering the . . . Fields."

16. See Cynthia Young (1997), who discusses the increasing collaboration between fashion and art and the explicit patronage of shows by the likes of Hugo Boss and Madonna, whose career epitomizes the power of look and style. States Young: "Perhaps it is ironic that today, when the possibilities for the future are imagined in simulated or cybernetic terms, that fashion, often handmade and economically elitist, and its entourage are both a critical point of reference for identity and a new mainstay for art institutions" (4). Raymond Williams has also caught the contradictory relationship between fashion and "high art" and technology: "High technology can distribute low culture: no problem. But high culture can persist at low levels of technology: that is how most of it was produced. It is at plausible but hopeless conclusions of this kind that most current thinking about the relations between culture and technology arrives and stops" (quoted in Harris 1993, 72).

17. Hugh Southam, deputy chair of the NEA, quoted in Cohnstaedt 1989, 52.

18. Peter Roberts, director of Canada Council, quoted in Cohnstaedt 1989, 52. Another example indicative of the different political temperaments in Canada and the U.S.A. can be seen in the ways that feminist artists protest women's continued marginalization: the *Guerrilla Girls* formed in 1985 to protest and combat sexism in the art world of New York (mainly). Since then, they have been keeping score of the lack of changes while dressed up in gorilla suits. They claim that they cover up and remain anonymous "in order to draw attention to issues rather than *personalities*" (my emphasis; Guerrilla Girls 1989, 35). On the other hand, in Canada the feminist art magazine *Matriart,* under the heading "Who 'counts' and who's 'counting,' " has also been keeping score eponymously and thus in politically accountable fashion. For additional discussion of the dispositional differences between Canadians and Americans see Gaile McGregor, *The Wacousta Syndrome* (1985).

19. Bourdieu, quoted in Moi 1991, 1027.

20. The exhibit was widely reviewed in the local press, before its opening and after. For details, see Pizanias "Considering the . . . Fields." Cheang has not only been reviewed widely in the U.S.A., she has also been reviewed in Canada (Marks 1995) in *Parachute* art magazine, one of three or four that are nationally distributed. The following instances

will demonstrate the position of Canada's artistic fields as dominated by that of New York: France Morin, a cofounder of *Parachute,* has been living and working in New York for a number of years as curator to the New Museum of Contemporary Arts; Shu Lea Cheang has sat on selection committees and acted as resource person at the Banff School for the Arts on a number of occasions.

21. Susan Stewart as a member of *Kiss & Tell* went back to local politics with her performance in *That Long Distance Feeling: Perverts, Politics, and Prozac,* at Vancouver's Roundhouse Community Centre in November 1997 (Pizanias 1998a).

22. Judith Butler (1996) reads the *habitus* as a "reformulation of Althusser's notion of ideology," freeing her (like others before her) from having to deal with, as Richard Nice so aptly put it, "the difference between practice and discourse about practice" (1978, 25). The interesting, albeit obvious, aspect of her polemic is that she supports her arguments by quoting Charles Taylor's contribution in *Bourdieu: Critical Perspectives* (1993) while ignoring two essays in the same anthology on other ways of reading Bourdieu, one by Loïc Wacquant and the other by Bourdieu himself. To paraphrase Fox Keller, she acts (as do others) as if the production of knowledge is not done for a particular "we."

23. See for example Soper 1989 and 1991, Probyn 1990 and 1991, and DiStefano 1990.

24. Since this chapter was accepted for publication my travels (with Bourdieu) have taken me to Vancouver and Calgary, to two artistic fields and two more acts of *misrecognition*: in Vancouver to examine *Artropolis 97,* the city's occasional supposedly "countercultural" visual arts exhibit (Pizanias, 1998b, 1998c) and in Calgary where painter Jed Irwin gave away twenty paintings to "spoil" a nonexisting market for his work (Pizanias 1998).

BIBLIOGRAPHY

Berger, Maurice. *How Art Becomes History: Essays on Art, Society, and Culture in Post-New Deal America.* New York: Icon Editions, 1992.

Bourdieu, Pierre. *Outline of a Theory of Practice.* Translated by Richard Nice. Cambridge: Cambridge UP, 1977.

———. "Les trois états du capital culturel." *Actes de la Recherche en Sciences Sociales* 30 (1979a): 3–6.

———. *The Inheritors: French Students and Their Relation to Culture.* Trans. R. Nice. Chicago: University of Chicago Press, 1979b.

———. "The Production of Belief: Contribution to an Economy of Symbolic Goods." *Media, Culture, and Society* 2 (1980): 261–93.

———. "The Field of Cultural Production or the Economic World Reversed." *Poetics* 12 (1983): 311–56.

———. "The Market of Symbolic Goods." *Poetics* 14 (1985): 13–44.

———. "Flaubert's Point of View." *Critical Inquiry* 14 (1988): 539–62.

———. *The Political Ontology of Martin Heidegger.* Translated by Peter Collier. Stanford: Stanford UP, 1991.

———. "Concluding Remarks: for a Sociogenetic Understanding of Intellectual Works." In *Bourdieu: Critical Perspectives,* edited by Craig Calhoun, Edward LiPuma, and Moishe Postone. Chicago: U of Chicago P, 1993.

———. *In Other Words: Essays toward a Reflexive Sociology.* Translated by M. Adamson. Cambridge: Polity Press, 1994.

———. *The Rules of Art.* Translated by S. Emanuel. Cambridge: Polity Press, 1996.

Bourdieu, Pierre, and Y. Delsaut. "Le couturier et sa griffe: Contribution à une theorie de la magic." *Actes de la Recherche en Science Sociales* 1 (1975): 7–36.

Bourdieu, Pierre, and Jean-Claude Passeron. *The Inheritors: French Students and their Relation to Culture.* Translated by Richard Nice. Chicago: U of Chicago P, 1979.

Bürger, Peter. "The Problem of Aesthetic Value." In *Literary Theory Today,* edited by Peter Collier and Helga Geyer-Ryan. Ithaca, N.Y.: Cornell UP, 1990.

Butler, Judith. 1996. "Performativity's Social Margin." In *The Social and Political Body,* edited by Theodore R. Schatzki and Wolfgang Natter. New York and London: Guilford Press, 1996.

———. *Excitable Speech: A Politic of the Performative.* New York and London: Routledge, 1997.

Caniglia, Julie. "Gutter Ball: The Walker Art Center Gets Lost in Cyberspace." *City Pages* (December 13, 1995): 21–22.

Cohnstaedt, Joy. "Human Rights and Canadian Cultural Policy." *Canadian Issues* 11 (1989): 51–63.

Dinkla, Söke. "From Participation to Interaction: Toward the Origins of Interactive Art." In *Clicking In: Hot Links to a Digital Culture,* edited by Lynn Hershman Leeson. Seattle: Bay Press, 1996.

DiStefano, Christine. 1990. "Dilemmas of Difference: Feminism, Modernity, and Postmodernism." In *Feminism/Postmodernism,* edited by Linda J. Nicholson. New York and London: Routledge, 1990.

Douglas, Stan, ed. *Vancouver Anthology: The Institutional Politics of Art.* Vancouver: Talon Books, 1991.

Fowler, Bridget. *Pierre Bourdieu and Culture Theory.* London: Sage, 1997.

Guerrilla Girls. "The Advantages of Being a Woman Artist." *Heresies* 6, no. 4 (1989): 35.

Guilbaut, Serge. 1985. "The New Adventures of the Avant-Garde in America." In *Pollock and After: The Theoretical Debate,* edited by Francis Francina. London: Harper & Row, 1985.

Guillory, John. "Bourdieu's Refusal." In this volume.

Harris, Jonathan. "Modernism and Culture in the U.S.A., 1930–1960." In *Modernism in Dispute: Art since the Forties,* edited by Paul Wood, Francis Francina, Jonathan Harris, and Charles Harrison. New Haven and London: Yale University Press and Open University, 1993.

Hüyssen, Andreas. "Mapping the Postmodern." In *Feminism/Postmodernism,* edited by Linda Nicholson. New York and London: Routledge, 1990.

Kiss & Tell. Her Tongue on My Theory: Images, Essays, and Fantasies. Vancouver: Press Gang Publishers, 1994.

Lemmon, Nadine. "The Sherman Phenomenon: A Foreclosure of Dialectical Reasoning." *Discourse* 16, no. 2 (1993–94): 101–17.

Marks, Laura. "Sexual Hybrids: From Oriental Exotic to Postcolonial Grotesque." *Parachute* 70 (1993): 22–29.

McGregor, Gaile. *The Wacousta Syndrome: Explorations in the Canadian Langscape.* Toronto: U Toronto P, 1985.

ppropriating Bourdieu: Feminist Theory and Pierre Bourdieu's Sociology of Culture." *New Literary History* 22 (1991): 1017–49.

———. "The Challenge of the Particular Case: Bourdieu's Sociology of Culture and Literary Criticism." *Modern Languages Quarterly* 58, no. 4 (1997): 497–508.

Nice, Richard. "Bourdieu: A 'Vulgar Materialist' in the Sociology of Culture." *Screen Education* 28 (1978): 23–33.

Phelan, Peggy. *Unmarked: The Politics of Performance.* London: Routledge, 1993.

Pizanias, Caterina. "Reviewing Modernist Painting and Criticism in the Canadian Prairies: A Case Study from Edmonton." *International Journal of Canadian Studies* 13 (1993): 139–69.

———"*Habitus*: From the Inside Out and the Outside In." *Theory and Psychology* 6, no. 4 (1996a): 647–65.

———. "(Re)thinking the Ethnic Body: Performing 'Greekness' in Canada." *Journal of the Hellenic Diaspora* 22, no. 1 (1996b): 7–60.

———. "That Long Distance Feeling: Perverts, Politics, and Prozac—a Performance by *Kiss & Tell.*" *Canadian Theatre Review* 95 (summer 1998a): 93–95.

———. "Ceci n'est pas un archive: Browser '97." *FUSE Magazine about Issues of Art and Culture,* 21, no. 2 (1998b): 38–40.

———. "Descent from the Artropolis: Browser '97." Unpublished paper presented at the "Working the Field: Bourdieu's Sociology of the Cultural Field session" of the 1998 Midwestern Languages Association Conference in St. Louis, Missouri, on November 7, 1998c.

———. "Priceless Paintings: All Dressed up and Nowhere to Go." *Artichoke: Writings About the Visual Arts,* 10, no. 3 (1998d): 22–25.

Probyn, Elspeth. "Travels in the Postmodern: Making Sense of the Local." In *Feminism/Postmodernism,* edited by Linda Nicholson. New York and London: Routledge, 1990.

———. "This Body Which Is Not One: Speaking an Embodied Self." *Hypatia* 6, no. 3 (1991): 111–24.

Rissatti, Howard. "Some Questions on Interventionist Art." *Art Papers* (January–February 1990): 6–9.

Robbins, Derek. *The Work of Pierre Bourdieu.* Boulder, Colo.: Westview Press, 1991.

Schneemann, Carolee. *More than Meat Joy: Complete Performance Works and Selected Writings.* New Paltz, N.Y.: B. McPherson Editors, 1979.

Soper, Kate. "Feminism as Critique." *New Left Review* (July–August 1989): 91–112.

———. "Postmodernism, Subjectivity, and the Question of Value." *New Left Review* (March–April 1991): 120–28.

Swartz, David. *Culture and Power.* Chicago: U Chicago P, 1997.

Taylor, Charles. "To Follow a Rule." In *Bourdieu: Critical Perspectives,* edited by Craig Calhoun, Edward LiPuma, and Moishe Postone. Chicago: U Chicago P, 1993.

Tippett, Maria. *Making Culture: English-Canadian Institutions and the Arts before the Massey Commission.* Toronto: U Toronto P, 1990.

Wacquant, Loïc J. D. "The Structure and Logic of Bourdieu's Sociology." In *An Invitation to Reflexive Sociology,* by Pierre Bourdieu and Loïc J. D. Wacquant. Chicago: U Chicago P, 1992.

———. "Bourdieu in America: Notes on the Transatlantic Importation of Social Theory." In *Bourdieu: Critical Perspectives,* edited by Craig Calhoun, Edward LiPuma, and Moishe Postone. Chicago: U Chicago P, 1993.

Walker Art Center. *Shu Lea Cheang's "Bowling Alley": Exhibit Catalogue.* Minneapolis: Walker Art Center, 1995.

Young, Cynthia. "Fashioning Art." *Afterimage* (May–June 1997): 4.

Zukin, Sharon. "Art in the Arms of Power: Marked Relations and Collective Patronage in the United States." *Theory and Society* 11 (1982): 423–51.

9

Pierre Bourdieu's Fields of Cultural Production: A Case Study of Modern Jazz

Paul Lopes

The appearance of "modern" jazz in the national spotlight in the 1950s presented at the time a unique hybrid aesthetic in American music. In the mid-twentieth century, American music was divided institutionally between a high art music and a popular art music represented respectively by a classical music establishment and a popular music industry. Modern jazz was a hybridization by popular musicians of popular idioms and popular practices with high art performance practices and claims to high art aesthetics. Modern jazz was also viewed by many jazz musicians as a rebellion against the popular and the commercial—a claim to the legitimacy of a pure and an authentic art. These elements of modern jazz were to express themselves in different degrees, and in strikingly different ways, depending on the jazz style, jazz musician, or others active in the jazz art world. This hybridization and rebellion, however, was the expression of a general modern jazz paradigm that evolved over a twenty-year period from the thirties until modern jazz's national prominence in the fifties.

If in the mid-twentieth century American music was divided institutionally between a high art music and a popular art music, the obvious question is how and why did a hybrid aesthetic like the modern jazz paradigm appear? Why was it popular big band musicians who articulated this new hybrid? Why was "jazz" for musicians, critics, and others positioned as a distinct genre from the "popular" and the "classical"? And finally, why was it important to jazz musicians and others in the modern jazz art world to claim a fine art status for jazz?

During my search for the answers to these questions about modern jazz, I was struck by how sociological analysis of this cultural hybridization invariably led to an argument that jazz musicians following World War II were distinctly different from their predecessors in jazz. The claimed difference was that unlike their predecessors, postwar jazz musicians were middle class and/or conservatory-college trained, a claim never once supported with empirical evidence.[1] It seemed that certain class assumptions, and assumptions about cultural production, were implicitly expressing themselves. Empirical studies on jazz musicians that addressed class and my own research on jazz musicians suggest that this transformation was not completed until the 1960s.[2] In the present chapter, I argue against the adequacy of this explanation for the rise of a modern jazz paradigm.

It was the use of high art aesthetics and high art performance practices in modern jazz that prompted these scholars to argue that a class and educational transformation was necessary. This argument involved three assumptions. The first assumption was that high art aesthetics and high art performance practices were absent from the artistic culture of popular musicians prior to the postwar period. The second assumption was that the use of high art aesthetics and high art performance practices was dependent on formal music education. The third assumption was that jazz musicians of lower-class origins could not possibly have the "disposition" for such high art practices. All three assumptions stemmed in large part from a lack of attention given to the artistic culture of urban popular musicians in the first half of the twentieth century.

The above explanation of modern jazz was further biased by approaching modern jazz in isolation from the general field of music production in the United States. The explanation does not acknowledge that the transformation in jazz music might have been generated by specific dynamics in this field. In particular, as Pierre Bourdieu would argue, the proponents of this explanation did not acknowledge the possibility that the transformation was the product of specific struggles between different positions within the music field, that is, that the modern jazz paradigm was a specific strategy adopted in these struggles.

Pierre Bourdieu argues that any cultural form or cultural practice is embedded in a broader *field* of cultural production. It exists in relation to other forms and practices, and also to artists and other individuals involved in the production and valuation of these forms and practices. The field is conceived as *objectively structured* by the given *positions* that actors can occupy, the relations between these positions, and the *space of possible strategies*. For Bourdieu, the aesthetic strategy (*position-taking*) of actors in any given position in the field is determined by the struggle for symbolic profit and/or economic profit, that is, cultural status and/or material gain, determined in the first instance by the structure of the field itself. This is where any sociological analysis of an art form and its practitioners should begin. Then from this vantage point, questions of the social origins of actors, and their associated cultural dispositions, can be addressed as they are *refracted* through the field.[3]

This chapter argues that from Bourdieu's vantage point one can discover the genealogy of the modern jazz paradigm. The position of jazz music and jazz musicians in the musical field in the United States in the 1930s and 1940s led to the transformation of jazz as a cultural practice. The evolution of a modern jazz paradigm and a jazz art world was a gradual response to the rejection of jazz practices by the popular music industry during this period. It also was a response to the exclusion of urban popular musicians from practicing high art aesthetics and high art performance practices co-opted by the classical music establishment. This rise of a new aesthetic and new art world in American music was also linked to the boundaries of race distinction and racial subordination in American culture, which marginalized black music and black artists. The artistic culture of jazz where this paradigm evolved was a socially heterogeneous artistic formation—by race, class, and education—whose members were united in their opposition to the processes of exclusion and subordination in the musical field in the United States.[4]

The case study of modern jazz demonstrates the power of the analytical model Bourdieu provides for the investigation of cultural production. It also provides an opportunity to expand his conceptual framework. While Bourdieu has emphasized the problematic, or the misrecognition of a problematic, between restricted high art and bourgeois high art, he has placed all popular art production within a subfield of industrial art. He fails to recognize the tensions between modern culture industries and popular artists and other independent producers outside these industries. The case of modern jazz demonstrates a need to expand Bourdieu's general framing of the cultural field.

This chapter on modern jazz also presents a critique of Bourdieu's generalizations on the distinctions and the struggles at play in a cultural field. Bourdieu's concept of social class tends to resolve itself into a concept of economic class with cultural capital as an ancillary form of power within the dominant class. This conceptualization presents cultural struggle as a struggle between class fractions of the dominant class with the dominated classes culturally disempowered. Such a view leads to the portrayal of cultural struggle in art production as more of a parlor game than a fundamental struggle to transform the social status hierarchy in a cultural formation. The case of jazz shows how the dominated classes do participate in cultural production and their struggles are more significant than simply a misrecognition of a shared parlor game. Bourdieu's conceptualization of social class also inadequately considers the significance of noneconomic social group dynamics. In particular, the case of jazz shows the fundamental importance of race distinction and race subordination in the American cultural field.

THE MODERN JAZZ PARADIGM

In the mid-fifties, "jazz" gained national recognition in both media coverage and in a booming recorded and live performance market. The jazz press hailed a final victory for a jazz art world that had struggled over two decades to gain the type of prominence that jazz music so richly deserved. "Modern" jazz was at the forefront of this cultural coup, but while jazz musicians were innovating new styles of jazz music, previous styles of jazz and older jazz musicians were also part of the modern renaissance in jazz. In this sense, what I refer to as the "modern jazz paradigm" was a general position in the field of American music shared by all jazz musicians, even though they were to apply themselves in distinctly different ways to this new position.

The modern jazz paradigm as it appeared in the fifties was a generally shared position equivalent to the classical and the popular in the American musical field. Just as the classical position and the popular position supported a variety of sub-genres, the modern jazz position demonstrated its generality in the breadth of *trajectories* jazz music would follow as this position emerged in the musical field. The fact that a variety of musical styles would fall within the category of jazz, ignoring for the purposes of this chapter the numerous disagreements in the jazz art world over what deserved to be included within the jazz rubric, demonstrated that jazz had evolved to represent a general orientation and aesthetic in American music. The basic performance practices in jazz were instrumental performances for a listening audience with improvisation as the core "art."

The basically hybrid nature of the jazz paradigm was revealed in its use of popular idioms and popular practices in a mode of performance that at the time was considered restricted to classical music—performance for attentive listening audiences. The new jazz paradigm also positioned jazz musicians as serious and autonomous artists. The articulation of this high art aesthetic, however, was not the same for all jazz performance and among all jazz musicians. What constituted a "high art" aesthetic was in itself socially constructed. The very hybridity of the jazz position in terms of its practices and the dispositions of its artists was a serious ideological challenge to the rigidly constructed high art aesthetics of the classical music establishment. Some jazz musicians would attempt a full emulation of classical music performance, but the majority of jazz musicians would not follow that path. The point is to recognize a general orientation in jazz, in which artists and groups of artists would choose specific strategies that would lead to different artistic trajectories.

The importance of my specific use of the term "modern" is to avoid viewing this transformation in jazz only as a consequence of "modernist" jazz musicians in the postwar period. First, both older and younger musicians applied themselves to the new modern jazz paradigm from the jazz elder Louis Armstrong to the young lion Miles Davis, although jazz musicians schooled in urban big bands from the 1920s onwards such as Duke Ellington, Coleman Hawkins, John Lewis, and Gerry Mulligan, would adopt a far greater degree of the "high art" jazz aesthetic than their jazz folk predecessors. Second, the roots of the modern jazz paradigm reach far back before the postwar period. What became the modern jazz paradigm was the rearticulation of musical orientations and musical practices already preexisting in the artistic culture of urban popular musicians from the turn of the century to the postwar period. The question is: why did this rearticulation occur and why did "jazz" signify this new position in the musical field? To understand this we need to look at the field of American music during the first half of the twentieth century.

THE MUSICAL FIELD: POSITIONING JAZZ PRACTICES

The modern jazz paradigm was a response in large part to the *institutionalization* of American music in the first half of the twentieth century. It was the result of the struggle of urban popular musicians subjected to this process of "symbolic violence." This process entailed two moments. The first moment was the institutionalization of high art music that began in the late nineteenth century and continued into the early twentieth century. The second moment was the institutionalization of popular music that occurred rapidly following the Depression of the late 1920s and early 1930s. These two processes of co-optation of cultural production led in part to the distinct separation of two narrowly defined music aesthetics in American music, the classical and the popular, leading into the mid-twentieth century.

The institutionalization of classical "high art" music occurred when urban elites in the United States gradually created high culture establishments at the end of the nineteenth century and on into the twentieth century. This institutionalization has been well documented in the work of Paul DiMaggio and Lawrence Levine.[5] Elite-run symphony orchestras and opera companies co-opted European classical and operatic music and laid claim to exclusive rights to the legitimacy of a high art aesthetic. This co-optation involved the creation of a distinct high art classical music aesthetic, the consecration of specific musical genres and works, the creation of separate social spaces for performances quarantined from the popular classes, and the separation of classical musicians from popular musicians and popular performance. The strategy of containment was accomplished first by exclusive contracts with American musicians that excluded performance of popular music and by recruiting European musicians. This was later replaced by the separate training of classical musicians as exclusive music conservatories were established in the United States in the early twentieth century. By the late 1920s, this elite establishment of high art music had consolidated an organizational field of music with well defined boundaries distinguishing it from the subfield of popular music.

By the 1930s, the urban elite-created classical high art music was being disseminated outward through music education programs supported by governmental and educational organizations and the promotion of classical music by the popular music industry. All these institutions accepted the dichotomy of classical high art music versus popular art music.[6] The period following the Depression is significant in that it marked the greater dissemination beyond elite institutions of the new ideology of classical music and classical artists as the *exclusive* carriers of high art aesthetics.

What is of prime importance in viewing this first moment in the institutionalization of American music is that urban "popular" musicians in the late nineteenth and early twentieth century played an eclectic repertoire of musical genres that encompassed, from our contemporary perspective, both "popular" and "classical" aesthetics, idioms, and performance settings.[7] Further, urban popular musicians viewed themselves as more or less professional musicians. From turn-of-the-century marching bands like John Phillip Sousa's to popular society orchestras in the early twentieth century like James Reese Europe's, Vincent Lopez's, and Paul Whiteman's, popular bands and orchestras performed the "high" to the "popular." Of course, many carried their own biased elitism towards folk musicians ("musical illiterates") who migrated to major metropolises, although by the 1920s urban popular musicians would be infected by these folk musicians' "jazzy" music. In fact, most urban popular musicians outside the high culture establishment continued this eclectic practice during the first moment of institutionalization. It was only with the collapse of live popular music performance and independently recorded popular music during the Depression and the subsequent second moment in the institutionalization of American music in the thirties that urban popular musicians were subjected to the "symbolic violence" of a narrowly conceived "popular" music market.

The process of institutionalizing the production of popular music proceeded rapidly following the Depression with the rise of a cohesive organizational field of popular music production in the early thirties. This oligopolistic field was maintained through the interlinking interests established between major record companies, national radio networks, major film companies, and the American Society of Composers, Authors, and Publishers (ASCAP), which had virtually exclusive access to these three industries. Each of the industries relied on a closed system of production that prevented significant access to radio, film, and record audiences—that is, access to mass media, the emerging dominant field of popular cultural production and popular cultural reception in America. The conservative and narrowly defined parameters of what constituted popular music for the radio industry and film industry, augmented by the exclusive membership of ASCAP, which excluded black ("race") composers and country ("hillbilly") composers, defined in large part the decisions of the record industry and major big bands, which were dependent on radio and film for sales of their recordings. With mass media having a major impact on the musical tastes of listeners, this oligopolistic field also affected live performance as audiences' tastes were shaped by records, film, and radio.[8]

This emergence of a musical field of what Bourdieu calls *industrial art* had a major impact on determining what constituted "popular" idioms and "popular" aesthetics, particularly in terms of national recognition and distribution. With the success of radio and sound film in the twenties, coupled with recorded sound, *mass media* appeared to make the national cohesion of a musical field possible. This occurred also at a time in which a major avenue of popular music production in the first two decades of the twentieth century, vaudeville theater, had collapsed under the triple blow of film entertainment, recorded sound, and the Depression. The Depression also destroyed the base for independent record producers. In the thirties, therefore, the new oligopolistic industry had the institutional capacity to impose nationally a clearly demarcated *objective structure* of musical genre positions by a process of inclusion and exclusion.

In the thirties and forties, white vocal big band dance music was the oligopolistic industry's exclusive product. It tended to prefer what jazz musicians pejoratively referred to as "sweet" or "corny" big band music as represented by Guy Lombardo's Royal Canadians, that is, big band music barely influenced by African American idioms. Even when white "swing" big band music like Benny Goodman's, which was an articulation of African American big band music, became a national "craze" in the late thirties, corn syrupy sweet remained the preferred taste of the music oligopoly.

Underlying this preference for "sweet" music was the industry's segregation of African American musical idioms and African American musicians in the musical field. Conventionality was racially constructed by the industry in its strategy to protect its oligopoly from scrutiny, in part in response to the elite outpouring against the popular success of African American music during the "Jazz Age" of the twenties.[9] In general, the oligopoly produced a more or less homogeneous and standardized product, and therefore popular aesthetic, one which excluded to a large degree the African American music practices enjoyed by black urban popular musicians and many white urban popular musicians. Further, "jazz" remained, regardless of the musician or mode of performance, associated with both African American culture and Prohibition urban nightlife—the "noncommercial" claim of the industry against jazz was a thinly veiled subordination of both black culture and the nonconventional, socially heterogeneous culture of urban nightlife.

It is important to note that the "top down" control of the industry was replicated at the level of live performance and recorded music through the power of big band leaders. The career path of an aspiring young musician was through preexisting local, regional, and for a lucky few, national big bands. Established big band leaders had a monopoly over most performance sites and recording sessions. The conservatism of the industry, therefore, tended to be reflected in the older, particularly white, big band leaders.

The position of a big band musician tended to be that of a "professional" yeoman following the dictates of the bandleader. This explains how even with the success of the swing craze in the late thirties many young white popular musicians continued to be frustrated as many older band leaders maintained their "corny" ways. Black urban popular musicians were even more frustrated with the general segregation and subordination of black musicians. This was made even more apparent when the swing craze brought far more attention and money to white musicians than to the community of black musicians who had created its foundations. Black musicians, however, were also subject to the dictates of the established black big band leaders.

While African American music idioms and music practices in general struggled against the forces of the oligopoly, it was the African American practice of improvisation in an ensemble setting popular among black musicians and many white musicians that was the crux of these musicians' frustrations with the industry. Running parallel to commercial big band entertainment was a late-hour artistic urban subculture of improvisational performance. In this subculture, popular big band musicians, both black and white, maintained a distinctly different "popular" performance aesthetic from the industry's big band dance aesthetic. As already mentioned, the post-Depression music oligopoly rejected the African American jazz practices that became popular among urban musicians beginning as early as the twenties. This popularity continued into the thirties and forties, and also spread among a larger and larger number of young white musicians.

As the popularity of jazz practices continued to grow among popular big band musicians, the industry continued to reject jazz as "noncommercial." The result was that many popular big band musicians lived dual artistic lives: one as popular dance band musicians during regular entertainment hours, and the other as jazz musicians active in a late-hour artistic subculture and small urban club scene. This artistic culture of jazz musicians became an ongoing "subculture" that existed in opposition to these musicians' roles in the industrial machine of the music oligopoly. It was in this subculture that the modern jazz paradigm was generated among musicians.[10] From this subculture, a jazz art world of records, clubs, concerts, and publications was gradually erected that eventually established jazz as a national music genre by the fifties.

In the thirties and forties, the popular music oligopoly set the stage for a rearticulation of jazz performance in three ways. First, the industry's demand for only "entertaining" vocal dance music placed the original eclecticism of high art aesthetics and popular art aesthetics in urban popular performance in a latent state from which it could be rearticulated in a more autonomous subculture of popular big band musicians. Second, the rejection of the popular practices associated with jazz led these to become the defining practices of the autonomous subculture of both black and white big band musicians. And third, the rearticulation was a product of the specific struggle for cultural legitimacy by black artists that coalesced with the struggles of white musicians against the dictates of the music industry. In essence, the industry accepted the dichotomy of high and popular promulgated by the high culture establishment, relegating the industry to promoting entertaining, mainstream music. Popular musicians were confronted with an extremely conservative and racist music industry that subjected them to a highly rationalized and homogenous system of music production. It was the dual position as "popular dance band musician" and "jazz musician" in the musical field that set the parameters of the generation of a modern jazz paradigm.

By the early fifties, the oligopolistic music industry had lost effective control over the production of music in the United States. As national networks abandoned radio for television, a large number of new independent radio stations across the country searched for music to broadcast over the airwaves. With new technologies in recording and manufacturing, independent record labels were able to supply these new stations at the same time as reaching new audiences through independent distribution of recorded music. These changes in the organizational field of music production allowed modern jazz along with "popular" genres like rhythm and blues and rock 'n' roll to successfully enter the national field. The institutionally imposed *objective structure* of the music field dissolved as artists, producers, and others realigned the field.

THE MUSICAL FIELD: POSITIONS AND POSITION-TAKING

As mentioned previously, Pierre Bourdieu argues that to explain the content and form of a genre, and the strategies of its practitioners, one must situate it in relation to its artistic field. To understand the evolution of a hybrid jazz paradigm, one must recognize how jazz was positioned in the field described above. To do this, however, we need to extend Bourdieu's original conceptualization of three general artistic subfields: the restricted subfield of art, the subfield of commercial bourgeois art, and the subfield of commercial-industrial (popular) art.[11] At least in the case of the musical field in the United States, a fourth subfield exists, that of the restricted subfield of popular art. Bourdieu's original idea of the restricted subfield of art is limited to "high art" production and does not take into account popular art production that is not part of the culture industry. This restricted subfield of popular art is not the same as that of high art and represents a distinct position in cultural production in its relation to all the subfields. As table 9.1

Table 9.1   Field of Music Production, United States

Bourgeois Art	Industrial Art
Institutionalized Consecration	Mediated Mass Market
Restricted High art	Restricted Popular Art
Charismatic Consecration	Charismatic Consecration

shows, the musical field is bifurcated into two poles of opposition: restricted high art and bourgeois art; and restricted popular art and industrial art.

The two moments of institutionalization in American music described above represent the historical development of this two-pole objective structure for the musical field. The classical music establishment generated the "high art" pole in music production and music reception in America. As Bourdieu argues in the case of the literary field in France, this pole involved principles of legitimacy between bourgeois art and restricted high art. These principles were determined for bourgeois art by the general demand of high art music audiences, patrons, and professionals, what Bourdieu refers to as *institutional consecration*. The principles for restricted high art were determined by an artistic culture of composers and critics based on *charismatic consecration*.[12] The popular music industry generated the "popular art" pole in music production and music reception. This pole involved principles of legitimacy between industrial art and restricted popular art. These principles were determined for industrial art by the general demand of popular music audiences, mass media professionals, and mass media gatekeepers, based on an industrial *mediated mass market*. The principles of legitimacy for restricted popular art were determined by artistic subcultures of musicians, audiences, producers, and critics, based on the *charismatic consecration* provided by subcultures whose cultural identities often were more intimately tied to a genre of music.

What this model suggests is that the musical field during its institutionalization refracted a broad cultural struggle for legitimacy between a bourgeois art pole and a popular art pole—an "elite culture" versus a "popular culture" in American music. In addition to this struggle, however, there were two other cultural struggles: one struggle over the principles of legitimacy for bourgeois art and then another struggle over the principles of legitimacy for popular art—separate struggles over defining "elite culture" and defining "popular culture" in American music. In fact, once these poles were institutionalized, and therefore gained relative autonomy from each other, it would be the struggles over principles of legitimacy within each pole that would determine positions and strategies among artists more than the broader struggle between the elite and the popular, although the broader struggle would remain. Each pole would develop its own "history" of struggle, although artists in each pole occasionally would borrow from the other pole in their particular strategies, as was the case in modern jazz.

As Bourdieu would argue, these two poles are homologous, yet distinct; there is a certain affinity between bourgeois art and industrial art, as there is between restricted high art and restricted popular art. One example of these homologous links was the link in the forties and fifties between bohemian beat writers in the literary subfield of restricted high art and popular big band "jazz" musicians in the musical subfield of restricted popular art. Unfortunately, Bourdieu never acknowledges the existence of restricted popular art; it is merely "culture" that high art bohemians like the beats co-opt or develop an affinity towards. This may in part explain Bourdieu's claim that artists come from the dominated fraction of the dominant class—that is, he ignores artists among the dominated classes. This claim could also be a result of music (and dance) in the twentieth century being one of the last significant independent areas of cultural production for large numbers of the dominated classes to be practitioners of (rap, heavy metal, punk, country, etc.).

The struggles over principles of legitimacy in the American musical field in the first half of the twentieth century must be seen as multidimensional in the overlapping of specific struggles of cultural distinction. The struggle between an "elite" culture and a "popular" culture was entwined with struggles over race distinctions and class distinctions in the field. Both the bourgeois art subfield and the industrial art subfield during this period were actively working to construct homogeneous and conventional cultures that excluded the heterogeneous culture of American urban life. Clearly the most dominant symbolic violence was against black culture and black artists. Bourgeois high art music and industrial popular art music were determinedly "white" culture.

The jazz subculture existed in the subfield of restricted popular art. In the thirties, forties, and fifties it was composed of mostly, but not exclusively, members of the dominated classes, that is, members of the working class, ethnic minorities, and racial minorities. Jazz practices were popular music practices, first found in southern African American folk music traditions, and then in the twenties integrated into urban popular music performance. Jazz performance in the thirties, forties, and fifties was found in both "bohemian haunts" and the "haunts" frequented by the dominated classes, particularly African Americans. The importance of jazz music's location can not be overstressed. Its location in social space, in the social status hierarchy, and in the musical field are interrelated in the difficulty of jazz musicians in the thirties and forties in trying to "convert" their cultural practices into symbolic value either in the popular music industry or the classical music establishment.[13]

What is clear is that jazz musicians and their artistic subculture were forced into a position in opposition to, or at least distinguishable from, industrial art due to this subfield's rejection of jazz. That is, the music industry's rejection of jazz as "noncommercial" and its segregation of black music from the "popular" led jazz musicians to develop an "anticommercial" ideology and a stance against the "popular" to legitimize their practices.[14] Forced into a marginal subculture, jazz musicians also used the claim to "pure art" and the high-art aesthetic to counteract their genre's "commercial" rejection by the industry. Such a disposition was possible for two reasons. First, the artistic subculture of urban popular big band musicians still retained its earlier eclectic aesthetic including what by then were considered separate high and popular aesthetics. Second, the leading musicians, both black and white, applying the modern jazz paradigm were mostly the top professionals at the national, regional, and local levels; that is, a proven "professional" musician had the position to claim superior talents. The rejection by the culture industry, aided by the high culture establishment, of (1) black music and black artists; (2) the jazz practices shared by black and white big band musicians; and (3) the previous aesthetic eclecticism of popular musicians led to the coalescence of these elements around an evolving modern jazz paradigm.

In general, a distinct jazz aesthetic was necessary to create an independent symbolic value for jazz in order to generate symbolic profit and economic profit. In other words, the cultural practices of jazz musicians had to be converted into symbolic capital. Only by making its difference, that is, rejection by the industry, symbolically valuable could jazz music succeed in becoming a major genre in American music. The anticommercial and fine-art ethic became an essential position-taking in the jazz art world's strategy. From such a general position-taking, each jazz musician, jazz critic, and jazz entrepreneur would bring his or her own cultural dispositions to bear. This accounts for the hybridization of modern jazz, as the general paradigm refracted the various dispositions of its practitioners, promoters, and audiences.

This account of the position of jazz music in the field of music production in the United States provides the explanation of how musicians of working-class background and without formal education would participate in the hybridization of a jazz paradigm. In joining the jazz artistic subculture with its roots in urban popular performance, musicians acquired this subculture's slowly evolving strategies of legitimization and the general eclectic dispositions still latent among urban popular musicians. As with all popular musical traditions, musicians learn collectively through performance and interaction in artistic cultures, that is, through informal education. The assumption that a musician needs formal education to articulate high art aesthetics, or even acquire knowledge of high art forms, is patently a class-biased view of how cultural practice works (and of how supposedly "difficult" high art music is compared to popular music).

What becomes apparent once jazz practices and jazz artists are situated in the general field of music production in the United States leading into the mid-twentieth century is that the *objective structures* of the field set the parameters of the strategies adopted. Given the relationship between the position of popular musician in the industry and that of jazz musician, the *logic of the field* set a strategy of anticommercialism and pure art as the best alternative. Given the overarching dichotomy between "commercial" popular art and "autonomous" high art that was a virtual *doxa* in American culture, it should not be surprising that a high art ideology was adopted by jazz musicians and adapted to their own musical dispositions. Such a strategy was "logical" regardless of one's social class background or formal music education. Nor should we forget how this strategy with regard to popular musicians' position vis-à-vis the classical music establishment circumvented the co-optation of cultural legitimacy undertaken by urban elites in the first part of the twentieth century. Maybe, considering the narrow parameters enforced by the music oligopoly and the classical music establishment, those cultural dispositions active in American urban culture excluded from these parameters would eventually find expression through a "third position."

Race, class, and education obviously were important in the directions the artistic culture of jazz musicians would take. The very heterogeneity of this artistic culture allowed for the hybridization of music practices and music aesthetics. Ironically, the symbolic violence of the music oligopoly forced musicians of diverse background into a shared professional big band culture. For the community of black artists, economic and cultural segregation in the twentieth century made the big band profession something of a "middle-class" profession, which attracted college-educated artists such as black big band leaders Don Redman, Fletcher Henderson, and Jimmy Lunceford, and black musicians Coleman Hawkins and Ben Webster, all of whom began their careers in the twenties. At the same time, however, the celebrated big band leader and jazz composer Duke Ellington had neither college education nor formal training in music composition; nor did such "modernist" leaders in the forties as Dizzy Gillespie and Charlie Parker. In addition, the artistic culture of urban big band musicians since the turn of the century performed for a variety of "popular" urban audiences that included the middle class and the working class. In this sense, it must be emphasized that "popular" urban culture in America was more heterogeneous by class and race in the first half of the twentieth century than most accounts of jazz acknowledge.

The accounts of modern jazz that emphasized postwar changes in class and educational background assumed the high-popular dichotomy that linked music practices to class and educational dispositions. They failed to take into account the fact that this very dichotomy was institutionally imposed in the musical field. Class and education were important factors in the field, but not in the way portrayed in these accounts. Once again, the heterogeneity of the jazz artistic subculture was an essential part of the evolution of the modern jazz paradigm since the 1920s, but through the fifties the majority of jazz musicians were working class with no formal music education.[15]

ARTISTIC STRATEGIES AND SOCIAL CLASS IN MODERN JAZZ

Jazz musicians did follow different artistic strategies as they applied themselves to the modern jazz paradigm. This paradigm in combination with the cultural dispositions of jazz musicians created what Bourdieu calls a *space of possible strategies*. It would be misleading, however, to assume a "sociological determinism" similar to the postwar argument on modern jazz that would posit each individual jazz musician's artistic strategy within the modern jazz paradigm as a direct manifestation of social class background—whether economic, racial, or educational. The collective nature of jazz performance and the heterogeneity of social class in the artistic culture of jazz as a whole made an individual jazz musician's social class less deterministic than one would assume even following

Bourdieu's arguments on artistic strategies and social class. At the same time, however, social class was expressed in certain general approaches to jazz and in certain strategies used by jazz musicians. In this sense, the term *refraction* remains appropriate in pointing to the way in which the modern jazz paradigm and the artistic culture of jazz musicians acted in refracting the cultural dispositions of social class among individual jazz musicians or groups of jazz musicians.

The clearest expressions of social class in modern jazz were the differences in artistic strategies between black jazz musicians and white jazz musicians. Certain new styles in modern jazz in the forties and fifties, from bebop to hard bop to soul jazz, were created by black musicians and viewed by many of these musicians as a distinctly "black" jazz. The new modern jazz style of cool jazz in the fifties was performed by predominantly white jazz musicians and was associated with them in the jazz art world. Besides specific styles, differences in strategies between black musicians and white musicians were evident even in more shared approaches to jazz music. Black musicians, unlike white musicians, used black popular idioms and associations with black culture in approaches to jazz music such as big band composition, classical pretension, the avant-garde, and the commercial popular.

This general difference between black jazz musicians and white jazz musicians was in part the result of differences in the practices they acquired as artists from different music cultures. While both black musicians and white musicians shared in their participation in jazz music, they still came from segregated music cultures. The big band artistic culture was a segregated culture regardless of the interchange between black musicians and white musicians in jamming sessions, in jazz clubs, and through recorded music. Apprentices in black bands learned different practices and idioms from those learned by apprentices in white bands, and groupings of jazz musicians remained mostly racially segregated. Unlike white musicians, black musicians were familiar with popular black idioms such as gospel music and rhythm and blues music, with a considerable number performing in rhythm and blues bands in the forties and fifties. While black musicians and white musicians shared the modern jazz paradigm, their different musical dispositions would lead to distinct artistic strategies and often distinct stylistic approaches.

The difference between artistic strategies and jazz styles of black jazz musicians and white jazz musicians was also a reflection of a more conscious artistic position-taking within the general jazz position. For many black jazz musicians, the historical co-optation of black music by white musicians led to the assertion of a distinct "black" jazz. This assertion led to controversial debates in the jazz press about the distinction between "black" jazz and "white" jazz. Whether such a distinction was warranted, and I believe in general it was, this strategy of distinction was commonly used by black musicians and record producers. The strategy allowed black jazz musicians to assert a unique position within the general jazz position that over time successfully established black jazz musicians as the dominant artists in the jazz art world.

The position-taking of "black" jazz might simply be viewed as an instrumental move to secure a major market in jazz music by black jazz musicians and record producers. But such a view ignores the fact that the associative qualities of music are an important part of their meaning. The musical association of jazz with black culture was a meaning black jazz musicians worked to maintain. These associative qualities expressed in modern jazz performance did not always have to be an overtly conscious strategy, as black musicians simply worked to create a "meaningful" music for themselves and for their black audiences. For white musicians, a strong association of jazz with their social class identity was far less important and less "meaningful," and therefore, their strategies were more oriented to direct musical associations with jazz music, mainstream American pop music, classical music, or international music such as Brazilian music or Indian music.[16]

The associative qualities of black jazz also point out the importance of jazz as a vehicle for the legitimization of black culture for many black jazz musicians. The modern jazz position inherited the black nationalist agenda of the early twentieth century to "lift up" black culture from its subordinate position in American culture. The use of black idioms and thematic associations with black culture in modern jazz continued the black nationalism prominent during the Harlem Renaissance in the twenties when jazz first entered urban popular performance. This general agenda would eventually link a number of black jazz musicians with the black arts movement of the sixties and lead some to disavow the term "jazz" and to claim their work as "black music."

While the black jazz approach was a clearly recognizable strategy in modern jazz, it was not the only strategy employed by black musicians. Black musicians would participate in other strategies and styles in modern jazz with no overt association with black idioms or black culture. White jazz musicians would also employ "black" styles, particularly bebop, which for many was the first modern style of jazz. In terms of patterns of social class distinction in modern jazz, however, "black" jazz was the most clearly recognizable pattern whether as an overtly conscious strategy, as a result of the continued segregation of musicians, as simply the consequence of different musical dispositions, or as a result of the ultimate signification of skin color in American culture. Race as a *structuring category* of position-taking in jazz was *overdetermined* by the various dynamics of race distinction and race segregation in America.

The economic class and education level of jazz musicians did affect a pattern in approaches to modern jazz music. The turn towards classical pretension in both musical composition and performance presentation was a strategy adopted by predominantly middle-class and college-educated jazz musicians. This would take the form of either orchestral composition common in third stream jazz or of jazz ensembles emulating classical chamber music performance. The turn towards classical pretension, however, was not a common strategy in modern jazz

music in the fifties and sixties, although several jazz musicians were quite successful in applying it. Middle-class and working-class, college-educated and non-
college-educated, jazz musicians in general pursued other strategies.

The avant-garde strategy of free jazz in the sixties demonstrated the importance of the jazz paradigm and collective collaboration in jazz music versus strategies determined by musicians' social class. One could easily assume that an
avant-garde strategy would be followed predominantly by middle-class and college-educated jazz musicians, but this was not the case. The free jazz strategy
was adopted by jazz musicians of different social classes, and many of the most
important and successful musicians in free jazz were working class with no college education. Free jazz was easily adapted to the practice of jazz improvisation
and open to the articulation of a variety of musical dispositions and idioms. In
this case, the general modern jazz paradigm provided the foundation from within
which musicians of different social class backgrounds would choose the avant-
garde strategy.

Jazz musicians applied a number of different strategies to the modern jazz paradigm. I have focused on the three strategies of black, classical, and avant-garde
jazz to look at the relationship between artistic strategies and social class in modern jazz. The strategies of black jazz and classical jazz demonstrate that the refraction of social class was an important part of modern jazz performance. At the
same time, however, the avant-garde strategy shows that the collective nature of
the modern jazz paradigm created a space of possible strategies in which jazz
musicians from different social class backgrounds could share similar strategies.
In many ways, the hybrid nature of the modern jazz position both in aesthetics
and in social class created a more complex articulation of artistic strategies and
social class expression than in either the classical or the popular positions.

CONTRIBUTIONS TO PIERRE BOURDIEU'S
CONCEPTUAL FRAMEWORK

I have already suggested that Bourdieu's framework on cultural production needs
to incorporate a restricted subfield of popular art into a two-pole field of cultural
production. Linked to this additional subfield is an argument against Bourdieu's
view of the nature of industrial art. In his various claims on industrial art, Bourdieu reveals a belief that industrial art reflects market demand *unmediated* by
industrial gatekeepers.[17] This is not the case: gatekeepers are important media-
tors, and the struggle between the restricted subfield of popular art and the subfield of industrial art is often over the culture industry's circumvention of restricted popular art's ability to reach audiences. This suggests further that
symbolic capital is important in the popular art pole both in what symbolic capital gatekeepers in industrial art give to specific popular cultural forms, that is,
what industrial gatekeepers consider marketable, and in how subcultures of popu-

lar artists and popular audiences generate their own independent symbolic capital.

It is important to note, however, that given the nature of the relation between industrial art and restricted popular art, the logic of reverse economics Bourdieu finds in the subfield of restricted high art is not the pre-given case in the restricted subfield of popular art.[18] "Selling out" is not always the issue. The issue is often lamenting the inability of restricted popular artists to reach audiences due to the hold that industrial art professionals and industrial art gatekeepers have over access to the popular market.

Given that reverse economics is not the modus operandi of the restricted subfield of popular art, however, does not mean that issues of "autonomy" or "authenticity" are not structured into its relationship to industrial art, issues similar to those structured into the relationship of the restricted subfield of high art to bourgeois art. The difference is in the lapse into formalism of restricted high art in its quest for autonomy and its elaborate history of competencies. Autonomy and authenticity are not linked to abstract formalism and elaborate competencies in the restricted subfield of popular art but are linked to expressing the culture of a popular subculture community further linked to its collective social group identity (class, race, gender, sexuality, etc.)—an identity often subordinated by the "hierarchy of symbolic value" in the cultural field. "Selling out" is usually viewed not directly in terms of financial gain but in terms of whether one retains the aesthetics and the identity of the original subculture, although admittedly the most commonly held view is that someone who makes it into the industry will face intense pressures to "assimilate."

The hybridity of modern jazz is revealed in this very juxtaposition of formalism versus collective identity in restricted art. One trajectory of jazz was towards the formalism of restricted high art seen in free jazz and avant-garde jazz. Also, over time, a history of elaborate competencies was established in the jazz art world that were internal to this artistic culture. At the same time, however, jazz in the fifties and sixties was very much part of the collective identity of urban popular culture for both blacks and whites, although it had a vastly greater associative power for black musicians and their collective identity with African American culture. This associative power of jazz remains for contemporary black jazz musicians and black audiences, while jazz's trajectory away from any urban subculture community has left contemporary white jazz musicians with little linkage between jazz and any collective identity outside of being jazz musicians.

Finally, the dynamic of subcultures and the industrial art industry leads one to question whether Bourdieu's idea of "playing the game" as a critique of the misrecognition of the imposed legitimacy of the dominant class forgets that for those in the dominated classes cultural production might not always be simply a game. Further, the authenticity question of the subfield of restricted popular art and that of the restricted subfield of high art might be homologous by structure, but each speaks to distinct questions in terms of the link between cultural hierarchy, social status hierarchy, and the misrecognition of cultural, economic, and political domination. Such "cultural politics" in the American cultural field have been not simply a struggle between economic classes, but a fundamental struggle over a racial order in America that has subordinated African Americans economically, politically, and culturally.

CONCLUSION

This chapter has argued that the generation of a modern jazz paradigm was the consequence of long-term conflicts in the American field of music in the first half of the twentieth century. While modern jazz appeared on the national scene in the fifties, the *generation* of this position in the American field of music began with the initial infusion of folk jazz practices into urban professional performance in the twenties and the subsequent struggles of urban popular musicians against a powerful music oligopoly in the thirties and forties. The modern jazz paradigm was an expression of the struggles over principles of cultural legitimacy in America as expressed in the music practices and idioms of popular performance.

The story of modern jazz reveals the historical and complex relationships between aesthetics, cultural practices, and social class in America. I argue against deterministic interpretations that assume a static and direct relationship between social class and artistic expression. This relationship must be viewed in its historical context and in the social context of the art worlds in which art is produced. Retrospective interpretations of modern jazz that assumed a direct correspondence between social class and aesthetics failed to recognize that the high-popular dichotomy in America was historically constructed and openly contested in the cultural field. These interpretations also failed to examine the artistic culture of modern jazz and its aesthetics in the context of the general field of music in the United States. Modern jazz was the collective expression of a socially diverse artistic subculture responding to the institutional enforcement of a rigid high-popular dichotomy that subordinated popular artists in the musical field.

While modern jazz was an expression of struggles over the high and the popular in American culture, the struggle over racial subordination was crucial in the generation of this new position. Race subordination was the major social force that engendered a "third" position in the American field of music. It was black culture and black artists during this period who were excluded from participation in both the "high" and the "popular." White big band musicians, as they adopted an affinity towards jazz practices, were to join, consciously or not, in this struggle over the position of black music in America. In turn, they would participate with black big band musicians in the more general struggle against the formation of an exclusive elite high culture in American music. But the rejection of jazz in the thirties and forties was fundamentally based on the subordination of black culture in America. The modern jazz position as a product of fundamental struggles over cultural legitimacy in America was not merely another card to be dealt in a parlor game of social class misrecognition. The principles of cultural legitimacy evoked in modern jazz were tied to struggles over the constitution of the American social status hierarchy. Modern jazz was the first significant assault against an elitist and racist construction of cultural legitimacy and social status in America. While one could argue about the success of this assault and its strategic paradigm, its legacy persists in contemporary cultural politics.

Pierre Bourdieu has challenged those who wish to understand the social forces behind cultural production to avoid the reductionism of failing to take into account the place of a cultural form in the broader field of cultural production. He further poses a challenge to elucidate how broader struggles over social group legitimacy and social group distinction are expressed in the field of cultural production. While this chapter has criticized Bourdieu's assumptions about popular art and the importance of noneconomic social group distinctions in cultural production, it has done so in the spirit of acknowledging the powerful tools of analysis that he has created. It is unfortunate that Bourdieu's analysis of cultural production has yet to receive adequate attention from American scholars. I hope this chapter will lead others to consider Bourdieu's framework, whether in critical engagement or in the integration of his insights into their own analyses of cultural production.

NOTES

1. See Crane (1992), Erenberg (1989), Ross (1989), Peterson (1972), and Jones (1963).
2. See Lopes (1994), Harvey (1967), Becker (1951), and Lastrucci (1941).
3. See *FCP* and *RA* for Bourdieu's general analysis of cultural production. See *FCP*, 29–73, and *RA*, 214–77, for his specific explication of cultural fields.
4. On "unity of opposition" of individuals of divergent social origin see *FCP*, 66.
5. See DiMaggio (1982, 1991) and Levine (1988).
6. See Lopes (1994) and DiMaggio (1991) on the dissemination of the classical high art music paradigm.
7. See DiMaggio (1982), Levine (1989), and Lopes (1994) on eclecticism of popular music.
8. The importance of the oligopoly can be seen in the fact that following its collapse in the early 1950s, American music saw the advent of a whole new set of musical genres— rhythm 'n' blues, rock 'n' roll, and modern jazz. See Peterson and Berger (1975), Ryan (1985), and Lopes (1992, 1994) on the importance of the oligopoly.
9. See Ogren (1989) and Leonard (1962) on elite response to jazz in the 1920s.
10. In addition, jazz critics were important in generating the paradigm. See Lopes (1994).

11. See *FCP*, 37–40 and *RA*, 215–23 on these three subfields.

12. For examples of music critics' expression of this "struggle" between bourgeois art music and restricted art music, see Horowitz's (1987) lament of bourgeois art music and Pleasants' (1955) lament of restricted art music.

13. See Berger (1947) on the social status of jazz.

14. It must be remembered that the industry's claim of jazz not being commercially viable was a self-fulfilling prophecy, since they refused to allow it to prove itself in the market.

15. See Lopes (1994) and Harvey (1967) on the class and educational background of 1950s jazz musicians.

16. One could argue that the orientation to American pop music and classical music was a refraction of the less acknowledged associative qualities of this music as "white" culture.

17. See *FCP*, 97.

18. See *FCP*, 74–76; *RA*, 215–16.

BIBLIOGRAPHY

Becker, Howard S. "The Professional Dance Musician and His Audience." *American Journal of Sociology* 57 (1951): 136–44.

Berger, Morroe. "Jazz: Resistance to the Diffusion of a Culture Pattern." *The Journal of Negro History* (October 1947).

Bourdieu, Pierre. *The Field of Cultural Production*. Edited by Randal Johnson. New York: Columbia University Press, 1993.

———. *The Rules of Art*. Stanford, Calif.: Stanford University Press, 1996.

Crane, Diana. *The Production of Culture: Media and the Urban Arts*. London: Sage, 1992.

DiMaggio, Paul. "Social Structure, Institutions, and Cultural Goods: The Case of the United States." In *Social Theory for a Changing Society*, edited by P. Bourdieu and J. S. Coleman. San Francisco: Westview Press, 1991: 133–55.

———. "Cultural Entrepreneurship in Nineteenth-Century Boston," *Media, Culture and Society* 4 (1 and 2) (1982): 33–50, 303–22.

Erenberg, Lewis A. "Things to Come: Swing Bands, Bebop, and the Rise of a Post War Jazz Scene." In *Recasting America: Politics and Culture in the Age of the Cold War*, edited by L. May. Chicago: University of Chicago Press, 1989.

Harvey, Edward. "Social Change and the Jazz Musician." *Social Forces* 46 (1967): 34–42.

Horowitz, Joseph. 1987. *Understanding Toscanini*. New York: Alfred A. Knopf, 1987.

Jones, Leroi. *Blues People*. New York: Morrow Quill, 1963.

Lastrucci, Carlo L. "The Professional Dance Musician." *Journal of Musicology* 3 (winter 1941): 168–72.

Leonard, Neil. *Jazz and the White Americans*. Chicago: University of Chicago Press, 1962.

Levine, Lawrence. *Highbrow/Lowbrow: The Emergence of Cultural Hierarchy in America*. Cambridge, Mass.: Harvard University Press, 1988.

———. "Jazz and American Culture." *Journal of American Folklore* (1989).

Lopes, Paul. "Innovation and Diversity in the Popular Music Industry, 1969–1990." *American Sociological Review* 57 (1992): 56–71.

———. "The Rise of a Jazz Art World and the Modern Jazz Renaissance." Ph.D. dissertation, University of California at Berkeley, 1994.

Ogren, Kathy J. *The Jazz Revolution: Twenties America and the Meaning of Jazz.* New York: Oxford University Press, 1989.

Peterson, Richard A. "A Process Model of the Folk, Pop, and Fine Art Phases of Jazz." In *American Music: From Storyville to Woodstock,* edited by C. Nanry. New Brunswick, N.J.: Transaction Books, 1972.

Peterson, Richard A. and David G. Berger. "Cycles in Symbolic Production: The Case of Popular Music." *American Sociological Review* 40 (1975): 158–73.

Pleasants, Henry. 1955. *The Agony of Modern Music.* New York: Simon and Schuster, 1955.

Ross, Andrew. *No Respect: Intellectuals and Popular Culture.* New York: Routledge, 1989.

Ryan, John. *The Production of Culture in the Music Industry.* New York: University Press of America, 1985.

10

Romancing Bourdieu: A Case Study in Gender Politics in the Literary Field

Marty Hipsky

How can Bourdieu's cultural theory illuminate literary history? There are a number of possible answers to this question; given the ambitious scope and depth of Bourdieu's theoretical work in culture,[1] we might do well first to consider what the term "literary history" currently connotes. In the wake of new historicist and cultural studies-inspired projects in literary criticism, it is important to condition our understanding of the term "literary history" with the reminder that any such history is, if not a text per se, "inaccessible to us except in textual form" (Jameson, 35). In the field of literary and cultural studies, of course, conceptions of textuality have broadened to include signifying practices of all kinds, including any number of extra- or nonliterary discourses, depending on the time and place in question. From the outset, then, we perceive that Bourdieu comes in at a somewhat oblique angle to much current intellectual work in literary history, informed as such literary history is by such a multitude of complex theories of textuality; for after all, as Toril Moi asserts, "insofar as his is not a theory of textuality at all, a *purely* Bourdieuian reading is unthinkable" (1040). Bourdieu's is not a theory of discourse or textuality, that is, in the Bakhtinian, Derridean, or Foucauldian senses; an important dimension of his work has been to analyze both the social and the individual determinants of agency and subjectivity in cultural production, without being delimited by any theory of discourse or epistemology that takes language (in whatever sense, with whatever emphases) as its final horizon. Yet if, as Moi asserts, a *purely* Bourdieuian interpretation of texts is "unthinkable," it may nonetheless be his insistent focus on the particular social practices surrounding the production, distribution, and reception (or consumption) of liter-

ary works that makes his theoretical apparatus a salutary complement to the ideo-
logical-discursive focus of much literary history currently being written.

I believe this to be the case with respect to literary criticism in, for example,
the area of Victorian studies. A number of superb studies centrally concerned
with mid- to late nineteenth-century fiction have demonstrated that feminist, psy-
choanalytic, and discourse-theoretical approaches can be productive and compel-
ling in their heterogeneous explorations of their literary objects' discursive ter-
rains and ideological layerings.[2] We might partly attribute this recent critical
engagement with, above all, issues of gender and class to the fact that no traditionally delimited literary period lends itself better to contemporary theoretical
applications—whether because Victoriana offer such sheer volume and diversity
of material (much of it still tempting *terra incognita* to literary scholars), or because many of the features of modernity that have precipitated twentieth-century
sociocritical theory took early form in Victorian Britain, or even because certain
of the thinkers in whose works we find the genesis of critical and literary theory—Marx, Freud, Nietzsche, Saussure—were formed intellectually during the
mid- to late nineteenth century. Whatever the broader reasons, more theoretically
minded scholars of recent years have broken open the formerly functional and
regulative discourses of traditionally professionalized, humanistic scholarship on
Victorian culture generally, and Victorian literature in particular. While most of
us do still look upon *Jane Eyre* and *Middlemarch* as great art, we are, with the
literary-theoretical illuminations of the best of the newer scholarship, less likely
to see such classics as the ornate repositories of statically conceived humanistic
values, as revered Grecian urns high on the shelf of the Great Tradition.

Nonetheless, we might also suspect that precisely the above critical methodologies, the fresh approaches that have so productively complicated our understandings of Victorian literature, also run the risk of retrofitting their historical object
with conceptual models so powerfully motivated by the intellectual contests of
our own moment that—especially in the case of Foucault-inspired, discursively
focused theoretical reading—this work may potentially fall prey to a kind of
poststructuralist idealism, reading the texts in question *exclusively* for symptoms
of discursively constituted historical structures, forces, or pressures: gender construction, national or colonial projects, the consolidation and maintenance of hegemonic regimes of power, and so on.[3] While offering useful correctives to literary history as the story of the leading Great Authors or as the Hegelian unfolding
of the history of ideas, such accounts may also tend to underplay the idiosyncratic
historical agencies of individuals and groups, and to refigure these irreducible
contingencies as the marionettes—much like Walter Benjamin's chess automaton—of sociohistorical forces that are only ever accessible to us via discourse.
Moreover, although such accounts properly acknowledge the overdetermination
behind concrete shifts, evolutions, and novelties in cultural practice, they nonetheless may tend to overemphasize more abstract causes—this or that form of
broadly conceived power or desire—at the expense of exploring the specificities

of really existing, simultaneously discursive and extra-discursive agents of change: in the case of Victorian literature, the writers, agents, publishers, and others who acted both individually and through formal and informal institutions.

Bourdieu's theorized dialectic between the subject's *habitus* and the objective conditions of the cultural field,[4] sometimes known as "genetic structuralism,"[5] might allow us to retain the insights of the above readings while enabling a more thorough accounting for the intentions and actions of the creators of Victorian literary culture—to see them, that is, as more than ciphers of epistemic possibilities. I therefore want to employ a Bourdieuian framework in this chapter, in order to shed some light on a question of late-Victorian-through-Edwardian literary history: how do we account for the turn-of-the-century emergence of the modern, mass-market romance novel? At the risk of oversimplifying or reifying Bourdieu's supple cultural theory, I hope to demonstrate here how his models both of the various species of capital—economic, social, symbolic, cultural, educational, political (terms to be defined in what follows)—and of the embedded fields of cultural production, power, and class relations have been enormously helpful in the attempt to explain the evolution of the romance into its modern, mass-market form.[6] I am going to tell part of this story through an individual writer, Mary Arnold (Mrs. Humphry Ward), whose somewhat unenviable career vector—from Victorian totem of propriety to modernists' lightning rod of abuse—illuminates the various material, social, and ideological energies that served to shape the woman's romance novel into its recognizably secularized, liberal individualist form. There are therefore two interpretive horizons in play here: first, that of the great methodological potential of Bourdieu's theoretical apparatus in cultural historicizing projects such as this one; second, that of the history of a particular literary field, whereby this evolution of the romance contributes to our understanding of the twentieth-century's "Great Divide" between the "mass" and the "high" in culture. All the while, my metacritical goal is to demonstrate via this instance the compatibility between the textualist approaches glossed above and an approach that foregrounds institutions and social processes.[7]

THE LITERARY FIELD OF LATE VICTORIAN ENGLAND

I want to start this story with the judgment of a recent literary historian, who tells us that

> around the turn of the century, there were no women novelists of a literary stature remotely comparable to that of James, Hardy, Conrad, Meredith, Bennett, Wells, Gissing, or a dozen other men. This situation was itself a specifically late Victorian phenomenon . . . from the death of George Eliot in 1880 until the publication of Virginia Woolf's first novel *The Voyage Out* (1915), there was a break in the great

tradition . . . even though there were more women publishing fiction and earning a good living from it than ever before. (Keating, 175)

However we may feel about the mystical continuity of "the Great Tradition," the period 1880–1914 does seem to offer a conspicuous hiatus in contemporary canons of fiction by English women. Between the death of George Eliot and the publication of Virginia Woolf's first novels, we witness the yawning emptiness of what Raymond Williams, referring to British literature as a whole, calls "The Interregnum."[8] Observers of the period were in fact noticing this hiatus in significant literary output from women authors. There is much evidence to suggest that in the mid-Victorian period, the popular image of female literary output in Britain had bifurcated into two general categories: popular "sensation" fiction, meant for light entertainment, and the morally serious novel, devoted to exploring ethical questions stemming from the relationship between individual and society. By 1880, the year of George Eliot's death, we might posit that there existed in the world of English letters these two ready-made roles for any would-be fiction writer who happened to be female: on the one hand, there was the "serious lady novelist," staking her claim to verisimilitude and the complex portrayal of moral problems and psychological truths, and to the mantle of Jane Austen, Charlotte Brontë, Elizabeth Gaskell, and Eliot; on the other, there were the many writers of popular novels for the entertainment of a less educated audience, in a tradition spanning from Fanny Burney to Mary Elizabeth Braddon. The former category was understood to be a very small club, yet its members were accepted as the peers of the greatest male novelists. In fact, late Victorian male critics in positions of cultural power regularly listed women writers as among the best in the English tradition, as attested by this catalogue from an 1877 article in *Nineteenth Century*: "our great English novelists—Miss Austen, Scott, Dickens, Thackeray," with "the greatest name of all, George Eliot, in the present" (Meyers, 229). One midcentury critic, François Guizot, went so far as to rhapsodize on how "[m]y delight is to read English novels, particularly those written by women. *C'est tout une école de morale.* Miss Austen, Miss Ferrier, Charlotte Brontë, George Eliot, Mrs. Gaskell, and many others almost as remarkable, form a school which . . . resembles the cloud of dramatic poets of the great Athenian age."[9] The latter category, by contrast, had been belittled by none other than George Eliot herself, in her well-known derogation of "silly novels by lady novelists."[10] On the occasion of Eliot's death, a female critic approvingly cited the great author's dictum:

> As an artist, [Eliot] wrote in 1852, Miss Austen surpasses all the male novelists that ever lived, and for eloquence and depth of feeling no man approaches George Sand. But in general the literature of women may be compared to that of Rome—a literature of imitation. (Simcox, 782)

By critical consensus, female literary genius exhibited two special features: it expressed moral vision, and it was exceedingly rare. By the closing decades of the century, moreover, these women authors of genius had begun to be perceived as a phenomenon of the past.

The categories of "woman novelist of genius" and "silly lady novelist"—the one embracing a select few, the other an undifferentiated mass—might be said to correspond to two positional poles on the late Victorian literary field, as hypothetically charted in table 10.1. Bourdieu defines the field generally as a competi-

Table 10.1 Hypothetical Configuration of the Literary Field in Britain, 1880–1900

	+ **HIGH CONSECRATION** (older figures)	
intellectual audience		*bourgeois audience*
Carlyle		Dickens
M. Arnold	realist novel	Scott
Ruskin	George Eliot	
	Charlotte Brontë	
Pater	**"woman novelist of genius"**	
Swinburne, Rosetti		
psychological novel	**MRS. HUMPHRY WARD**	"high" theatre
← Henry James		
Aestheticism	Charlotte Yonge	
	Mrs. Henry Wood	
POETRY	*NOVEL*	*DRAMA*
+ AUTONOMY	← Oscar Wilde →	HETERONOMY —
The Yellow Book	serial novel	Mrs. Oliphant
	magazine story	
William Morris	journalism	
George Meredith		Marie Corelli
Decadence		**"silly lady novelist"**
	Thomas Hardy	sensation novel
		comic opera
		music halls
George Gissing	**"New Woman novelist"** (post-1890)	
	Olive Schreiner, Beatrice Harraden,	
	Ella D'Arcy, George Egerton, et al.	
Bohemia		
no audience	**LOW CONSECRATION** (younger figures) —	*mass audience*

Literature no longer holds its former high prestige,—there are too many in the field,—too many newspaper-scribblers, all believing they are geniuses,—too many ill-educated lady-paragraphists and 'new' women, who think they are as gifted as Georges Sand. (Marie Corelli, *The Sorrows of Satan,* 1895, 260)

tive system of social relations, operating under the rules specific to its do-main—be it the economic, the political, the educational, the cultural, the social, or any other. It is important in the context of cultural analysis to remember that, though the broadest field of class relations encompasses the just-listed fields, each of these fields is nonetheless semiautonomous and functions by its own rules.[11] Thus would Bourdieu attempt to avoid reductionism, for instance the notion that economics or politics must inevitably determine the relations of the agents on a given field. What the fields *do* share is a homologous functioning, whereby agents take positions on the field, and engage in competition for control of the interests and resources that are specific to the field in question.[12]

Bourdieu describes the literary field, which for our purposes here can be considered a subset of the field of cultural production, as

> neither a vague social background nor even a *milieu artistique* like a universe of personal relations between artists and writers (perspectives adopted by those who study "influences"). It is a veritable social universe where, in accordance with its particular laws, there accumulates a particular form of capital and where relations of force of a particular type are exerted. This universe is the place of entirely specific struggles, notably concerning the question of knowing who is part of the universe, who is a real writer and who is not. (*FCP*, 163–64)

According to this view, the literary field is best envisioned as a two-dimensional, metaphorical arena of cultural reception, in which are constelled the dominant works, authors, and genres of a given historical moment. The field's horizontal axis measures the relative popularity and profitability of a given work or writer or genre; figures' and texts' relative positions are, in an obvious borrowing from Marx, calculable via their "economic capital," which in this specifically cultural context signifies their commercial success. The vertical axis measures the relative prestige of the work, writer, or genre in question; its measure of success is what Bourdieu calls above "a particular form of capital"—*symbolic* capital, or relative cultural prestige (although the term is not strictly synonymous with traditionally understood "prestige," as we will see below). This second form of "capital" here is clearly figurative; it conveys the risks of the original venture of seeking recognition on the literary field, as well as the propensity of cultural prestige, once established, to maintain itself or accumulate if it is carefully "managed." The metaphor vividly connotes the investment, accumulation, and convertibility of such prestige within the social context of a given field.

Bourdieu further suggests that the study of a given literary field is

> a form of *analysis situs* which establishes that each position—e.g. the one which corresponds to a genre such as the novel or, within this, to a sub-category such as the "society novel" or the "popular" novel—is subjectively defined by the system of distinctive properties by which it can be situated relative to other positions; that every position, even the dominant one, depends for its very existence, and for the

determinations it imposes on its occupants, on the other positions constituting the field; and that the structure of the field, i.e. the open space of positions, is nothing other than the structure of the distribution of capital of specific properties which governs success in the field and the winning of external or specific profits (such as literary prestige) which are at stake in the field. (*FCP*, 30)

Here Bourdieu reveals the structuralist underpinnings of his theory. He posits that the field is not ontologically grounded, but rather constituted of ever-changing relations—it is not a static thing, but a dynamic process, in which fluid relationality is the source of structure. He also refers to a universal aspect of all fields, cultural and otherwise: each involves specific forms of capital, which the agents aim to accumulate and increase through their varying "strategies."[13] The term "capital," again, while used literally in the case of "economic capital," is in its other designations figurative, and functions as incarnated through the "specific properties" (cultural, symbolic, political, educational, linguistic, etc.) that govern success in a given field.

The three forms of (noneconomic) capital most important to us here are the cultural, social, and symbolic. "Cultural capital" refers to cultural knowledge as a resource of power; it consists in "the incorporation of symbolic, cognitive, and aesthetic competences via implicit learning processes mainly within the family socialization" (Joppke, 57). Cultural capital can take objective form in cultural goods, artifacts, books, and so on; beyond the family, it is accrued through social associations and formal and informal schooling. "Social capital" refers generally to the power that comes of social associations, such as membership in various kinds of groups, both formal and informal; the strategic use and accumulation of such capital can bring the profit of improved position, as through "social climbing." "Symbolic capital" is perhaps the trickiest (and most important) form of noneconomic capital in Bourdieu's theory. It effectively embraces all the other species of capital, and is the most abstract form, constituted as it is within the recognition (*reconnaissance*) of others. Neither one's literary allusions nor one's *objets d'art* nor one's social connections can function as valuable unless they are recognized as valuable by those individuals and groups who form one's social context. As Christian Joppke asserts, "Because symbolic capital is dependent on its activation and affirmation by actual communicative practices, and in this regard cannot be objectified, institutionalized, or incorporated, it is merely a subjective reflection, acknowledgement and legitimation of a given distribution of economic, cultural, and social capital" (60). Symbolic capital might thus be said to have a dialectical relationship with the other forms of capital; as a concept it underscores the fact that none of the positive properties that circulate on the literary field ever *permanently* or *objectively* inhere in any of the individuals, groups, works, or literary forms that are held to partake of those properties. The structure of the literary field is always contingent and evolving as a matrix of subjective perceptions, power relations, and objectified embodiments of symbolic capital.

Though it is a complex structure, then, the literary field does in large measure take its form through the identifiable exertions of individual and collective will and agency. Not only do literary writers compete, through their strategies, to improve their relative positions on the cultural field; they have also historically "struggled" (Bourdieu's term is quite deliberate here) for the opportunity to claim a position on it in the first place, to be considered "real writers." For the field is also "the site of struggles in which what is at stake is the power to impose the dominant definition of the writer and therefore to delimit the population of those entitled to take part in the struggle to define the writer" (*FCP*, 44). Such struggles, individual and collective, return us to the case study at hand. In the literary history of the nineteenth century (as in any era), the literary field was experienced differently by female and male writers; while all strove individually or in movements to stake their claim in what it meant to be a writer, only female aspirants had the added challenge of struggling to legitimate themselves as *women* writers—to overcome, that is, powerful gender prejudice against their cultural productions. While this observation may seem self-evident, the point here is that, in the case of late Victorian and Edwardian women novelists, authorial gender is one crucial, symbolic "property" among the others—economic capital, social capital, and cultural capital—that together and in complex fashion help determine an author's or a text's success on the literary field. As we will see in the case of Mrs. Humphry Ward, advantages in certain of these forms of capital could occasionally help overcome the social handicap of gender. As Toril Moi asserts,

> In general, the impact of femaleness as negative capital may be assumed to decline in direct proportion to the amount of other forms of symbolic capital amassed. Or to put it the other way around: although a woman rich in symbolic capital may lose *some* legitimacy because of her gender, she still has more than enough capital left to make her impact on the field. In the case of exceptionally high amounts of capital, femaleness may play a very small part indeed. (1038)

While Moi is here referring primarily to female cultural figures of the twentieth century (for example, Simone de Beauvoir), the point holds—though to a somewhat lesser extent—for the Victorian literary field. As we have seen, by the late Victorian period the positions available to the woman writer consisted mainly in the two roles or constructs described above—at one end, "the woman novelist of genius," with her high symbolic capital (at that historical moment, perhaps the highest ever accorded the female writer); at the other, the scribbling, "silly lady novelist," with her low symbolic capital, but ever-increasing potential for high financial capital—that is, massive popular sales, and the very real possibility of the author's economic independence. Thus the wider field of positions made possible by "the distribution of specific properties"—in this case, the degree of institutional consecration and the degree of success in the market—is in the case of the woman writer's works narrowed down dramatically by the possession of yet another "distinctive property," namely, the author's gender. If the potential for institutional consecration had come only gradually to the woman writer, and almost exclusively through the genre of the novel, her artistic autonomy from market forces was, by virtue of that genre's heteronomous[14] position in the field, essentially nonexistent. But if by 1880 women novelists' victories on the literary field were few and hard won, they were nonetheless incontestable. The title "lady novelist of genius" could be said to have occupied a position of middle-range economic capital, and relatively high symbolic capital, given its synonymity with the names of Jane Austen and George Eliot. The "silly lady novelist," by contrast, could be said to occupy a low corner of the field, given her high earning potential and abysmally low status in the eyes of the masculine arbiters of culture.

Another important element here, however, is the fact that literary genres themselves can acquire, maintain, or lose both economic and symbolic capital. Just as they can become more or less commercially viable, so too can their relative prestige as cultural forms rise or fall over time—and the relationship between these two indices is never fully predictable. In the case of the Victorian novel, as Gaye Tuchman and Nina Fortin (1989) have carefully demonstrated, both the genre's profitability and its prestige rose considerably between 1840 and 1900, but the gender distribution of low-culture versus high-culture novelists underwent a transformation:

> Before 1840 the British cultural elite accorded little prestige to the writing of novels, and most English novelists were women. By the turn of the twentieth century "men of letters" acclaimed novels as a form of literature, and most critically successful novelists were men. These two transitions—in the prestige of novel-writing and the gender distribution of lauded novelists—were related processes, constituting complementary elements in a classic confrontation between men and women in the same white-collar occupation. (Tuchman and Fortin, 1)

Through a detailed study of the publishing records of such houses as Macmillan and Company, Tuchman and Fortin have shown how once such women writers as Austen, Gaskell, and the Brontës helped to establish the prestige of the novel as a preeminent English literary form, the male publishers and critics began to redefine the serious novel as a male province, and to exclude *new* women writers from the "high end" of the field. By the turn of the century, in this well-documented account, "women were not edged out of all fiction writing; they were edged out of writing high-culture novels" (Tuchman and Fortin, 93). On the literary field, in other words, the novel as a genre began in this period to bifurcate clearly into "high" and "low" embodiments; women writers were generally assumed to be capable of producing only the latter. If the examples of Austen, Gaskell, the Brontës, and Eliot offered towering refutations of this assumption, the overwhelmingly male publishing and critical establishments made no attempt to belittle their achievements; in a neat ideological contradiction, the widespread belief in female literary exceptionalism allowed them both to revere these precedents and routinely to dismiss ambitious new women novelists.

As Tuchman and Fortin's terms for this evolution in the literary field should indicate—"a classic confrontation between men and women in the same white-collar occupation"—this account of the Victorian "lady novelist" is a sociological one, and as such focuses on the institutional and ideological structures of the period. It is certainly true that women writers were collective victims of male-dominated institutions and ideologies, yet the very language of the description— women "were edged out of writing high-culture novels"—reveals through its passive construction how focusing on these levels exclusively may obscure women writers' own agency in this literary history. For this evolution is also the history of the interplay between, on the one hand, the patriarchal structures of the publishing industry and wider Victorian society, and on the other, the actions of certain (relatively) empowered women themselves, as individual agents, in the evolving social constructions of "the lady novelist." Certainly it must be true that, given the lopsided binary of a very few "serious" novel-writing precedents versus the mass of "frivolous" ones (with virtually no role models in-between), any aspiring young woman writer of the time must have felt powerfully the limited possibilities of the literary field. (How many, for instance, felt encouraged to designate themselves "poet" or "playwright"—not simply as amateurs, but vocationally?) Yet in the years following George Eliot's death, the list of those who did attempt to match her kind of novelistic achievement is a long one, including Eliza Lynn Linton, Olive Schreiner, "John Oliver Hobbes," and Vernon Lee.[15] Patriarchal ideologies notwithstanding, the existence of such an "officially" belaurelled predecessor served as a powerful encouragement to ambitious women novelists coming of intellectual age in the 1880s and 1890s.

MRS. HUMPHRY WARD TAKES A POSITION

Nowhere is the aspiration to become "the next George Eliot" more apparent than in the history of how the young Mrs. Humphry Ward, née Mary Arnold, came to publish one of the best-selling novels of nineteenth-century England. As the granddaughter of Dr. Thomas Arnold, niece of Matthew Arnold, and friend to Walter Pater, Robert Browning, T. H. Huxley, and Henry James, Mary Ward was arguably as well provided with educational and cultural advantages—with high-cultural capital—as any woman of the period could possibly have been. Her first youthful efforts at becoming a woman of letters consisted of a poetry primer, a translation of the Swiss philosopher Amiel, and a Jamesian novella entitled *Miss Bretherton* (1884). Although her uncle Matthew pooh-poohed these efforts— reportedly announcing, "No Arnold can write a novel; if they could, I should have done it"[16]—Ward did manage, through her considerable social connections, to get her first novel published, and she was undaunted by its indifferent reception. As capable and energetic as she was ambitious, she now took her publisher Macmillan's advice and set out to write on a more "generally popular subject";[17] yet she also clearly hoped that the new work would identify her as a novelist of ideas—as, that is, the potential successor to George Eliot. As she explains in her autobiography, Ward wanted to write a novel simultaneously popular and intellectually challenging (*A Writer's Recollections*, 233). Implicit in this self-description was the desire to assay the highest position on the literary field now imaginable to the woman writer, by publishing a work in the same vein of high seriousness as were Eliot's late, most philosophical works, *Romola* and *Daniel Deronda*.

To aim for this high position in the literary field, Ward required a theme equal to the task. Happily, her social experience among the male Oxford intelligentsia of the 1870s and 1880s provided her with a complex and controversial *donnée* for a novel—the loss of Christian faith. Harnessed to a traditional romance, this theme might, as she put it, "touch two zones of thought . . . that of the scholar, and that of what one may call the educated populace" (*A Writer's Recollections*, 233)—might, that is, bring her symbolic capital both in the general literary field, and, within that, amid the exclusively male domain of the Oxford academic-intellectual milieu. The resulting novel, *Robert Elsmere* (1888), is at once a passionate love story, a compendium of allusions to most major British thinkers of the nineteenth century (in a zealous and excessive display of its author's cultural capital), and the tale of a man's rejection of Christianity in favor of an ethical theism. Ward herself would later describe the impetus behind the work as her desire to appeal to "the floating interest and passion surrounding a great controversy—the *second* religious battle of the nineteenth century—with which it had seemed to me both in London and in Oxford that the intellectual air was charged" (*A Writer's Recollections*, 233). She refers here to the multiple challenges to established religious thought at Oxford during the 1860s and 1870s, the liberalizing Christian "heresies" being propounded by Benjamin Jowett, T. H. Green, Mark Pattison, and others. We need not revisit here the substance of these religious controversies to recognize how brilliantly Ward appropriated them to effect her successful arrival as a woman novelist.

If, in a structural sense, George Eliot's precedent offered Ward an imaginable position for the ambitiously intellectual female novelist on the field, then on the thematic level, the religious novel offered her the safe means for what Bourdieu calls an effective "position-taking" (*prise de position*) on the field. As Randal Johnson suggests,

> The dynamic of the [cultural] field is based on the struggles between . . . positions, a struggle often expressed in the conflict between the orthodoxy of established tradi-

tions and the heretical challenge of new modes of cultural practice, manifested as *prises de position* or position-takings. (In *FCP*, 16–17)

In publishing *Robert Elsmere*, Ward participated in this metaphorical struggle between literary "orthodoxy" and "heterodoxy" (Bourdieuian terms), by championing a literally heretical movement in religious thought. Certainly she saw herself as doing so; she lists as her literary models for *Robert Elsmere* certain controversial mid-Victorian male literary figures: "There were great precedents—Froude's 'Nemesis of Faith,' Newman's 'Loss and Gain,' Kingsley's 'Alton Locke,'—for the novel of religious or social propaganda" (*A Writer's Recollections*, 229). Few literary historians today would deny that *Robert Elsmere*'s profound treatment of the title character's complex spiritual and religious crises earns Ward an irrefutable place on this list. The brilliance of her strategy here, however, lies in the fact that, behind her overt and successful tactic of religio-philosophical provocation, Ward was effectively camouflaging the challenge of what Johnson calls above a "new mode of cultural practice": a woman "novelist of ideas" asking to be taken as seriously as the most controversial male thinkers—and not *only* male novelists—of the time. It was Eliot and Eliot alone who had recently made a successful bid to extend the female novelist's authority beyond exclusively moral questions and into a more philosophical purview. This particular kind of intellectual ambition, coming from a female novelist, was still virtually unheard of. As if to divert attention from this fact, Ward offers in *Robert Elsmere* a throughgoing ideology of male intellectual superiority over women. If the novel's religious explorations were daring and progressive in their time, the social universe within which she environs them is profoundly retrograde in its gender relations. Catherine, the novel's heroine, is as passionate in her self-denying adulation of her husband Robert as she is incapable of understanding his radical ideas about the nature of Christianity. Catherine's sister, Rose, who has artistic ambitions and an urge toward independence, is duly punished by the narrative for placing these goals before her feminine self-subordination to the right kind of man. The divide between the male and female characters has in fact been an aspect of the novel most striking to contemporary critics; as Clyde Ryals notes, "the men in *Robert Elsmere* sometimes seem to be personifications of ideas more than flesh-and-blood human beings," whereas the women are "vivid" and intuitive characters who "gain in moral awareness through love and suffering" (Ryals, introduction to *Robert Elsmere*, xxxiii–xxxvi).

In fact, *Robert Elsmere*'s vastly different representations of male and female characters could be seen as the novel's structuring tension, a faultline at once thematic and formal, ideological and generic. As noted above, the novel embodies both philosophico-religious treatise and romantic love story, and while the former dimension is achieved through a set of debating male characters, the latter is experienced primarily through the heroine's self-subjection to her lover/husband. The romantic plotline is the simple and time-honored tale of the hero's wooing, winning, losing (in this case, spiritually), and rewinning of the heroine. As Laura Fasick suggests, Ward here (and in her subsequent novels) "makes her love stories a conversion experience as well" (150)—the conversion of intellectually and psychologically dependent women to the beliefs of their superior male lover/husbands. We therefore see this thematic and ideological pattern at both the level of overt theme and the level of genre itself; Ward hybridizes or cross-pollinates the genres of the philosophical novel and the romance novel. Just as the male characters serve as the vehicles of ideas to be learned by the female characters, so the "feminine" genre of the love story helps sustain the reader's interest in the "masculine" genre of the "novel of ideas." Thus, in the same stroke, Ward both shields her "unwomanly" literary ambition by representing a profoundly patriarchal vision and aims for wide popular appeal by delivering her provocative religious philosophy through the vehicle of a romantic love story.

This complex strategy worked phenomenally well, establishing her virtually overnight as a serious literary-intellectual contender. Published in late February 1888, *Robert Elsmere* at first received little notice. But Ward was frenetic behind the scenes, shrewdly manipulating her connections, calling in her various investments of social capital among the producers of cultural meaning and value. She asked for and received a favorable review of the novel from Walter Pater; she had a copy sent to W. Knowles, the editor of the highbrow journal *Nineteenth Century*, with the very audacious request that he pass it on to his mentor, ex-Prime Minister William Gladstone. On 14 March 1888, three weeks after the novel's publication, she wrote to her publisher that Knowles "seems to be enthusiastic, and is handing his copy on to Mr. Gladstone. But I am afraid R. E.'s [her main character Robert Elsmere's] opinions will hardly be . . . congenial to the G.O.M. ['Grand Old Man']." While the ex-leader of England did not find the protagonist's theism exactly "congenial," he did take the novel very seriously, considering it be a "propagandist romance" symptomatic of England's religious decay (Gladstone, 766). Passing through Oxford in early April, a week after he had read *Robert Elsmere,* Gladstone summoned its author for a discussion of the novel. Ward had been standing vigil over her dying mother, but would not let this get in the way of a career-making encounter; within twenty-four hours of her mother's death she appeared at Gladstone's door for the requested interview, and proceeded to argue with him about Christian miracles at great length.[18] Seven days later, uncle Matthew Arnold—astonished perhaps by the news of this imperial summons of his niece—dropped dead of cardiac arrest in a street in Liverpool. Nor were the newspapers unimpressed; their reported rumors of this encounter sparked the novel's sales dramatically. A month later, Gladstone published a long review essay attacking the novel's theological positions, and the resulting notoriety soon caused the work to become the best-selling English novel of the nineteenth century to date.

W. E. Gladstone, a powerful individual from the dominant fraction of the nation's dominant class, had by taking issue with this "propaganda romance" not only effectively legitimated Mary Ward as a significant novelist, but also, on another level, helped to consolidate and sustain the high symbolic capital that, after Brontë and Eliot, could potentially infuse the female-authored romance novel. Mary Ward had parlayed both her own and others' cultural, social, and even political capital into a firm basis of symbolic capital on which to launch a stunningly successful early career as late Victorian Britain's premiere female novelist. Ward herself immediately sensed as much; she soon dared, in private correspondence with her editor, to invoke Eliot's example as a parallel to her own:

> I am very glad to hear that the 4th edition [of *Elsmere*] is doing so well. But do you anticipate a speedy slackening in the sale that you are only printing 250 copies instead of 500 in the 5th edition? On looking back at the facts of George Eliot's circulation, I see that her great success in the case of Adam Bede was made with a 2 vol. edition which came out after about 2750 copies of the third edition had been dispensed of. . . . I don't mean to compare myself to G.E., whatever foolish and 'irresponsible reviewers' may do! (Letter to George Smith, 2 May 1888)

Both the practical concern with sales figures and the coyness about her own literary stature are characteristic Ward; her ambition takes cover under a "feminine" self-effacement, yet she is never afraid to reveal to her editors a hard-nosed business sense. For if she had an uncanny "sense of the game" in the literary field—a well-developed *habitus*—she had an attendant knack for converting her symbolic capital into the more concrete form of money.

WOMEN WRITERS AND THE LITERARY FIELD
UNDER WARD'S DOMINANCE

Hereafter, until the early Edwardian period, Mrs. Humphry Ward managed to maintain both her vast popularity and her role as the standard-bearer of the "respectable lady novelist." During these years, the fate of the female "novelist of genius," as social construct and repository of symbolic capital, arguably lay in her hands as in no one else's. Nevertheless, despite a string of intellectually sophisticated (if effectively antifeminist) novels between 1888 and 1898—*Elsmere, The History of David Grieve* (1892), *Marcella* (1894), *Helbeck of Bannisdale* (1898)—and despite her successful self-promotion among the institutions of literary legitimation and consecration, she soon went on to help delegitimate and deconsecrate the same prestigious image of the high-end "lady novelist" that she had seemingly carried on.

In part, as one might well imagine, her unfaltering advocacy of women's relegation to the private and domestic spheres would meet with increasing distaste among younger readers, especially those influenced by the New Women novelists of the early to mid-1890s; yet her status as ideological reactionary only reinforced her prestige among the conservative establishment through the Edwardian era. She was invited, for instance, to visit with Teddy Roosevelt at the White House in 1908. The subtitle of John Sutherland's biography tells this story of her institutionalization in four words: *Mrs. Humphry Ward: Eminent Victorian, Pre-Eminent Edwardian.*

However, Ward's most important influence on the symbolic and economic capital of women novelists as a group arguably had less to do with her gender ideology than with her role in the rapidly changing economy of the publishing industry. Soon after her blockbuster religious romance had lifted Ward and her family out of shabby gentility and into the realm of the *nouveau riche*, Ward and her family assumed a new life of country houses, aristocratic affectations, philanthropic projects, and elite education for the children. In order to sustain this upward mobility, Ward began to transform herself, in the words of her biographer, into a "money-generating fiction machine" (Sutherland, 133). All pretense of intellectual autonomy in her art—as a literary practice that would at least appear to resist marketing and literary codification—was by the early 1900s draining out of her work. After her reputation's apogee in the mid-1890s, when critics crowned her as "the greatest woman novelist of her day" (Sutherland, 151), her writing became more and more simplistic. In a series of novels written between 1902 and 1914—*Lady Rose's Daughter* (1903), *Fenwick's Career* (1906), *The Testing of Diana Mallory* (1908), *The Case of Richard Meynell* (1911), *The Mating of Lydia* (1913), and *Delia Blanchflower* (1914)—she shifted her writing's emphasis from characterization and ideas to plot and simple-minded didacticism. In order to maintain her tremendous popular appeal (especially in the United States), she made her fallen antiheroines' subplots racier and more scandalous, even as she moralistically decried both the feminist explorations of the "New Woman" novelists and the women's suffrage movement itself.

Thus, Mary Ward was making a deliberate transition into writing solely for the field of large-scale production. According to Bourdieu, another feature of nineteenth- and twentieth-century literary fields is the distinction between the field of restricted production, in which culture is produced primarily for other cultural producers, and the field of large-scale production, in which culture is produced for the widest possible audience, and is conceived primarily as a commodity on the market. (These fields correspond respectively to the "autonomous" versus "heteronomous" spheres of cultural production). While the field of restricted production is embedded within the field of large-scale production, and consequently dominated by this larger field economically, the former achieves a kind of revenge on the latter, by reversing its terms of value, and excluding those writers and artists who achieve popular acclaim. Early on, Ward had been a rare instance of the writer who achieved success in both fields; increasingly, however, she strove to make her novels' ideological messages appeal unchallengingly to the broadest audience possible, and to flatter her audience's chauvinisms and unexamined prejudices. The protagonist of *Fenwick's Career* is pitted against the newfangled corruption of French impressionist painting; the heroine of *The Test-*

ing of Diana Mallory is fanatically pro-imperialist; the villain of *Delia Blanch-flower* is a militant suffragette (based on Christabel Pankhurst). Increasingly, Ward pitted herself against the ideological heterodoxies associated with the burgeoning cultural and political avant-gardes of the pre-World War I years.

It is perhaps ironic, however, that Ward's most significant influence on the literary field through these years arguably had nothing to do with the powerfully traditionalist ideologies of her conservative romance novels. Perhaps most important of all for the future of the woman-authored romance was the effect of Ward's newfound power in the publishing industry. Desiring a greater share of personal profit from her work—in order to sustain her suddenly elevated social status—Ward arranged with her publishers to bring out the cheaper, fast-selling single-volume editions of her novels ever faster after their triple-volume publication for the lending libraries. By so doing, Mary Ward in 1894 became one of the proximate causes of a phenomenon that would in some senses enable the twentieth-century mass marketing of fiction in Britain: namely, the extinction of that Victorian institution, the triple-decker novel. This moment had of course been coming for a while, given recent advances in publishing technologies, along with the massive book-buying public that had been swelling since the 1870 Education Act. In the early 1890s, a number of publishers who wished to avoid the censorship of the circulating libraries—notably, John Lane, T. Fisher Unwin, Heinemann's, and Ward, Lock, and Bowen—had begun to depart from the usual three-decker format and to sell novels directly to the public in cheap, single-volume format. Nevertheless, it was Mary Ward, probably the highest-paid woman in 1890s Britain (Sutherland, 159), who was powerful enough by 1894 to achieve what no male author had yet achieved, and successfully take on the once all-powerful institution of the circulating libraries, with their patriarchal arbiters, Mudie and W. H. Smith. Against their explicit wishes, Ward convinced her publisher George Smith to bring out the six-shilling, one-volume edition of *Marcella* a mere three months after the three-volume edition. (The usual delay was at least twice as long, to ensure the profits of the lending libraries.) As Ward's biographer, John Sutherland, asserts, "The reprint of *Marcella* was the torpedo that sunk the three-decker and by so doing stripped Mudie of his dictatorial powers" (148).

Ward's publishing coup had wide-ranging emancipatory effects, inasmuch as it helped decrease the circulating libraries' censorious and socially normative control of women's production and consumption of fiction. Indeed, after the mid-1890s there would be be virtually no mediating cultural institutions between popular women writers and market forces; together with material gains in publishers' efficiency and tremendous leaps in literacy among the lower classes, the demise of the triple-decker irrevocably changed the structure of the literary field as a whole. But of course direct exposure to the market also brought with it those negative effects with which we, at this end of the twentieth century, are all too familiar. With uncensored access to the ever-growing reading market, publishers increasingly expected female novelists to produce—as Ward soon did herself—

that more immediately sensational and less morally complex romantic fiction which provided publishers their best profit margins. With less and less of the overt attention to gender politics that had characterized the New Woman fiction, and more and more adherence to formulaic love stories, a handful of female fiction writers in Edwardian England now successfully realized the writing profession for women even as they weakened its potential autonomy and lowered its cultural status in the field. The day of the so-called "sex novel," that embryo of the contemporary mass-market romance, had arrived; its most successful practitioners—Elinor Glyn, Florence Barclay, Ethel Dell—had by 1914 supplanted the more cautious and residually Victorian Mary Ward in this burgeoning new subgenre. Mills & Boon, the British equivalent of Harlequin Romance, was founded in 1908. Writing popular romance was becoming a vocation of what Bourdieu labels "industrial art," heteronomously determined by market forces. The irony here—the ruse of literary history—may thus be that Ward helped materially to enable the widespread distribution of "sex-novels" whose implicit ideologies of women's right to erotic pleasure Ward abhorred. It was at precisely the moment of these more "licentious" new novels' appearance within the field of large-scale literary production—circa 1910—that saw the beginning of Ward's popular decline. Almost overnight, the mass readership on both sides of the Atlantic began to find her romances too "Victorian" in their treatments of women's public and romantic lives.

The female novelist was now capable of wider popular success and greater financial independence than ever before in British history; at the same time, her symbolic capital had sunk dramatically since the mid-Victorian "golden age." It would now take the highbrow modernism of such women writers as Virginia Woolf, Rebecca West, Katherine Mansfield, Dorothy Richardson, and others, reacting against the twentieth-century stampede of mass-market romanciers, to redeem the symbolic capital of the female literary writer as a social construct. But they did so at a familiar price: the increased polarization of the literary field. By 1920, such female modernists were doing their utmost to distance themselves from the romance-writers of large-scale literary production. Rebecca West was decrying the novels of Dell and Barclay and Marie Corelli as "tosh," and proclaiming that Mrs. Humphry Ward's career had been "one long specialization in the *mot injuste*" (West, 106). Had Ward lived to read these words, she would have been offended in more ways than one. Not only had she been lumped in with her ideological foes, the new breed of mass-market novelist; she had even become the anti-Flaubert, triply reviled by the bohemian avant-garde for her bourgeois institutionalization, her formal and thematic conservatism, and her (one-time) mass appeal. Whether explicitly or intuitively, the female renegades of modernism could now define themselves as Ward's determinate negation, her converse image on the literary field. For by 1920, the year of her death, she had offered the model of female predominance in both symbolic and economic capital on the literary field, with a power that was only just beginning to wane; yet her institutionalization was of such a nature that it precluded any sense of gender solidarity with her on the part of the literary avant-garde. It was her kind who had helped to structure the orthodox positions in the literary field upon which these modernist writers were now taking their unorthodox positions. The feminist modernists, of course, would in their turn accrue symbolic capital and ascend to positions of dominance and orthodoxy, as the literary field evolved through the 1920s and thereafter. But that is another story.

NOTES

1. Most systematically laid out, perhaps, in *Distinction: A Social Critique of the Judgement of Taste* (1979; Eng. trans., 1984), *The Field of Cultural Production* (1993), and *The Rules of Art: Genesis and Structure of the Literary Field* (1992; Eng. trans. 1996).

2. To name a few of the best: Elaine Showalter (1977), Eve Sedgwick (1985), Nancy Armstrong (1987), D. A. Miller (1988), Mary Poovey (1988), Anne Cvetkovich (1992), and Anne McClintock (1995).

3. Thus it is, for instance, that D. A. Miller's *The Novel and the Police* (1988) employs Foucault's theories of incarceral discipline, and Nancy Armstrong's *Desire and Domestic Fiction* (1987) uses Foucault's theories of the history of sexuality, in incisive efforts to demonstrate how both the content and the reading of Victorian novels produced and perpetuated middle-class cultural hegemony. Yet, as Elizabeth Langland points out, each of these critics may be seen to offer too totalizing and neatly continuous a narrative of the development of "the bourgeois subject" (1994, 5).

4. Bourdieu has variously defined these two central terms, *habitus* and "field." In perhaps the best-known definition of the former, he calls it a system of "durable, transposable dispositions, structured structures predisposed to function as structuring structures, that is, as principles which generate and organize practices and representations that can be objectively adapted to their outcomes without presupposing a conscious aiming at ends or an express mastery of the operations necessary to attain them" (1977, 72). "A field," he says, "is a space in which a game takes place [*espace de jeu*], a field of objective relations between individuals or institutions who are competing for the same stake" (quoted in Moi, 1021).

5. Bourdieu's thought has also at times been called *genetic sociology*. The term "genetic"—from the Greek *genesis*, or "becoming"—carries this theory's fundamental difference from other structuralist modes of perceiving sociocultural phenomena. Genetic structuralism, fully accounting for the agency of the individual or collective subject, is perhaps more effectively dialectical than Saussurean semiology, structural anthropology, or Althusserian marxism. Central to its readdressing of subjectivity is the notion, borrowed from Scholastic philosophy, of the *habitus*. This concept accounts for the creative, active, and inventive capacities of human agents, without reducing their agency to any "universal mind." Genetic structuralism is also dialectical inasmuch as it defines class members by their *being-perceived* as much as by their *being*, that is, by their consumption as much as by their position in the relations of production. It therefore describes both those members' *becoming-in-being*, as structurally evolving class positionalities, and those members *be-*

coming-in-appearing, as volitional, consuming agents with a special emphasis on the latter phenomenon.

6. The larger project out of which I have lifted this chapter was originally inspired by Jan Radway's *Reading the Romance* (1984), which investigates the contemporary American practice of reading Harlequin-style romances. I had wanted to scrutinize the popular woman-authored romance in the place and period that I study—namely, Britain at the turn of the twentieth century—but Radway's exemplary study is largely based on ethnographic research among the romance readers themselves, whereas the original readers of romance novels between 1880 and 1914 are by now, in the main, deceased. I was able to fill this methodological gap by recourse to the theoretical apparatus of Bourdieu.

7. Toril Moi, in discussing the appropriation of Bourdieu for femininist criticism, expresses such compatibility in terms borrowed from Emile Benveniste: "Bourdieu's sociology of culture, I would argue, is promising terrain for feminists precisely because it allows us to produce highly concrete and specific analyses of the social determinants of the literary *énonciation*. This is not to say that such determinants are the only ones we need to consider, nor that feminist critics should not concern themselves with the *énoncé*, or the actual statement itself . . . feminist criticism fails in its political and literary task if it does not study literature both at the level of texts and at the level of institutions and social processes" (1018).

8. What we might call (in the context of my argument here) non-Foucauldian feminist studies of the woman author in Britain in this "Interregnum" period have also, of course, been useful and illuminating, and have tended to swing between individualist accounts and broadly historical ones. An example of the first is Elaine Showalter's highly influential *A Literature of Their Own*—which may idealize women writers at the expense of a full accounting for social structures and material conditions of existence. An example of the second, a more traditionally sociological approach, is Gaye Tuchman and Nina Fortin's *Edging Women Out*, which surveys women writers and their works exclusively through their relation to institutional structures, without entering into those works' thematic and ideological content.

9. Quoted in Hugh Walker, *The Literature of the Victorian Period* (Cambridge: Cambridge University Press, 1910).

10. This is in fact the title of an article by George Eliot in the *Westminster Review*, October 1856.

11. See "The Field of Cultural Production, or: The Economic World Reversed," the first chapter of *The Field of Cultural Production*, especially 37–40.

12. Here I borrow from the gloss provided by Randal Johnson in his superb introduction to the English translation of *The Field of Cultural Production* (6).

13. In Bourdieu's lexicon, "strategy" is a crucial notion, indicating the mode of individual agency on the field. It conveys the possible effectivity of conscious intention, while allowing as well that the actant's tactics often half succeed, fail entirely, or produce unintended effects.

14. "Heteronomous" is a useful term here in contradistinction to "autonomous"—it indicates how success for the mass-market novelist is determined by a form of capital—economic—that strictly speaking does not find its value within the field of cultural production, but in effect "impinges from outside," from the broader general field of (economic) power in society at large.

15. On these writers, see especially Colby (*Singular Anomaly*, chapter 1).
16. Quoted in Sutherland, 100.
17. Letter from G. L. Craik to Ward, 27 February 1885 (quoted in Sutherland, 107).
18. Their debate took place over the course of two days—Ward was resummoned the next day after breakfast.

BIBLIOGRAPHY

Armstrong, Nancy. *Desire and Domestic Fiction: A Political History of the Novel.* New York: Oxford University Press, 1987.

Bourdieu, Pierre. *Outline of a Theory of Practice.* Translated by Richard Nice. Cambridge: Cambridge University Press, 1977.

————. *Distinction: A Social Critique of the Judgement of Taste.* Translated by Richard Nice. Cambridge, Mass.: Harvard University Press, 1984.

————. *The Field of Cultural Production.* Edited by Randal Johnson. New York: Columbia University Press, 1993.

————. *The Rules of Art: Genesis and Structure of the Literary Field.* Translated by Susan Emanuel. Stanford, Calif.: Stanford University Press, 1996.

Brown, Marshall, ed. *The Uses of Literary History.* Durham, N.C.: Duke University Press, 1995.

Colby, Vineta. *The Singular Anomaly: Women Novelists of the Nineteenth Century.* New York: New York University Press, 1970.

Cvetkovich, Ann. *Mixed Feelings: Feminism, Mass Culture, and Victorian Sensationalism.* New Brunswick, N.J.: Rutgers University Press, 1992.

Davis, Lennard J. *Resisting Novels: Ideology and Fiction.* New York: Methuen, 1987.

Fasick, Laura. "The Ambivalence of Influence: The Case of Mary Ward and Charlotte Yonge." *English Literature in Transition,* 37, no. 2 (1994): 141–54.

Feltes, N. N. *Literary Capital and the Late Victorian Novel.* Madison, Wis.: University of Wisconsin Press, 1993.

Flint, Kate. *The Woman Reader, 1837–1914.* Oxford: Clarendon Press, 1993.

Gladstone, W. E. " 'Robert Elsmere' and the Battle of Belief." *Nineteenth Century* 23 (May 1888): 766–88.

Jameson, Fredric. *The Political Unconscious: Narrative as Socially Symbolic Act.* Ithaca, N.Y.: Cornell University Press, 1981.

Jones, Enid Huws. *Mrs. Humphry Ward.* London: Heinemann, 1973.

Joppke, Christian. "The Cultural Dimensions of Class Formation and Class Struggle: On the Social Theory of Pierre Bourdieu." *Berkeley Journal of Sociology* 31 (1986): 51–78.

Keating, Peter. *The Haunted Study: A Social History of the English Novel.* London: Secker & Warburg, 1989.

Langland, Elizabeth. *Nobody's Angels: Middle-Class Women and Domestic Ideology in Victorian Culture.* Ithaca, N.Y.: Cornell University Press, 1995.

McClintock, Anne. *Imperial Leather: Race, Gender, and Sexuality in the Colonial Conquest.* New York: Routledge, 1995.

Meyers, W. H. "George Sand," *Nineteenth Century* 1 (April 1877): 221–41.

Miller, David A. *The Novel and the Police.* Berkeley: University of California Press, 1988.

Miller, Jane Eldridge. *Rebel Women: Feminism, Modernism, and the Edwardian Novel.* London: Virago Press, 1994.

Moi, Toril. "Appropriating Bourdieu: Feminist Theory and Pierre Bourdieu's Sociology of Culture." *New Literary History* 22 (1991): 1017–49.

Peterson, William S. *Victorian Heretic: Mrs. Humphry Ward's* Robert Elsmere. Leicester, U.K.: Leicester University Press, 1976.

Poovey, Mary. *Uneven Developments: The Ideological Work of Gender in Mid-Victorian England.* Chicago: University of Chicago Press, 1988.

Radway, Jan. *Reading the Romance.* Chapel Hill, N.C.: University of North Carolina Press, 1984.

Sedgwick, Eve Kosofsky. *Between Men: English Literature and Male Homosocial Desire.* New York: Columbia University Press, 1985.

Showalter, Elaine. *A Literature of Their Own: British Women Novelists from Brontë to Lessing.* Princeton: Princeton University Press, 1977.

Simcox, Edith. "George Eliot." *Nineteenth Century* 9 (May 1881): 778–801.

Stubbs, Patricia. *Women and Fiction: Feminism and the Novel, 1880–1920.* Brighton, U.K.: Harvester Press, 1979.

Sutherland, John. *Mrs. Humphry Ward: Eminent Victorian, Pre-Eminent Edwardian.* Oxford: Clarendon Press, 1990.

Tuchman, Gaye, and Nina Fortin. *Edging Women Out: Victorian Novelists, Publishers, and Social Change.* New Haven: Yale University Press, 1989.

Walker, Hugh. *The Literature of the Victorian Period.* Cambridge: Cambridge University Press, 1910.

Ward, Mrs. Humphry. *Robert Elsmere.* London: George Smith: 1888.

———. *A Writer's Recollections.* London: W. Collins Sons & Company, Ltd., 1918.

West, Rebecca. Review of Ward's *A Writer's Recollections, Bookman* 45 (December 1918): 106–7.

11

The Prestige of the Oppressed: Symbolic Capital in a Guilt Economy

Carolyn Betensky

Throughout his book *Representing the Holocaust*, Dominick LaCapra uses the term "symbolic capital," always in quotation marks, to describe the "self-legitimating or self-righteous" uses to which the Holocaust may be put by its victims or their descendants.[1] For LaCapra, the Holocaust may be converted into symbolic capital when the memory of the genocide is used, sometimes unscrupulously, to the strategic advantage of those who have suffered from it.

I must make it clear right away that in his book, LaCapra refrains from accusing anyone of exploiting the Holocaust as " 'symbolic capital' or as a pretext for self-serving monumentalization" (63). Indeed, the notion of symbolic capital plays a very minor role in LaCapra's thesis. Rather, when he employs the term "symbolic capital" in *Representing the Holocaust*, LaCapra is characterizing the way certain people, including some of his subjects—a variety of Holocaust historians ranging from German revisionists to Pierre Vidal-Nacquet—have come to view and represent the Holocaust, or more accurately, the way some of them have appraised *others'* representations of the Holocaust. He uses the expression almost casually, in the context of his discursive analyses of the historians' work.

What interests me in LaCapra's use of the term "symbolic capital" is that he should choose the term at all. Certainly, Pierre Bourdieu has no patent on the expression, but it is striking that LaCapra uses it so differently from Bourdieu, with whom the expression is most often associated. Is LaCapra's consistent application of the quotation marks his way of indicating that he is borrowing and modifying Bourdieu's concept, or do the quotation marks just suggest contempt for jargon LaCapra feels for some reason constrained to use? Elsewhere in the book LaCapra cites Bourdieu's work on Heidegger (139), so it is fair to assume

207

he is acquainted with Bourdieu's work. In any case, the question I am interested in asking is how LaCapra's symbolic capital can make sense in the same world as Bourdieu's. For Bourdieu's symbolic capital is capital that says it is not capital; LaCapra's symbolic capital is the extreme negation of capital—abject victimization—that is said to be capital. *Said to be* capital: as I will explain shortly, this kind of symbolic capital seldom actually *operates* in the manner of capital so much as *it is said*, or hoped, or expected—or strategically and even cynically declared, generally by those who would dispute its claim to legitimacy—to operate as capital.

Generally, for Bourdieu, the term "symbolic capital" designates what is considered (in a given cultural context) to be honor or prestige, systematically misrecognized as economically disinterested.[2] Like the extravagant feast for an entire village thrown by the host who would seem from all appearances to be spending his money against his better interests, symbolic capital establishes one's "credit" within a community. Symbolic capital in Bourdieu's sense is a kind of implicit debt I may cause to accumulate in others, a debt I have created by "giving freely"—honorably, "disinterestedly"—of myself, a debt I will call on later for my own benefit. This debt may be interpreted in the widest ways possible, with economic, social, and moral pressures all coming together to enforce its repayment.

An important aspect of Bourdieu's symbolic capital is that it is by definition convertible into material, "economic" (in the most common sense of the term) capital, and his symbolic capitalist necessarily makes good in some extrasymbolic way. LaCapra's symbolic capital, by contrast, does not go hand in hand with material profit. LaCapra's symbolic capital presupposes what might be called a guilt economy.[3] A guilt economy is a symbolic economy such as that characterized by LaCapra in which your oppression is transformed, by means of your former oppressor's debt to you, into your symbolic wealth. Your suffering is transformed into something of value to you, into something you can expect to work for you; it becomes a kind of capital that enables you to get certain things done because you have something good coming to you. Yet as opposed to the eventual opportunity to cash in that Bourdieu's symbolic capital promises, in a guilt economy the payoff remains overwhelmingly within the realm of the symbolic. And herein lies the initial problem with LaCapra's symbolic capital: while paths leading from "self-legitimation" or "self-righteousness" to material success can be imagined without too much difficulty, they are nonetheless far from inevitable. As Bourdieu insists in *The Logic of Practice*, communities must adhere to certain rules in order for symbolic capital to exist: each kind of capital "produces its specific effects only in specific conditions" (*LP* 122). In a guilt economy, there is no dependable way to redeem the symbolic capital that is derived from one's status as a victim. Perhaps we could envision a transcendental exchequer evening the scores, but it is all too clear that people in this world are generally not rewarded for their suffering. Sometimes they are, when there are rules governing the compensation for certain sorts of suffering, but in most cases, of course, they are not.

It is no accident that LaCapra should have adopted Bourdieu's term to signify its operational opposite, for the economies that produce each variety of capital have long been intertwined, confused, and conflated. This traditional conflation of economies ultimately functions as a sophisticated mechanism in the service of what Bourdieu would call "soft domination"—and this is the second, and more serious, implication of the term in LaCapra's usage.[4] The misidentification of the two economies allows the dominant to dominate with increased efficiency. The losers in one economy (the victims of the symbolic economy of the "real") are said—by those who stand to gain by ascribing such a status to others—to be the winners in the other (the guilt economy). Although compensation within the guilt economy is dependably only of a symbolic nature, the conflation of the two economies establishes an equivalence between the two kinds of compensation, an equivalence between the "real" capital lurking in Bourdieu's symbolic economy and the overwhelmingly purely symbolic capital in the guilt economy.

The consequences of this assumption of equivalence—the consequences of considering victimization on a par with officially misrecognized, culturally calculated, lavish financial output—are subtle and insidious. In the United States in the late 1990s, this assumption, or ascription, of equivalence is made so regularly that we are perhaps numb to it. The "real" (profitable) and the exclusively symbolic (explicitly unprofitable) guilt economies are commonly elided by those engaged in the recent backlash against "political correctness." By ascribing inherent symbolic capital to a wide range of "victims" (a term applied with a sneer), the proudly "politically incorrect" may reposition them for yet another beating. Fighting "capital" with Capital, imaginary weapons with the artillery of what is for too many a police state, the opponents of those rich in poverty unabashedly argue for keeping them where they are—or lowering them still further.

Yet these economies are conflated not only by right-wing adversaries of what used to be called social and economic justice. The misidentification of symbolic capital in LaCapra's sense and symbolic capital in Bourdieu's may take place on the left as well. Whenever the recognition of oppression—responsibility established, consciousness raised—is viewed as valuable unto itself, whenever symbolic empowerment is asserted to be empowerment *tout court*, "capital" is allowed to stand in, however temporarily, for Capital.

In her 1840 novel, *Le compagnon du tour de France*, George Sand depicts a microclass struggle with surprising clarity by pitting symbolic capital in Bourdieu's sense against symbolic capital in LaCapra's. By showing what stakes lie beneath the attempts of certain characters to disregard the distinctions between these economies and the attempts of others to keep them apart, Sand lets us see how the possessors of material capital may deny the differences between the economies in order to consolidate their power.

Le compagnon du tour de France is a rather unusual novel for its time because instead of featuring mostly passive and stoically suffering poor, it stars a man of the people whose suffering is more intellectual than physical or even material: a journeyman carpenter named Pierre Huguenin who is hired by the Count de Villepreux to restore his ancestral château. In this novel, upper-class characters appeal to Pierre as a superior man for various kinds of satisfaction. Mostly they want to know what he thinks, not about carpentry but about revolution; and in this respect, what they are *most* interested in, perhaps not unsurprisingly, is in what he thinks of them. Some of them also want his cooperation in a Carbonarist conspiracy; one of them wants to snare him as a husband. You should also know that Pierre is portrayed as being devastatingly beautiful—represented as something of an it-boy, he is a magnet for free-floating sociosexual desire.

The richer characters who favor revolution are constantly telling Pierre of the superiority of the People and of his own exceptional standing within his own class. But what is remarkable is that this worker, a journeyman carpenter, refuses to be drawn out and to be put on a pedestal. Although his bourgeois and aristocratic petitioners insist throughout the novel, with excruciating candor—as does the noble Yseult de Villepreux, the count's granddaughter—"[V]ous sortez des opprimés, et moi des oppresseurs. J'envie beaucoup votre noblesse, maître Pierre" (320) ["Your ancestors were the oppressed, and mine were the oppressors. How I envy you your nobility, master Pierre"][5]—Pierre does not accept this characterization of himself; he does not buy into this idea of the prestige of the oppressed. Rather than accept the terms of the imaginary economy whose rewards remain totally symbolic—for they are the wealthy, after all, and he is only a poor carpenter—Pierre admits only to the existence of the standard economy. He does not want to be told of his own prestige by those whose prestige obviously extends beyond his. He wants what he wants, according to the rules of the economy that counts: he wants to do his job well, he wants his carpentry to be appreciated, he wants to get paid. He also wants to know what his social superiors think about the arrangement of society—he wants answers from the class that is making the rules. The worker does not dare to want what he knows he cannot have, according to the rules that are in force; he does not dare to conceive his own desire for Yseult in a coherent, practical, marriage-prone way, much less to come forward with his desire, nor does he dare to expect to be treated as a real equal by his employers. It is not that he is conservative, modest, stupid, or happy with his lot; it is just that he is very suspicious of the imaginary economy held out to him as real.

Because he is aware of his fragile position in the real economy, Pierre must avoid confrontation with those whose real capital is greater than his. At one point in the novel, he gets in trouble for teasing a bumbling Carbonarist conspirator, a bourgeois wine merchant named Achille Lefort. Achille had been pestering Pierre to participate in revolutionary activities for some time before Pierre found a card with notches in it that marked its bearer as a full-fledged member of the conspiracy brotherhood. Pierre shows this card to Achille, and Achille is by turns astonished, reduced to a sputtering, hysterical idiot, embarrassed and sycophantic, but when he finds out that Pierre has merely stumbled across the card in a desk and guessed at its significance, he gets truly angry. Pierre quickly extends his hand in a gesture of friendship. Achille welcomes the handshake, but scolds Pierre in the following terms:

> "Mon rôle est plus difficile que le vôtre," reprit Achille. "Vous êtes le peuple, c'est-à-dire l'aristocrate, le souverain, que nous autres conspirateurs du tiers-état nous venons implorer pour la cause de la justice et de la vérité. Vous nous traitez en subalternes; vous nous questionnez avec hauteur, avec méfiance; vous nous demandez si nous sommes des fous ou des intrigants; vous nous faites subir mille affronts, convenez de cela! Et quand nous ne poussons pas l'esprit de propagande jusqu'à l'humilité chrétienne, quand notre sang tressaille dans nos veines, et que nous prétendons être traités par vous comme vos égaux, vous nous dites que nous n'étions pas sincères, que nous portons au dedans de nous la haine et l'orgueil; en un mot, que nous sommes des imposteurs et des lâches qui descendons à vous implorer pour vous exploiter." (273)
>
> [My role is more difficult than yours. You are the people, that is to say, the aristocrat, the sovereign, whom we third-estate conspirators come to implore in the cause of justice and truth. You treat us as subalterns; you question us with haughtiness, with mistrust; you ask us whether we are lunatics or schemers; you make us take a thousand insults, believe me! And when we do not live out the spirit of propaganda to the extreme of Christian humility, when our blood throbs in our veins, and when we ask you to treat us as equals, you tell us we haven't been sincere, that we harbor hatred and pride within our hearts; in the end, you call us impostors and cowards who have come to beseech you just to exploit you.]

It is passages like this that let you appreciate how truly weird, how perverted the guilt economy can become. Only in the make-believe, topsy-turvy economy asserted by all three of the main upper-class characters can a declaration such as Achille's—"You are the people, that is to say the aristocrat, the sovereign"— make sense. The novel takes place during the Restoration, a time of relative security for the real aristocrats. Revolutionary gains notwithstanding, the masses were still mostly poor and decidedly unpowerful, and that included journeymen carpenters. Yet Achille, a well-enough-off bourgeois merchant, insists on the existence of an alternative economy that puts him at a disadvantage and the poor at a great advantage. While it is true that the conspirators depend on the cooperation of the people, there is more than this cooperation at issue in Achille's hyperbolic vision of the people having the bourgeoisie at their mercy.

So what is going on here? Achille is first of all offended that Pierre has stepped out of line by producing a membership card that established him as an equal. But this practical joke has clearly unleashed a much more deeply felt, pent-up aggression and resentment on the part of the "friend of the people" toward the people, who, to the despair of the bourgeoisie, will not do their bidding and sacrifice themselves in an uprising conceived by the bourgeoisie. By putting the people on this unlikely pedestal, by calling them the real aristocrats, Achille is making a statement of what I call *peuple oblige*, obliging them so that they will be obliging, positioning them on high so as to rationalize telling them off and putting them down when they do not behave as nobles should. The "thousand insults" that Achille and the third-estate conspirators have had to suffer, the suspicions and accusations and lack of faith that they have encountered in the people, all screen and justify a backlash against them.

This kind of thing happens all through this novel, and we can see how the *peuple oblige* approach is used as a strategy of soft domination either when upper-class characters want something from the worker or on the rare occasion when, as in the case I just discussed, the worker steps slightly out of line. The prestige the upper-class characters impose on the carpenter can twist things around so much, the statements can be so bald, that the exchanges can be rather funny. At one point Pierre is summoned to talk to the count. Yseult has found him in a flower bed on the château grounds, weeping over the difficulty of achieving social justice. She has suggested that he tell her grandfather his problems, an offer Pierre politely, as usual, attempts to turn down. Using a pretext relating to his work, however, the count forces the carpenter to pay him a visit. Like his granddaughter and Achille, he harbors a "vif désir"—a "burning desire"—to commune at ease with "l'homme du peuple"—"the man of the people" (257).

In the exchange that ensues, the count attempts to pierce Pierre's reserve in order to ferret out what he takes to be his secrets. He does so by appealing to Pierre as a superior man, but his flattery is issued from above and in the inescapable character of an order. As Pierre enters the area of the Villepreux park in which the count likes to take tea, he announces as he hesitates to take a seat, "Je venais pour prendre vos ordres." ["I've come to take your orders."] The count responds to Pierre's reminder of their respective stations with a denial of the real economy: "Il ne s'agit pas d'ordres ici . . . on ne donne pas d'ordres à un homme tel que vous. Dieu-merci, nous avons abjuré ces vieilles formules de maître à compagnon. D'ailleurs, n'êtes-vous pas maître vous-même dans votre art?" (264) ["We don't give orders around here. . . . One doesn't give orders to a man like you. Thank heavens, we've done away with those old formulas between master and laborer. In any case, aren't you yourself a master of your art?"]

Pierre resists the count's dismissal of convention and insistence upon his own position as master. He replies with typical diffident reticence, "Mon art n'est qu'un obscur métier" (264). ["My art is just an obscure trade."] The count, however, is scarcely put off by such a show. He persists in his characterization of Pierre as a member of an elite, hinting that there might be some financial support in store for him should he affirm his membership, but Pierre turns him down.

Pierre's refusal to take the bait and to adopt a more congenial, though false, economy perturbs the aristocrat. So he persists:

Elle [Yseult] vous a fait, en mon nom, des offres de services, des promesses d'amitié; elle a parlé selon mon coeur. Vous avez rejeté ces offres avec une fierté qui vous rend encore plus estimable à mes yeux, et qui me fait un devoir de vous servir malgré vous. Prenez donc garde d'être injuste, Pierre! Je sais d'avance tout ce que votre vieux républicain de père a pu vous dire pour vous mettre en garde contre moi. J'estime infiniment votre père, et ne veux pas blesser ses préjugés; mais il y a une différence entre lui et moi, qu'il est l'homme du passé, et que moi, son aîné, je suis pourtant l'homme du présent. Je me flatte de mieux comprendre l'égalité que lui; et si vous refusez de me confier le secret de votre peine, je croirai comprendre la fraternité humaine mieux que vous aussi. (264–65)

[She has offered you my services and has promised you my friendship; she has spoken according to my wishes. You have rejected those offers with a degree of pride that makes you even more honorable in my view, and this pride of yours makes it my duty to serve you in spite of your wishes. Take care not to be unfair, Pierre! I know in advance everything your old republican of a father must have told you to put you on guard against me. I have an infinite amount of respect for your father, and I don't want to rattle his prejudices; but there is a difference between him and me, and that is that he is a man of the past, and I, his elder, am nonetheless a man of the present. I like to think that I understand equality better than he; and if you refuse to entrust me with your secret, I will believe that I understand human fraternity better than you, as well.]

The count insists on his duty to serve Pierre, in defiance both of Pierre's wishes and of the rules of the economy that obtain even as he makes his pronouncement. Noting Pierre's obstinate refusal to partake in a make-believe economy, he casts the carpenter in the role of the disdainful seigneur and himself in that of the forward-looking republican. The aristocrat, blood-heir to the fortune of Villepreux, latest in a long line of nobles left intact by the Revolution, declares himself the true progressive and castigates Pierre's father, the laborer, for clinging to the ways of times past. In a final irony, the count challenges Pierre to reveal his secrets to him with the taunt that, should Pierre keep to himself, then he, the count, would be the better keeper of the Revolution.

The upper-class characters in *Le compagnon du tour de France* invoke the prestige of the oppressed in order to dominate them more efficiently and ever more gently. I do not mean to suggest that each of them has some nefarious, conscious plan to seize (or hold onto) power and crush the proletariat. These are characters, after all, who consider themselves the "friends of the people." But they have adopted a strategy, or a rather a strategy has adopted them, that seems to satisfy two of their desires at once: to spread the wealth and power around, and to keep the wealth and power to themselves.

It is to Sand's credit that she portrays Pierre as resisting the imaginary guilt economy with such fortitude, and with such skepticism. What he is doing, really, by rejecting the prestige conferred upon him, is denying the very basis of what LaCapra calls symbolic capital. By refusing to accept what seems to be a good deal—your poverty is now your wealth—Pierre is very shrewdly looking the gift horse in the mouth, and affirming what Bourdieu says is a fundamental characteristic of symbolic capital: that the exhibition of symbolic capital—which is in the end what most of the largeness of spirit on the part of the richer characters amounts to—is "one of the mechanisms which (no doubt universally) make capital go to capital" (*LP,* 120).

NOTES

1. See 48 et seq.

2. For Bourdieu's most sustained accounts of this notion, see *OTP,* especially 171–83; and *LP,* most particularly 112–21.

3. In his second essay in *On the Genealogy of Morals* (" 'Guilt,' 'Bad Conscience,' and the Like"), Nietzsche locates the origins of guilt in the concept of debt. Nietzsche's concept of a guilt economy does not explicitly address the conditions prevailing here, though, with some modification, it could accommodate them.

4. "Soft domination" is, according to Bourdieu, a particular mode of domination made possible by the accumulation of symbolic capital. Soft domination is violence or overt exploitation in its "gentle, disguised"—or "euphemised"—forms. See *LP,* 122–34.

5. All translations of Sand's novel in this article are mine.

BIBLIOGRAPHY

Bourdieu, Pierre. *Outline of a Theory of Practice.* Trans. Richard Nice. Cambridge: Cambridge University Press, 1977.

———. *The Logic of Practice.* Trans. Richard Nice. Stanford: Stanford University Press, 1990.

LaCapra, Dominick. *Representing the Holocaust: History, Theory, Trauma.* Ithaca, N.Y.: Cornell University Press, 1994.

Nietzsche, Friedrich. *On the Genealogy of Morals and Ecce Homo.* Ed. Walter Kaufmann, trans. W. Kaufmann and R. J. Hollingdale. New York: Vintage, 1969.

Sand, George. *Le compagnon du tour de France.* [1840] Grenoble: Presses Universitaires de Grenoble, 1988.

12

Space, Time, and John Gardner

Bo G. Ekelund

Resurrection and the survival of ghosts were privileged themes and even formal strategies of Gardner's works, and while it is not the aim of this chapter to perform the academic ritual of literary resurrection, it will be necessary to conjure up Gardner's ghost. It is hard to resist quoting Gardner in his titanic mode, when his philosophical bent made him seize on the universe, no less, or all of human history as a suitable matter for fiction to deal with: "I've been working with that old question everybody works with, time and space. The thing that I'm doing is trying to work out the connections between all our human cultures . . .—you know, modern physicists, the ancient Sumerians, the tump-builders" (quoted in Harvey, 87). We are in metaphysical, universalizing territory with a vengeance, 1970s pop-science occultism set to maximum overdrive; a man infatuated with "philosophy," rummaging through different realms of ideas which, despite his ability to dramatize them in a necessarily ironic way, he took only too seriously. But even false universalism entertains intimate relations with the productions of time, and it is my aim in this chapter to put Gardner's work and self-representation—reinforced as it has been by sympathetic and hostile criticism alike—to the question that Pierre Bourdieu's relational sociology helps pose. More particularly, I will seek to demonstrate how a conception of socially constituted, differentially constructed temporalities will yield a better analysis of Gardner's career than the organic and even charismatic model that his own guiding commentary invites. Understanding the pressures that Gardner negotiated as his embodied history was inserted into social time frames where it had no given place will perhaps make it clearer why the leap to the higher plane of metaphysics came so "naturally" to him.

215

ACCIDENTS

That leap often sprang, in Gardner's case, from the specific category of the accident. Accidents will happen. They certainly happened to Gardner, who died in one well before his time. And theory will find it hard to accommodate them, by virtue of their sheer contingency, their being no part of statistical probability. Accidents do not conform to tendencies, which are really the only phenomena available to models. It will have to be shown, when it comes to an accident-prone individual like Gardner, that, even so, the sociological approach is more adequate than the types of criticism that are led to their descriptive findings "by accident" or by the resolute rejection of the very notion of the accidental in terms of a higher, overriding principle, a solution that Gardner himself preferred.

One of Gardner's most insightful, but also excessively sympathetic critics, John M. Howell, has drawn the kind of connection we need to focus on, a connection between the accidental and the essential. In an article titled "The Wound and the Albatross," he discusses the effect on Gardner of a traumatic childhood accident. When Gardner was twelve, his younger brother Gilbert fell and was crushed by a heavy roller, a cultipacker, drawn by the tractor Gardner was driving. Howell then quotes from two books that Gardner wrote about fiction writing, the polemical *On Moral Fiction*, and a book addressed to budding novelists, *On Becoming a Novelist*, to show that a conception of a primal wound as the origin of artistic work was constant in Gardner, and that it flowed from this accident (1). The accident forms the essence of a creative career, the seed for its unfolding movement. Howell gains strength for his thesis from the fact that the two textual instances are fifteen years or so apart, even as he acknowledges that the comments from *On Moral Fiction* were not published until 1978, only four years before *On Becoming a Novelist* was finished; and in that gap between the initial expression of strongly felt sentiments and their finally being made public we must locate the principle that undoes the illusion of the organically unfolding career. In other words, we cannot account for accidents, but we can analyze how they are made socially meaningful, how they take their place in a socially determined time frame.

In the comments that Howell quotes, Gardner makes the typical connection between the individual wound and "the universality of woundedness in the human condition" (1). Between the accident and metaphysical truth the individual artist stands as a conscious and active mediator. As Howell puts it, the accident forced Gardner to deal with the question of "determinism and free will, and he would spend the rest of his life trying to reconcile these competing forces" (2). Howell may overemphasize this aspect, but that is his prerogative in an article pursuing precisely those interconnected motifs; what his article helps me focus on is a kind of gap that even the best accidental-essential criticism is unable to close. Howell claims that Gardner explored this philosophical dilemma from the beginning of his career to its end, but that he did so "using many different masks" until "finally" he threw off the mask in 1975 (3). It is to an account that will give to this word "finally" a coherent meaning that my own discussion of Gardner and time is directed. I agree on a very basic level that Gardner had a drive to express certain experiences—and let us by all means call them accidents—and that this "expressive drive" found its outlet in fiction. In Howell's analysis, the accident had to be given expression, but there is no telling, then, why Gardner did not give it full, unmasked expression right away. Why did he do so only "finally"?

To give a proper answer the analysis must avoid accident as well as necessity, the entirely contingent as well as the essential. In this respect, the immediate correlation that Howell makes between the original accident and the authoritative self-interpretation Gardner supplied later on is helpful for a delimitation of the sociological analysis. In this juxtaposition, which is posed as an explanation, two principles for the analysis of a writer's career are articulated. One of them supports the biographical, psychologizing method, which finds in individual events—the meaningful accidents of a life story—determining factors; the other one is the retrospective analysis of intentions, which fastens on ideas expressed by an author at a certain point in his career and utilizes them to "explain" aesthetic choices made long before as well as after that point. Both these methods owe more to what Bourdieu has termed "spontaneous thinking" than to any strict methodology, and they have come under a great deal of fire, especially from formalistically inclined criticism. Relevant to this line of questioning but insufficient on their own are the New Critical rejection of the "intentional fallacy" and the aversion among deconstructionists and structuralists to any reference to a reality outside the text. In either guise, this sort of privileging of relations within and between texts has no greater justification than the privilege accorded to the author's self-representation or the reference to biographical facts. The self-imposed restrictions of this type of textualism are obvious: it is like a project analyzing the role of money in society that would limit its analysis to a close scrutiny of banknotes. The production of texts is no less complex a thing than the circulation of money; it takes place in constant interaction with a whole world of events, processes, and structures—literary as well as non-literary—and the tendency to restrict this world of possible explanatory factors to some single category is as understandable, and as regrettable, as the choice to abandon explanatory modes altogether in favor of hermeneutics.

BEYOND THE ACCIDENT

Bourdieu's method, however, with its emphasis on the constitutive role of relations, leads past the either/or dilemma posed by biographical and formalist methods. The concept of the field allows us to anchor the classic Marxist problematic of mediation in a sociological model that can account for the relatively autonomous structures of a modern society without reducing the individual to a passive carrier of social forms.

In the sociological approach, the data we referred to above—the accidents of life and texts—are not simply excluded as irrelevant. What must be done, however, is to objectify each of these "keys," that is, they must be brought into the model as something asking for an explanation, not as transcendent tools for understanding the rest. Events and "facts" of disparate provenance—private experiences, political developments, discoveries in the sciences, and so on—enter the field only after having passed through a filter of formal demands and a process of translation into those expressions recognized by the field; moreover, they are entered into the field among strategies that depend on a sense of the game, a sensitivity to its tempo.

For a study of a single author's trajectory, however, Bourdieu's method presents various problems. The point with the field model is to have the analysis grasp the entire world in which the author moves as author: it is the sum of taken and available positions within the relevant field that orients the individual's strategies. Moreover, it is certainly plausible to assume that the relations between the literary field and the fields of education and of power are decisive for each trajectory, and with this assumption one is obliged to map out thousands of positions and trajectories. Counting only American prose writers of the sixties and seventies with a degree of academic recognition, the figure is over fourteen hundred.

Is there, then, any way to keep faith with the logic of the field model in the absence of a well-staffed research center of one's own? There is reason to suspect that one may start with the proper intentions and yet end up with a combination of a biographical "career study," an analysis of literary institutions, and a basic ideological critique. Short of a complete mapping of the field, what sort of tools can we use to avoid lapsing into what Fredric Jameson once condemned as "conventional sociology"?

My answer to this question is to claim, somewhat paradoxically, that the field concept, this spatial paradigm, can yield temporal structures with which individual trajectories can be analyzed. The kind of understanding produced in this way will be vastly different, in for example Gardner's case, than the image of organic development drawn by earlier studies. If we understand Gardner's career as a trajectory through a field that imposes its own rules on all those who enter it, we discover that Gardner's writing was marked by what Bourdieu, using a Freudian term, calls compromise formations. *On Moral Fiction* can then be understood as a failed attempt to break with the rules of the field. This failure had everything to do with bad timing.

I have elsewhere made a comprehensive analysis of Gardner's trajectory (1995). What I wish to dwell on here are the temporal structures that are involved in Bourdieu's field model and to illustrate them with Gardner's case.

Three analytical levels seem indispensable for the study of a single agent, or a restricted group of agents, and each level points up certain problems. The first level is that of the crisis, which indicates the horizon of an encompassing social field of fields, and the conflicts and coordination of separate fields; on the second level we find the individual field, whose relative autonomy frames a struggle over the time of the field that in turn produces the phenomenon of literary generations with their characteristic variations; finally, the third level is that of the *habitus*, where time can be seen as an element of inertia that sets limits to the adaptation any single agent can accomplish vis-à-vis the history of the field.

BOURDIEU AND TIME

Bourdieu's advice to beginning sociologists in *The Craft of Sociology* centers on the object of study, an object that must be conquered, constructed, and confirmed. This is the brief formula for the "epistemological hierarchy of scientific acts which subordinates validation to construction and construction to the break with self-evident appearances" (Bourdieu, Chamboredon, and Passeron, 1968/1991, 11). The conquest of the object is the most important step, since it has to do with a conscious break with spontaneous thinking and thus with the pre-constructed objects of such thought, a break that, as Bourdieu notes, "is more often proclaimed than performed." (13). It is this first step that my discussion will focus on.

In the case of Gardner's practice seen as a trajectory, the choice to treat it within the general model developed by Bourdieu and to use some of his tools serves as a break with an earlier understanding that treats the works as stages in an ideal development seemingly called into being by Gardner's own pronouncements in *On Moral Fiction* and elsewhere. This is the tendency of earlier Gardner criticism, and a familiar model for many mainstream literary studies. Familiar as it is, the way this approach constructs its object is seldom made explicit. The following quotation from a book by David Wyatt urging scholars to return to a study of careers comes very close, I think, to articulating the kind of logic that underlies a great many other studies: "A student of careers begins by valuing the tension between fact and wish that gives the work power and momentum. He then searches for some destination which, when reached, relieves the tension" (151). What will inevitably follow from such presuppositions is a teleological reasoning by which the "destination" will serve to explain what has led up to it. The "resolution of tension" is of course an aesthetic rather than a scientific concept, and any such concept will generate an idealist, self-contained space and time within which the object of study is approached. Another, more sophisticated variant is the idealist psychologizing of strong poets' struggles with their predecessors in the studies of Harold Bloom.

These strictly idealist versions of the writer's practice are scholastic illusions that sociology must counter, and the necessary break can be articulated as follows: the illusion that the producer of art also produces his or her own career, and thus his or her own history, must be broken by resituating the practices making up that career in a time that is not of their making. This time is one created by a space, namely that of the field and its internal and external relations.

Although it would go firmly against the grain of Bourdieu's work to raise the question of time to the pinnacles of philosophy where it has traditionally been kept, this relationship between temporal and spatial structure must first be set out at the most general level. One place to start would be with Bourdieu's discussion of Heidegger's project, which held at bay all questions regarding the temporal foundations of ontological philosophizing, "by using the eternalization of temporality and of history in order to avoid the historicization of the eternal" (*POMH*, 63). That unwillingness to historicize the eternal is contrary to the sociological line of inquiry. As Donald Broady observes, the tendency in Bourdieu's work is to follow the Durkheimian school and Bachelard in precisely the move to historicize that which philosophy treats as unchanging; that is, the categories of thought, like time, may be "*primitive* forms of classification" but like other forms of classification they are subject to change. As Durkheim and Mauss famously put it, "even ideas so abstract as those of time and space are, at each point in their history, closely connected with the corresponding social organization" (Durkheim and Mauss, 88).

Bourdieu's early work displays an emphasis on time understood in this way: in his study of Kabylian society, the forms of temporal consciousness are accorded greater importance than the forms of economic consciousness, and the transformation of traditional Kabylian society to a capitalist economic order is shown to involve a new way of relating to time: a calculating attitude appears, the day is divided into working time and leisure time etc. At the same time, the fact that the past exists in the individuals, in their bodies, means that the transformation is incomplete: it is through an incorporated past as a category of temporal perception that modern milieux are then perceived. This is the *hysteresis* effect, to which we will return. This example also illustrates the fact that temporality is constructed on crucially separate levels, and that tensions between the social totality and the dispositions of the individual are expressed in partly incompatible ways of relating to time. Even at the most abstract level, then, time is to be conceptualized as a relatively inert category, but not impervious to the structuring powers of social structures.

TIME, CRISIS, AND TOTALITY

Bourdieu's ideas about relatively autonomous fields—fields that gain independence as agents within them invoke differentiated principles—follows up and makes more precise Weber's perception of institutional and functional differentiation in modern society. Accordingly it appears less fitting to speak about a time in common, such as the one Bourdieu found in Kabylia, when it comes to modern societies. Yet there are glimpses of such an encompassing time frame in Bour-dieu's studies of contemporary France as well. They appear in connection with what Bourdieu terms "crises" and "historical events." In *Homo Academicus* the crisis (in this case the events of May 1968) is seen as a conjuncture, a "conjunc-tion of independent causal series" (174). Essentially, this conclusion is identical with Marx's perception that "[t]he crisis thus makes manifest the unity of proc-esses which had become individually independent" (quoted by Lukács, 32). That is, the relatively autonomous fields, worlds that are separate but participate in the same universe, are synchronized, and the fact that this can happen points to "their relative dependence as regards the fundamental structures—*especially the eco-nomic ones*—which determine the logics of the different fields" (*HA*, 174).[1] It is this relative dependence, Bourdieu argues, that makes possible the "historical event." It is important to realize that this argument pertains to societies that have reached the complexity that produces history, "societies without history being perhaps societies so undifferentiated that there is no place for the properly histor-ical event which is born at the crossroads of relatively autonomous histories" (*HA*, 174). Bourdieu's analysis here refers both to an "objective time," time as *chronology*, an order marked by historical dates (which I think we should inter-pret as relatively transhistorical), and specific orders of time, which must then be understood as the effects of autonomous fields, and which may or may not in-clude the chronological events of other fields. The point is of course that most events of objective time enter the time of a specific field, if at all, only after the crucial mediation that relative autonomy applies to everything external to the field. Each field imposes a certain structure of censorship on the material that enters it. On the other hand, there are events that effect a synchronization. Bour-dieu notes that "one of the major effects of great historical crises, of the events which *make history* [*font date*], is that they synchronize the times of fields de-fined by specific structural durations" (*FCP*, 107). Normally, the struggle within and between fields "*produces* contemporaneity in the form of the confrontation of different times," but at certain critical conjunctures, then, these different times are fused into one and the same "structural duration."

This notion seems to be stated in a weaker sense in the book on Heidegger, where Bourdieu recognizes a crisis in Heidegger's precarious time: a critical mo-ment that includes, for Germany, World War I, the abortive revolution of Novem-ber 1918, the political assassinations, Kapp's putsch, the military defeat, the Treaty of Versailles, the occupation of the Ruhr by French troops, the inflation, the brief, rationalization-crazy prosperity of the twenties, and the Depression. This concatenation of events created a traumatic experience that stamped the so-cial thinking of intellectuals and was articulated in more or less euphemized ex-pressions, such as "the age of the masses," "the era of technology," "the discon-tents of civilization." According to Bourdieu, the crisis and Heidegger's practice stand in a close relationship: the crisis "never ceased to be reflected and ex-pressed through [Heidegger]" (*POMH*, 7). It appears, however, that this "German crisis" did not attain the kind of synchronization that characterized May 1968. We must conclude that we are dealing with a weaker sense of the concept, a relative convergence of different temporalities that may best be labelled a zeit-geist.

From my perspective the concept of a crisis lifts the veil from a latent totality, a social and historical wholeness that exists as a possibility beneath and beyond the divisions of modernity. This is a principle of totality that perhaps can be seen to contain the reason or telos for critical analysis: not a field constituted by a single specific type of capital, but a field carrying the notion of total transforma-tion. An enduring synchronization may be a utopian notion, but it is clear that the logic of convergence we have touched on here harbors possibilities beyond the narrowly analytical ones.

However, it is these latter concerns that interest us here, and in particular what the weaker sense of crisis can imply, the case where field autonomy is weakened and the tendencies of one field become tendencies in other fields as well.[2] Here we are offered opportunities to study partial "synchronizations" as signs of het-eronomy, that is, of a breach of the independence of the field. On the other hand, we can detect signs of autonomy in the capacity of the field to "translate" chro-nological events into the field's temporal schemas.

CONVERGENCES AND STRATEGIES

If we apply this line of reasoning to the study of an individual agent, we can note the significance of the moments of conflation or convergence of fields in terms of strategies: agents can "seize the opportunity created by the critical break in the ordinary order, to advance their own claims or defend their own interests" (*HA*, 175). Moreover, as dominant fields create themes and forms that impinge on the general habits of apprehending the social world, writers can introduce such extraneous materials and forms into the literary field. Given these strategic op-portunities, it is of the utmost importance to attend to tangible "transactions" between different fields, and in particular the literary field on the one hand, and the fields of politics, education, and economics on the other hand. For the U.S., after World War II, there were a number of cases of partial convergence which had an impact on Gardner's trajectory.

Gardner belonged to the first generation that enjoyed the opportunities pro-vided by the explosive growth of higher education after the war. He shared in the harvest of increased economic investment in the domain of culture in the 1960s, when the U.S. for the first time after the Depression experimented with federal support of cultural production by establishing institutions like the National En-dowment of the Arts, and at the same time private sponsors increased their contri-butions. As a fairly typical example, Gardner received an NEA grant in 1972 and a Guggenheim grant in 1973. All of this must be seen in the context of the unique, unbroken economic growth that marked the years up to 1969.

The great transfer of funds to higher education also created opportunities for individuals who had systematically been deprived of access to advanced positions in the field of education to mobilize as groups and thereby make a collective social breakthrough, upsetting relations of power across many different fields (See Karen, 208–37). Gardner's works frequently register the political and cultural mobilization of groups that identified themselves on the basis of race, ethnicity, or gender. The traces are there in every text Gardner wrote, but they are most obvious in the novella "The King's Indian," in which a symbolically charged ship, a veritable ship of state, is claimed by a "multicultural" crew that mutinies against a New England captain, and in *October Light*, where the conflict between two octogenarian Vermont siblings contains a veiled commentary on "the new immigration."[3]

The most striking example of how forces from a dominant field are translated into the categories of the literary field is to be found in Gardner's book of criticism, *On Moral Fiction*. Even Gardner's contemporaries gave vent to suspicions concerning the way this book articulated the renewed conservative hegemonic pressure that was applied from the middle of the 1970s. When it came out, the "moral majority" was a media phenomenon, and both the populist "new right" and the more intellectual "neoconservatives" had wind in their sails. *On Moral Fiction* can be understood as an expression of this ideological offensive, and this thesis can be supported by the book's institutional position just as much as by an analysis of the text's veiled expressions of a populist right stance. A brief look at the institutional context will demonstrate how precisely the insertion of the book into an ideological conflict took place. When Knopf, which had published all of Gardner's major works, rejected the book, he went to Basic Books editor Midge Decter, who proved more understanding. Basic Books at this time published writers like Daniel Bell, Irving Kristol, and Robert Nozick, and Midge Decter was married to Norman Podhoretz, all of them leading neoconservative intellectuals. In addition, Decter herself had made her name in the 1970s as a polemical author who had published three acrid attacks on the women's movement and the alleged moral laxity of the sixties generation. More than chance, less than a conspiracy, the institutional space where *On Moral Fiction* was posted represents a meaningful coincidence. To paraphrase Bourdieu's analysis of Heidegger, Gardner *was situated* in a given moment of the political history of the U.S., at the same time that he *situated himself* at a stage in the internal history of literature, by producing a "back to basics" text published by Midge Decter at Basic Books.[4]

THE TIME OF THE FIELD

The Russian formalist Yuri Tynyanov pointed out the necessity of taking into account relations to other "historical series" when trying to understand the events of literary history, but he would not have been a formalist if he had not given greater weight to internal relationships. If we think sociologically no such conclusion is given a priori, but if the field we are studying has achieved relative autonomy it is within its time frame that we will find the most significant factors for an individual trajectory.

According to Bourdieu the struggle is the principle that creates field time:

> It is not sufficient to say that the history of the field is the history of the struggle for the monopolistic power to impose the legitimate categories of perception and appreciation. The *struggle itself* creates the history of the field; through the struggle the field is given a temporal dimension. . . . On one side are the dominant figures, who want continuity, identity, reproduction; on the other, the newcomers, who seek discontinuity, rupture, difference, revolution etc. etc. . . . To introduce difference is to produce time. (*FCP*, 106)

In the inevitable Bourdieusian mise-en-scène, we see the dominant and the dominated pitted against each other. However, this is not just rigid schematicism: in strategies, in field-specific capital, in the relation to other fields, we find factors that will confer dynamism and substance to the model. Is it, then, not just a matter of generational wars, of parricides and matricides? The sociological emphasis complicates the commonsense assumption: biological age has no significance in itself; it is only a matter of probability—since the accumulation of cultural capital takes time—that sets the biologically young against the old. Even so, Bourdieu's formula for the generation of time within the field is certainly that of an order of succession: in terms borrowed from religious wars, heretics challenge the orthodox, with the successful heterodoxy itself turning into orthodoxy with time. In this way, the struggle creates specific time. And it is in relation to the results of this struggle that individual writers devise their strategies.

What all this implies is the most crucial operation that must be made in a single-trajectory study. It is easy enough to situate the writer's position-takings, in the form of publications, in a chronology, a succession of neutral dates. The question we then must ask is: How do we get from a chronology to the *real time of the field*?

GENERATING GENERATIONS

First of all, the specific temporality of the field differs from the neutral time of a strict chronology in being the outcome of a collective effort. Different agents in the field have different interests in how this temporality is shaped. It is an obvious pattern that labels and names of "schools" and "movements" are more liable to be accepted by individual agents when they enter the field, that is, when individual symbolic profit is hard won; in the next phase all "brand names" are rejected: the unique personality of the author must be cultivated in order to maximize symbolic profits (at this stage, however, latecomers can profit from established group symbols); finally, when younger contenders appear, a certain, almost nostalgic affirmation of generational identity may be expressed again. To take an example from the sixties generation of writers, Robert Coover, many years after the fact, acknowledged in conversation that he and a number of other writers—John Barth, Stanley Elkin, William H. Gass, etc.—"did feel a little like a literary generation." They had, over the years, achieved sufficient recognition to be branded as a school, or anyway branded with names: they were singled out by the critics, those cocreators and arbiters of literary capital, as fabulists, metafictionists, postmodernists, or new fictionists. This sense of belonging to a generation had been sharpened, Coover said, after they had come under fire from a new generation of writers, branded in similar ways as "dirty realists" or minimalists (personal interview 1992). In this example we can see that it is a struggle over definitions that generates the representations through which the agents in the field recognize themselves, while at the same time it determines the distribution of literary capital. By virtue of these mechanisms, ideas about things become things themselves. At certain points, representations are interfused with objective conditions. "Words," Bourdieu reminds us, "the names of schools or groups, proper names—are so important only because they make things" (*FCP* 106).

If time comes into being by the introduction of differences, then names and labels clearly are the constituent parts of time. Things are made by words, but as Bourdieu has pointed out in polemics against speech act theory, words have this effect only if spoken with authority. That is, words make things only if at the same time they confirm the holding of capital. In the case of heresy, no doubt the cultural field, which is constituted by a sense of newness, confers a surplus of symbolic capital to young challengers, who could otherwise not match the older agents, with their amassed capital. In any case, the importance of labels can hardly be understated.

One influential critic who helped to devise that curious object, a literary generation, by imposing the proper name was, in the case of the sixties, Robert Scholes. Discussing the reasons underlying his 1967 study *The Fabulators*, he later claimed that "[a]t that time . . . it seemed that a movement of great importance in contemporary fiction was being ignored, misinterpreted, or critically abused because it lacked a name" (1). Only three years before the publication of *The Fabulators*, another critic, Alan Trachtenberg, had applied the label "fabulists" to John Barth—Scholes's main example as well—and John Hawkes, but not to the same effect. Names must be conferred at the right moment: the truth of the field's temporality lies somewhere between the chronology and the individual agent's sense of who belongs with whom. There is a precarious objectivity in the recognition granted to individual and collective bids to introduce difference, to bracket the past. The crucial unit for the project of constructing the individual trajectory as an object of study, then, is the break, the successful claim to represent something new. As Sartre claimed in *Search for a Method*: "It is of primary

importance . . . not to pass over one fact which the Marxists systematically neglect—the *rupture* between the generations" (137). It appears of equal importance to avoid the humanist mistake of seeing in each generation a group of individuals with unique personal experiences who, by virtue of their charismatic
vision, are able to overturn "the sclerosis of old forms" in their search for authentic expression.[5]

By focusing on the break we can take a shortcut and bypass the complete mapping of the field. As long as we do not mistake the world of representations that
is produced within the field for the objective conditions of their possibility, it is
at least certain that those representations and the discourses that carry them in
diverse ways *register* the objective break between the generations. In other words,
an appearance of change installs itself as the actuality of change by virtue of the
cumulative weight of self-fulfilling prophecies and stock-takings pronounced in
all the different genres that the field acknowledges, by those agents it recognizes.

Two such breaks can be observed for the period 1945–90: the first break came
around 1960 and a second break, less marked, occurred around 1975. Two
breaks: this gives us three generations after World War II. One should be wary of
making too-sharp demarcations, but it is clear that many writers themselves oriented their strategies according to these shifts.

The fact that these challenges succeeded depended on a number of factors that
supported the magic of naming. It seems fairly clear from my data that the dominant writers of the second generation brought in a higher degree of specialized
educational capital, mainly accumulated in English departments, and thus many
of them were familiar with the New Criticism. The third generation, on the other
hand, had a greater share of educational capital directly geared towards writing,
as creative writing courses expanded in the sixties. What particularly marked the
third-generation challenge, however, was its relation to the mobilization of
women and minorities during the sixties, especially in the field of education, so
that their products drew on symbolic resources having to do with different experiences specific to the groups they represented, and these experiences could be put
into the service of new realist or "magic realist" fictional modes.

THE LATECOMER'S DILEMMA

Through the collective recognition gained by these three generations the differences that generated the real time of the field were introduced, and it is within
this temporal framework that Gardner's trajectory unfolds. In a simplified model,
this career can be illustrated as in figure 12.1. What is important in this context
is the fact that Gardner was a johnny-come-lately in "his" generation, and his
arrival as a relative latecomer had profound effects on his strategies. Several other
prominent writers of the second postwar generation made their debut in 1966,
the same year as Gardner, but they achieved the crucial critical recognition that

Figure 12.1   Three Postwar Generations and Gardner's Trajectory

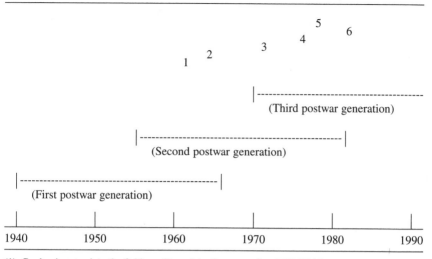

(1) Gardner's entry into the field as editor of the literary review *MSS* (1961).
(2) Gardner's book debut, *The Resurrection* (1966), to little critical recognition.
(3) Gardner's breakthrough with *Grendel* (1971) and *The Sunlight Dialogues* (1972).
(4) Gardner receives the *National Book Critics Circle Award* for best work of fiction, *October Light* (1976).
(5) *On Moral Fiction* is published (1978).
(6) Gardner dies in a motorcycle accident soon after publication of the novel *Mickelsson's Ghosts* (1982).

Gardner's debut went without. His breakthrough did not come until 1971 and 1972, with *Grendel* and *The Sunlight Dialogues*.

The second postwar generation had truly arrived by the early seventies. In this arrival of a generation of writers, Gardner stood at an ambivalent crossroads. He could easily claim to belong to the fabulists: in the objectivity of the field, he was one, unless he rejected the objective positioning. For that was the other alternative: to defect from the camp in favor of a new position-taking. The logic determining this choice of alternatives is twofold. As part of the generation of writers then earning peer recognition in due order, Gardner was a latecomer and thus subordinated to the predecession of Barth, Barthelme, Pynchon, and Vonnegut. He was becoming established, but these other writers were established before him, taking up positions ahead of him according to an inexorable logic of temporal irreversibility. On the other hand, he was slightly younger, and he was perceived by the field as a younger, because more recently arrived, writer.[6] To play with the time of the field, Gardner had an objective possibility of staking out new claims, opposed to those of Barth and the others, which would effectively date the achievements of the postmodernist generation.

With *On Moral Fiction*, this is the strategy Gardner chose. The position he tried to establish in the late seventies was in effect a third-generation position (and at the same time a move towards the "popular" pole of the field), and thus an attempt to contribute to the necessary historical bracketing of the second generation. It is in this light that one must view the resentment with which Gardner's attacks on fellow writers were met. According to this logic, for all that it is rarely made explicit, Gardner's attack was an act of apostasy.

If we take into consideration the new time structures created by the generational breaks we can account not only for Gardner's campaign for moral fiction, but also for the compromises that preceded it and that built up a pressure of bitter and righteous envy in Gardner. Finally his *ressentiment* towards those writers who had taken his rightful place issued in this morally self-righteous burst of outrage.

THE TIME OF THE RETROSPECTIVE ILLUSION

Alternatives to such an account exist. They make use of a time frame that is closer to the ideal time that Gardner located in the world of fiction than to the sociological temporalities we are concerned with here. David Cowart and Gregory P. Morris devoted book-length studies to Gardner's work in 1983 and 1984, respectively, and three collections of essays devoted to Gardner's work were published between 1982 and 1985.[7] With few exceptions these studies were laudatory and deferential to Gardner's particular creative genius, and they effectively erase the social temporality that determined his career. Cowart may be taken to represent the position taken by many critics in the early eighties, all of whom tended to see *On Moral Fiction* as central to any understanding of Gardner's work. For Cowart, the argument of *On Moral Fiction* is not to be reckoned as a product of particular circumstances, but appears rather as a telos of Gardner's career. Gardner, claims Cowart, advocated "life-supporting art . . . consistently throughout his extraordinary career." Cowart's method here is to take two separate statements, one from 1958—the dissertation abstract for Gardner's "The Old Men"—and one from 1974, and by noting likenesses he concludes that Gardner's view of art remained consistent throughout his career. As I have demonstrated in greater detail elsewhere, there is no such consistency if we look at specific aesthetic strategies, although there is certainly a core of fiercely held opinions, modulated according to situation. Cowart's position is not one open to such inconsistencies. He belongs to the school of critics who take the interests of their cherished author as their own; taking sides with Gardner's moral fiction campaign, he is driven to extravagant claims. For example, regarding the controversy over *On Moral Fiction*, Cowart claims that Gardner's position "does not surprise those familiar with the career of its author, whose every public statement, every poem, and every work of fiction illustrate the book's argument" (13). This vision of absolute constancy and faithful "illustration" is made possible by disregarding all evidence of vacillation. Gardner's tortuous career goes through the critic's refinery and comes out with no impurities, untouched by the ravages of time. Even so, the contradictions inherent in Gardner's practice generate descriptions that qualify matters by assigning a certain waywardness to Gardner's temperament.[8] "Not that Gardner despised fabulation. It should be clear by now that he found simple realism somewhat misguided" (Cowart, 13). There is no attempt at discussing the method of "simple realism," whatever that may be, nor is Gardner's fabulation and game-playing and his fascination with the dark side of existence distinguished from the bad examples set, according to Cowart, by John Barth and William H. Gass, Eugene O'Neill and T. S. Eliot (!) except by the claim that Gardner's practice was founded in a good cause.

Taken within its own charmed circle of philosophical and literary references, *On Moral Fiction* does not lead us to the social conditions that made its argument possible. On the contrary, it leads those interpreters who prefer to stay within that circle only to a metaphysical vantage point from which all practice appears as "representation and will." Another lengthy quote from Bourdieu will help me characterize the kind of vision that has accompanied Gardner's practice within the critical field:

> Nothing is more misleading than the illusion created by hindsight in which all the traces of a life, such as the works of an artist or the events at [*sic*] a biography, appear as the realization of an essence that seems to pre-exist them. Just as a mature artistic style is not contained, like a seed, in an original inspiration but is continuously defined and redefined in the dialectic between the objectifying intention and the already objectified intention, so too the unity of meaning which, after the event, may seem to have preceded the acts and works announcing the final significance, retrospectively transforming the various stages of the temporal series into mere preparatory sketches, is constituted through the confrontation between questions that only exist in and for a mind armed with a particular type of schemes and the solutions obtained through application of these same schemes. (*LP*, 55)

An illustration of such application can be found in Gregory P. Morris's study. Like Cowart, he finds a remarkable "philosophic consistency" in Gardner's vision, and finds it helpful to use *On Moral Fiction* as a manual for reading Gardner's fiction, especially *October Light*, which is seen as "a fictional companion piece to the criticism" (Morris, 146). In this type of criticism we find precisely that unity of meaning that precedes all the acts and works. The fundamental mistake is one and the same. What are essentially pieces written in the course of one undivided but internally differentiated practice, with all the coherence and the necessary limits to that coherence that belong to the logic of practice and the negotiations of censorship that literary production is subject to, are divided into the separate categories of theory and practice in order to argue for a speciously constructed ideal coherence.

On Moral Fiction does pose certain problems precisely because of the effects it had on Gardner's position in the field. Most Gardner scholars make note of this, usually as an occasion to berate the smallmindedness of those critics and authors who took offence, but in Gardner scholarship it is seldom the case that these effects lead on to reflections over the place of *On Moral Fiction* in Gardner's career. Instead, its field-determined effects are imported into the criticism and continue to riddle it. Since the questions posed are always the same—how do we see Gardner's fictions through the lens provided by *On Moral Fiction*? How do we define the essence of Gardner's aesthetic in the vocabulary generated by *On Moral Fiction*?—the critics are led into a circle of vicious essentializations: Gardner's fictional oeuvre as an organic whole and Gardner's "theory" as the principle of generating that whole. To discuss *On Moral Fiction* in these terms is to return to an entirely artificial inaugurating moment, a beginning constructed by critics from one event in Gardner's trajectory, a telescoping that places the content of a complex, discontinuous, trajectory-specific text as the origin of the entire career. The time of the entire individual history of compromises, challenges, and overreaching is rolled up into the capsule of a metaphysical time frame, the illusion caused by hindsight and the academic's armchair perspective.

While it should be clear that this brand of Gardner criticism failed in constructing its object properly, these critics' failure does not simply lie in the interest they take in the writer's personality. The "vulgar anti-biographism" of so many theoretical approaches of the late twentieth century is as much at fault as the "vulgar biographism" of earlier literary scholarship when it comes to grasping the sociological truth of literary phenomena. The writer's embodied logic must not be bracketed, nor should it be treated as a case for psychoanalysis, nor simply elevated for analysis to charismatic first-order importance. In order to come to a clearer sociological understanding of this aspect I will finish with a discussion of the third level of socially constructed time, that is, time in its embodied aspect: social time as an effect of the *habitus*, the *habitus* as the active container of an agent's history.

TIME DEPOSITED IN THE *HABITUS*

The concept of the *habitus* is part of Bourdieu's dual materialism. The schema of the *habitus* supplies us with the basic grids that direct our perception of the social world and the way we orient ourselves in it. While providing the principles for strategies concerned with future practice, the *habitus* is necessarily the product of an agent's past relations to the social totality. That is, the entire history of any social field is present in each moment in two forms: materialized (as institutions and objects, such as literary works) and incorporated (as dispositions of those involved in the struggle over these materialized social products) (*LSP*, 247). As embodied history, the *habitus* "ensures the active presence of past experiences, which, which, deposited in each organism in the form of schemes of perception, thought and action, tend to guarantee the 'correctness' of practices and their constancy over time, more reliably than all formal rules and explicit norms" (*LP*, 54). *Habitus*, then, tends to generate practices that are adapted to circumstances resembling those conditions that shaped the *habitus*. Bourdieu's model has been criticized for being restricted to the *reproduction* of the status quo, with the *habitus* functioning as the principle of the continuity and regularity. Generally, the active presence of past experiences will tend towards reproduction and harmonious insertion in a social world of familiarity, but as trajectories cross the boundaries of a differentiated and hierarchized social world, the *habitus*, the principle of regulated integration, can also figure just as much as an obstacle to assimilation.

If the *habitus*, as Bourdieu tells us, produces actions that are preadapted to conditions that are similar to the conditions that produced the *habitus*, then a change in those conditions will create a problematical insertion of the subject into a new situation. Early experiences carry special weight in this formation, and thus there is a persistence of a basic social imaginary that derives from the family and class conditions of childhood and adolescence. These residual charges may play tricks on the individual who changes social milieux. Bourdieu writes:

> The presence of the past in this kind of false anticipation of the future performed by the *habitus* is, paradoxically, most clearly seen when the sense of the probable future is belied and when dispositions ill-adjusted to the objective chances because of a hysteresis effect (Marx's favourite example of this was Don Quixote) are negatively sanctioned because the environment they actually encounter is too different from the one to which they are objectively adjusted. (*LP* 62)

In Gardner's case, it is abundantly clear that the presence of the past—both as the individually embodied schemes of a collective social experience and as the privileging of the past in his discourse—was considerable.

How then, can the concept of the *habitus* help us understand Gardner's career? The time of the field, as we have seen, is the product of a collective labor to open up new positions, and in the process earlier positions are transcended. The constellation of possible positions that are available at any given moment also presupposes a set of specifically literary *habitus* which allows access to them. With the help of the *habitus*, writers orient themselves towards this space of possible positions. In the ideal-typical case the dispositions of the writer coincide with the dispositions presupposed by the position to be taken, but in other cases, when *habitus* and position are imperfectly orchestrated, the shoe will pinch.

Gardner's outlook did not comfortably match the positions he took within the literary field. Put very roughly we can say that as a result of a strongly inculcated "home culture," which was rural, Presbyterian, upstate New York Republican, Gardner privileged a "deep seriousness" in art. What was to be taken seriously was above all the primacy of human character and human emotions. This *gravitas*, with its humanist pathos, differed to a very significant degree from the playfully ironic attitude that, so to speak, *went with the territory* that Gardner entered along with the other writers of the second postwar generation. When he took a position, he moved into an already furnished room where his most beloved heirlooms had no place. It is no wonder that his literary works display constant tensions that derive from this predicament. The strong home culture persists throughout Gardner's trajectory, even when it is censored by the demands of the field.

On the thematic level, all of Gardner's novels deal with situations where the transmission of the past in different forms constantly fails or is distorted. For example, in the old Vermont farmer James Page's history lesson in *October Light*, given to his daughter's adopted son, the main motif is corruption, and this principle of decay and disfiguration turns out to be a formal element in the novel as well, in the form of a "trash paperback" novel read by James's sister and shared by the reader. Its presence is made more significant with the knowledge that Gardner had, at an earlier stage, submitted a version of this novel-within-the-novel for publication to his literary agent. The final fate of this narrative, to be rejected by the "good reader" Sally Page, has to do with Gardner's gradual return to the principles he had had to compromise and "corrupt" during his dominated period.

The dominant writers of the second postwar generation distinguished themselves through the mastery of conspicuous literary form and a stance of irreverence towards traditional realism and humanism. Gardner could adapt to the demands of form but was unable to reconcile himself to the ethos that attached to them, and he was thus forced to submit to a mode of "double irony" as a way of negotiating this imposition. This double irony is in evidence particularly in the early novels, *The Wreckage of Agathon* and *Grendel*. The method borders on schizophrenia, but a careful analysis of the texts is required to reveal it. In lieu of a detailed discussion, a quote from Gardner's breakthrough year, 1972, must suffice to illustrate the underlying attitude.[9] In an interview Gardner discusses the ironic stance of the new generation of writers and adds that for his own part he creates grotesque characters as mouthpieces whenever he feels an "inclination toward a message. . . . The character undercuts what I say" (Natale, 16). Negotiating the orthodoxy established by "his" generation, Gardner was driven to distort precisely those elements that mattered the most to him, and to make them appear ironic even in contrast to a given ironic context.

If the incompatibility of *habitus* and position reveals itself in the compromises of double irony during the first half of the 1970s, the final period of Gardner's trajectory appears as an attempt not only to assert the values he had repressed, but also as a bid to change the rules of the game. *On Moral Fiction* is the release into a new space of articulation of the deeply felt convictions that had been expressed in distorted and restricted forms during the years when Gardner negotiated a field that resisted the inherent moralism of his expressive drive and cramped his style. The polemical book represents Gardner's ambition to carve out a new position, and it describes an imagined, ideal field created by an alternative history, a field where the *traditional* view of literature would not sound like "strange news." In Gardner's eyes, his contemporaries had deviated from the true path, and the transmission of the good tradition had been disrupted. The fact that Gardner sounded like an Old-Testament prophet during the moral fiction campaign (he always had a weakness for Amos) is no coincidence, nor is it just another instance of art as a "displaced prophetic vocation" (Bloch, quoted in Jameson's *Marxism and Form*, 156). Fundamentally, Gardner spoke with a religious as much as a secular voice, and as a prophet he berated his age for not being the kind of age that would have welcomed his own way of speaking and writing. The new and yet old literary world he prophesied, however, had no real equivalent. That is, Gardner misjudged both the strength of his position and the strength of the values dominating the field of restricted production. The difference between the ideal field that Gardner imagined for the purposes of his campaign and the objective relations of symbolic power was too great, and this objectivity simply failed to match Gardner's perceptions, which were formed as much by the inertia of his *habitus* as by the actual practices of his contemporaries.

Was there an element of wishful thinking in Gardner's campaign? I think there should be no doubt that Gardner's oft-repeated belief that the field had somehow swung over to his way of seeing things was a real belief, but it was also an attempt at a kind of self-fulfilling prophecy. He really believed, I would claim, that he was voicing a new consensus, an opportunity for heroism, for a newfound purpose. With an astounding ingenuousness Gardner would say, after *On Moral Fiction* had met with sharp rebukes, that he had had no idea that his fellow writers would mind so very much being called to task for their literary misdeeds. The obvious confusion that characterizes Gardner's statements in the wake of the debate contradicts any cynical interpretation that would see in Gardner's manifesto nothing but cool opportunistic calculation. A more convincing explanation is to be found in the incompatibility of two structures. Like two tectonic plates, Gardner's *habitus* and the objectivity of the field grated against one another until *On Moral Fiction* spewed out the accumulated grief and *ressentiment* like so much fire and brimstone.

In *On Moral Fiction* we can find the imprints of all the temporal series I have discussed. On one level the book represents the hysteresis effect, the inertia of embodied history set against the continually renewed challenges of the field. Secondly, according to the later logic of orthodoxy and heresy, *On Moral Fiction* is the manifestation of a strategy by which Gardner sought to reinsert his project in the new time that was generated by the third postwar generation in its ambition to supersede the fiction of the sixties. As such, it can be analyzed in the framework of a temporal logic of struggles and strategies. Thirdly, the book euphemized the political positions being established by the rise of the new right in the political field, and in this respect it functioned as a veiled expression of a zeit-geist—or rather, a hegemonic offensive—which countered the radicalism of the sixties and early seventies.

TOTALIZATION AND FIELD ANALYSIS

If traces of different temporal series can be detected in Gardner's polemical book, this clearly implies the advantages of an analytical method that proceeds accord-ing to a notion of sociologically divided time frames. Nevertheless, this should not be taken as saying that the overall object of study, a "modern" society with its various specialized functions, necessarily lacks unity, or that it is somehow profoundly "disarticulated," or that its "reality" has been "de-stabilized" as Scott Lash, for example, seems to claim (14). Bourdieu's sociology does not lead to the fragmented, static perception of relations that is characteristic of a tradi-tional sociological analysis. In an important passage in *The Political Uncon-scious*, Fredric Jameson correctly claims that "the conventional sociology of lit-erature or culture, which modestly limits itself to the identification of class motifs or values in a given text, and feels that its work is done when it shows how a given artifact 'reflects' its social background, is utterly unacceptable" (80–81). What Bourdieu's field model helps construct as an object of study is something vastly more dynamic than the empirically discernible subject of John Gardner's biography, fleshed out with the help of psychoanalysis or given a social meaning by his ability to mechanically reflect a fixed social background; it also gives us a more deeply mediated view of literature than the "reading" of the hypostatized "texts" seen as symbolic acts mediating the contradictions of a sociopolitical structure without regard to the specific social trajectory of the author. Instead of the static pairs of text and society or life and times, Bourdieu's model focuses a moving point in social space and time, which is concretized by being endowed with a *habitus*—a class-specific and individual repository of internalized struc-tures and schemes of practice, carrying within it a socially specific past as well as projecting and orienting itself towards its possible futures—a point that can be traced because it produces a discourse that speaks equally about its own trajec-tory, about the formal impositions of the field it traverses, and about a complex social totality articulated in relatively autonomous fields, including those contra-dictions that Jameson sees as the fundamental object of textual analysis. Obvi-ously, any simple "reflection" of a static "social background" is out of the ques-tion if the analysis proceeds by respecting the dynamics of a temporal discontinuity that is a function of the divisions generated by a totality according to a historical development of differentiation. What is gained, in comparison with Jameson's project of textual hermeneutics, is precisely that dimension of media-tion that Jameson discusses at length in the introduction to *The Political Uncon-scious*, but that he too often leaves by the roadside as he goes on to configure individual texts into the "collective or class discourse," the referent of which is the social totality. By introducing Bourdieu's concepts of *habitus* and field in their temporal aspects a ground is provided to the "symbolic act" that is fundamental to Jameson's scheme, but that is left strangely hanging in a state of spontaneous self-generation within it.

As Alex Callinicos points out, we can and indeed should concede Althusser's point that the social totality is internally differentiated[10] and for that reason even "unrepresentable" as such without giving up the notion of an encompassing totality. It seems to me that Bourdieu's field model and its related concepts provide precisely the complex set of tools that could match this conception.

ECONOMIC PROCESSES AS A HISTORICAL HORIZON

Finally I raise the claim that the ideological shifts negotiated by Gardner in the 1970s are interwoven in complex ways with a more fundamental time frame, the inner dynamic of the capitalist system. Some prudence is called for in this context. Too often materialist literary criticism has tried to point out direct connections between economic processes and literary forms of expression, lapsing into that schematic totalization of the Lukácsian variety that Perry Anderson termed "evolutionism." Tynyanov and Jakobson insisted that the critic must analyze "the correlation between the literary series and other historical series" (50), and in this respect they anticipated Bourdieu's field model as an attempt to do methodological justice to processes that indeed have become, in Marx's words, "individually independent." Postulating that these series with their internally determined processes were situated at different distances from one another, Tynyanov warned the critic not to seek direct correlations between the series of economic events and the series of literature, since they were too distant from one another. Granted that the literary expression of these distant conditions for the very existence of literature are euphemized to a high degree, there is still reason to attend to the tangible presence of two expressions, in Gardner's works, for the workings of capital, one of them concrete and unmistakable, the other one less transparent. The first one is the narrative of a lost world. In fragments one can find in *On Moral Fiction* the story of a real, sociohistorical loss: the obliteration of the world of the family farm. This narrative is given greater density in the novels *The Sunlight Dialogues* and *Nickel Mountain*. Accordingly, Gardner's work can be inserted into an encompassing time frame, in which the independent small-hold farmer, Jefferson's ideal American, is replaced by "agribusiness." Between 1954 and 1973 the share (numbers of peole involved) of self-employed and "family workers" decreased from 31 percent to 17 percent, figures that tell precisely this story—about a mass migration from the countryside, about young men and women who, like Gardner, found their way to the expanding sector of education, or to other means of employment (Armstrong et al., 170). In the novels this story can be followed as an underlying narrative, which treats the loss in two ways: on the one hand, the lost world is described as the site of universal, truly human values; on the other hand, the process by which it is eliminated is still affirmed as the expression of a transcendent principle. It is in this principle that we find the abstract formulation I mentioned. In Gardner's work it is reiterated as the image of "creative destruction," a term he borrowed from the philosopher Alfred North Whitehead, but which may be found in a more influential source for modernity, in John Locke's "perpetual perishing." Closer to Gardner, and closer to the economic processes that destroyed the conditions for small-scale agriculture, we find the same principle in Joseph Schumpeter's description of the capitalist system as a "perennial gale of creative destruction." In comprehending the way that Gardner solved the contradiction between regretting the tragical loss of a lifeworld carrying essential values and affirming the principle behind its destruction, we come closer to an understanding of the specific functions of the literary text. Gardner once said that the basic purpose of fiction is "to take us right out of temporality, right out of this world, this universe, into the eternal sunlit world where novels take place" (Edwards). Accordingly, it was within the ideal time of art that Gardner, time and again, sought to resurrect a social content that the time of economic rationality had pushed into the past, by giving it a symbolic existence. Beneath the surface of the polemical pamphlet the same complex negotiation of affirmation and lament is taking place, and out of this process Gardner produced a text that was both conservative and antiestablishment, a text easily inserted into the rhetoric of moral rearmament and yet (romantically) anticapitalist; in short, a condensation of new right populism, and as such indicative of the false universalism through which Gardner's metaphysical vision consistently sought to compensate for temporal, secular wreckage.

This is how we may condemn Gardner, and the type of fiction he represented, in a tribunal that asks for the power of literature to reveal or to hide the socioeconomic forces that see nothing in the individual or the art work but fuel for a constant process of creative destruction. Let us see. In Gardner's symbolic world we can discern three different time structures. There is the time of real losses, which evoke sorrow and anger and an overpowering "will to speak" about them and to "resurrect" them, the "magic motive" of "preserving things I value: people, places, modes of feeling" (Letter to Gass). Above this series of never-ending obliteration and unhealed wounds there is a chain of cosmic inevitability, an abstract time that Gardner can only approach philosophically, as a metaphysical truth. In the time outside of time created by the novel, these two series meet and pain is ennobled to selfless resignation and an affirmation of the superordinate, sublime process. From these lofty heights Gardner stoically dramatizes Whitehead's sober musing that the world "craves for novelty and yet is haunted by terror at the loss of the past, with its familiarities and its loved ones. It seeks escape from time in its character of 'perpetually perishing' " (481). If, as readers, we follow Gardner all the way to these pinnacles of metaphysical wisdom there is no doubt that we participate in what Bourdieu calls the shared denial of the social reality indicated by the text. If instead we intercept the anger, the grief, and the sense of loss, before it has been "purged" into acceptance, we may in Gardner's work perceive the traces of a critique that was not capable of encompassing the literary conventions it relied on. Indeed we may read the traces of an inability to turn the sense of loss into a projection of a future. The utopian wish in Gardner is often curtailed or absent so that the future can only to be implied as something that will make one's own sacrifice appear worthwhile. If Gardner never aims at disclosing the character of such a future, and appears instead to be stuck with celebrating that which has been lost and denigrating the present as that which does not make sense of the sacrifice, he nevertheless insists that literature must deal with the seriousness of loss in terms that are collective rather than private. The scandal with *On Moral Fiction* was, after all, that Gardner demanded from serious writers that they speak of real problems and address "ordinary readers." This category may be just as metaphysical as the notion of creative-destructive process, but broaching it leads into a problem concerning the sociology of literature, a problem that is no less urgent for being perennial in critical aesthetics: is the virtue of autonomy enough in its own right, or should we require of autonomy that it attempt to reach out beyond its own limits? Bourdieu approaches this question in his dialogue with the artist Hans Haacke and in his manifesto for a "universal corporatism." In the latter he emphasizes the value of the relative autonomy attained by the intellectual field and the field of art: a primary task is to maintain that autonomy vis-à-vis the political and economic fields, so as to preserve the capacity for criticism. In the conversation with Haacke some of the difficulties with this position become obvious: constitutive of that autonomy are the conventions that are understood by the initiates but inevitably strike outsiders as esoteric; how then can the critical thought that is cultivated within the field affect anyone outside it? Should we not demand from those who enjoy the protection and advantages of the autonomy of, say, the field of literary production, that they should risk that immunity in order to reach outside the limits of the field? This was Gardner's demand on his fellow writers, that they should ignore trends (that is, the logic of shifts between orthodoxy and heterodoxy) and formalism (that is, specific literary capital) in order to speak to the "ordinary reader" about real values that are constantly under threat. Gardner's way of formulating the problem may have been naive and lacking in self-reflexive knowledge of the conditions for his own position, and it was certainly reactionary in its general ideological thrust, but it still remains as a problem.

There is a lesson to be learned, perhaps. The specificity of time in circumscribed fields gives notice that time is not yet universal. This should not lead us to a denial of the notion of a social totality, but to investigations into the social conditions for the contradictory nature of that totality and, on the metatheoretical level, the conditions for that denial itself.

NOTES

This chapter was previously published as "Författaren och fältets tid," in *Kulturens fält*, edited by Donald Broady, Göteborg: Daidalos, 1998. It is reprinted by permission of Donald Broady.

1. Emphasis added: it is clear that Bourdieu confers special significance on the economic base, and it seems important that we can retain the notion of the primacy of the economic within Bourdieu's model.

2. See Gisèle Sapiro's analysis of the French literary field during the German occupation, "Académie française et Académie Goncourt dans les années 40: Fonction et fonctionnement des institutions de la vie littéraire en période de crise nationale." *Texte: Revue de critique et de théorie littéraire* 12 (1992): 151–96.

3. See Ekelund 1995, chapter 9, for an analysis of "The King's Indian"; and Ekelund 1997 for a critical reading of *October Light* and immigration.

4. See Ekelund 1995 for an extensive analysis of *On Moral Fiction*.

5. The phrase is borrowed from Robert Coover talking about his generation's wish to break with the past ("An Encounter," 302).

6. As Tom Wolfe put the matter of sociological and biological age in an introductory speech for an educational TV workshop with Gardner: "one nice thing about being a writer is that you can be considered a young man up until about the age forty-five, until the stiff hairs begin sprouting out of your ears."

7. Cowart, Morris, Henderson, Morace and VanSpanckeren, and Mendez-Egle. Ten years later a second harvest came: Butts, McWilliams, and Winther. Winther's study, however, was available as an unpublished Ph.D. thesis in 1984.

8. Boris Eikhenbaum clearly diagnosed this tendency in the type of criticism that tends to see the work as "the direct emanation of [the writer's] soul or as a manifestation of his individual, self-enclosed 'linguistic consciousness.' " Since such scholars are all but invariably faced with contradictions, they "are compelled to classify practically all writers as 'dual' natures" (2).

9. For a full discussion of *Grendel*, see Ekelund 1995, chapter 8.

10. And of course Althusser's and Balibar's notion, in *Reading Capital*, of different temporalities peculiar to different levels of a social formation is quite similar to Bourdieu's account.

BIBLIOGRAPHY

Althusser, Louis and Étienne Balibar. *Reading Capital*. Trans. Ben Brewster. London: NLB 1970.

Anderson, Perry. "Modernity and Revolution." In *Marxism and the Interpretation of Culture*, edited by Cary Nelson and Lawrence Grossberg. Urbana: U of Illinois P, 1988.

Armstrong, Philip, Andrew Glyn, and John Harrison, *Capitalism Since 1945*. Cambridge: Cambridge UP, 1991.

Bourdieu, Pierre. *Homo Academicus*. Trans. Peter Collier. Stanford: Stanford UP, 1988.

———. *The Logic of Practice*. Trans. Richard Nice. Stanford: Stanford UP, 1990.

————. "Fourth Lecture. Universal Corporatism: The Role of Intellectuals in the Modern World." *Poetics Today* 12, no. 4 (winter 1991): 655–69.

————. *Language and Symbolic Power.* Trans. Gino Raymond and Mathew Adamson. Ed. John B. Thompson. Cambridge: Harvard UP, 1991.

————. *The Political Ontology of Martin Heidegger.* Stanford: Stanford UP, 1991.

————. *The Field of Cultural Production.* Ed. Randal Johnson. New York: Columbia UP, 1993.

Bourdieu, Pierre, and Hans Haacke. *Free Exchange.* Stanford: Stanford UP, 1995.

Bourdieu, Pierre, Jean-Claude Chamboredon, and Jean-Claude Passeron, eds. *The Craft of Sociology: Epistemological Preliminaries.* 1968. Engl. ed. by Beate Krais. Trans. Richard Nice. Berlin: de Gruyter, 1991.

Broady, Donald. *Sociologi och epistemologi.* Stockholm: HLS förlag, 1990.

Callinicos, Alex. *Against Postmodernism: A Marxist Critique.* Cambridge: Polity Press, 1989.

Butts, Leonard C. *The Novels of John Gardner.* Baton Rouge: Louisiana State UP, 1988.

Coover, Robert. "An Encounter with Robert Coover." Interviewed by Thomas Alden Bass. *Antioch Review* 40, no. 3 (summer 1982): 287–302.

Cowart, David. *Arches and Light: The Fiction of John Gardner.* Carbondale: Southern Illinois UP, 1983.

Durkheim, Émile, and Marcel Mauss. *Primitive Classification.* Trans. and ed. Rodney Needham. Chicago: U of Chicago P, 1963.

Edwards, Bob. Radio interview with John Gardner, September 1982. National Public Radio.

Eikhenbaum, Boris. "Some Principles of Literary History: The Study of Lermontov." In *Formalism: History, Comparison, Genre.* Vol. 5 of *Russian Poetics in Translation.* Oxford: Holdan Books, 1978.

Ekelund, Bo G. *In the Pathless Forest: John Gardner's Literary Project.* Uppsala: Acta Universitatis Upsaliensis, 1995.

————. "The Alien in our Midst: Trash Culture and Good Americans in John Gardner's *October Light.*" *Novel* 30, no. 3 (spring 1997): 381–404.

Gardner, John. *The Resurrection.* 1966. Rev. ed. New York: Vintage, 1974.

————. *Wreckage of Agathon.* New York: Harper, 1970.

————. Letter to William H. Gass, dated November 18, 1971. John Gardner Collection. University of Rochester, Rochester, N.Y. [Probably never sent, since it is filed in original typescript.]

————. *Grendel.* New York: Knopf, 1971.

————. *The Sunlight Dialogues.* New York: Knopf, 1972.

————. *Nickel Mountain: A Pastoral Novel.* New York: Knopf, 1973.

————. "The King's Indian." In *The King's Indian: Stories and Tales.* New York: Knopf, 1974.

————. *The King's Indian: Stories and Tales.* New York: Knopf, 1974.

————. *October Light.* New York: Knopf, 1976.

————. *On Moral Fiction.* New York: Basic Books, 1978.

————. *Mickelsson's Ghosts.* New York: Knopf, 1982.

————. *On Becoming a Novelist.* New York: Harper, 1983.

————. *Conversations with John Gardner.* Ed. Allan Chavkin. Jackson, Miss.: UP of Mississippi, 1993.

Harvey, Marshall. "Where Philosophy and Fiction Meet: An Interview with John Gardner." *Chicago Review* 29 (spring 1978): 73–87. Reprinted in Gardner 1993: 84–98.

Henderson, Jeff, ed. *Thor's Hammer: Essays on John Gardner.* n.p.: U of Central Arkansas P, 1985.

Howell, John M. "The Wound and the Albatross: John Gardner's Apprenticeship." In Henderson 1985.

Jameson, Fredric. *Marxism and Form.* Princeton: Princeton UP, 1974.

———. *The Political Unconscious: Narrative as a Socially Symbolic Act.* London: Routledge, 1983.

Johnson, Charles. Letter to John Gardner, March 22, 1977. John Gardner Collection. University of Rochester, Rochester, N.Y.

Karen, David. "The Politics of Class, Race and Gender." *American Journal of Education* 99, no.2 (1991): 208–37.

Lash, Scott. *Sociology of Postmodernism.* London: Routledge, 1990.

Lukács, Georg. "Realism in the Balance." In *Aesthetics and Politics.* London: Verso, 1980. 28–59.

McWilliams, Dean. *John Gardner.* Boston: Twayne Publishers, 1990.

Mendez-Egle, Beatrice, ed. *John Gardner: True Art: Moral Art.* Edinburg, Tex.: Pan American University School of Humanities, 1983.

Morace, Robert A., and Katherine VanSpanckeren, eds. *John Gardner: Critical Perspectives.* Carbondale: Southern Illinois UP, 1982.

Morris, Gregory P. *A World of Order and Light: The Fiction of John Gardner.* Athens: U of Georgia P, 1984.

Natale, Richard. "John Gardner: 'Great Age of the Novel Is Returning.' " Interview with John Gardner. *Women's Wear Daily* (8 December 1972): 16.

Sartre, Jean-Paul. *Search for a Method.* Trans. Hazel E. Barnes. New York: Knopf, 1963.

Scholes, Robert. *Fabulation and Metafiction.* Urbana: U of Illinois P, 1979.

Tynyanov, Yuri, and Jakobson, Roman. "Problems of Research in Literature and Language." In *Russian Poetics in Translation.* Vol 4. Oxford: Holdan Books, 1978.

Whitehead, Alfred North. *Process and Reality: An Essay in Cosmology.* Cambridge: Cambridge UP, 1929.

Winther, Per. *The Art of John Gardner: Instruction and Exploration.* Albany: SUNY Press, 1992.

Wolfe, Tom. Introductory remarks. "John Gardner." *University of South Carolina Writer's Workshop*, Video Recording. Columbia, S.C.: University of South Carolina and South Carolina Educational Television Network, 1982.

Wyatt, David. *Prodigal Sons: A Study in Authorship and Authority.* Baltimore: Johns Hopkins UP, 1980.

13

Passport to Duke

Pierre Bourdieu

"Ceci est de la poésie philosophique
—Qu'est-ce que la poésie philosophique?
—Qu'est-ce que M. Edgard Quinet?
—Un philosophe?
—Euh! euh!
—Un poète?
—Oh! oh!"

—Charles Baudelaire

I would have liked to be here, amongst you, with you, during this conference. First to thank its organizers and all those who heeded their invitation, but also to present myself to you *en personne,* in the flesh, and thus give you an idea of who I am and of what I do at once more lively and less abstract than the idea one may form solely from reading texts.

I have the habit, in such circumstances, of recalling an intuition that Marx has in passing in *The Communist Manifesto* according to which texts circulate without their context. It follows that texts such as mine, produced in a definite position in a definite state of the French intellectual or academic field, have little chance of being grasped without distortion or deformation in the American field (as, for instance, is the case here and now, in this university, which occupies a determinate position in the space of American universities) given the considerable gap that separates these two fields, notwithstanding their apparent growing interpenetration.

Now this gap is most often ignored. For instance, French authors such as Foucault, Derrida, or Lyotard who have been "incorporated," more or less completely, and according to very different modalities, in this or that subsector of the American academic field (in literary studies more often than in philosophy, their originating point in France), were embedded in a whole network of relations. These *objective* relations, irreducible to personal interactions, which united them

241

to each other as well as to a whole series of institutions (for instance disciplines whose structure, history, and hierarchy are not the same on the two sides of the Atlantic) and to an entire galaxy of agents (philosophers, social scientists, writers, artists, journalists, etc.) most of whom are unknown in the United States, helped shape the creative project of which their work is the expression. Transformed into isolated asteroids by inter-national import which typically tears them from the constellation of which they are but elements, such French authors (I fear I am about to enjoy, or suffer, from such a strain of "French flu," as my late friend E. P. Thompson used to say) become available for all manners of interpretation as they may be freely subjected to categories (such as the fadish opposition between modern and postmodern, hardly ever invoked in France) and problematics specific to the American field.

This is where being present in person can play an irreplaceable role. The questions, inevitably ambiguous, on the relations that the guest speaker may entertain with other absent authors ("What do you think of Derrida?" or, to be more precise, "I read that you recently led a series of political interventions with Derrida, what are we to make of this?"), such questions, and many others you might have in mind, can trigger so many explicit or implicit position-takings—as would no doubt be the case if I were before you at this moment: an amused and somewhat ironic smile for Lyotard, a loud silence concerning Baudrillard. Such position-takings would at least allow you to see how the invited author situates himself, consciously, in relation to other authors.

This is all very well but would it suffice to overcome the structural disjuncture to which I was referring at the outset? I do not believe so. Having dealt, through a series of negative clarifications, with all of the misunderstandings that result from the effect of *allodoxia* produced by the distance (and not only geographical) that separates national intellectual fields, and having cleared up interferences between the historical traditions these have engendered, I would still have to effect two *apparently* contradictory operations in order to achieve better communication with you.

First I would have to show the coherence and empirical adequacy, that is, the *scientificity*, of the theory, or the *system of relational concepts* I have developed and which can be engaged in the construction, at once theoretical and empirical, of objects phenomenally very different and typically assigned to different disciplines (history of literature, history of sciences, history of philosophy, history of art, and so on. I could enumerate here the diverse and manifold disciplines represented at this conference, much to my satisfaction). Second I would outline the structure of the field, and the corresponding space of possible theoretical stances (that is, the system of negative and positive determinations), within which this conceptual framework has been constructed and to which it owes its virtues but also its limitations, some of them unapparent to me in spite of all my efforts to shun national particularities and particularisms through a deliberate (and early) commitment to scientific internationalism.

On the second point, the structure of the academic field and the relations it
entertains with the literary, artistic, and political field in France (relations that
are profoundly different from their counterparts in the United States), I can refer
you to my book *Homo Academicus* and in particular to the "Preface" to the En-
glish-language translation (Stanford, Stanford University Press, 1988, orig.
1984). In it, I try, based on the diagrammatic mapping of a multifactorial correspondence analysis, to uncover the characteristics of the position occupied by the
main contenders in the French academic field, which comprise those authors best
known in the United States, Foucault, Derrida, Barthes, and many others, myself
included. I show how, taking into account variations introduced by discrepancies
in social and academic trajectories, this structural location is at the root of the
critical, anti-institutional stances these authors took in their works. To gain a
more thorough understanding of commonalities and differences between them,
you could read a paper entitled "An Aspiring Philosopher" ("Un aspirant philosophe: Un point de vue sur le champ universitaire dans les années 50," in *Les
enjeux philosophiques des années 50,* Paris, Editions du Centre Pompidou, 1989,
pp. 15–24), where I try to specify, through a sort of retrospective self-analysis,
the dispositions (or, more precisely, the intellectual ambitions and pretentions)
associated with being a philosophy student in a French elite school, the Ecole
normale supérieure, around the time of its apogee. You will also find in this paper
instruments to understand one of the factors which, along with my social origins,
distinguish me most strongly from the most illustrious of my contemporaries:
namely, the choice I made to leave the *superior caste* of the philosophers and
turn first towards anthropology (with my field work in Kabylia) and later—an
even more grievous derogation—towards the sociology of work (see *Travail et
travailleurs en Algérie,* 1963) and the sociology of education (with *The Inheritors* and *Reproduction,* published in 1964 and 1970 respectively), at that time two
of the most despised subsectors of a pariah discipline. I effected this reconversion
precisely during that period, the sixties, when those who would later discover, no
doubt due partly to the sociology of education and of science, the question of
power in academic and scientific life, were surfing on the structuralist tide.

It is an understatement to say that I did not partake of those semiologico-literary fads, exemplified in my eyes by Roland Barthes and, at the intersection between the scientific and the literary fields, the fanatics of *Tel Quel:* mixing Mao
and Sade (in those years, virtually all French intellectuals, Simone de Beauvoir
included, wrote their dissertation on the author of *Justine*), Sollers, Kristeva, and
their little coterie of minor writers with grandiose pretentions tried to institute, in
the intellectual field, the aestheticist cult of gratuitous transgression, erotic or political (on this point, see my "Sollers Tel Quel," *Liber, revue européenne des
livres,* 21–22, March 1995, p. 40). I was scarcely more indulgent towards those
who, culminating the prestige of philosophy, preferably Nietzschean as with De-
leuze and Foucault, or Heideggerian in the case of Derrida, and the aura of literature, with the compulsive and compulsory reference to Artaud, Bataille, or Blan-

chot, contributed to blurring the frontier between science and literature, when they did not go so far as to breathe life back into the dullest commonplaces that the arrogance of philosophers has produced against the social sciences and which periodically take them to the brink of nihilism (for excellent demonstrations on this, I can refer you here to two books by my companion in *resistance,* Jacques Bouveresse: *Le philosophe chez les autophages,* Paris: Editions de Minuit, 1984, and *Rationalité et cynisme,* Paris: Editions de Minuit, 1989).

This is why I am more than a little surprised when I see myself placed, through a typical effect of *allodoxia,* on the side of those so-called "post-modern" writers whom I have ceaselessly fought on intellectual grounds, even when I might have shared political grounds on account of the fact that, as I noted earlier, we had similar subversive or anti-institutional dispositions linked to the propinquity of our positions in academic space.

This leads me to the second point of my intended demonstration, namely the space of theoretical options in relation to which my own specifically scientific project (founded upon a total social break with the mundane games of literary philosophy and philosophical literature) was constituted. It is clear that if I reacted forcefully against the authors most directly engaged in the semiologico-literary fashion of the time and if I quite consciously denied myself the benefits of the accelerated international circulation of ideas that the latter have enjoyed, thanks to the prestige still accorded to Parisian literary avant-gardes, in particular via the French departments of select American universities, I was actively engaged in confronting structuralism as incarnated by the Lévi-Strauss of *The Elementary Structures of Kinship, The Savage Mind,* and *Mythologiques,* and this, in my research practice rather than solely at the level of discourse (as with philosophers, save for Foucault). In the prologue to my book *Le sens pratique (The Logic of Practice,* 1980/1990), I draw out the intellectual context of my research work during the sixties and I try to show, in the first two chapters of that same book, how I strove to overcome the opposition, still salient in all the social sciences today (for a discussion with reference to history, see my interview with the German historian Lutz Raphael in *Actes de la recherche en sciences sociales,* 106–107, March 1995, pp. 108–22), between objectivism, represented in exemplary fashion by Lévi-Strauss, and subjectivism, taken to its outer limits by Sartre. The concept of *habitus* is intended to give a stenographic expression to the overcoming of this antinomy.

But to understand the other instruments I employ in my analyses of cultural works, law, science, art (as with my work in progress—for much too long now—on Manet), literature (cf. my study of Flaubert and, more recently, Baudelaire), philosophy (with the study of the German philosophical field in Heidegger's time), one would need to draw out the totality of the space of theoretical contributions to the analysis of symbolic power that I have been led to cumulate and to synthesize, step by step, to resolve the problems posed, very concretely, by the analysis of Kabyle ritual or religious practices or yet the literary and artistic productions of differentiated societies (I presented a sort of simplified synopsis of these theories for the first time in 1972, at the University of Chicago, before an audience of positivistically-inclined, and thoroughly befuddled, sociologists: see "On Symbolic Power," reprinted in *Language and Symbolic Power,* Cambridge: Polity Press, 1991).

The concept of literary field, as a space of objective positions to which corresponds a homologous space of stances or position-takings (which operates as a space of possibles or options given to participants in the field at any given moment), was itself works to which it is opposed at the same time as it annexes and integrates them in a non-eclectic manner (you will find a map of this space of theories of literary or artistic products in "Principles for a Sociology of Cultural Works," in *The Field of Cultural Production: Essays on Art and Literature,* New York, Columbia University Press, 1993, as well as in *Les règles de l'art,* Paris, Editions du Seuil, 1993, pp. 271–92; translated as *The Rules of Art,* Cambridge, Polity Press, 1996).

If I had the time, I could show you how one can critique symbolic structuralism, as conceived by Foucault and the Russian formalists, and yet preserve its achievements (the idea of a space of strategic possibilities or intertextuality) within a framework that transcends the opposition between internal analysis (text) and external analysis (context) by relating the literary (philosophical, juridical, scientific, etc.) field in which producers evolve, and where they occupy dominant or dominated, central or marginal, positions, on the one hand, and the field of works, defined relationally in their form, style, and manner, on the other. This is tantamount to saying that, instead of being one approach among many, an analysis in terms of field allows us methodically to integrate the achievements of all the other approaches in currency, approaches that the field of literary criticism itself causes us to perceive as irreconcilable.

Lastly, I would need to show you how an analysis armed with knowledge of the general properties of fields produced by the theory of fields can discover in each of the various fields (for instance, the literary field or the field of painting) properties that the naive (and native) vision would overlook. Such an analysis can bring to light, thanks to methodical comparison made possible by the notion of field, properties that uniquely characterize the functioning of each of the different fields, which leads in particular to refuting the conflation between the scientific field and the literary field fostered by a certain "post-modern" vision of literature and science (I think of the nihilistic critiques of the social sciences that have proliferated recently in the name of the "linguistic turn").

As I tried to demonstrate in what would seem to be the most unlikely case, that of sociology (see "La cause de la science," *Actes de la recherche en sciences sociales,* 106–7, March 1995, pp. 3–10), if science, even the purest science, presents a number of structural and functional traits in common with the political field, it remains that it has its own *nomos,* its (relative) autonomy, which insulates it more or less completely from the intrusion of external constraints. This explains that truths produced in this relatively autonomous field can be historical through and through, as is the field itself, without for that being either deducible from historical conditions or reducible to the external conditionings they impose. This is because the field opposes to external forces the shield, or the prism, of its own history, warrant of its autonomy, that is, the history of the "languages" (in the broadest possible sense of the word) specific to each field or subfield.

These are some of the arguments I would have liked to make before you, had I been able to travel to Duke University and to be there with you on this day. I would have liked also to tell you how grateful I am for the interest you have shown in my work, and this in the manner which pleases me the most: by treating it as an intellectual machinery capable of generating new products and thus by working together to design whatever improvements are needed.

Paris, March 1995
Translation by Loïc J. D. Wacquant

NOTES

This chapter was prepared as a paper for the conference on "Bourdieu: Fieldwork in Literature, Art, Philosophy," Duke University, Durham, NC, U.S.A., April 1995, and read in absentia. It was published in the *International Journal of Contemporary Sociology*, vol. 33, no. 2 (October 1996). It is reprinted by permission of the *International Journal of Contemporary Sociology*.

Index

About the Contributors

Jon Beasley-Murray works in the Department of Hispanic Studies at the University of Aberdeen. He received his Ph.D. from Duke University's literature program for his dissertation entitled "Outline of a Theory of Culture: The Relation between the State, Culture, and Civil Society in Latin America from Peronism to the Zapatistas."

Carolyn Betensky is assistant professor of English and Honors at George Washington University in Washington, D.C. She is currently working on a book on guilt and symbolic capital.

Pierre Bourdieu is professor of sociology at the Collège de France and the director of studies at the Ecole des Hautes Etudes en Sciences Sociales. He is the author of numerous books, including *Distinction, Homo Academicus, The Rules of Art,* and *On Television.*

Nicholas Brown is assistant professor of English at the University of Illinois at Chicago. He has written on modernism and on African literature, and he is currently working on a book that traces the relationships between these two fields, entitled *Narratives of Utopia Inchoate: African Fiction and British Modernism.*

Bo G. Ekelund currently holds a postdoctoral fellowship in American literature at Uppsala University, Sweden. He has published an extensive study of the U.S. novelist John Gardner, *In the Pathless Forest: John Gardner's Literary Project,* which drew on Pierre Bourdieu's sociological model. He has also published an article in *Novel,* "The Alien in Our Midst: Trash Culture and Good Americans in John Gardner's *October Light.*" At present he is finishing a study of contemporary British and American fiction and critical social theory, called "Studies in an Undead Culture: Conceptions of Value in Fiction and Social Theory, 1980–2000."

251

John Guillory is professor of English at New York University and the author of *Cultural Capital: The Problem of Literary Canon Formation.* He is currently completing a book on the sociology of literary study.

Robert Holton teaches literature and critical theory at Okanagan University College in Kelowna, British Columbia. His publications include *Jarring Witnesses: Modern Fiction and the Representation of History,* a study that employs Bourdieusian notions of *doxa* in an analysis of modernism.

Marty Hipsky is assistant professor of English at Ohio Wesleyan University. He has published on narrative and film, and he is currently working on a book that examines the relationship of the turn-of-the-century romance novel to literary realism and modernism.

Marie-Pierre Le Hir is the Elizabeth M. and William C. Treuhaft associate professor of French and comparative literature and chair of the department of modern languages and literatures at Case Western Reserve University. A specialist in nineteenth-century French literature and culture, she is the author of *Le romantisme aux enchères,* a book on French romantic drama. She has also published journal articles that examine fields of cultural production in nineteenth-century France and issues such as authorship and "popular" culture. She is the coeditor, with Dana Strand, of *French Cultural Studies: Criticism at the Crossroads,* forthcoming from SUNY Press.

Paul Lopes is assistant professor of sociology and director of the communications and media studies program at Tufts University. His field of research is cultural sociology with special emphasis on mass media and popular culture. He is presently completing a book on the transformation of jazz music in the twentieth century.

Caterina Pizanias is an itinerant academic who received her Ph. D. in 1992 in the sociology of knowledge from the University of Alberta. Her research documents art works that best reveal the restrictive subtexts of modernity. She has found Pierre Bourdieu's theories to be an excellent companion in her travels across the art worlds of North America and Europe.

Daniel Simeoni is a member of the Faculty of Graduate Studies at York University (Toronto), and a research associate at the Centre de Linguistique Théorique of the Ecole des Hautes Etudes en Sciences Sociales (Paris). His publications are in the fields of linguistics, pragmatics, translation, and intercultural studies.

Carol Stabile is associate professor of communication at the University of Pittsburgh. She is the author of *Feminism and the Technological Fix* and is currently working on a book on media coverage of crime from 1892 to the present.

Imre Szeman is assistant professor of English and a member of the Institute on Globalization and Social Change at McMaster University in Hamilton, Ontario. He is coeditor of the forthcoming second edition of *The Johns Hopkins Guide to Literary Theory and Criticism* and is completing work on a book entitled *Zones of Instability: Literature, Postcolonialism, and the Nation.*